LAWYER

LAWYER

A Life of
Counsel and Controversy

ARTHUR L. LIMAN

with the assistance of
PETER ISRAEL

PUBLICAFFAIRS
New York

Library of Congress Cataloging-in-Publication Data
Liman, Arthur L.
 Lawyer : a life of counsel and controversy / Arthur L. Liman.
 p. cm.
 ISBN 1-891620-04-5 (hc. : acid-free paper)
 1. Liman, Arthur L. 2. Lawyers—United States—Biography.
I. Title.
KF373.L496A3 1998
340'.092—dc21

[B]   98-27279
                                                                          CIP

First Edition

ISBN - 1-58648-177-0

CONTENTS

Foreword   *vii*

Family   *xi*

Acknowledgments   *xv*

Opening Statement   *xvii*

I

Two Mentors (and a Menace)

1. Roy Cohn Made Me a Lawyer   *3*

2. The Judge: Simon H. Rifkind   *15*

3. The Boss: Robert M. Morgenthau   *33*

II

Private Practice

4. Paul, Weiss, Rifkind, Wharton & Garrison   *57*

5. American Express, Tino De Angelis, and the
Great Salad Oil Scandal   *67*

6. *U.S. v. Wolfson:* My Introduction to Defending
White-Collar Crime   *85*

7. Charles Bluhdorn Awards Us the Gulf & Western
Good-American Medal   *94*

8. Continental Grain Chases the Silver Sheiks   *107*

9. The Rise and Rise of Steve Ross and
the Mega Merger of Time and Warner   *125*

10. Keeping the Eye Was Bill Paley's Prize   *159*

III

PUBLIC SERVICE

11. As Natural as Breathing   *171*

12. The Attica Uprising: Investigation and Implications   *175*

13. The Case of New York's Collapsing Subway Cars   *195*

14. Representing the Unrepresented: The Legal Action Center,
the Legal Aid Society, and the Capital Defender Office   *209*

15. Was the New York City Medical Examiner Covering up
Police Brutality?   *220*

IV

A THUMB ON THE SCALE OF JUSTICE

16. The Runaway Prosecutors   *229*

17. *Pennzoil v. Texaco:* The $10 Billion Handshake   *239*

18. *U.S. v. GAF:* Good Things Don't Always Come in Threes   *249*

19. Michael Milken: The Demon of Wall Street   *265*

V

THE IRAN-CONTRA INVESTIGATION

20. Flouting the Constitution   *297*

21. Contraband, Contra-Aid, Controversy   *300*

22. Public Hearings in the Television Age   *317*

23. North and Poindexter: Covert Acts and Cover-Ups   *328*

24. Implausible Deniability: Why Reagan Was Not Impeached   *343*

25. Presidential Accountability and Criminal Liability   *351*

Summation   *357*

Afterword   *361*

Index   *365*

FOREWORD

THE RULES OF MORAL CONDUCT that a lawyer must obey are few and easily stated. The principal ones can be written down on the back of an envelope. "Serve your client with zeal and a heartfelt devotion to his cause." "Keep the confidences with which you are entrusted." "Remember that you are an officer of the court, bound to serve the law and to advance the work of justice." "Remember, too, that the law protects the poor as well as the rich, the unpopular and feared as well as the celebrated and successful."

How simple it is to list these basic norms of professional life, but how difficult—how exquisitely difficult—to meet their demands and keep them all in balance. Many treatises have been written explaining how this can be done, but more valuable than all the learned dissertations on legal ethics is the example of a life lived well and fully in the vortex of the law, with its clashing demands and extraordinary pressures on the simple ideal of justice. Arthur Liman's life in the law, chronicled in these pages, is such an example and those who wish to know how an ethical man conducts himself in the fields of the law will find here wonderful material for reflection.

Several features of Arthur Liman's multifaceted career are worthy of notice. One was his profound appreciation of the lawyer-client relationship, the fundamental building block on which the practice of law in all its forms is based. Arthur understood—he felt intuitively—the client's need for an ally who would stand with him through thick and thin and be his friend in the center of the storm. Arthur knew how lonely a person caught in a legal dispute can be, and how unsure even the most self-confident client often becomes. He appreciated the client's need for a steady hand and a calm supportive voice. But Arthur also understood how important it is, how truly essential, for a lawyer to maintain a moral independence from his client and to tell the client "no" when "no" is the right advice. In the glare of the cameras and the crush of reporters, no lawyer has ever been a more steadfast supporter of his clients than Arthur Liman was. But in the quiet privacy of the office, no lawyer has spoken more bluntly or with greater moral candor to his clients than Arthur did. This is a difficult balancing act which requires considerable agility and a nuanced understanding of human psychology, as well as the law. It is easy to say that a lawyer must be loyal to his clients, while adding that such loyalty must always include an element of moral independence. But how hard it is to live in accordance with this complex conception of loyalty, and how instructive Arthur's relations with his clients are in showing us the way to maintain the needed balance.

Arthur's career is instructive for a second reason. For most of his years in practice, Arthur was a partner at the Paul, Weiss firm in New York, where he represented clients of great wealth and renown. But Arthur's private practice was punctuated by periods of remarkable public service, in the United States Attorney's Office, as counsel to the New York State Special Commission on Attica, and as counsel to the Senate Iran-Contra Committee. This last assignment brought Arthur into the national spotlight, and of course what the world saw then was the man Arthur had been all along: a devoted champion of the rule of law, a true lover of justice, but one whose passion for the law was tempered by a human compassion for the frightened and the weak. Arthur was a great prosecutor but he was no grand inquisitor, and in the Iran-Contra hearings the American people saw a lawyer of decency and character, very much like the lawyer they saw three decades earlier when Joseph Welch took on the Senator from Wisconsin in the Army-McCarthy hearings.

Arthur believed that every lawyer, whatever his station and whoever his clients, has a duty to serve the public good. His own career, with its mix of private practice and public service, gives us a fine contemporary example of what this duty means when a lawyer takes it seriously.

Third, Arthur knew, as we all do, that the inequalities of wealth and power that exist in our society, or in any society for that matter, can spoil the grand equalities of the law. But unlike many, Arthur acted on this knowledge and throughout his career vigorously defended the need to bring legal services to the poor and unrepresented. As president of the Legal Aid Society of New York, Arthur was as forceful as any lawyer in the city in pressing the claim which the poor have on the legal profession, with its special influence and privileged access to the castle of the law. Arthur possessed a transparent humanity that made it possible—even natural, I would say—for him to reach across the gulf that separated the world of his Paul, Weiss clients from that of the Legal Aid Society and, even more remotely, from the world of the inmates of Attica Prison. Anyone who reads this book will remember forever the image of Arthur sitting in the cafeteria at Attica on Christmas Eve, beginning to get to know the prisoners with whom he had come to break bread.

This brings me to the last point I would make about the episodes that are recounted in this book. Perhaps the most important lesson that anyone can draw from them is that decency and honor in professional life are inseparable from decency and honor in life generally. Arthur Liman was a good lawyer because he was a good man, because his values were sound and his character strong. This is an important lesson, especially for lawyers, who need to remember that the great ethical challenges of their profession are in the end no different from the great ethical challenges of life, and who will be equipped to meet the first only if they are prepared for the second. Arthur was a mensch, and that is the secret not only of his greatness as a human being but of his greatness as a lawyer. How fortunate we are to have his example and the wonderful stories contained in this book. All of us—lawyers and non-lawyers alike—will do well to take their lessons to heart.

—ANTHONY KRONMAN,
Dean of the Yale Law School

FAMILY

ALTHOUGH THIS IS A BOOK about my career as a lawyer, my work has been just a part of my life. My family is, and always has been, my foundation and my joy, and if I failed to acknowledge this, and the great support they have always given me, I would be telling less than half the story.

My wife, Ellen, made a home for me, raised our three children, encouraged me in all my endeavors, lifted my spirits when I was down, and kept me from ever taking myself too seriously. Along the way, she herself wrote five books on design, became an accomplished painter, headed New York City's Commission for Cultural Affairs, and served on the boards of several art organizations, museums, and a philanthropic foundation.

Every busy father feels guilty about the limited time he has for his children, but by stretching my schedule here and there, I managed to help mine with their homework, give them advice (sometimes gratuitously), take them on vacations, play tennis (poorly) with them, take them waterskiing and deep-sea fishing (whether they liked it or not), and initiate them into the mysteries of golf. Seeing them grow into responsible adults and delightful people has been my greatest joy.

In addition, they are all different. My oldest, Lewis, is a lawyer who now serves as a federal prosecutor in the same U.S. Attorney's Office I worked in more than thirty-five years ago. I am proudest of his values. It serves as proof to me that we are passing the best traditions of the bar on to the next generation.

My daughter Emily is a neurobiologist with a Ph.D. from Harvard, and so is her husband Don. I have tried to read all of her scientific papers. She may have inherited my love of investigation and discovery, but her wondrous skills in science and math are not of the immediate paternal gene pool.

My youngest, Douglas, is a movie director with a very successful and funny first feature film to his credit, called *Swingers*. Of course, I like to think he inherited from me a lawyer's ability to tell a story. I once even let him cast and direct me in a bit part in the movie, *Getting In*. (No greater love does a parent have for a child.)

What Arthur doesn't tell you is that we often couldn't get a word in edgewise or win an argument—he cajoled, cross-examined, and frequently convinced us, always with warmth and humor, honing his skills as much in our living room, perhaps, as in the courtroom. But sadly his fierce determination and sheer will power failed him in his final battle, against nature. So now we do have the last word and they are words that would have been otherwise left unsaid because of Arthur's modesty, pride, and shyness.

He was to us—as he was to so many clients—our close friend and trusted confidante: a counselor, teacher, psychiatrist who was always accessible and available. Both impatient and patient, tender and tough, passionate and compassionate, he worked too hard and held us all to a high standard. (And he played hard too, getting up at 6 A.M. for a golf game, to catch a fish, or to ferret out at a flea market an old game for his collection.)

Arthur was asked many times to write a book. He resisted because, for him, learning the next case (moving forward) was always more interesting than recounting the last. Besides, he did not like talking about himself. Who would be interested, he said. He finally capitulated when he became ill, not because he wanted to tell all about his clients, but because he wanted us to understand his life as a lawyer, his commitment to his profession, and the joys and hardships of being a practicing attorney.

As Arthur's illness progressed, the number of his handwritten yellow pads telling his tales proliferated. His greatest difficulty was in selecting from so many stories those that would be the most interesting and instructive while simultaneously maintaining the attorney-client privilege.

In fact, he was so fiercely protective of his clients' lives that the chapter he jokingly titled "To Hate and to Punish/Family Disputes" was cut from the final manuscript because it was too short and lacked juicy material. This brevity in no way reflected reality.

Not as well known to most, his common sense was valued by the many he constantly counseled on critical, personal challenges. He was reachable at anytime (he insisted on having all of his phone numbers listed), anywhere (often on weekends or late at night) and by anyone. Somehow, he found time, often when there was none, for those in trouble. His clients were not just the prominent and powerful paying clients depicted in these pages, but frequently the neighbor or friend who needed help or the stranger whose case just simply called out for justice. We tolerated this endless intrusion and shared him because witnessing his wisdom and the lessons learned enriched and inspired us.

—ELLEN LIMAN

ACKNOWLEDGMENTS

In ADDITION TO PETER ISRAEL, special mention must be made of Peter Sistrom who was instrumental in the formation of this book, and of the talented staff of PublicAffairs who recognized its importance and saw it through to its final completion.

It would be impossible in a book of this length to acknowledge all the many friends, family members, clients, partners and associates who enriched Arthur's life and who contributed to his many successes or the many cases and clients about which or whom he felt passionate. Ever modest, Arthur tried to list most of them in his early drafts. The names overwhelmed the text. To those many whose names did not make the final draft, you know who you are. Words cannot convey the depth of our (and Arthur's) gratitude to you.

Finally, it should be noted that Arthur's Iran-Contra diaries were not discovered until after he died. We have decided to include them in the book because they so clearly reflect his feelings at the time.

OPENING STATEMENT

Almost forty years have passed since I stood in that courtroom in downtown Brooklyn with a group of my peers, waiting to take the oath. It was 1958, and I was fresh out of law school, newly a member of the New York bar. The presiding judge sternly reminded us of our moral obligation as lawyers: we were to be more than advocates; we were to be servants of justice and officers of the court.

Luckier than some, I already knew where I was going next—to an established and in many ways unique New York law firm. I knew too that, somehow, I was going to combine private practice with public service, and that someday I would face the greatest challenge that awaits any lawyer, that of trying my own cases before judge and jury. For me, as for all lawyers of my generation, the reigning trial of the century was the celebrated Scopes "Monkey Trial." The state of Tennessee had banned the teaching of evolution in its public schools, and in the summer of 1925, Clarence Darrow, the foremost advocate of his time, challenged the constitutionality of that law, while William Jennings Bryan, the silver-tongued orator who had twice run for president, defended it.

To the extent that I had a model in my mind, it would certainly have been Clarence Darrow.

At the same time, I had little inkling of what was in store for me. I was nervous inside, and excited—ambitious too, idealistic, impatient to get going—but I could never have envisaged the great variety of cases and clients that awaited me in the decades ahead. I would represent the rich, the poor, the famous, the infamous, the unknown. I would counsel, among others, Steve Ross, who began with his father-in-law's funeral business and created in Time Warner a media and entertainment giant; William Paley, who built CBS from a handful of radio stations; Michel Fribourg, whose Continental Grain Company, a huge, secretive, family-owned business, has long dominated the world's grain trade; Felix Rohatyn of Lazard Frères, who saved New York City; and entrepreneurs like Herb Siegel of Chris-Craft; David Margolis of Colt Industries; Tony O'Reilly, the Irish rugby player who became head of H. J. Heinz; and Charles Bluhdorn, who created the first great conglomerate, Gulf & Western, which at one time owned everything from zinc mines and sugar plantations to Paramount Pictures. In the course of my work, I would find myself in the midst of the great economic and social upheavals of our times, ranging from the freewheeling stock market swindles of the 1950s to the Attica prison rebellion of 1971, which became the searing subject of an independent investigation, led by me, and which changed irrevocably my views on race in America and our criminal justice system. The city of New York would be my client—the state too—and in 1987, appointed chief counsel to the Select Committee of the U.S. Senate investigating Iran-Contra, I would interrogate John Poindexter and Oliver North on national television. And then there would be Michael Milken, who, during the financial scandals of the 1980s, became for many the symbol of all that was wrong with America, yet who remains, to my mind, the most enigmatic and least understood figure of his age.

I want to tell the stories of many of these cases and clients because they are interesting in their own right, and because they have marked my life as a lawyer, but I also have another motive in writing this book. In a sense, it is the trial for murder of O. J. Simpson that has spurred me. To my way of thinking, this courtroom spectacle brought into the American home as distorted and unflattering an image of the legal profession at work as any that can be found in the pages of Charles Dickens, but it also brought to my mind the countless movies of recent years, and the television shows and novels about lawyers, and the realization that we, as a profession, have never been on display as much as we are today. We are the guests, sometimes even the hosts, of innumerable television talk shows, discussing our own cases, commenting on others. Even the newest medium, the Internet, has discovered us. Like it or not, lawyers no longer work behind the scenes.

Whether we are cast as villains and charlatans on the one hand or heroes and saviors on the other, I maintain that people know surprisingly little about what lawyers' lives are really like, and further, that this general ignorance is at least in part our own fault. In public, in our memoirs, even among ourselves, we like to strut our successes. We boast of the big deals we've negotiated, the verdicts we've won. We leave the impression of going from mountaintop to mountaintop without ever descending, without toiling long hours, without doubt, certainly without failure. For me at least, and for the lawyers I've known, there have, on the contrary, been triumphs but also losses, exhilaration but also frustration, a sense of purpose and direction but also, at times, the bewilderment of being lost in the fog. In reality, the more success a trial lawyer achieves, the harder his cases become.

But there is a further reality, one I believe the trial lawyer himself only comes to recognize after many years of experience. The courtroom may in fact resemble a stage set and the trial a theatrical drama in which the advocates play key roles, but the measure of my success as a lawyer, I believe, has been neither my advocacy nor my courtroom performance, but the value of my counsel. I am referring to that far less glamorous, behind-the-scenes effort to guide my clients not only through the mazes of what is legal and illegal but in the direction of what is right, and to try to do so consistently with discretion, sound judgment, and common sense. Elihu Root, a leading New York lawyer in the early part of the century, once admonished the bar, "It may be legal, but if it's rotten, tell your client not to do it." To my mind, this is a fine way of describing the lawyer's key role as counselor and conscience.

It is this aspect of a lawyer's life, even more than the great cases I have participated in, that has made my career so richly rewarding. If, in writing about that career near the end of my century, I can succeed in convincing young or aspiring lawyers to go for it at the beginning of theirs, well, then I will have fulfilled my task.

LAWYER

I

Two Mentors (and a Menace)

Roy Cohn Made Me a Lawyer

IT WAS NO SMALL irony that I served as chief counsel to the Senate Select Committee that investigated the Iran-Contra affair in 1987, for I became a lawyer in the first place because of the abuses of due process of another Senate committee—the Permanent Subcommittee on Investigations headed by Senator Joe McCarthy and Roy M. Cohn. In the middle of my senior year at Harvard, in 1954, Joe McCarthy brought his Red-baiting circus to Boston for two days of public hearings. Just four years before, he'd been an obscure, first-year senator from Wisconsin, but in February 1950, with a speech charging that the State Department was full of Communists and that he knew their names, he began his swift and noisy ride to notoriety. Crude, reckless, and vulgar, McCarthy had a genius for creating tumult. His wild charges of subversion and espionage tapped some dark fear in the country, one that echoed the Bolshevik panic and the Palmer raids of an earlier generation. In 1953 the Republicans in Congress had put him in charge of the Senate's Committee on Government Operations and its Permanent Subcommittee on Investigations, and he hired Roy Cohn as his chief counsel. Cohn did all the work, but when he dug up something good—an alleged Communist at the Voice of America, or a Communist's novel in a government library—McCarthy came in for the kill. Naturally, McCarthy's two days of hearings were an advance sensation in Boston. "Red Hearing on TV Opens Tomorrow" said the front-page headline in the *Boston Herald;* two television stations and one radio station carried the hearings live. Since I was writing my senior thesis on the threat that McCarthy-style congressional investigations posed to our concepts of civil liberties and limited government, I was eager to see McCarthy at work. Besides, it would be a welcome break from tedious hours in the library reading transcripts of long-ago hearings.

The first day of the hearings, January 15, dawned raw and gray. Well before 9:00 A.M., the scheduled start, Sam Huntington, a young political science professor I was friendly with, and I were at the Federal Building in downtown Boston. We stood outside the hearing room with hundreds of others jostling to get in. I wore gray flannel trousers and a navy blazer, the only jacket I owned, because a Senate committee hearing, I'd thought naively, would be a formal, august occasion.

McCarthy took over the grand and spacious federal courtroom as a committee of one. The summer before, his subcommittee's three Democratic members had quit in disgust, and no Republican bothered attending his road show. McCarthy sat alone at the marble and wood desk, high above the room, where a judge usually sat. At his side was Cohn, whispering in his ear, often giggling, sometimes scowling.

Cohn was a brash New York lawyer, only twenty-five years old, barely four years older than me. He was undeniably smart, like me a Jew, and was shrewder and considerably meaner than his boss. McCarthy may have had a bully's instinct for weakness and fear in others, and a con man's instincts for improvisation and publicity, but he was a lazy demagogue. Cohn did the work. Both of them loved publicity, but Cohn loved the hunt for its own sake. I came to watch McCarthy that day, but it turned out to be Cohn who captured my attention.

Their target was Harvard, which McCarthy hated. As a propagandist, he knew the university could be made to symbolize naive, sissified, un-American intellectuals, men like Dean Acheson who were not awake to the dangers of communism, or worse, men like Alger Hiss. Two Harvard teachers had been summoned that morning—a physics professor named Wendell Furry and a young research assistant in psychology, Leon Kamin. During the war, Furry had done radar research for the government, while Kamin, as a college student, had worked one summer in a low-level job reading simulated radar. Questioned by other congressional committees, they had invoked their Fifth Amendment right not to incriminate themselves and refused to answer questions. McCarthy accused neither of them directly of espionage or disloyalty. By his own logic, he didn't have to: their refusal to testify proved their guilt. After all, if they had done nothing illegal, how could telling the truth incriminate them? And how could a company that did defense-related work for the government, or a university, or a government agency, employ someone who refused to deny being a Communist? Someone who was, in McCarthy's coinage, a "Fifth Amendment Communist?"

Forty-odd years later, reviewing the transcript of those hearings, I find it difficult to believe they actually took place. Testifying first, Kamin didn't take the Fifth. He said he would answer questions about his own political activities and views but not about those of others, and not because to do so would incriminate him, but because it was wrong. I could hear people in the audience around me whispering. Turning to Huntington, I asked whether he thought McCarthy could jail Kamin for refusing to answer his questions, now that he'd renounced his Fifth Amendment right to remain silent. Huntington nodded. I glanced back at Kamin. Like Cohn, he was only a few years older than me, and he looked scared but determined.

For a moment, McCarthy was startled by Kamin's response. He and Cohn huddled, and then he pushed on. Kamin admitted having been a Communist in the 1940s, and writing articles for the *Daily Worker.* Knowing he would refuse, McCarthy then asked Kamin to name names. Kamin replied that his sense of duty to his country didn't require him to become a political informer. Back now on familiar ground, McCarthy shouted at Kamin: "You're not here to protect Communist spies and conspirators. You are *ordered* to answer the question—if a number of Communists you have known for years are now working in defense plants!"

Cohn sat grinning beside McCarthy. When Kamin refused to answer, McCarthy told him that he would have him prosecuted for contempt. "As much as I hate to decimate the Harvard faculty," the senator from Wisconsin added.

The audience hooted at this, and then McCarthy dismissed the witness.

Next up was Professor Furry. This was his second time before McCarthy. The previous November, at a secret session, he had refused to cooperate and McCarthy had demanded that Harvard fire him. This time, Furry too waived his right to refuse to answer. He read a statement saying that, while his past claims to the Fifth Amendment were legally justified and morally right, he would now answer questions about his own activities in the hope that, by telling his own political history, he would "dispel suspicion and contribute to public understanding."

At the same time, like Kamin, he said he wouldn't answer questions about other people.

"If I knew of any person whose conduct as I saw it was criminal, I should feel bound to reveal the facts," Furry said. "I am not seeking to protect the guilty from prosecution. I wish merely to shield the innocent from persecution. I hope that on this matter the committee will respect my conscience."

Brave as Furry's statement sounded, I wondered whether he could hold up under McCarthy's questions. He seemed timid to me, and befuddled, the type whom people at the time were quick to label an egghead. Furry admitted that he'd been a Communist for a dozen years, but that he'd quit the party in 1951. He said he'd worked with several other Communists at a government radar laboratory during World War II. Who were they? McCarthy demanded. Furry wouldn't answer. He said they were loyal Americans, devoted to the war effort, and besides, none were now working on government research projects. Then came a cat-and-mouse game in which McCarthy and Cohn tried repeatedly to trick or coerce Furry into naming names:

McCARTHY: You have been ordered to give us the names of all people known to be Communists and working in the radar laboratory when you were there.

FURRY: Will you repeat that question?

McCARTHY: It is not a question! It is an order!

FURRY: I refused to answer that question some time ago and I still refuse.

McCARTHY: We will ask you the name of each one and cite you for contempt for each refusal. That will be one way of helping President Pusey get rid of some Harvard Fifth Amendment Communists.

McCarthy pressed on. To the delight of many in his packed audience, he asked Furry to name anyone at Harvard who had ever been a member of the Communist Party. Then, when Furry refused again, McCarthy erupted:

This, in the opinion of the chair, is one of the most aggravated cases of contempt that we have had before us, as I see it. Here you have a man teaching at one of our large universities. He knows that there were six Communists handling secret government work, radar work, atomic work. He refuses to give either this committee or the FBI or anyone else this information which he has. To me, it is inconceivable that a university which has had the reputation of being a great university would keep this type of a creature on, teaching our children. Because of men like this who have refused to give the government the information which they have in their own minds about Communists who are working on our secret work, many young men have died in the past, and if we lose a war in the future it will be the result of the lack of loyalty—complete immorality—of these individuals who continue to protect the conspirators.

People in the audience around me now clapped and yelled their approval. I had the strange, and decidedly uneasy, feeling that all of them knew I was a Harvard student, and not only that but a Russian Jew from New York. Moments later, after threatening to jail Furry for contempt, McCarthy ended the hearings for the day.

For a moment, I sat in disbelief. McCarthy and Cohn had uncovered nothing. All they'd done—all they'd evidently wanted to do—was to browbeat two nervous, harmless academics and create a divisive ruckus. As Furry left the courtroom, a woman sitting near me spat on him. Later, while Sam Huntington and I rode the subway back to Cambridge, a belligerent drunk, who'd apparently watched the hearings on television in a bar, confronted us. He must have spotted my gray flannel trousers. "Who're you for?" he taunted us. "The government? Or Harvard?"

At nine the next morning, I was back in the federal courtroom, this time alone. I couldn't stay away. Riding the subway into the city, I read the morning papers, which McCarthy dominated. "Furry Refuses to Name Five Red Ex-Aides," read one. Another said: "Harvard Prof Tells of Reds in Radar Lab."

That second day was a stormy farce. McCarthy had subpoenaed five men, supposedly members of a Communist cell, who worked at the General Electric plant in nearby Lynn on military jet engines. This time the senator did not even permit witnesses to read statements. When one tried, McCarthy ordered federal marshals to remove him.

"I'll hear no speech of any Fifth Amendment Communist," McCarthy intoned.

The witness's lawyer asked permission to read the statement for him. "Remove the counsel," McCarthy shouted, and as U.S. marshals led the lawyer away, the senator announced, "If a man doesn't have the guts to stand up here and say he is a Communist and believes in the Communist revolution, he can't make statements."

The audience cheered. Then a man behind me yelled out that what McCarthy really was doing was helping General Electric purge union organizers. On McCarthy's orders, marshals picked the man up by the arms and carried him out.

Then a lawyer for another witness asked whether he could file a motion objecting to the validity of the proceedings.

McCarthy, after consulting with Cohn, answered no. Lawyers, he said, could not take part in the committee's proceedings, adding, "We have found in the past that Communist lawyers oftentimes try to use the committee room as a transmission belt for filibusters."

Later, when the same lawyer objected to one of McCarthy's questions to his client, McCarthy asked whether he—the lawyer—was himself a Communist, and then ordered him to stand and be sworn as a witness. When the lawyer refused, McCarthy had him removed too.

By the time the spectacle ended, I was shaken to the core. McCarthy and Cohn had abused people without qualm, even seeming to enjoy it, and that enraged me. Not that I knew Furry or Kamin or any of the other witnesses. I was no Communist either, not even a left-winger; in fact, I thought anyone who remained a Communist after Stalin was either a fool or blind. I'd more or less inherited my parents' moderate Jewish Democratic views, and if I'd been old enough to vote in the 1952 elections, I'd have voted enthusiastically for Adlai Stevenson. So it wasn't for ideological reasons that I found Cohn and McCarthy repugnant; my disgust was much deeper, much more instinctual. Furry's and Kamin's only sin was holding unpopular and, to me, foolish political views. But I'd watched a reckless demagogue play to a mob by bullying them. McCarthy stirred up fear, confusion, and suspicion, then used it as license to trash basic civil liberties. He turned a congressional investigation into government-sponsored terrorism.

As bad as he was, though, Cohn to me was even worse. Short and short-tempered, sullen in manner, brutal in speech, Cohn had a cruel streak. Worse still, he reminded me in some ways of myself—I too was young, smart, and a Jew—and these similarities bothered me more than I can say. How could a Jew, a man trained in the law, himself the son of a respected judge, ally himself with a rabble-rousing demagogue spouting intolerance and hate?

———

Dogmatism, intolerance, and hate were things about which I knew something, if at secondhand. I was born in 1932, in Far Rockaway, Queens, a grandchild of Russian Jews who had emigrated to the United States. My grandparents on both sides had come from the Pale, the one part of czarist Russia where Jews were legally allowed to settle. Like many Jews, they had fled religious persecution and economic hardship. Pogroms had been a reality for them, and so were military conscription, legal restrictions on schools and jobs, and special taxes imposed on Jews.

My father's father, Louis Liman, came from a shtetl called Orla, which is now part of Poland. His family had run a one-room tavern. When he was twenty-one years old, he and his siblings had made their way to Rotterdam, bought steerage tickets, and emigrated to the United States. He arrived in New York in July 1891. An immigration officer trimmed his name from Limanski to Liman. Years later, when I was at Harvard, people sometimes asked me whether I was related to the Lymans of Beacon Hill. No, I would say, I'm from the Limanskis of Orla.

With some pots and pans he got from a relative, Louis Liman walked from town to town throughout the South, his inventory clanking on his back. A peddler's life, though, was not to his liking. When he had scraped together enough money, he rented a cigar store on 124th Street in New York City and lived above it with his family. My father, Harry Liman, was born above that store. Eventually, Louis Liman brought his own parents to the United States. His father, Chaim, was beaten to death on the Lower East Side, soon after he arrived in New York, by an anti-Semitic Irish immigrant. For this and other reasons, Louis Liman's life in the United States could not have been an easy one, but I never heard him speak of Orla. It was as if his life began only after he arrived here. He was fiercely proud that he was a naturalized American citizen and could read and write English. That he also was fluent in Russian and Polish he never mentioned.

Growing up a Jew in the 1930s and 1940s, it was virtually impossible to not learn at a very early age to value tolerance, due process, and civil liberties almost as much as life itself since for many Jews they were often the same. During the first two decades of my life, there occurred the most deadly and relentless persecution of Jews since the Crusades. In Germany the Nazis were burning and ransacking Jewish homes, businesses, and synagogues. Here at home, in the 1930s, Father Charles E. Coughlin, on his weekly radio broadcasts, stirred up virulent anti-Semitism by blaming the Depression, the coming war, and everything else that was troublesome on the Jews. Saturday mornings in temple, our rabbi told us horrifying, nearly unbelievable stories about the slave-labor camps in Poland. In the late 1930s, before the war began, my family corresponded with a relative in Poland, hoping to bring him to the United States, but suddenly, ominously, the letters went unanswered. And then came the Holocaust.

So, for a Jewish child, even in a calm, mostly Jewish suburb like Lawrence, the small Long Island town I grew up in, it was an insecure and scary time. Although I was never physically attacked, as my great-grandfather was, more than once, after Hebrew school, I was taunted as a Christ-killer. Anti-Semitism was real. We Jews knew our place. We could not live in certain towns. Even Lawrence had a restricted neighborhood, what we called the Back Country. It was an enclave of expensive houses with wide lawns owned by men who took the train to Wall Street banks, wore seersucker suits and white straw hats in the summer, sent their children to private schools, and gathered at restricted clubs like the Rockaway Hunt Club and the Lawrence Beach Club. We were proud of prominent Jews like Henry Morgenthau, Roosevelt's Treasury Secretary, and Felix Frankfurter, who sat on the Supreme Court, yet we also knew that many Jews worried when Roosevelt appointed Frankfurter in 1939, convinced that it would increase anti-Semitism. We knew too that many universities had strict Jewish quotas. It was regarded as a breakthrough in 1946 when my sister, Gladys, was admitted to Smith College—where, of course, she was assigned a Jewish roommate. Hotels displayed "No Jews Permitted" signs. Certain industries did not hire Jews. Homeowners signed restrictive covenants agreeing not to sell to them. Some of my friends, ashamed of their Jewishness, tried to pass themselves off as Episcopalians.

My parents, along with others of their generation, never quite shook their instinctual fear of government authority. Even safe in America, in a calm and comfortable suburb, they could not rid themselves of the history of persecution, the knowledge of how swiftly fear, ignorance, and hatred could sweep through a people. On the one hand, Jews depended on tolerance for their very survival. On the other hand, our history had been a two-thousand-year-old story of never quite belonging.

Small wonder that I grew up fearing the demagogue, the rabble-rouser, the hater, and the dogmatist and treasuring tolerance, fairness, and respect for individual liberties. I was wary of anyone, myself perhaps most of all, who thought he knew the true religion or political ideology, and I was downright scared of any such person who was in a position of authority and power. When I was in law school, I read a speech that Learned Hand, the great federal judge, had made in May 1944, just two weeks before D-day, to 150,000 newly naturalized citizens who had gathered for an "I Am an American Day" ceremony on the Great Lawn in Central Park. "What is the spirit of liberty?" he asked.

> I cannot define it; I can only tell you my own faith. The spirit of liberty is the spirit which is not too sure that it is right; the spirit of liberty is the spirit which seeks to understand the minds of other men and women; the spirit of liberty is the spirit which weighs their interests alongside its own without bias.

Hand's words expressed perfectly my skeptical, tolerant inclinations and the commitment I felt to fairness and equal respect for all members of the community. And fifty years later, when I read them again, they still do.

————

Like most Jewish immigrants, my family valued education for its own sake and as the surest way to a secure, happy life. My mother had been the valedictorian of her high school class, graduated Phi Beta Kappa from Hunter College, and taught Latin. My father was the first Liman to attend college—the tuition-free City College of New York—and for a while he taught history in the New York City public schools. Eventually, in 1920, he joined his father in a dressmaking business.

Operating out of a cramped factory on Seventh Avenue in the Garment District, the firm of L. Liman & Son produced what were known as "popular-priced" dresses, which sold for less than five dollars each. My father would buy an expensive dress at a department store, copy the style and pattern, and then return the original dress to the store. It is one of the pleasing ironies of my career that, many years later, I represented designers such as Calvin Klein and Ralph Lauren, whose designs my father would eagerly have knocked off if he'd lived long enough.

Harry Liman regarded the dressmaking business as just a business; he derogatorily referred to it as the *schmata* business, or the rag trade. The people he really admired were those who earned a living using their education and intellect. One summer I worked in my father's shipping room, folding and packing dresses in boxes for shipping to stores, and was a total failure. I was unable to master the art of folding and every box I packed and shipped came back because the dresses arrived so badly wrinkled the customer couldn't sell them. My father didn't care. The dressmaking business gave us a comfortable middle-class life, but he never wanted me to follow him into it.

When Harvard College accepted me in 1950, it was like a dream coming true—for both the family and me. Harvard was the oldest university in the country. It was Roosevelt's college. In our naïveté, we thought that a Harvard degree not only symbolized acceptance but ensured a successful career. It was, of course, nothing like that. Harvard couldn't even get me a summer job. I worked at Long Island beach clubs, first as a cabana boy and then as a parking attendant. Parking was a promotion because I received a one-dollar tip per car and got to drive the latest models. But Wall Street and corporate America, at the time, were not beating down the doors to hire Harvard graduates, and in my class, only the premed students knew definitely where they were headed.

When I was growing up in Lawrence, the only lawyers I knew were a man who played handball with my father and handled house closings and a bankruptcy lawyer who had moved onto our street just before I left for college. Yet watching McCarthy, a former judge, and Cohn, a former federal prosecutor, abuse their lawyerly skills for such ugly ends, I knew what I wanted to do. The lawyers I saw at the hearings may have been courageous, but they were ineffectual. Too deferential by far, they gave the farcically unfair proceedings an air of legitimacy, and as I sat in that Boston courtroom, watching them and their clients being dragged away one by one for trying to speak while the gleeful mob shouted and clapped, I was sure for the first time that I wanted to be a lawyer.

So, in the fall of 1954, I entered Yale Law School. It was the ideal place for a young man wary of orthodoxy. Yale taught a skeptical and pragmatic approach to the law called legal realism. Orthodox legal theory held that judges decide difficult or controversial lawsuits by applying fixed and abstract rules based on previous judicial decisions, or precedent. Legal realism, however, held that judges decide cases according to their own political and moral views and use appropriate legal rules to explain the results. Legal realism said that judges must do so because the law should be an instrument for social change, and Yale taught that the best judges were those willing to abandon precedent and its fixed rules if the facts of the case and a changing world demanded it. In May 1954, several months before I entered law school, the Supreme Court outlawed racial segregation in schools in *Brown v. Board of Education*. *Brown* was a vivid example of a court discarding years of judicial precedent, but it was just one of many such cases. We read hundreds of others in which judges shook off archaic rules that would have prevented them from compensating victims, nullifying unconscionable contracts, or ensuring civil liberties. This was a time of great ferment in the law, and Yale taught me, above all, that lawyers could make a difference in the type of society we had.

Roy Cohn lasted only a short time as McCarthy's counsel. In the fall of 1953, he and the senator from Wisconsin went after the U.S. Army. For a few months, they garnered headlines by making flimsy charges of disloyalty and espionage in the Army, but the Army did not cave in. The showdown—the Army-McCarthy hearings in the late spring of 1954—was televised nationally. For thirty-five days, millions of Americans watched as the Army's lawyer, the canny and courtly Joseph L. Welch of Boston, stood up to Cohn and McCarthy. By the time it was over, McCarthy's arrogance and vulgarity had done him in. The Senate voted to condemn him in December, and he died three years later, in May 1957, probably from heavy drinking.

Roy Cohn resigned as McCarthy's chief counsel in August 1954, after the Army-McCarthy hearings, and returned to New York to practice law. Over the next twenty years, I had several encounters with him. There were times when we found ourselves on the same side of a case, but even then Cohn was as ruthless as he'd been as McCarthy's counsel. An intimidator and a bluffer, he was famous among lawyers for winning cases by delays, evasions, and lies. He even boasted that he bribed judges. For Cohn, the law was a contest without rules and apparently had no purpose other than increasing the wealth and celebrity of Roy M. Cohn. Just before he died in 1986, New York disbarred him. He had deceived a dying client into signing a codicil to his will making Cohn one of his executors. Cohn had also refused to repay a $100,000 loan from a client, mishandled escrowed funds, including the insurance proceeds from a yacht that had mysteriously burned and sank, and lied on his application to the District of Columbia bar.

One day after court—I remember it well—Cohn offered me a ride back to my office. Not relishing the thought of driving around town in his white Cadillac convertible limousine, with the top down no less, I respectfully declined, but as he was leaving, the impulse seized me.

"You know, Roy," I said to him, "it was because of you that I became a lawyer."

Arrogant as always, Cohn was delighted. He took it as a compliment, a way of praising his skill in the courtroom. It was unimaginable to him that I might loathe his brutal tactics, his dishonesty, his contempt for fairness, and above all else his amorality.

I failed to enlighten him.

2

The Judge: Simon H. Rifkind

I F ROY COHN AND Joe McCarthy made me want to be a lawyer, it was Simon Hirsch Rifkind—the greatest courtroom advocate of his time—who taught me how to be one.

Rifkind was born in 1901, and he spent the first nine years of his life in the tiny village of Meretz in Lithuania, which was then part of imperial Russia. He often said he'd been born in the sixteenth century. During his years as a young boy in Meretz, he never wore a factory-made garment and never saw a newspaper. Villagers drew their water from a common well and carried it home in buckets suspended from shoulder harnesses. Rifkind spoke only Yiddish and read only Hebrew. He never spoke or heard a word of English until he was nine years old. His father had left for America when Rifkind was just an infant, and it wasn't until 1910 that he could finally afford to send for his wife and children.

When I first met him, in 1957, Rifkind was fifty-five, a small, trim, elegant man, with round glasses and a small mustache. Though he hadn't become fluent in English until high school, he had no trace of an accent—either Russian or Bronx. I often thought he must have memorized the dictionary—his was the widest and most arresting vocabulary of anyone I have ever known. His diction was elegant, and he chose words with care and flair. He liked to call himself a ham, but despite his enormous intellect, he was neither affected nor ponderous nor arch. He was wise without being pedantic, and persuasive without being overbearing.

For a time, in the 1940s, Rifkind had been a federal trial judge, and after that everyone called him "Judge," even his partners. Eventually, I got used to calling him Si rather than Judge, but that was only after I'd been his partner for fifteen years. The man wasn't at all haughty, though. He was civil, almost courtly, in manner. If he ever raised his voice in anger or complaint, I never heard it. As fierce an advocate as he was in court, he used reason and logic, not personal attack, and he treated everyone with equal courtesy, even when he was eroding a witness's credibility on cross-examination or flaying an adversary's argument.

If he'd been born, as he said, in the sixteenth century, Rifkind caught up with the twentieth in a hurry. After high school, he attended City College and then Columbia Law School, where he met William O. Douglas, the future Supreme Court justice, who became a lifelong friend. What a delightfully odd pair the two of them must have made—Douglas, the tall, rugged, plain-spoken westerner from Walla Walla, Washington, and Rifkind, the spare Russian immigrant from New York City. Rifkind's legal career began in 1927, when New York's newly elected senator, Robert F. Wagner, a former judge and labor lawyer, hired him as his sole legislative assistant. Wagner's Senate staff was tiny—just Rifkind and two stenographers. Rifkind wrote bills and committee reports for his boss and simultaneously ran Wagner's law practice in New York. During the Depression, Wagner was responsible for the enactment of extensive labor legislation, and Rifkind helped him draft bills that became the core of the New Deal's economic and social policies.

Of all the bills Rifkind worked on, the best known was the National Industrial Recovery Act, which Congress passed a few months after Roosevelt took office in 1933. It was the most comprehensive program for industrial recovery, public works, and unemployment relief ever enacted in this country, and it created the National Recovery Administration (NRA), which had the authority to control prices, restrict production, set minimum wages and maximum work hours, and establish industrywide codes of fair competition. Rifkind wrote a section of the bill that firmly announced the right of American workers to organize, to engage in collective bargaining, and to strike. Section 7(a), as it was called, declared that every industrial code must provide that "employees shall have the right to organize and bargain collectively through representatives of their own choosing, and shall be free from the interference, restraint, or coercion of employers . . . in the designation of such representatives." The new law also created the National Labor Relations Board to supervise collective bargaining and stop unfair labor practices. Although, in 1935, the Supreme Court declared parts of the law unconstitutional, Congress reenacted Rifkind's section 7(a) provisions in what is now called the Wagner Act. It is an eloquent and concise statute, and Judge Rifkind wrote it on one sheet of a legal pad, a fact he delighted in reminding us of, particularly when President Clinton's health care reform legislation ran to thousands of pages.

Rifkind left Washington on June 16, 1933, the day the Senate passed the National Industrial Recovery Act, and returned to New York City to run the Wagner law firm. By this time, he was Wagner's law partner. In 1941, at Wagner's urging, President Roosevelt appointed Rifkind to be a United States District Judge in New York. Rifkind was only forty, but he quickly won a reputation as one of the ablest judges in the country. In October 1945, just after the defeat of Germany, he took a six-month leave from his judgeship to advise General Eisenhower on Jewish affairs in Europe, then returned to the bench for four more years. In May 1950, unable to afford sending his children to college on the modest salary then paid to federal judges—$15,000 a year—he resigned and was invited by Louis Weiss to join him and his twelve other partners in the firm then called Paul, Weiss, Wharton & Garrison to build a litigation practice.

The firm that eventually became Paul, Weiss had been formed before World War I by several Jewish lawyers, among them Louis Weiss's father. It had had a general commercial practice for a small group of prosperous German Jews—the Cullman family, tobacco merchants who later formed Phillip Morris, the Straus family, who owned the Macy's department store, and others. Then, in 1923, Louis Weiss started his own firm with a classmate from Columbia Law School, John F. Wharton. Weiss was a Jew, and Wharton a Protestant, and they resolved that their firm, Weiss & Wharton, would be one in which

Gentiles and Jews would be at home as partners, employees, and clients. A few years later, they merged with the original Weiss firm.

Louis Weiss was the soul of the firm. His liberalism and open-mindedness attracted clients like Marshall Field in 1941, when Field wanted to start a new newspaper in Chicago, the *Sun*, to challenge Colonel Robert McCormick's reactionary *Tribune*. John Wharton became a specialist in theatrical law. He pioneered the use of a uniform partnership agreement that spelled out the different interests of backers of theatrical productions. He also devised a contract that allowed an author to sell motion picture rights to a play before it was produced on the stage. In 1942 he became Cole Porter's lawyer and, after Porter's death, the sole trustee of the Cole Porter Musical and Literary Property Trusts, which controlled the rights to Porter's songs. Wharton also represented clients in the fledgling television industry and the movie producer David Selznick, who made *Gone with the Wind*.

Weiss & Wharton thrived. One early recruit to the firm was Walter Pollak, a talented civil liberties lawyer who represented the "Scottsboro Boys"—four young black men who were summarily tried and convicted of a rape they did not commit and were headed for the electric chair. Another was Randolph Paul, the tax lawyer, who left his position as counsel to the U.S. Treasury Department in 1944 to join the firm. Lloyd K. Garrison, the great-grandson of William Lloyd Garrison, the abolitionist editor, came along in 1946. A delightful, gentle, and self-effacing man, Garrison had been the first chairman of the National Labor Relations Board (created by one of the bills that Rifkind had written for Senator Wagner) and dean of the University of Wisconsin Law School. Roosevelt had considered him for the Supreme Court seat filled by William O. Douglas.

When Rifkind joined, in May 1950, the firm had just a dozen partners. Only one did trial work, so Rifkind set about building up a trial practice. He soon won attention for the firm with some highly publicized successes. One was a libel action against the popular commentator Walter Winchell, for branding the *New York Post* editor a Communist. Rifkind also represented Madame Chiang Kai-shek, wife of the Chinese Nationalist leader, when she sued the columnist Drew Pearson for allegedly defaming her, and he defended Supreme Court Justice Douglas against an impeachment attempt led by then-Congressman Gerald Ford. Later he was Jacqueline Kennedy's lawyer when she tried to have portions deleted from William Manchester's book *The Death of a President*. He used to say that the lawyer's prayer is "Give me a rich, scared client," and he seemed to attract all of them.

By the time I went to work for Paul Weiss, Rifkind was bringing in most of the firm's new cases, and other lawyers commonly called us "the Rifkind firm." Given his dominance, Rifkind could have ruled the firm as a dictator if he'd wanted to, but he was no autocrat. He believed that every partner, even the youngest, should have the same vote as he, and he wrote a statement of firm principles that have remained unchanged to this day:

> Our objectives are, by pooling our energies, talents and resources, to achieve the highest order of excellence in the practice of the art, the science and the profession of the law; through such practice to earn a living and to derive the stimulation and pleasure of worthwhile adventure; and in all things to govern ourselves as members of a free democratic society with responsibilities both to our profession and our country.
>
> We believe in maintaining, by affirmative efforts, a membership of partners and associates reflecting a wide variety of religious, political, ethnic and social backgrounds, characteristic of that community. We believe that through this policy we may bring to the service of our clients greater breadth of understanding and wider contacts with the world at large, while enriching our personal lives and demonstrating the value of democratic principles as applied to the organization of a law firm.

Despite his busy private practice, Rifkind found time to take on important public assignments. He believed lawyers owed their livelihood to the community and were obliged to contribute their skills to its welfare. In 1955, for example, the Supreme Court asked for his help in resolving a complex dispute between California and Arizona over rights to the waters of the Colorado River. Twenty years later, in 1975, when New York City was nearly bankrupt, Governor Hugh Carey asked for his advice on how to rescue the city's finances. Billions of dollars of New York City bonds were coming due. The city could scarcely afford to redeem them, yet no one would lend the city more money to pay its debts. Though others recommended that the city default on its bonds and file for bankruptcy, Rifkind knew that would be ruinous. With his help, the city declared a moratorium. It deferred paying its creditors for a time, without, however, defaulting on its obligations. Courts eventually ruled against the moratorium, but meanwhile Rifkind bought the city time and saved it from a disastrous bankruptcy. It was his proudest achievement.

He never retired from the practice of law. In 1986, when he was eighty-five, Pennzoil hired Rifkind in its fight with Texaco. As I will relate later, a Texas jury awarded Pennzoil $11 billion because Texaco had unlawfully wrested control of Getty Oil from Pennzoil, and Texaco was now appealing that verdict. Pennzoil knew it needed an exceptional advocate to defend what even Pennzoil knew might be undefendable, but Pennzoil executives were skeptical when I recommended they talk to Judge Rifkind. They looked him up in *Who's Who*, and they said, "But, Arthur, he's eighty-five!" "Don't worry," I replied. "Just meet him." This they did, and the Pennzoil executives were quickly convinced. In fact, Judge Rifkind was so persuasive that they turned down an extraordinary settlement offer. He then went to Houston and argued the case brilliantly. The judgment was upheld.

Judge Rifkind died in November 1995 at the age of ninety-four. Some years before, on his eightieth birthday, he'd made me swear to him that I would tell him if I ever saw his mind slip in any respect, so that he could withdraw immediately as a partner and not embarrass himself or the rest of us. But there was no such occasion. His mind remained as keen as when I first met him.

When I graduated from Yale Law in 1957, New York law firms were mostly Jewish or non-Jewish. The prestigious and elite Wall Street firms represented the blue-chip corporations and banks, and they rigidly excluded Jews. One writer called them the "last frigid citadel of Anglo-Saxon Protestantism." A partner at a leading Wall Street law firm told me to not even bother applying. I might have been first in my class, he said, but I was a Jew. His frankness, I believed, was sincerely meant to be helpful. He said he did not want me to be misled or disappointed. Some Wall Street firms, he said, though not his, might make an exception and take on a Jew as an associate, but none would ever make one a partner.

Yale nonetheless steered me toward the Wall Street firms, in the hope that, because of my grades, I would be taken on and that would make it easier for other Jewish applicants. I never so much as heard of Paul, Weiss until late in my second year. But then, at a Yale class reunion, a cousin of mine mentioned to a young Paul, Weiss lawyer, Ernie Ruben-stein, that I was first in my class at Yale and in need of a job that summer. Rubenstein, a former editor of the *Yale Law Journal* and Supreme Court clerk, was understandably skeptical since, by the testimony of cousins and other relatives, every Jewish law student was at the top of his class. The Yale placement office, however, confirmed the story. I happened to be home the following weekend. Ernie lived nearby, and he dropped by to talk to me about Paul, Weiss. As we stood in my driveway and he told me about the firm and what it stood for—the partners and clients from dif-ferent religious backgrounds, the lawyers who fought for civil liberties—I knew that was where I wanted to practice. I spent that summer working at Paul, Weiss, then finished school, and in November 1957, after taking the bar exam, I reported to work. I had just turned twenty-five. Except for leaves of absence to do government work, I've never left.

Initially, I thought I was going to be a tax lawyer. During that first sum-mer, before my last year at Yale, I was assigned to work on a complicated tax problem for the large Dutch electronics company Phillips NKV. Before the Second World War, Phillips owned and operated several sub-sidiary companies in North and South America. With war approaching, Phillips feared that its subsidiaries might be seized, either by the Nazis, if they invaded the Netherlands, or by foreign governments at war with Germany, and so the parent company formed a trust in the United States to hold the stock of its Western Hemisphere subsidiaries. It provided that if Germany invaded the Netherlands, Phillips's shareholders would be the beneficiaries of the trust, and because an American bank, not Phillips, would hold the stock as trustee, the Nazis could not seize it. It was an ingenious scheme, and it had worked. But now, eleven years after the war ended, the American bank still held the stock of the former subsidiaries, and Phillips had asked Paul, Weiss for advice on how to end the trust and recover the subsidiaries to Phillips without creating catastrophic tax consequences. I spent that summer working on a plan to accomplish this tax-free, and on a request to the Internal Revenue Service to approve the plan.

Evidently, my work was good enough that, when I joined the firm full-time, I was assigned to the tax department, even though I'd taken just one basic tax course in law school. I might have happily stayed there. The tax department was a small elite unit. Its work was always intellectually challenging. Bookish and awkward, I enjoyed tax law and its quiet, exquisitely complex puzzles. If there was someone whose career I thought I might follow, it was Dean Acheson, the New York corporate lawyer who had moved from his Wall Street practice to important government positions and back. He'd been Undersecretary of the Treasury under Roosevelt, then Secretary of State under Truman from 1949 to 1952. Trial lawyers, it seemed to me, were an altogether different breed. My image of the trial lawyer remained Clarence Darrow, who had sided with the working man, with minorities and radicals, and who had fought for due process and a fair trial and against bigotry, ignorance, and hate. But Darrow was larger than life, a man of impassioned eloquence whose power I could never imagine equaling.

But Ernie Rubenstein—the lawyer who had recruited me—once again intervened. He himself was in the litigation department, but after two years there he decided he wanted to be a tax lawyer. Because Paul, Weiss was so small, the partners wouldn't allow him to move unless he could persuade a tax lawyer to change places with him. Ernie asked me to do it, and there was no way I could turn him down. He promised that if I didn't like litigation, we would switch back, but I never took him up on it. In fact, I never looked back. And so, just a few months after I arrived at Paul, Weiss, I found myself a fledgling trial lawyer.

One of the cases I took over from Ernie was an appeal he'd been working on with Paul, Weiss's newest litigation partner, who was none other than Adlai Stevenson. Governor Stevenson, of course, had been the Democratic Party's presidential nominee in 1952 and 1956, but he'd been defeated twice by Eisenhower. He'd had a small law firm in Chicago, and at Judge Rifkind's urging, he combined his firm with Paul, Weiss in May 1957, several months before I joined the firm. For young liberal Democrats like me, Stevenson was an icon. In what had been, for us, a dark and difficult political period, he was a voice of calm rationality, of wit and elegance, and though he'd lost in the elections, he'd redeemed the Democratic Party for us and kept it vibrant and vital. Moreover, Stevenson was still active in politics and world affairs, and he seemed likely to run again for the Democratic presidential nomination in 1960. The chance to work with him, needless to say, was irresistible.

Stevenson spent most of his time in Chicago, but he was coming to New York to argue an important appeal. The owners of the Empire State Building had retained Judge Rifkind to challenge their property tax assessment. Rifkind had lost—a rarity—and the matter was now on appeal. He'd asked Stevenson to handle the appeal, and I was now assigned to the matter. Ernie Rubenstein and I would write the brief to the court, and then I would help Stevenson prepare for his oral argument. I couldn't help thinking that Stevenson ought to be working on a State of the Union message instead of preparing an argument on the appropriate depreciation rate for the Empire State Building, but the country's loss was my great fortune.

Stevenson read our brief in Chicago and then came east about a week before the argument, in May 1958, to prepare. Ernie and I had written an impassioned brief. To persuade the Court of Appeals that the taxes on the Empire State Building were unfairly high, we'd pointed out that the building was twenty-seven years old and almost obsolete—it had manually operated elevators and a primitive chilled water system rather than modern air conditioning. In calculating how much the building had depreciated, we argued, the city had totally overlooked the obsolescence factor. I made one awful mistake, though: I voiced no objection when Stevenson announced that, having never been inside the Empire State Building, he was going to stroll over by himself to have a look. If Judge Rifkind had visited the building, he would have noticed every sign of wear and tear that he could evoke in his argument, but Stevenson was more detached. After his inspection, his ardor for our position dimmed. "Having read your brief," he told me when he returned, "I expected to be hit by a falling brick, or to be stuck for a day in the elevators. By Chicago standards, it's actually a pretty nice building."

Whatever his misgivings about the merits of the case, Stevenson holed up in a suite in the old Sherry Netherland Hotel on Fifth Avenue, and he, Ernie, and I set about writing his argument for the Empire State Building appeal. Naturally, I couldn't help but be a little intimidated, in advance, by the idea of working with Stevenson. He turned out to be short, slightly overweight, rather aristocratic, bright, funny, and he seemed incapable of uttering a sentence that did not sound polished. But above all, he was offhandedly charming, and he put me immediately at ease.

He told us, to our surprise, that he planned to read his argument aloud to the court. The prevailing belief was that oral argument is more effective when extemporaneous and unstudied, and because most appellate courts often don't allow an advocate to complete a sentence without peppering him or her with questions, a prepared speech usually is of little use. But Stevenson read from a polished text whenever he delivered his speeches and was justly renowned for his witty, highly literate prose; he said he was going to present his argument the same way.

When we started, we had nothing—not a draft, not even an outline. We built the argument sentence by sentence, Stevenson selecting and placing each word just so. Was there a better, more precise synonym? Did the sentence have the right rhythm? Was the cadence perfect? This was in the days before faxes, of course, so when Stevenson was pleased with a couple of sentences, he would dictate them to his secretary over the phone, and shortly thereafter a typed version would arrive. Slowly, over several days, the argument unfolded until it reached twenty minutes when spoken aloud.

Stevenson and I fretted over the text for the entire three-hour train ride up the Hudson from New York City to Albany, where the Court of Appeals sits. Since oral arguments have a simple ending, usually a sentence or two asking the court to rule in the client's favor, Ernie and I hadn't bothered to write one out in full. I'd jotted just a few key words on a piece of paper in case Stevenson needed them to jog his memory. But now he wanted even the conclusion written out. We sat in the club car together and wrote, read aloud, and rewrote the last paragraph of his argument. Then, when we arrived at the Court of Appeals, Stevenson handed it to a court clerk and asked her to type it up for him—a remarkable request that only a celebrity like Stevenson could have gotten away with—and off we went to lunch. When we got back to court, the clerk handed Stevenson his new typewritten conclusion, and he quickly added it to the other pages.

Stevenson's argument to the Court of Appeals was utterly splendid. It was polished and graceful, and he read it with a stately formality—except for the very end. When he came to it, he first read the typed conclusion he and I had written on the train, but then, instead of finishing, he turned to the last page. There were my handwritten notes for the conclusion! I'd forgotten to throw them away, and evidently the court clerk had left them in place. I thought about interrupting him, but I was simply too petrified. I sat there, immobile, while out of his elegant voice came a string of disconnected phrases that made no sense whatsoever. There was a stunned silence. Stevenson must have realized he was reading my mnemonic devices. Fortunately, he was not only a gifted speechwriter but an adroit off-the-cuff speaker as well. He recovered instantaneously and finished his presentation with a second closing far more eloquent and spontaneous than the one we had penned on the train. While I thought my career was finished before it began, this courteous and elegant man never uttered so much as a word of complaint to me.

Stevenson left, immediately after the argument, on a trip to the Soviet Union. The judges had listened to him with rapt attention, enjoying his delivery so much they'd seemed reluctant to mar its elegance with questions. But the spell must have been broken with his departure. When the court announced its ruling—the judges had decided unanimously against us—Ernie and I sent Stevenson a cable in Moscow that said simply: "REGRET THAT COURT SAYS DEPRECIATION DOES NOT INCLUDE OBSOLESCENCE." I liked to think the KGB spent days trying to decipher that message.

The litigation department at Paul, Weiss, headed by Judge Rifkind, was small and collegial. We had only two full-time litigation partners and three senior associates, but together they formed an extraordinary group—all superb lawyers and teachers.

Samuel J. Silverman, then in his fifties, was second in command. He was a scholarly lawyer, the kind who carried all the key precedents in his head, and he read Proust in French on his subway ride in from Brooklyn. Unlike Rifkind, he wasn't a rainmaker, but every rainmaker needs a Silverman to make sure the work gets out. Sam, who almost always wore a smile—which could turn to a scowl if the work was beneath his standards—was a blunt, brilliant practitioner. He didn't dominate a courtroom the way Rifkind could, but his command of legal precedents overwhelmed the bench. He was a stickler for form, never tolerated mistakes, and believed intuition took a lawyer only so far. There was no substitute, Sam liked to say, for the law library. But he also delegated as much responsibility as he sensed a young lawyer was ready for, and in my first year at Paul, Weiss I was doing work that lawyers three years out of law school envision: drawing complaints, writing briefs and arguing motions, taking depositions.

When I first arrived at Paul Weiss, Silverman was in the midst of trying a case involving *The Diary of Anne Frank*. We represented the producer of the play, who was being sued by Meyer Levin. Levin had written the original adaptation for the theatrical version, but Otto Frank, Anne's father, was dissatisfied with Levin's script, which had made Anne into a specifically Jewish heroine. Frank saw his daughter as a more universal figure who, even at the end, was incapable of hate. New playwrights were hired, Frances Goodrich and Albert Hackett, and it was their version that had won the Pulitzer Prize. But then Levin brought a suit for plagiarism, and the jury found for him.

Every lawyer at Paul, Weiss had a passionate devotion to his clients, but Silverman was totally distraught at the jury's verdict. He told me, a lawyer a few months out of law school, that he was considering leaving the profession. He said he'd read the Levin script over and over, that the theme was entirely different from the play as it was produced, and that he'd lost confidence in a system that could permit so unfair a result.

I found myself consoling my mentor as best I could. I kept reminding him that, as every law student learns, juries are unpredictable and all we lawyers can do is use our abilities to achieve more just decisions. But I learned something too: not that I should maintain a distance from clients so as not to be hurt by disappointments, but that the best lawyers care so deeply that they are able to argue a case with passion and feeling. As for Sam Silverman, perhaps my platitudes did help him. In any case, he stayed on.

The other full-time litigation partner was Martin Kleinbard, then in his midforties. Martin was the very model of the insecure trial lawyer. He strove for perfection. Because he wrote his briefs over and over again, an associate working for him had to labor over every word, and he wouldn't think of questioning a witness unless the questions had been written out for him. But he had a disarming sense of humor that he could also use as a weapon, and a special skill in family disputes, which he could often settle where everyone else had failed.

In contrast to Kleinbard were two trial lawyers on the verge of becoming partners—Jay Topkis and Ed Costikyan. Topkis, who had been an editor of the *Columbia Spectator*, wrote his briefs with a dagger. No one could edit them—not a word was wasted. He was quick-witted, and his preparation seemed effortless. Yet Topkis also understood that associates should never be made to feel inferior, and he built up everyone who worked with him, myself included.

Costikyan was also a confident, efficient litigator. He could dictate all his briefs without having to make a change. In a time-honored Paul, Weiss tradition, he found time to enter politics and, as a reform leader in the Democratic Party, toppled Carmine DeSapio, then the head of Tammany Hall.

With Topkis, I worked on a brief for the Supreme Court. I thought I'd drafted a very persuasive piece of work, but Topkis took it to the beach over the weekend, and very few of my words survived. It was not that my brief was *lengthy*, but that Topkis used a punchy vernacular that made my prose seem ponderous. I learned from that. With Sam Silverman, I brought a series of stockholder suits against the management of a publicly held company, charging them with the waste of corporate assets. Sam taught me how to do everything, from drawing the complaints to taking pretrial examinations. Because I was less than thirty, I had to conceal my age. Otherwise, the client might have wondered why, when he had selected Rifkind and got Silverman, this associate Liman, just a couple of years out of law school, was doing all the work.

After some two years at Paul, Weiss, I got my first chance to work directly with Judge Rifkind. The case was a huge criminal antitrust prosecution against a large group of oil companies. Our client was a major oil company called Cities Service. In late 1956, a French-English-Israeli force had seized the Suez Canal, the major artery to and from the Middle East oil fields, and had interrupted the flow of oil. Soon after, crude oil and gasoline prices in the United States jumped. A federal grand jury had indicted Cities Service and dozens of other oil companies for conspiring to fix prices after the Suez crisis. At the time, it was the biggest criminal case ever brought by the federal government, and people on both sides of the case expected the trial to last for months.

The other oil companies had certainly prepared for a mammoth trial. Each had organized committees of lawyers, each assigned to develop various facts and research legal questions, with one or two lawyers from each firm appointed to each committee. Because Rifkind had only two of us helping him prepare for trial—Jay Topkis and me—we served on virtually all the committees. Too embarrassed to acknowledge the truth, we told the others that the many Paul, Weiss lawyers working on the case with us were simply too busy to spend time on the committees.

The trial began in December 1959, before Judge Royce Savage in federal court in Tulsa, Oklahoma. Rifkind arrived in Tulsa late the evening before, and I met him at the airport. With me at the wheel, and the two of us in animated conversation, we set off for the hotel, which was about twenty minutes away. We drove for a while past cows and oil wells, but the Tulsa skyline never appeared. Just as Rifkind began to ask gently whether I was sure we were going in the right direction, I saw a sign indicating we were three times farther away from Tulsa than when we'd started! I was mortified, but the judge was totally unruffled. The detour, he said happily, had simply given us some extra time to discuss the case together.

Every day, once the trial had begun, the other lawyers hauled crates of documents into the courtroom. We had the same documents, of course, but Judge Rifkind wanted only a few key ones handy in court. That was a relief to me. As the junior lawyer, custom dictated that I be responsible for organizing and retrieving the documents. Managing paper, unfortunately, has never been one of my skills. Once, in law school, I misplaced a footnote for a law review article I was editing. Its author, Guido Calabresi, who went on to become dean of the Yale Law School and is now a federal appeals judge, spread the rumor that I'd eaten his footnote. Nowadays computers have made it a lot easier to handle litigation documents, but this was in the days when a single mainframe computer would have filled the entire courtroom. Instead, we had a crude indexing system, but I found even that baffling. We punched slots in each of the thousands of documents in the case at a particular place along its margin, depending on the subject matter. To retrieve all the documents relating to a particular topic, all you had to do, in theory, was push a long knitting needle through the correct slot, shake the documents, and the ones you wanted would fall out. Never handy with gadgets, I couldn't master the technique. Topkis and Judge Rifkind often found me on the floor of our hotel room, picking up hundreds of fallen documents.

Once under way, though, the trial went at a gallop. Within a few weeks, the prosecutors had completed their case, and the defense lawyers met to decide what to do. This was an all-star team of the antitrust bar. Some had represented major oil companies in antitrust cases dating back to the 1930s, and all had towering reputations.

The other oil companies wanted to put on complex defenses to the government's allegations by calling dozens of witnesses and introducing batteries of documents. Rifkind, however, disagreed. His unique gift as an advocate, I should point out, was not his eloquence, although that was unmatched, but his common sense. He was unafraid to make the complex simple, staking his case on a few bold propositions. He was far from being an expert in antitrust, but in this case that proved an advantage. The antitrust specialists were utterly immersed in the complexities of oil industry pricing and the Supreme Court's antitrust precedents. Like the child who points out that the emperor has no clothes, Rifkind contended that the government had simply failed to prove a conspiracy, and so the defendants did not have to put on a defense. All the government had shown, he argued, was that the oil companies had raised their prices at the same time. But what did that prove? The conspiracy case should be dismissed, and any other defense was a waste of time.

Rifkind convinced the other defense lawyers to move to dismiss without calling any witnesses. I doubt that any of them believed the judge would do this without hearing the defense, but they didn't know Rifkind, and, they agreed, there was nothing to be lost in trying.

Rifkind fervently believed in his cause and that made him all the more persuasive. The government, he told Judge Savage, had furnished no proof of an actual conspiracy. Yes, the oil companies had all raised their prices at the same time—that was a fact—but so what? Every barrel of crude oil was just like every other barrel of crude, just as every bushel of wheat or corn was the same as every other bushel. Naturally, Rifkind said, oil companies would charge the same price for a barrel of oil, just as bushels of wheat and corn sold for the same price. Once the flow of oil from the Middle East had been suddenly interrupted, Rifkind argued, it was hardly surprising that the demand for oil in the United States had risen, and thus its price. All that proved was that the market was working, not that the oil companies had secretly conspired to raise their prices.

After hearing arguments in the morning, Judge Savage adjourned for lunch, but when he returned to the bench, he read his decision. He agreed with our motion and promptly acquitted all the defendants. The government had failed to establish guilt beyond a reasonable doubt, he said, and he added that he personally was convinced that none of the oil companies had conspired to fix prices.

The happiest man in the courtroom that afternoon was Jay Topkis, whose very pregnant wife had stayed in New York and was expected to go into labor at any moment. As soon as Judge Savage began to speak and we realized the case was over, Topkis began to fidget in his seat. He wanted to leave immediately, but he knew he couldn't get up from the counsel table and just walk out of the courtroom in the midst of Judge Savage's ruling.

Rifkind thought for a moment, leaned over, and told Topkis to start a coughing fit, then get up and cough his way out of the courtroom. This he did.

The prosecutors, meanwhile, were stunned—how could the court have rejected their case so completely?—and so were the antitrust specialists at the defense table. The big loser, however, wasn't the government but the court reporter, who'd expected to sell transcripts of each day's court proceedings to the oil company lawyers for a good year. When Judge Savage dismissed the case so quickly, his dreams of a bonanza ended, and as he typed the judge's decision, I remember how dejected he looked.

———

A trial, Judge Rifkind taught us, is like a good play: the trial lawyer is the playwright telling the story to the jury and the client is cast in the role of the hero. Rifkind believed that, if he could persuade the court or the jury that his client's cause was just and reasonable, he would win, but if the court or jury found his client undeserving, he would lose even if the law was on his side. In this sense, he was a Legal Realist. At the same time, we learned as his assistants always to be familiar with every fact of the case. The law, he once said, "has many faces and can be stitched together in a variety of ways. But the facts get kind of rugged, and they are hard to shift, and to me, the primary thing is the elaboration of fact, fact, fact." The trial lawyer's role, he taught, is to organize and present the facts in a way that leads to only one conclusion. The lawyer must appeal to the common sense of the court or jury, without bluster or fulminations or wheedling. He should be an actor, but never a ham.

It was sometimes a struggle for me and Judge Rifkind's other, less imaginative associates to think of a way to tell a story that would put the facts in a light sympathetic to the client, but somehow Rifkind could always do it. In one of my first years at Paul, Weiss, he was retained to represent S. J. Klein, a huge discount department store on Union Square in New York City. The New York Transit Authority had rented a small stall inside the Fourteenth Street subway station beneath the S. J. Klein store to a discounter called Subway Sam. Subway Sam's entire inventory would not have filled a counter at Klein's, but Klein's wanted to sue to stop Subway Sam from competing. It was a Goliath-against-David confrontation in which we could expect no sympathy from the court, but Judge Rifkind inimitably contrived to turn S. J. Klein from Goliath into David.

"Is the court aware," he asked, "that the Transit Authority has adopted a new policy of favoring one private business against another?"

No, the judge replied, and he asked Rifkind to explain.

Well, Rifkind elaborated, a person who took the subway could shop at Subway Sam's inside the subway station for the cost of a single fifteen-cent fare, but if he or she wanted to shop at S. J. Klein's aboveground, it cost two fares (since the shopper had to reenter the subway to ride home). Therefore, the Transit Authority, a public agency, was promoting and subsidizing unfair competition. Put that way, the case no longer pitted S. J. Klein against Subway Sam, but S. J. Klein against the power and might of the state. Having noted the Transit Authority's unfair policy, to the pleasure of all present, Rifkind then went on to the drier legal arguments on which our case rested and on which we ultimately prevailed.

Judge Rifkind never wanted imitators. Believing that trial lawyers are performers, he felt that good ones, like good actors or singers, have to develop their own particular style. "A trial lawyer," he once said, "has to be himself, natural to himself, compatible with his spirit, with his physical being, with his appearance, with his diction." Nevertheless, the only sure and safe and productive way to become a good trial lawyer, he maintained, was to watch and help a master of the art. "You're at the counsel table, you're sitting in chair no. 1, you're in charge of the case. Next to you is a young assistant. You project a question to the witness. The answer is unfolding. You know at once that you have a deposition in your file that contradicts the witness. You reach out—and that document is in your hand before you have to ask for it."

For three years I strove to play that role for Judge Rifkind. I was his apprentice, and I studied his craft—his manner with the jury or the judge, the way he framed questions, his gestures—coming to realize, in the process, that I could never mimic him. His air of sweet reasonableness, his vivid poet's skill with words, his authority, his sense of presence, his flair for the dramatic image—none of these could I emulate. I knew too that, as much as I loved the intensity and drama of the courtroom, I had yet to try a case on my own, and I began to doubt, with the passage of time, whether I would ever become really comfortable and effective in the courtroom. I felt like a sculptor training in Michelangelo's studio who, because of the genius of his master, was never able to pick up a chisel on his own. However reluctantly, I found myself less and less able to escape the conclusion that, if I stayed at Paul, Weiss, I might never really become a trial lawyer—or even know whether I had the stuff to become one.

3

The Boss: Robert M. Morgenthau

ONE DAY, early in 1961, I got a call from Robert Morgenthau, asking me to come see him. We'd never met, but I knew of him, of course, as the scion of an illustrious family and also as a successful corporate lawyer in his own right, at the prestigious New York firm of Patterson, Belknap & Webb. He was active in Democratic politics, had run John F. Kennedy's presidential campaign in the Bronx, and was now Kennedy's choice to become the U.S. Attorney for the Southern District of New York; the nation's largest federal prosecutor's office, the Southern District covers Manhattan, the Bronx, and several upstate counties. A partner at Paul, Weiss, he said, had recommended that he talk to me. I agreed to meet him in his office several days later.

Robert Morris Morgenthau was born into a prominent and wealthy New York German Jewish family. His grandfather, Henry Morgenthau, was a lawyer who made a fortune in New York City real estate. A close friend of Woodrow Wilson, he served as the Democratic Party's chief fund-raiser during Wilson's campaign in 1912, and Wilson made him ambassador to Turkey. Bob Morgenthau's father, Henry Morgenthau Jr., studied agriculture at Cornell and then bought a large farm in Hopewell Junction in New York's Duchess County, where he grew apples and raised cattle. The farm was about ten miles from Roosevelt's home at Hyde Park, and Henry Morgenthau Jr. was one of FDR's closest friends. When Roosevelt was elected governor of New York in 1928, he asked Morgenthau to advise him on agricultural policy, and four years later, when he was elected president, Morgenthau, as chair of the Federal Farm Board, reorganized the federal government's farm lending agencies. In 1934 Morgenthau became Secretary of the Treasury, which was an unusually vital cabinet position during the Depression years and on into the late 1930s and early 1940s, when the country had to figure out how to finance the war effort. He was one of my heroes when I was growing up—the Jewish member of the cabinet who spoke out against the persecution of Jews in Germany while the State Department remained silent.

Growing up in New York City and on his family's apple farm, Bob Morgenthau came from wealth, privilege, and an easy familiarity with power. Once, so the story went, while home at the family farm on leave from the Navy, he'd bartended for Roosevelt and Winston Churchill. I suppose I expected Morgenthau to be stuffy and aristocratic, but I couldn't have been more wrong. When I arrived at his office at Patterson, Belknap & Webb for our interview, I found a tall, scholarly-looking man with a hawk nose and tortoiseshell glasses. His suit jacket was slung carelessly over the back of a chair, and his shirtsleeves were rolled up. His office was crowded with piles of paper, pictures of his father with Roosevelt, and mementos from his service as an executive officer on destroyers during the war, and he was smoking a large cigar. He was shy, almost grave, but utterly without pretension, and he radiated energy.

Within moments, he was denouncing stock promoters, whose frauds, he said, were widespread and virtually unregulated. He talked about boiler-room operations selling worthless stock in mining and oil companies, using high-pressure telephone salesmen to gull naive investors. The Southern District included Wall Street, he pointed out, and he was already planning a vigorous attack, as U.S. Attorney, on stock fraud, tax evasion, and other types of white-collar crime. Unlike previous incumbents, he wanted to indict and bring to trial not just the stock promoters but the dishonest lawyers, accountants, and brokers who helped them devise and operate their swindles.

What he had in mind was a special unit to prosecute stock fraud cases only. What was more, he wanted me to run it.

While I knew he hadn't asked me to his office just to pass the time of day, I was taken aback. I had to admit that I knew almost nothing about stocks, let alone stock fraud. I had neither studied securities law at Yale nor ever so much as read the federal securities statutes.

"But, Arthur," Morgenthau countered, "neither have the crooks."

Besides, he went on, I could read everything I needed to know about the securities laws and regulations in less than a day, and then I *would* be an expert.

Even though I told him I wanted to think about his offer, I knew as we stood and shook hands that day that I was going to accept it. It was irresistible to me—in part because of the times. Kennedy's presidential campaign of 1960 had challenged many young men and women like me, stimulating our imaginations, arousing our hopes, and now I was being invited to join the new administration, which seemed so full of confidence, energy, and purpose. But along with the lure of public service came the personal challenge. As a prosecutor, I would have to handle cases on my own. I would find out in a hurry whether I had the skill and the nerves to be a trial lawyer, whether I could stand on my own feet in front of a judge and jury without suffering ulcers (I couldn't) or collapsing from stage fright (I could).

The time clearly had come.

Not that leaving Paul, Weiss was easy. I had been at the firm only three years, but I loved my work and had formed strong and, in some cases, lasting friendships with my colleagues. In Judge Rifkind and Sam Silverman, I'd been privileged to work with two totally different but equally influential mentors. I knew I would never encounter a more accomplished trial lawyer than Rifkind or a more generous and sensitive counselor than Silverman. On a more mundane level, I would also be taking a cut in pay. Law firms in 1961 hardly paid what they do now—I was making about $8,500 a year at Paul, Weiss—but my salary at the U.S. Attorney's Office would be only $6,000, and we would sorely miss the difference. I had married Ellen Fogelson, herself a lawyer's daughter, in 1959, and our first child, Lewis, had just been born.*

---

*The proud father in me can't resist pointing out that Lewis Liman is now a member of the very same securities fraud unit at the U.S. Attorney's Office that I formed thirty-six years ago. I suspect that if he opens one of the desk drawers, he'll discover one of the case files I was never able to find.

The hardest part about leaving I put off as long as I could, but the dreaded day came when I walked the now-familiar corridors at 575 Madison to the *sanctum sanctorum* where the rainmaker awaited me behind his massive desk. Wherever the firm moved, Rifkind's office would always be a nearly exact replica of his chambers as a judge. At 575, it was a large, imposing, and intimidating space, with two secretaries in an adjoining office and, separated from the Judge by a glass partition, the guardian at the gate, his private secretary, the redoubtable Miss Griffinger, who treated clients with almost the same reverence as the Judge—as long as they paid their bills—and watched associates' deadlines for Rifkind's work like a hawk. To be on her good side was to have a packed jury, and I was one of her favorites, receiving diaries and decorated pencil cups for Christmas. It was as if she had already anointed me one of Rifkind's successors.

I'm quite sure the Judge knew why I'd come that day. He listened attentively, though, while I made my announcement and fumbled my way through an explanation. But when I was done, he said, "I don't agree with you at all, Arthur. You don't have to leave here in order to learn how to try cases. Are you telling me Eddie Costikyan is not a fine trial lawyer? And Jay Topkis? I groomed them both."

His tone was mild, his logic unerring. For once in my life, I had trouble marshaling my thoughts. I just knew I was different from Costikyan and Topkis and that I could never be a trial lawyer in the Rifkind mold, could never match his eloquence, his courtroom style. I was going to have to try to find my own way, and I recognized instinctively that, if I remained Rifkind's apprentice, I would fail.

"We both know, Arthur," he observed, fixing me with his gaze, "that if you stay with the firm, you're going to make partner. That's no secret. You're already on your way up the ladder. But if you leave now and want to come back later, you may not find it as easy as you think. Other bright young lawyers will have taken your place on the ladder. You'll have to fight to get your position back. There's no telling what could happen."

His tone, as I say, was mild, not unfriendly, but the warning was unmistakable. Still, my mind was made up. We talked on, sparring, eyeing each other, already, across a certain distance. It wasn't a long conversation, in any event. Rifkind never took kindly to losing. At the end, though, realizing I was unshakable, he relented, and he offered me a piece of advice that was as prescient as it was sound.

"You're going to become enamored of trying cases before juries," he told me. "No question about it. You'd better mark a date on your calendar right now. Decide now how much time you're going to give them—two years, three years—but mark the date and make the commitment to leave when it comes, no matter what. Otherwise, they'll keep promising you bigger cases, better cases, and you won't be able to resist."

I followed his advice. I told Morgenthau I'd stay for at least two years, no more than two and a half. That March of 1961, with Ellen looking on, I was sworn in as an Assistant U.S. Attorney, and I moved downtown to the federal courthouse on Foley Square. Built during the Depression, the building was ornate with bronze, the judges' chambers handsomely paneled and with elegant antique furnishings. But two floors of the building were, to say the least, less handsomely decorated. They were home to the Assistant U.S. Attorneys, all forty of us packed together, with few secretaries, few typewriters, and few of the other amenities of the modern office. It was a vastly different world.

Bob Morgenthau and Simon Rifkind had nothing in common. Rifkind was a brilliant courtroom advocate, the best I have ever seen. To this day, Bob Morgenthau has never tried a single case and has rarely even argued in court. Rifkind was a short, well-organized, and meticulous man. Morgenthau is a tall, reedy, absentminded, and rumpled introvert, with none of Rifkind's loquaciousness or social ease. He is grave with strangers and often shy in public. In private, he can be terse and blunt and obstinate, but he can also be merry with friends and has a dry, acerbic wit. Nearly deaf in one ear because of a childhood infection—he cheated on the hearing test to get into the Navy—Morgenthau sometimes simply ignored dissenting views by literally turning the deaf ear.

The year after he became U.S. Attorney, Morgenthau took a leave of absence to run for governor of New York. He was badly beaten by the Republican incumbent, Nelson Rockefeller. He tried again in 1970 but withdrew before the Democratic primary. His critics called him a stiff, wooden, even tongue-tied candidate, but to his assistants, like me, he was very different, and we idolized him. He has been a spectacularly effective chief prosecutor for more than thirty years, first as U.S. Attorney, and then, after he was elected District Attorney for Manhattan in a special election in 1974, through six more terms with little opposition.

Everyone who worked for Morgenthau called him "the Boss," and he was unmistakably a born leader. He may not have appeared in court, but he knew every last detail of what was going on in the office. He loved to prowl the corridors with an unlit cigar in his mouth and stop at his assistants' offices to drop off apples from his farm and talk case strategy. Although he himself didn't try cases, he had superb instincts as a prosecutor, especially when it came to white-collar crime. Follow the flow of the money, he liked to say. One day, the story goes, he was shopping in the old Abercrombie & Fitch for clothes (an infrequent event), and for some reason he tried on a luxurious and lavishly expensive vicuña suit. The sales clerk said it looked good on him and asked whether he wanted it. "It *is* a beautiful suit," Morgenthau agreed. "But what I'd really like is a list of everyone who's bought it."

Above all, Morgenthau hated the abuse of power and the betrayal of the public trust. Corrupt politicians, dishonest financiers and businessmen, organized crime bosses, and crooked labor leaders were all targets for his prosecutions. Once a powerful Bronx politician pleaded with him to delay for a few weeks indicting an important constituent who was then under investigation. Custom dictated that Morgenthau grant the request, but instead, as soon as the politician left his office, Morgenthau called the assistant in charge of the case and asked when he was planning to indict the man. The assistant said, "Next Wednesday." Morgenthau told him to move it up to Tuesday.

No one, no matter how powerful or prominent, was above the law, and no one could violate the law with impunity. With just one tiny exception, that is. Morgenthau loved cigars. His grandfather had promised to pay him $1,000 if he didn't smoke before he was twenty-one. Morgenthau collected on the bet, used the money for a sports car, and then promptly took up cigars. Cuban cigars, then as now, could not be brought into the United States, but federal customs agents would confiscate them from travelers arriving at New York's airports. Morgenthau would check to see what was in inventory. When he was told that there were far fewer cigars in inventory than had been reported as seized, he would comment, I guess the evidence went up in smoke.

A good deal of the credit for training us as prosecutors belonged to Silvio Mollo, a career prosecutor who had seen U.S. Attorneys come and go and whom Morgenthau made head of the criminal division. Mollo was a by-the-book prosecutor. He also conveyed to all of us that we carried the honor of the U.S. Attorney's Office with us every time we went into court. We were not to be gamesmen. When I was preparing for one of my first trials, Mollo asked me to show him my list of questions. Trying to imitate Rifkind, the questions I drafted were melodramatic and leading. Worse, they were all improper. Mollo tore up my script. I was a novice, he said. As such, I was to ask basic, nonleading questions, such as, "What happened at 8:00 P.M. on the night of August 12?" Of course I protested bitterly. I'd joined Morgenthau's office to learn how to be a trial lawyer, I said, not to ask questions in court like a robot. Eventually, as we learned our craft, Mollo gave me and the other assistants some latitude, but he insisted that all of us master the technically correct way to question witnesses.

It was the Boss, though, who grasped intuitively how to give inexperienced young lawyers the requisite confidence and freedom so that they blossomed into skilled prosecutors. We all came with little experience in the courtroom and from different backgrounds. Some of us were from Ivy League schools; others had worked their way through the city law schools, like Fordham or Brooklyn Law. Some were extremely conservative, others liberal. Morgenthau made us a close-knit group with high morale, and we learned on the job and from each other. Many of us went on to have distinguished careers in the public sector as lawyers and judges—including Pierre Leval, a federal appeals court judge; John Martin, Harold Baer, John Sprizzo, Tony Sifton, Sterling Johnson, Roy Daly, and Vincent Broderick, all federal trial judges; Charles Rangel of the House of Representatives; Franklin Thomas, former head of the Ford Foundation; Andrew Mahoney, who became U.S. Attorney for Brooklyn; and Steve Kaufman, with whom I later worked. To this day, we hold a dinner once a year to celebrate and reminisce about our time with the Boss—one of the happiest and proudest passages of our careers.

As an Assistant U.S. Attorney, downtown in those rabbit-warren offices, my hours were long, and I rarely got home before late evening. I worked Saturdays, sometimes Sundays. Securities cases usually require lengthy investigations, and they commonly end in pleas, not trials, so while I was becoming expert in the securities industry—particularly the underside of it—I wasn't acquiring the trial experience I'd come to Morgenthau's office to get. True, my skills at examining a witness were being honed in grand jury investigations, where I interrogated scores of witnesses, many of them hostile to enforcement of the securities laws. But cross-examining a witness before a grand jury, where no lawyer for the other side is present, was a far cry from the courtroom. I had to find other ways of getting trial experience. The easiest way was to take on drug cases, and I soon became the garbage pail for the narcotics unit. Any cases the prosecutors there didn't want to try, I would take on, sometimes on a few hours' notice.

For an experienced prosecutor, I suppose, these cases were boring. Certainly they were simple and routine. An undercover agent, relying on a tip from a confidential source, would have arranged to buy drugs from a source, then arrested the source as soon as the deal was consummated. At trial, the Assistant U.S. Attorney would put the undercover agent on the witness stand, pass among the jurors an envelope filled with a white powder that the agent had bought from the defendant, and call a chemist to identify the white powder as heroin. Occasionally, the defendant would take the stand, and the prosecutor would have to cross-examine him. Narcotics cases were easy to try, but they helped me begin to build confidence in front of a jury. I experimented and made mistakes, and slowly I began to find my own style in the courtroom.

My first trial was one such unremarkable narcotics case called *United States v. Leroy Samuels.* Leroy Samuels was a young black man from New York who had served in the Army in Korea and was now a heroin addict. The man Samuels bought heroin from had been caught, agreed to cooperate with the government, and named Samuels. Then an undercover agent had persuaded Samuels to sell him some heroin. Now Samuels was charged with being a dealer. When, late one afternoon, the head of the narcotics unit asked whether I wanted the case, he handed me a thin case file—it contained little more than the undercover agent's brief report—and said that it was going to trial in the morning.

It took less than a day to try Leroy Samuels, and even less time for the jury to convict him. But when the jury foreman announced the jury's guilty verdict, instead of pride I felt only sadness and a great frustration. Under the federal drug laws, Samuels faced the same long mandatory minimum prison sentence he would have received as a serious drug dealer. While I knew he'd broken the law, I didn't believe for a minute that he was a drug kingpin, or even a regular dealer; he was just an addict who'd sold a minor quantity of narcotics to a government agent to support his habit. Samuels needed treatment for his addiction, and help getting and keeping a job, a lot more than he needed a long jail sentence. Most defendants in his position would have pleaded guilty to a less serious charge and agreed to cooperate, but Samuels had nothing to bargain with, no information the government wanted. Other than a few other addicts like himself, the only person he could give them in the heroin trade was his own dealer, and they already had him.

There's little a prosecutor can do in such a case. Because the law required that the judge impose a sentence no less than the specified minimum, sentencing was largely a formality. Typically in such cases the prosecutor would say nothing at all, but when the day arrived for Samuels to be sentenced, I couldn't remain silent. Having prosecuted him, I now felt somehow responsible. So I explained to the judge that Samuels had served in the Army during the Korean War and was honorably discharged, and that he was a heroin addict who needed treatment more than anything else.

The judge looked perplexed.

"Mr. Liman," he said, "don't you know that the law requires me to impose a mandatory sentence?"

I must have nodded.

"Then why are you telling me all this?" the irritation now clear in his voice.

Too late, I realized how I seemed to him—the impertinent young prosecutor reminding him of what he knew all too well: that the sentence he had no choice but to impose was unfairly severe, and ineffective besides. I managed to say something to the effect that, while I knew he was obliged to give the minimum sentence, the law didn't bar him from imposing an even longer one, and I therefore had wanted to put Samuels's offense in perspective.

Morgenthau didn't fire me for it, nor did any of my colleagues criticize me. As often happened in my career, they indulged me. "Arthur can't control his conscience," they would say. What's more, they were right.

Like most young prosecutors, I was fervently convinced that anyone who violated the law deserved to be vigorously prosecuted. Once I prosecuted a man who owned a bar in New York and was accused of adding water to half-empty bottles of whiskey and serving the diluted whiskey to his unsuspecting patrons. That was a violation of the federal alcohol tax laws because it deprived the government of revenue. No one else in the office wanted the case, but I of course was always ready and willing.

As with the narcotics cases, my job was easy. All I had to prove was that the man was serving drinks from bottles containing diluted whiskey. I called a chemist, who told the jury that he had compared open bottles seized from behind the bar to other bottles with unbroken seals and found that the open ones were watered down. As it happened, I didn't even need an expert. The trial took place in the summer during a New York heat wave. It was hot in the courtroom, so the court clerk raised the blinds and opened the windows. Sunlight streamed in and backlit the bottles from the bar that I'd lined up on my table. The jurors started staring at the bottles. The open ones that had been seized at the bar contained a pale liquid, while the others had the dark hues of whiskey. This was my first experience with the unmatchable, visceral power of demonstrative evidence.

It took the jury only a few minutes to convict. It took the judge even less time to give the defendant a short and suspended sentence. The only one who got a lecture was me. It turned out that the judge's father was a bartender, and the judge made it plain that he thought it was a sound and wholly unremarkable business practice for a bartender to dilute liquor, and hardly a federal offense.

"Mr. Liman," he admonished me, "the next time you want undiluted whiskey, go to a liquor store, not a bar."

In the meantime, I was preparing to bring the new securities fraud unit's first cases to trial. Most of these came from the Securities and Exchange Commission (SEC), which cannot itself prosecute criminal securities law violations, but Morgenthau had superb sources of his own on Wall Street. From time to time, he would call me into his office to tell me about a tip he'd been given and ask me to investigate. His nose for wrongdoing was impeccable.

The 1950s and early 1960s were a time of extraordinarily bold stock frauds. The main targets were unsophisticated small investors—retired persons, widows, others who might fall for a sucker's pitch. In a typical scheme, a promoter would form a corporate shell, often in Canada, buy some speculative uranium mining claims or oil leases, issue worthless stock at low prices, and then use high-pressure salesmen, working for unsavory brokerage operations called boiler rooms, to sell the stock over the phone. Some promoters even dispensed with an office and simply operated with lists of names from pay phones.

In 1933 Congress had tried to protect investors with a law that required stock promoters to register stock they wanted to sell to the public and to give potential buyers detailed, honest financial statements describing the operations and finances of the company in question. However, the stock swindlers devised ways of evading the law. Worse yet, the Securities and Exchange Commission, the new regulatory agency set up to enforce the law, had had its budget progressively cut after the war, and its efforts to control stock swindlers had all but stopped. Because federal prosecutors relied on the SEC's investigations and referrals, very few stock promoters or boiler rooms were prosecuted for their crimes, and stock fraud had become rampant again.

Prosecuting stock fraud requires much investigation and preparation, and my first major stock fraud trial, the Gulf Coast Leaseholds case, didn't begin until November 1962, about eighteen months after I joined Morgenthau's office. But this was the case that made me a trial lawyer. Once under way, the trial lasted for nine months, which made it one of the longest criminal cases ever tried at the time. Trying a case for that long a period, and with so many witnesses, gave me more courtroom experience than if I'd tried a dozen more typical criminal cases.

The Gulf Coast Leaseholds scheme was as sophisticated as it was brazen. Cecil Hagen, a petroleum engineer, and a Washington lawyer named Roy B. Kelly formed a small oil exploration company called Gulf Coast Leaseholds, a marginal operation that posted only losses. Its stock was selling for about a dollar a share and may have been overpriced. If Hagen and Kelly had wanted to sell shares of Gulf Coast Leaseholds lawfully to the public, they would have had to file financial statements with the SEC and give them to potential investors. Honest financial statements would have revealed the company's dismal state of affairs. Instead, Hagen and Kelly made a deal with a notorious con man named John Van Allen to sell millions of unregistered shares of Gulf Coast Leaseholds stock to the public by grossly manipulating the stock price and issuing bogus reports about the company's prospects.

John Van Allen had used too many fictitious birth certificates for anyone to be able to discover his real age, but he was probably about seventy-five. He'd never earned an honest dollar. His rap sheet ran forever, with convictions in Europe and America. He'd been deported from England for bilking a parson. He'd been banned from ocean liners between the wars for running a card-shark ring. Along the way, he'd acquired an English accent and fancy English clothes. He characteristically wore a black homburg on his balding head. After the Second World War, he'd gone into the business of promoting penny stocks, and in the 1940s New York State had banned Van Allen for life from the securities business. Gulf Coast Leaseholds was his biggest swindle.

It worked this way. Hagen and Kelly agreed to sell 750,000 shares of Gulf Coast Leaseholds stock at penny prices to the Brandel Trust, an entity Van Allen had set up in the duchy of Liechtenstein. Some wealthy Europeans, Van Allen claimed, owned the Brandel Trust and he was merely carrying out their orders, but that was a lie. To avoid having to register the stock with the SEC, Hagen, Kelly, and Van Allen swore that Brandel Trust was purchasing their stock solely as an investment, not for resale to the public. In fact, Van Allen manipulated the price of Gulf Coast Leaseholds by paying brokers to do phony buying and selling, and then he sold all the Brandel Trust's shares of the stock to American investors, using high-pressure boiler rooms in New York. The operation lasted for two years. Gulf Coast Leaseholds' stock price rose at one point to $15 a share, but it soon collapsed. By December 1957, it was selling for less than a dollar. Van Allen divided his profits with Hagen and Kelly by paying kickbacks to a secret Swiss trust he helped them organize, called Universal Finance Company.

I took over the Gulf Coast Leaseholds case from a predecessor in June 1962. Several defendants had already been indicted—Hagen, Kelly, Van Allen, Van Allen's Swiss lawyer, Paul Hagenbach, and several New York boiler rooms—but none had been tried, and the case was nowhere near ready for trial. Van Allen had pleaded guilty several months before and agreed to cooperate with the government by testifying against Hagen and Kelly. According to him, Hagen and Kelly were his partners in the illegal scheme to distribute Gulf Coast Leaseholds stock, and he had paid them through their Swiss trust. Hagen and Kelly, however, claimed that Van Allen had duped them. They said they'd never known Brandel Trust was planning to resell their shares. They denied helping Van Allen manipulate the stock, and they denied owning Universal Finance, the secret Swiss trust. Despite Van Allen's cooperation, no one in the U.S. Attorney's Office wanted to pursue the case against Hagen and Kelly because it would depend solely on Van Allen's uncorroborated testimony.

To convict Hagen and Kelly, I knew I'd have to convince a jury that they'd shared in the profits with Van Allen. I needed cooperation in Switzerland. The prosecutor who'd handled the case before me had met with Van Allen's Swiss lawyer, Hagenbach, who administered the Brandel Trust. He'd promised Hagenbach in writing that we would drop his indictment if Hagenbach turned over the records of the trust. This promise was crucial to Hagenbach. Though the U.S. government couldn't have extradited him from Switzerland, he loved to take long winter vacations in Florida. As long as he was under indictment, though, he could have been arrested if he'd so much as set foot in the United States. Based on my predecessor's written promise, Hagenbach had turned over the records.

The only trouble was that no one had authorized the prosecutor to make such a promise, and he'd told no one in the office about it. Nor had he honored it by having the indictment dropped.

When I took over the case, I had no idea why Hagenbach was now refusing to cooperate. He wouldn't even testify that the records he'd turned over were authentic. Without that, I couldn't introduce the records as evidence, because I had no way of proving they were the Brandel Trust's records. It was several months before I found out about our broken promise. Once I did, I insisted that we honor it—not only because I needed Hagenbach's testimony, but because it was the right thing to do. The Justice Department didn't want to dismiss Hagenbach's indictment, but after the Boss intervened, the charges were dropped. Hagenbach's testimony marked the first time that federal prosecutors had ever obtained cooperation concerning secret Swiss banking records.

The trust records, in fact, were a gold mine. They showed receipts and disbursements of cash from the sale of the Gulf Coast Leaseholds stock. Most important of all, they recorded cash payments that Van Allen had made to Universal Finance, the Swiss trust that Van Allen said was owned by Hagen and Kelly.

But that was what Van Allen said. Hagenbach's records themselves only proved that payments had been made, not that Hagen and Kelly owned Universal Finance. In setting it up, they had a different Swiss lawyer, and now he refused to cooperate with us.

Temporarily, I was stumped. I knew I couldn't hang the whole case on Van Allen's testimony. But one file that Hagenbach turned over happened to contain an unsigned, typewritten letter giving the trustee of Universal Finance instructions on how to distribute its cash. Whoever had typed the letter was a mystery, but I deduced that whoever it was had to have owned Universal Finance. If Van Allen was telling me the truth, that meant Hagen and Kelly did own Universal Finance. So I set out to link Hagen and Kelly to that typewriter.

To do that, I needed a typewriter expert. At the time, there were only two whom I could possibly use as witnesses, and both raised problems. One worked for the FBI. Unfortunately, it was an SEC investigation that had led to the Gulf Coast Leaseholds prosecution, and since the FBI regarded the SEC as a rival, it refused to permit me to use its typewriter expert. This may sound strange today, but J. Edgar Hoover, the head of the FBI, was powerful enough to get away with that kind of jealous turf-guarding. The other typewriter expert presented a different kind of problem. He had testified for Alger Hiss at his perjury trial in 1950. Hiss was accused of lying about stealing secret State Department documents and passing them to the Communists. The government's key evidence against Hiss was a sheaf of secret documents that Hiss allegedly took from his office, gave to his wife to copy at home on an old typewriter, and then passed to his Communist confederate and now accuser, Whittaker Chambers. Hiss was convicted and sent to jail despite this expert's testimony, which had been hotly disputed in court. I worried that putting him on the witness stand might put Morgenthau in an awkward spot politically, if it were interpreted as a tacit endorsement of Hiss.

I laid out the problem for the Boss. He asked me whether the expert's testimony in Gulf Coast Leaseholds would have anything whatsoever to do with the substance of his testimony in the Hiss case. No, I replied. So your only concern is embarrassing publicity, Morgenthau asked? Yes, I said, it was. Well, then, he said, you worry about winning the case and leave that to me.

When we came to trial, the expert's testimony was powerful indeed. He compared several letters typed on a typewriter in Kelly's office to the mysterious Universal Finance letter. One key on Kelly's typewriter had worn unevenly and left a distinctive imprint. The exact same imprint appeared on the Universal Finance document, proving that both documents had been typed on the same typewriter. There was only one conclusion to be drawn: Kelly and Hagen owned Universal Finance, just as Van Allen said.

Meanwhile, I had spent long days with Van Allen, trying to master the Brandel Trust records that Hagenbach turned over so that I could explain them to the jury. That was virtually a trial within a trial. Like any con man, Van Allen was eagerly ingratiating, but he fixated on trivial and irrelevant details. Worse, whenever the federal marshals brought him from jail to my office, they allowed his wife to pay him a visit, and she always brought his favorite lunch—a huge pastrami sandwich and garlicky dill pickles. After each visit, I had to air my office for hours. It got so bad that I feared that, when we tried the case, the defense lawyers would attack the Swiss records as forgeries, since they now had the fragrant odor of the Lower East Side, not of a musty Zurich bank vault.

Hagen and Kelly went to trial in November 1962. Van Allen wasn't a defendant, and I was reluctant to let him testify, for several reasons. His spectacular career as a stock swindler hardly made him a credible witness, even if he told the truth. I didn't entirely trust him to tell the truth myself, and if I decided he wouldn't, I would be ethically barred from putting him on the stand. Besides, I didn't really need his testimony. There was enough other evidence to connect Hagen and Kelly to the fraud. On the other hand, if I didn't call him, Hagen and Kelly's lawyers would surely exploit his absence to the fullest. They might even convince the court to instruct the jury that it must *presume* that Van Allen's testimony would have hurt the government's case. A missing-witness instruction, so called, would have been devastating to my case.

I decided to wait until the end of my case, when most of the other evidence had already been presented. Then I put Van Allen on the stand, asked him a few innocuous questions about the Swiss documents, then turned him over to the defense for cross-examination.

Van Allen's cross-examination lasted for six weeks! The defense lawyers did an absolutely spectacular job proving to the jury that the witness was an unrepentant con man, but the longer they went on, the more I came to believe they were making a colossal mistake. Hagen and Kelly had admitted knowing Van Allen for years, and if Van Allen's dishonesty was as obvious as the cross-examination made it seem, Hagen and Kelly had to have known he was a crook. The defense, in other words, proved my point, and I planned to make the most of it in my summation to the jury.

Needless to say, I learned an important lesson in the process, one I would never forget. The defense lawyers may have destroyed Van Allen on the witness stand, and they'd put on a splendid show, but they had also, however inadvertently, destroyed their own clients in the process. Cross-examination is a two-edged sword, to be handled with care.

At the end of the trial, the defense spent days summing up the case for the jury. Ignoring the documents entirely, they devoted their energy to Van Allen. When my turn came, I dealt with him in just a few sentences. If my case depended solely on his testimony, I told the jury, I would never be asking them to convict Hagen and Kelly. I had called Van Allen as a witness simply so that the jury could see firsthand the con man Hagen and Kelly had relied on to sell Gulf Coast Leaseholds' stock. The defense, I said, had proved beyond any doubt that Hagen and Kelly could not possibly have thought Van Allen was a responsible and honest securities dealer. Van Allen, I said, was demonstrative evidence, in and of himself, that Hagen and Kelly were themselves crooks.

Then I turned to the documents, and I spent almost two days reviewing and discussing them, one by one.

I will return more than once I'm sure to that agonizing passage of waiting after the jury has retired to deliberate, a time when the lawyer, whether prosecutor or defender, is reduced to searching for portents and signs wherever he may find them. No lawyer, no matter how seasoned or experienced, ever suffers the wait with equanimity. But in this case there were what I thought of as two highly propitious signs for the prosecution. First, the jury sent the judge a note asking for a transcript of my summation. The judge correctly told them they couldn't have that—courts usually permit juries to have evidence only in the jury room. But then, a little while later, out came a second note, asking not only for the documents I'd used in my summation but in the order in which I'd discussed them. In other words, they seemed to be reconstructing my summation! How could that not be good?

Although I would learn, many times over, that the omens are often inscrutable and sometimes downright misleading, in this instance the gods must have been smiling on me.

The verdict was guilty.

Gulf Coast Leaseholds was a milestone for me. When the trial started, I was still awkward and stiff in the courtroom. Rereading the transcript of my opening statement, I've discovered only in one paragraph glimmers of the sparkle and sense of the dramatic that I'd tried to learn from Judge Rifkind. But over the course of the trial, I grew increasingly comfortable in front of the jury, and as the weeks and then months unfolded, my own courtroom style emerged. Unlike Judge Rifkind, I wasn't eloquent. My style was plain, simple, orderly, and sincere. I tended neither to embellish nor to exaggerate. I also learned how to listen and concentrate. Outside the courtroom, I often interrupt people, but inside I have trained myself to listen with rapt attention. Every gesture a witness makes, every pause or vocal emphasis, is a clue, especially when a witness is uncomfortable with his or her own testimony. I also found that sarcasm and anger in confronting witnesses were less effective, at least for me, than the subtler effort of turning a witness's own testimony to my advantage. When I cross-examined the defense's expert witnesses, I tried to make them my own. I succeeded in getting one to agree that his opinion had been based entirely on assumptions given to him by the defense. Then, using a document that proved those assumptions false, I led him to admit not only that his original opinion appeared incorrect but, based on the evidence, that he could only conclude in my favor.

Later, after court, this same witness confronted me in the hallway. He said the government should now pay his fee as an expert, because the defendants no longer would! I could scarcely accommodate him, but the incident confirmed to me that I was on my way. The Boss himself once said that I could take a witness's socks off but leave his shoes still on and securely tied. While I learned later that sometimes I could and sometimes I couldn't, I took it as the highest compliment.

If Gulf Coast Leaseholds was my first big case as a stock fraud prosecutor, my last postdated my stay with the Boss. The most notorious stock swindler of the 1950s had been a man named Lowell McAfee Birrell, who was perhaps the leading wrecker of corporations and deluder of investors in the postwar era. When the SEC finally caught up with him in 1957, Birrell fled first to Havana and then to Brazil to escape prosecution. He left behind forty-six filing cabinets' worth of documents that eventually came into the government's possession and were deposited in a little room in Morgenthau's offices, where they sat in cardboard boxes. Yet with Birrell living beyond the range of indictments, no federal prosecutor had taken the time to look through them.

In the summer of 1961, a few months after I joined the U.S. Attorney's Office, I decided to browse through the papers. White-collar criminals rarely document their wrongdoing, so I was amazed to discover that Birrell had kept records—some even sketched out on place mats and napkins—of cash payments made to brokerage firms that he'd used to sell and manipulate his stocks. Hooked on Birrell's files, I spent days, then weeks, during that summer in a room with no air conditioning, sorting through the papers. We were quickly able to obtain two grand jury indictments, charging Birrell and his associates with securities fraud, but we decided that, as long as the kingpin himself remained in Brazil, there was little point in pursuing prosecution.

That same year, however, the United States and Brazil signed a new extradition treaty, and although ratifications were not formally exchanged until November 1964, Birrell had already elected to return voluntarily to the United States and had surrendered to the government. Surprisingly, he came home broke. He was given a court-appointed lawyer, and in December 1967, ten years after he'd fled to Brazil and six years after I'd indicted him, he was scheduled to stand trial.

I had already left the U.S. Attorney's Office and returned to Paul, Weiss, but I'd promised the Boss that I would return to try the Birrell case if he needed me, and now he called me back to head the prosecution team.

Lowell Birrell was a scoundrel by choice, not by necessity. He was a handsome and charming man, the son of a small-town Presbyterian minister, a graduate of Syracuse University and Michigan Law School. Apparently a brilliant lawyer, Birrell had worked at the aristocratic Wall Street law firm of Cadwalader, Wickersham and Taft but had left to seek fame and fortune in the stock market. After gaining control of several small companies, he issued huge quantities of unauthorized stock and then illegally unloaded the unregistered shares on the market, using loopholes he thought he'd found in the securities laws. He made millions of dollars on his swindles, and he bought a huge estate in Bucks County, Pennsylvania, on which he built a private lake for his yacht.

In 1954 Birrell got control of the Swan-Finch Oil Corporation. He authorized it to issue millions of new shares of stock, supposedly to be used for corporate acquisitions. Instead, he devised several illegal schemes to sell these shares to the public without, as the law specified, registering them with the SEC. One scheme involved a father-son team, named Re, who ran the American Stock Exchange's largest firm of specialists. Stock specialists are the broker-dealers who are key figures on the floor of every stock exchange. They execute orders for other brokers and take the responsibility for maintaining a fair and orderly market in the particular stocks assigned to them. They accomplish this by buying and selling shares on their own account, thus helping to cushion the market against wide and sudden price moves. As it happened, one stock the Res specialized in was Swan-Finch. Birrell recruited them, and paid them lavishly under the table, to manipulate the price of Swan-Finch and help him distribute the unregistered stock to the public. The Res, in turn, bribed the financial press, gave false tips, paid kickbacks to brokers, and generated the illusion of activity by arranging for fictitious trades to be recorded on the ticker tape. Also, they improperly distributed more than half a million shares of Swan-Finch by trading through dummy nominees, including a retired horse trainer named Charles A. Grande who had no experience in the securities business. Among their victims were political figures and celebrities, including Toots Shor, the restaurant owner, Chuck Dressen, the baseball manager, and the president of the American Stock Exchange himself.

Another of Birrell's swindles involved a Canadian company called American Leduc Petroleum Ltd., which supposedly explored for oil in Canada and Cuba. In the three years after Birrell became president of American Leduc in 1954, the company issued six million new shares of common stock, which Birrell then sold illegally, using a boiler-room telephone and mail campaign run by a New York brokerage firm, J. A. Winston & Company. American Leduc's actual production of oil in Cuba was minimal; the company had no earnings, and its prospects were doubtful, to say the least. For a time, the fraud was spectacularly successful. In one year, from August 1955 to August 1956, Birrell and J. A. Winston sold three and a half million shares of American Leduc at an average price of $1.05. Three months later, the price dropped to about fifty cents a share, and in July 1961, when I indicted Birrell and J. A. Winston, the stock was trading for about eight cents a share and was overpriced at that.

I returned to the U.S. Attorney's Office to try the American Leduc case in December 1967. Birrell was accused of illegal sales of unregistered stock and conspiracy, and he faced a possible sentence of fifty-five years and a $60,000 fine. The evidence against him was overwhelming. The J. A. Winston officers and salesmen had pleaded guilty and were willing to testify against Birrell. So was one of Birrell's Canadian associates who'd handled payoffs to brokers. Finally, Birrell's flight to Brazil and his extended stay there were, in and of themselves, powerful indications of his guilt.

We had the strongest case of all those I'd encountered to that point in the stock fraud field. Yet there was one enormous problem. We would be prohibited from using any of Birrell's documents as evidence at the trial. Nor could we use any evidence that we had obtained based on those documents. When Birrell fled in 1957, all documents relating to his various companies had seemingly vanished with him. It wasn't until 1959, during bankruptcy proceedings over Swan-Finch, that the treasure trove of files was discovered, in the custody of one of Birrell's lawyers. The government promptly obtained search warrants and seized them, and they eventually ended in Morgenthau's office. But after Birrell returned to the United States, he succeeded in convincing the court that the government had seized his documents unlawfully, using invalid search warrants. Not only did the court's ruling keep us from entering any of the seized documents in evidence, but worse yet, the court ruled that if the jury convicted Birrell, we would then have to prove, in a post-trial hearing, that none of the evidence we used had come from the unlawfully seized files. In other words, there would be two trials, assuming we prevailed in the first—one, before a jury, of Lowell Birrell, and the second, before Judge William B. Herlands, of the evidence.

The Boss was adamant that we go forward. So was I. Even with this handicap, we had, to my mind, an overwhelming case. In fact, the trial lasted only about three weeks, although Birrell tried everything imaginable. His lawyers called a foreign law expert and a handwriting expert, among other witnesses, none of whom said anything particularly relevant or helpful to Birrell's cause, but their tactic was clearly to try to confuse the jury. Then, in the middle of the case, I was hospitalized for internal bleeding, the result of taking too much aspirin for a persistent cold, and my assistant, Steven Hammerman, had to take my place. After all the years it had taken to reach this point, I was determined to deliver the summation myself, and against my doctor's advice, I did.

The jury came back quickly. Their verdict was guilty.

From the prosecution team's point of view, that verdict was all that counted. Birrell was already a ruined man, and Morgenthau's goal of developing a stock fraud unit that would put teeth into law enforcement had now been achieved. Nevertheless, six weeks later, in February 1968, we began the hearing before Judge Herlands to prove that we had not relied on Birrell's files. It promised to be a lengthy process, and Birrell set about to make it interminable. At one point, he tried to fire his court-appointed lawyer from the Legal Aid Society and demanded to represent himself. This brought the hearing to a halt. Judge Herlands knew that Birrell was taking Darvon for headaches and complained of memory loss, and that he also claimed to be a narcoleptic, but when he asked Birrell about his medical history, to determine whether he was capable of representing himself, Birrell refused to answer. Then Birrell sued the Legal Aid Society for malpractice and demanded $25 million in damages.

We struggled on. In fact, had it not been for an untoward event, we might still be struggling. But then, in the midst of the hearing, Judge Herlands died. This meant, practically, that we were going to have to start all over again—if, that is, we still wanted to try to put Birrell behind bars. The Boss and I weighed the options. We decided we could hardly justify using government resources to continue to pursue a man who was no longer a threat to anyone, except possibly his own lawyers.

So, at the end of the day, the conviction was dropped and my career as a government prosecutor came to a close. But the government's efforts to police the securities industry, through the SEC and the Justice Department, had barely begun, and soon enough we would find ourselves on opposing sides.

II

Private Practice

4

Paul, Weiss, Rifkind, Wharton & Garrison

As Judge Rifkind had predicted, Morgenthau tried to lure me into staying on. In addition, I'd begun to have doubts of my own about returning to private practice. How would I adapt to being an advocate for an individual's or a corporation's private cause? A federal prosecutor is an advocate too, of course, but his client is the United States. It is he, moreover, who decides whether to indict, and whether to accept a plea or go to trial. In the U.S. Attorney's Office, I would never have to prosecute a case I didn't believe in, and in addition to the autonomy and responsibility that went with the job, the cases I would be assigned would only get better as I gained in seniority and experience. If I went back to Paul, Weiss, wouldn't it somehow be a step backward?

And suppose I *didn't* make partner—what would become of my career?

It was at this time that I considered teaching, and Ellen and I went so far as to meet with members of the Yale Law School faculty who were trying to recruit me.

But litigation was now in my bloodstream. I wanted to try cases. I wanted to master the art of being a trial lawyer.

In the end, for the same reasons I'd chosen it when I graduated from law school—the uniqueness of its practice and the collegiality of its lawyers—I returned full-time to Paul, Weiss. This was in November 1963. I expected that I would leave again at some point to do public service, but when I did, I wanted the independence that would come from having established a solid private practice.

All my fears, though, about loss of independence were unfounded. For one thing, Paul, Weiss itself wasn't beholden to any one client. More established law firms typically represented a large bank or securities firm or insurance company that produced the lion's share of their work and therefore of their revenues. As a younger firm, we had no such bellwether client but earned our livelihoods, out of necessity, from a much greater diversity of sources.

As is often the case, what started as necessity would become, over time, a matter of choice, and one of the great attractions of Paul, Weiss, it's always seemed to me, has been the incredible diversity of our practice. Over the years, we've represented clients all over the world, institutions and individuals, Fortune 500 corporations and small entrepreneurs, employers and employees, media organizations accused of defamation and plaintiffs who were libeled, rich clients who could comfortably afford our services and poor ones who couldn't afford to pay anything. Unlike many firms, we've never specialized in any particular field of the law. Instead, we've immersed ourselves in hundreds of fields—antitrust cases, contract actions, will contests, property disputes, family controversies, white-collar criminal cases, libel suits, copyright actions, patent infringement suits. We have also taken on pro bono appeals in capital punishment cases. We brought the first environmental cases—opposing a proposed nuclear plant on the Hudson River. We have handled First Amendment cases and voters' rights cases. Every economic and social upheaval in the country has found its way into our office—the quiz show scandals, the salad oil fraud that nearly toppled American Express, the civil rights movement, the criminal case against Spiro Agnew, the asbestos cases, the back-office crisis on Wall Street in the 1960s, the takeover mania of the 1980s. Now, in the so-called global economy of the end of the century, we've been fast becoming a global law firm, with offices in Paris, Tokyo, Hong Kong, and Beijing. As my partner Ted Sorensen once noted, "We have represented a Sudanese-born Israeli, living in England with offices in Switzerland, seeking finance from Japan for telecommunications in Zaire, and Indians joining Saudis to form a Bahamian partnership to control a Netherlands Antilles corporation with Taiwanese and West African assets."

All true.

Sometimes I wonder who among us in the mid-1960s—even Judge Rifkind—could have imagined the firm of today. When I returned in 1963, there were but twenty-odd partners and about fifty lawyers, all told. In fact, we had recently lost our Chicago offices to the Kennedy administration—Stevenson, Willard Wirtz, and Newton Minow all served in Washington, and our Washington office, which specialized in taxes and was headed by our one female partner, Carolyn Agger, merged with the firm of her husband, Abe Fortas, the future Supreme Court justice. All of Paul, Weiss was then contained in one building on Madison Avenue. Everyone knew everyone else, and a number of us, partners and associates alike, ate lunch together whenever we could, most often at a French bistro called Larré's on Fifty-sixth Street near Sixth Avenue, where the *prix fixe* menu cost three dollars and joining the conversation was not only free but as stimulating and exciting as any law school seminar. Perhaps half the partners at the time were Jewish, and probably one-third were less than forty-five years old. The lion's share of the practice was generated by Rifkind himself, and a lot of it consisted of litigation. We had only a few corporate clients, but the younger partners, spurred by Rifkind, wanted to build the firm not just in tax, litigation, and entertainment law, where we already shone, but in the corporate field as well.

Rifkind, in fact, was constantly looking for talent outside the firm. One early recruit, in my time, was Morris Abram. Abram was from a small town in Georgia, a Rhodes scholar and an elegant trial lawyer. He helped argue the cases in which the Supreme Court struck down racially discriminatory voting districts and established the one-person-one-vote principle. After ten years at the firm, Abram left to become president of Brandeis University, where, however, he lasted only a year. This was during the Vietnam War era, when many students had grown impatient with reasoned discourse and the ideal of evolutionary social change. Even the civil liberties victories that Abram had helped win were regarded by student radicals as cosmetic. He was picketed repeatedly for no good reason, and after a year of it, in disgust, he chose to return to the firm.

Rifkind also recruited Ted Sorensen, one of President Kennedy's closest advisers, who became our first international lawyer and one of my best friends at the firm. Abram and Sorensen were fierce competitors. For a while, their competition was limited to the tennis court, but then they both decided to run for the Democratic nomination for senator of New York. As their partners, we could contribute to both campaigns, and many of us did, but New York not being Chicago, we could vote for only one. Fortunately, Abram soon dropped out of the race, but then Sorensen lost in the primary.

When President Johnson's Attorney General, Ramsey Clark, decided to leave government, Rifkind lured him too, in the hope that, with his Texas roots, he would bring in oil companies as clients. But Clark's practice took an unexpected turn. In 1970 he published *Crime in America*, a remarkable book about poverty and urban decay, and became a populist hero of the left, alongside such militant lawyers as William Kuntsler. It was only a matter of time before he decided to leave the firm to become a "people's lawyer" and champion of the underdog.

Rifkind's biggest catch of the period, however, was Arthur Goldberg, who, after serving as secretary of labor under Kennedy, was appointed a Supreme Court justice and then United Nations ambassador. When Johnson's term ended in 1969, Goldberg joined us. One of my heroes on the Supreme Court, he had written some of the major opinions of the Warren court. Although he attracted some exciting clients, including Curt Flood, the major league baseball player who had unsuccessfully challenged the reserve clause before the Supreme Court and was driven from baseball in retaliation, private practice was small potatoes for Goldberg, and he never really adjusted to it. He had the habit, whenever one of us approached him for advice on an issue, of saying that he had written an opinion on the Supreme Court that would provide guidance. Usually the opinion had nothing whatsoever to do with the question posed, but some of us, myself included, quickly became experts on Goldberg's Supreme Court opinions!

At the same time, Rifkind always encouraged expansion from within. When, at the yearly meeting at which new partners were voted in, some members of the firm turned unduly conservative, Rifkind, in his eloquent way, reassured them by likening a law firm to a boat. Those already on board, he would say, might well be afraid that adding anyone else might cause the boat to capsize. But he personally preferred to look at additional passengers as increased rowing power. In his view, every associate who came to work at Paul, Weiss should have the same opportunity to become a partner and to build a practice, and each partner, even the newest, should be free to choose and develop his or her own clients, subject only to the rules of conflict of interest. This open-door policy has clearly been one of the reasons Paul, Weiss has consistently been able to attract top law school graduates, and why, conversely, we have never lost a partner to another firm.

Another reason, I think, for both our success and our cohesiveness is that the firm has always been a robust democracy. Indeed, to borrow Rifkind's metaphor, we aren't just oarsmen, we're all coxswains guiding the boat. Thirty years ago, many large law firms were governed autocratically. Some, in fact, still are. A managing partner, selected by his predecessor or a small executive committee, ran the firm. Either alone or perhaps with a few other dominant partners, he chose the new partners, approved the new clients, and decided how much each partner earned. In one of New York City's largest firms, for instance, only the managing partner knew what every other partner earned. Each January he would privately tell each partner his share of the profits, and all were sworn to secrecy.

Given his importance as rainmaker to the firm, Rifkind could have run Paul, Weiss the same way, but that would have been totally antithetical to his values. At Paul, Weiss, it was one-person-one-vote, on every important issue, and it was far from unheard of for the rainmaker himself to be voted down. Not that every partner was comfortable with this democratic tradition. One who wasn't, in fact, was Arthur Goldberg, who'd written the stirring opinion in which the Supreme Court held that states must follow the principle of one-person-one-vote in their elections. When he was outvoted on an issue at the first firm meeting he attended, Goldberg confided to me—in jest, needless to say—that if he'd known at the time what one-person-one-vote, actually meant, he would have filed a dissenting opinion!

Not only has Paul, Weiss never had a managing partner, it has never even had an executive committee. Rifkind formed instead the Committee on Committees, which in turn appoints the committees that together run the firm. There are separate committees for finances, office administration, recruitment, compensation of associates and nonlegal personnel, and every other matter affecting our communal life. Every partner is encouraged to serve on the committees and to do his or her share of office administration.

For better or worse, compensation is the yardstick by which many partners measure their value. No matter how well paid, partners inevitably care how much their peers earn, as a symbol of their own standing, and many law firms have disintegrated because members felt that the sharing was unfair. Rifkind himself always took significantly less compensation from the firm than he deserved, and he devised a unique system for fixing the compensation of the partners.

He created a small committee of influential partners and called it the Deciding Group. Each year the partners must submit to the Deciding Group, and to each other, a report describing the fees they have contributed to the firm's income, their role in firm administration, and their pro bono work. The Deciding Group then determines each partner's share of the profits.

Paul, Weiss does have leaders, but their authority, as in all true democracies, comes from the consent of the governed; there is no royal family. Each year we elect the Deciding Group and the Committee on Committees. Long before term limits became fashionable, we had them at Paul, Weiss. I myself became a partner in 1966, and ten years later, in my forties, I became a leader of the firm, but I have never ruled Paul, Weiss.

———

Judge Rifkind and his partners welcomed me back, in 1963, as though I'd never left. Better still, they recognized that my experience as an Assistant U.S. Attorney had given me self-confidence and that I was no longer timid and halting in the courtroom. I was assigned quickly to the fray—that is, to some of the firm's most important matters—and little by little began to build relationships of my own with many of our clients.

In several respects, I was lucky. I may have arrived in Morgenthau's office, that day in 1961, never having read the federal securities statutes, but I now knew them inside and out. Furthermore, the 1960s not only witnessed great social turbulence and turmoil but marked the start of a period of burgeoning economic opportunity in the United States, a time when the corporate world went through epic changes in almost every respect. Large companies that had seemed virtually immutable were suddenly merged with other companies. Still others belonged to moribund industries or yielded to the pressures of the post–World War II international economy and were literally dissolved. Shareholders, who had been largely passive owners in the past, became more demanding of management, and management in turn became more entrepreneurial. New companies started up with a few dollars and an idea—Xerox is a prime example—and established companies were taken over in hostile transactions, previously viewed as too uncouth a practice in the quasi-closed world of American corporations. Spurred, as time went on, by the explosive development of the computer and other new technologies, whole new industries were in the process of being born, and with new businesses the need grew for new methods of financing and new legal requirements. All of these changes in the corporate world led to a new breed of lawyer, one more inventive and aggressive than those of the previous generation; to whole new firms specializing in mergers and acquisitions, like Skadden Arps and Wachtell Lipton, whose founders, contemporaries of mine like Joseph Flom and Martin Lipton, became friends and sometimes adversaries; and also to new laws and increasingly important regulatory agencies, including my former "client," the Securities and Exchange Commission.

I was fortunate to find myself at Paul, Weiss, where it was possible for me to practice as a so-called crossover lawyer—trying cases in the courtroom, on the one hand, but also developing, more deliberately, those long-term relationships in which I became a true counselor to my clients. Trial craft and trial work always brought me, I admit, a great personal "high," the testing period that, for the lawyer, demands the most intense concentration, vigilance, and control. But it is in that other function, that of counselor, that I think the lawyer may well perform his highest service.

Behind my desk hangs a nineteenth-century Old Testament sampler that Ellen found for me in a flea market. It is from the Book of Isaiah, and it reads "Fear Thou Not, For I Am With Thee." To me, the quotation expresses perfectly what every lawyer should strive for in the lawyer-client relationship, but oddly, the very idea—of the lawyer as counselor—is today rejected in certain professional quarters. There are lawyers—some of them eminent members of the bar—who regard themselves as hired for their technical legal expertise solely; they believe that, once they have identified and set forth possible adverse legal consequences, the rest is up to the client. In most other countries, lawyers do indeed play a reactive role— they answer legal questions posed by clients and they draft documents— but lawyers in our society occupy a unique place, and we always have. Lawyers dominate our legislatures. President Clinton is a lawyer, and so were some of our most highly rated presidents—Lincoln, Jefferson, Madison, Franklin Roosevelt. Virtually every social problem in America finds its way into a lawyer's office, and in the world of commerce, lawyers as much as chief executives and bankers have reshaped the corporate landscape. We are involved in planning and executing virtually every corporate decision, from mergers to downsizing. We advise our clients on what to do and how to do it, often proposing new ideas we've seen work elsewhere, and our advice is, or ought to be, based on considerations and judgments far broader than the question of whether a proposed act is legal.

Some critics of the profession—Ralph Nader comes to mind—have complained that corporate counselors do nothing but find loopholes in the law for their clients. That is not the way I see it or have experienced it. Yes, if there is a way to do a transaction lawfully, the lawyer will guide the client to and through it. But he will also tell the client when over-aggressive tactics are inappropriate and may well backfire. More often than not, the socially responsible act turns out to be the right thing for the client, and the good lawyer will so advise.

A fine illustration of this point is a case I wasn't involved in at all—the Pentagon Papers. When the *New York Times* received a set of classified government papers from a confidential source, it naturally sought legal advice from its regular law firm, Lord, Day & Lord, on whether it could publish them. The principal partner at Lord, Day & Lord was Herbert Brownell, who had been Attorney General under Eisenhower. He'd helped put Earl Warren and William Brennan on the Supreme Court and was no reactionary, yet Brownell felt strongly that publishing the secret document not only violated the law but was a dangerous act, since it contained classified information leaked by a government employee. The *Times* was his firm's most important client, yet Brownell said he and his firm would refuse to represent the paper if it published the Pentagon Papers.

Here he was giving far more than technical legal advice. He was helping his client deliberate about a complex decision, involving what was right not only for the client but for the country as well, and he was taking a stand.

The *Times* and its general counsel, James Goodale, weren't satisfied with Brownell's advice and called in Floyd Abrams, who was rapidly becoming the leading First Amendment lawyer of his time. A generation younger than Brownell, Abrams saw the law and public policy differently. He advised the *Times* that publishing the Pentagon Papers would be protected by the First Amendment and that it was in the interest of journalism, as well as the country, to expose the cover-up about how we'd gotten so deeply involved in Vietnam. The *Times*, of course, went ahead and published, and although the lower court initially enjoined the publication, the newspaper prevailed in the higher court and established the precedent that, under the First Amendment, the government cannot prevent even classified secrets from being published except in the most extraordinary circumstances.

The Pentagon Papers case changed journalism even more than Watergate. William Paley once told me that, during World War II, the press had seen it as a patriotic duty to support the war effort, even by disseminating propaganda. With the publication of the Pentagon Papers, that view changed definitively. The media would henceforth hold the government accountable, even in war.

My point, though, isn't that Abrams and Goodale were right and Brownell wrong. It is rather that all three lawyers gave their client independent advice without fear of the personal consequences. Brownell was willing to lose one of his most valued clients by telling the *Times* what he knew it didn't want to hear. Goodale and Abrams were willing to make a call that, if things had turned out differently, surely would have damaged their careers. In expressing their opinions, each of them was playing the unique role that American lawyers have occupied from the beginning—providing wise and independent counsel.

Two years after I returned to Paul, Weiss, Judge Rifkind called me into his office. I had been expecting him to tell me I was going to become a partner, although Paul, Weiss customarily didn't promote associates for nine years and I was just finishing my seventh. To my disappointment, however, he said that, although I was clearly ready for partnership, I was going to have to wait another year. Furthermore, great advocate that he was, even in personal relationships, he succeeded in convincing me that it was in my own interest that I stay an associate the extra year! Otherwise, as he explained, the other young partners would always resent my early promotion.

At home that night, when I tried telling Ellen the good news—that I had to wait another twelve months—she was not so easily persuaded. But then, I was no Rifkind.

It only hurt for a little while, as they say, and in the long run it mattered not at all. A year later, on the first of January 1966, I did become partner, the most junior of twenty-five of us, and as I said before, I've never looked back.

5

American Express, Tino De Angelis, and the Great Salad Oil Scandal

T HE SALAD OIL SCAM organized by Anthony "Tino" De Angelis was, for its time, the most remarkable business fraud of the century. It broke almost on the day of my return to Paul, Weiss in 1963, and by the time I closed the file on it, more than twelve years had gone by and I had become the senior member of a defense team interrogating Tino on the witness stand, after he had already served his prison term.

The case taught me, among other things, that there are times when a truly effective trial lawyer must be more than a zealous advocate. It was also my introduction to one of the country's most extraordinary corporations—Continental Grain Company—which became one of my most important clients.

Tino De Angelis was a rotund former butcher from the Bronx. He was convinced that the market potential for American salad oil, made from cottonseed and soybeans, in Europe, and particularly Spain, was virtually unlimited. His company, Allied Crude Vegetable Oil Refining Corporation, began to buy up all the soybean and cottonseed oil he could find— as well as futures contracts, using as his broker Ira Haupt & Company, one of the more prominent commodities firms on Wall Street.

De Angelis's goal was to monopolize the vegetable oil market, and his strategy was to buy high and not sell. By 1963 he was doing two-thirds of all of the vegetable oil business in the world. He bought the oil from domestic refineries and producers and sold it to exporters for resale abroad. The exporters, like Continental Grain and Bunge Corporation, couldn't deal directly with the domestic producers because De Angelis was there first, often buying from them at higher prices than the exporters would pay. When Continental and Bunge needed oil for export, they had to buy from De Angelis. But if demand for vegetable oil abroad slackened and prices fell, De Angelis stood to take a huge loss on his inventory.

De Angelis's operations were located in Bayonne, New Jersey, across from lower Manhattan. There he had the largest tank farms for vegetable oil in the country. He also had a refinery to convert cottonseed and soybeans into vegetable oil and the most modern facility for loading the oil onto ships for export abroad. He borrowed money from banks, including Chase and Continental Illinois, to carry his inventory of vegetable oil. He also demanded and received financing from exporters, like Continental Grain, on oil that would be delivered to them for export in coming months. As collateral for the financing, he gave his creditors warehouse receipts certifying that he had the oil stored in his tanks in Bayonne. The tanks were under the supervision of a subsidiary of American Express, and that subsidiary certified each receipt, representing that the oil was there.

Eventually, De Angelis issued more warehouse receipts than there was actual vegetable oil in the United States, but his lenders never caught on until he went bankrupt in November 1963. Then, when they scrambled to seize their collateral—the salad oil supposedly stored in his tanks—they discovered that the tanks were filled with sludge. As prices had fallen and he had needed more loans to cover his losses, De Angelis had deceived American Express into issuing the receipts on empty tanks. When American Express did inspections to certify that the oil was there, De Angelis had sometimes put a cylinder filled with oil inside a tank and then led the inspector to put his measuring equipment there. If that failed, he'd switch the sample of sludge the inspector would have obtained with real oil while the inspector was having a lunch . . . provided by De Angelis. When that was not sufficient, he'd simply counterfeit American Express receipts. At De Angelis's instructions, an employee had stolen a book of blank receipts from American Express and forged American Express's certification.

Unlike many swindlers, De Angelis didn't use the money he obtained to pursue a lavish lifestyle or make deposits in Swiss accounts. It all went to cover his losses in the vegetable oil business.

The salad oil scandal was unprecedented for its magnitude and for the sophistication of its victims. By the time De Angelis's fraud was exposed in November 1963, he had issued almost $200 million in worthless warehouse receipts. His victims included some of the largest banks and commodities companies. Ira Haupt, De Angelis's principal broker, which had lent him huge amounts of money, went bankrupt, as did several other firms. Even American Express's survival was in doubt.

———

The scandal broke, as I said, almost on the very day I returned to the firm in 1963. Lloyd Garrison was retained to represent Continental Grain and Keyser Ullman, a small English banking house that was stuck with the now-worthless American Express warehouse receipts. Garrison was the witty and much-loved Paul, Weiss partner, distinguished in many ways, including, at the tender age of seventy, sliding into third base at a firm picnic, taking out a terrified young associate! He and I were to spend almost two years struggling to find a solution to the salad oil problem.

Continental Grain had bought vegetable oil from De Angelis for export and lent him money, receiving American Express warehouse receipts as collateral. Keyser Ullman had also loaned De Angelis money and taken the warehouse receipts as collateral. Both should have been fully secured. They held receipts that on their face were twice the value of their loans, and they'd seen little risk in the transactions because of the financial strength of American Express, the parent company. Neither had realized that the receipts were in fact issued by a small subsidiary with few assets of its own, and that American Express might disaffirm any obligation for its subsidiary.

We could have pursued litigation and sued American Express for the value of the receipts. Doing so, however, might have destroyed American Express, for the face value of the receipts issued by De Angelis was greater than American Express's ability to pay. Indeed, few if any American companies at the time could have absorbed a loss of such dimension. Moreover, there was always the possibility that a court would hold that only the subsidiary, not American Express itself, was responsible for the receipts.

American Express's principal negotiator was Peter Kaminer of Winthrop Simpson & Ross, and he recognized, as we did, the need for an imaginative solution. But our problem wasn't just with American Express. We also needed to figure out how to divide among the receipt holders whatever money we could persuade or compel American Express to pay. Virtually every one of them was in a different position from the others. All they had in common was that De Angelis had given them worthless American Express warehouse receipts. Some, such as Continental Grain, held receipts supposedly worth twice the amount they had lent to De Angelis, while others had received receipts equal to their loans. Some receipts had been issued years earlier by yet another American Express subsidiary. In addition, there were creditors who suspected that some of the warehouse receipt holders had in fact been repaid in cash, in the months before De Angelis declared bankruptcy. Such cash payments, they believed, should be credited against their total loss. So, even after Kaminer and American Express had agreed to set up a fund for the warehouse receipt holders, the holders were fighting over who was to get what.

This dissension threatened to torpedo all our settlement efforts. As a last resort, a committee representing the creditors was appointed to try to come up with a fair and acceptable solution. As Lloyd Garrison's delegate, I was intimately involved with the facts relating to all of the holders and was therefore recruited for the committee.

The work occupied my time for months. It involved dealing with the attorneys for every receipt holder and trying to feel my way toward a compromise that might find general acceptance. Ultimately, my colleagues on the committee and I came up with a complex plan. Receipt holders who held receipts well in excess of their loans would receive, according to a formula, a larger share of their indebtedness than receipt holders who were undercollateralized and had receipts equal only to their indebtedness. Then we established a uniform interest rate for all of the indebtedness backed by receipts, so that those holders who had negotiated better interest rates wouldn't get favored treatment. The most difficult position of all to sell was our decision not to penalize any receipt holder who knew, or should have known, that De Angelis was engaging in shady operations. Of course, every receipt holder denied any such knowledge, all the while pointing the finger at others, but if we had tried for some sort of culpability discount, we would have been committing ourselves to fifty separate trials.

The formula we ultimately arrived at was so complicated that I believe only I and one other lawyer really understood it. Perhaps this was why no one tried to block us by holding out—this plus the receipt holders' recognition that a huge effort had gone into the negotiations. We needed unanimity, and we got it.

In 1967, four years after the De Angelis bankruptcy, the settlement was finally signed. American Express survived, and creditors like our clients, Continental Grain and Keyser Ullman, which had twice as much collateral as loans, received one hundred cents on the dollar. Others that had a lower ratio of receipts to debt received as much as 80 percent of their loss. This was a far better result, needless to say, than could have been achieved by litigation. We—the lawyers on both sides— could have had fifty trials, but no matter who won them, our clients would all have been worse off. American Express would have been bankrupt, and so would many of the creditors. Trained as we were to see all sides of an issue, we realized that compromise was in the best interests of all our clients, and we exercised a moderating influence on some understandably high emotions in order to get there.

———

There should be an expression, though: old cases never die, they just wait until the lawyers have turned their backs. How else to explain that, eight years later, in 1975, I found myself defending Continental Grain in court, in the only litigation that arose out of the scandal, and confronting Tony De Angelis on the witness stand?

In fact, the explanation was simple. The settlement we'd achieved with American Express had provided no money for parties that held only forged receipts. American Express considered itself—understandably—under no obligation to make good on receipts that had never been issued by its subsidiary. The largest holder of forged receipts had been Ira Haupt & Company, now bankrupt, and since it had received nothing in the settlement, its trustee in bankruptcy sued Continental Grain and other companies that traded on the commodities exchange where De Angelis had bought his oil.

De Angelis had not only bought all of the vegetable oil he could get from domestic producers, like Proctor & Gamble, but, beginning in 1963, traded vegetable oil as futures. Contracts for cottonseed oil were traded on the floor of the New York Produce Exchange, in lower Manhattan, where, as with all commodities futures, a contract enabled the holder to buy a railroad car of cottonseed oil at a set price for delivery at a given future date. In 1963 De Angelis began using Haupt & Company as his broker to buy contracts. Haupt was eager for the commissions involved and willing to lend De Angelis even his down payments. By November 1963, when the scandal broke, Haupt, acting in De Angelis's behalf, had accumulated roughly 80 percent of the contracts traded on the exchange.

As the price of cottonseed oil rose, Haupt received many millions of dollars in variation margin. It transmitted that money to De Angelis. As the price began to fall, however, the payment flow was reversed, and Haupt now had to make payments to the exchange representing the reduction in value. Rather than insisting that De Angelis reimburse Haupt for the money it was spending, Haupt kept lending him money. As collateral, it now began to accept warehouse receipts. When De Angelis ran out of receipts issued by American Express, he forged his own and gave them to Haupt.

Then, in November 1963, Haupt itself ran out of money. It decided to sell the contracts it was holding for De Angelis and, in addition, to collect the more than $40 million he owed by selling the warehouse receipts it had received as collateral.

There was no way, however, that Haupt could sell its huge 80 percent position in futures contracts without causing a total collapse of the market. For the first time, therefore, it disclosed the situation to the Produce Exchange and asked the exchange to order that all contracts be settled at a price to be set by the exchange. Several days later, the exchange did this, and at a price that Haupt believed would leave it in the black by some $3 million, once it had sold the warehouse receipts it had taken as collateral from De Angelis. When the receipts turned out to be forged, though, the huge resulting loss was more than Haupt could stand, and it filed for bankruptcy. Now, years later, looking for money to pay Haupt's creditors, the company's bankruptcy trustee sued the Produce Exchange, the exchange's directors, and the companies that employed them, claiming that the exchange ought to have detected that De Angelis was trying to monopolize, corner, and manipulate prices on the cottonseed oil market and should have intervened to stop him. Moreover, the Haupt trustee claimed that the exchange had not acted quickly enough in closing trading once Haupt told it that it was in trouble.

Harold Vogel, vice president of Continental Grain, was an outside director of the Produce Exchange. He and Continental Grain were named as defendants in Haupt's lawsuit. The case came to trial in September 1975, and I was retained to represent Vogel and Continental Grain.

As the most experienced trial lawyer among the defendants, even though I was only forty-three at the time, I took the lead role in court. In their opening statement, the trustee's lawyers emphasized that they were acting, not for Haupt, but for the creditors of Haupt, the real losers when Haupt had gone bankrupt. They told the jury they would call experts to testify that there had been ample warning signs that De Angelis, through Haupt, was accumulating a huge position in futures contracts. The Produce Exchange and its directors, they maintained, should have detected the signs and should have called a halt. Instead, they'd done nothing. The trustee's lawyers spent much of their opening statement defining the technical terms involved in trading on a futures exchange, and it became clear that, in addition to the expert testimony, they were going to deluge the jury with trading statistics.

I decided to use my opening to offer some definitions of my own and, in so doing, to spell out a theme for the defense that the jury would remember.

"You've heard a lot of technical terms defined today and yesterday," I began. "Now I'd like to define a term that I think will sum up the evidence that will come before you. The term is 'chutzpah.' If a man sets fire to his house, there is a chance that he will be caught in the ensuing explosion and be burned. Chutzpah is when the arsonist sues the fire department for not having stopped him from setting the fire or for not having put it out in time. And this, ladies and gentlemen of the jury, is above all a case of chutzpah."

I kept to that single theme.

"In any case, ladies and gentlemen, plaintiff's lawyers, with their considerable ability, will attempt to convince you that the victims are the villains, and to bury beneath a mountain of statistics and charts and exhibits the fact that it's the villain who is suing.

"Harold Vogel's own employer, Continental Grain Company, was one of the victims of Tino De Angelis's $100 million swindle.

"As you now know, Ira Haupt was De Angelis's broker—and, I submit, accomplice. And I won't call him Tino [as Haupt's lawyers had], I will call him De Angelis, because I'm not on such intimate terms with him.

"The complaint in this case reads like a confession of sin by the plaintiff. We are told that in 1963 De Angelis was out to corner the futures market—he was out to manipulate the market—and Haupt was acting as his broker in these activities. And when De Angelis's scheme collapsed and he went bankrupt, Haupt, which was not only acting as his broker but also his financier in these futures operations, went bankrupt also.

"Now, twelve years later, plaintiff's attorneys are in court trying to blame the Produce Exchange, its board of governors, and the companies that employed them for the fact that they didn't discover that Haupt was engaging in this scheme and stop Haupt from doing it.

"The main point is that if there was an effort at cornering the market, it was Haupt on behalf of Allied that was doing it. If there was an effort at manipulating the market, it was Haupt on behalf of Allied that was doing it. And it is Haupt on whose behalf this claim is being asserted now."

I knew from Haupt's witness list that it would not be calling any of the company's executives. I wanted the jury to appreciate the significance of that omission:

"But there is one other fact that I would ask you to consider when you judge the speculative theories that are being proffered to you by plaintiff, and that is that they are not calling a single partner or executive of the Haupt firm in 1963. Not one of them will take the stand and point an accusing finger at Harold Vogel, Continental Grain, or any other defendant. But we are not going to let them forget their client. We will present testimony from these Haupt officials, and we will present the statement of the Haupt trustee himself that Haupt's loss was due to the dishonesty of its own employees, for which they are now trying to blame all of us.

"Ladies and gentlemen, as I conclude, I'd like to leave you with some really final words about what this case really means. Trials are always very interesting. They lend—maybe not for the jurors but for spectators anyway—they lend themselves to great drama, television, movies, series based on them. This case belongs in the category of the theater of the absurd. To accept the claims that are being advanced here you would have to really descend down the rabbit hole into the land of Alice in Wonderland. You would have to impute knowledge to Harold Vogel on November 14 which he didn't have until November 19. You would have to find bad faith as to all the defendants, where there was only good faith. You would have to find that Continental Grain was a seller, when it was a buyer. You would have to find, above all, that the policeman is to blame, not the wrongdoer. The evidence in this case, I submit to you, will permit only one verdict, and that is of no liability. But if the law permitted you to bring in a verdict of shame, shame for dragging these people into this courtroom on such baseless charges, I submit that the evidence in this case would cry out for that verdict."

Openings ought never be too long—mine, in this case, lasted half an hour—but they must state and elaborate the trial theme that will be inherent in all the ensuing evidence and argument, and impress that theme on the jurors' minds. The plaintiff's evidence in this case could take up as much as a month of their time, and that very duration might suggest that the case had to be taken seriously. I wanted them to understand, from the outset, that the case was not only bizarre but an insult to their intelligence.

———

Just before the trial, I met Tino De Angelis for the first time. He had long since pleaded guilty to fraud and was already out of jail. The lawyers for Haupt's trustee had put him on their witness list to testify about his goal of supporting the market price of cottonseed oil through his purchases through Haupt, as well as to the fact that he had done business with two of the defendant companies, Bunge Corporation and my client, Continental Grain.

I traveled to Bayonne, New Jersey, to interview him in the company of Judith Kaye, then a very young lawyer whose boss, Jack O'Donnell, was representing the Produce Exchange. Visiting De Angelis was an adventure for us. The onetime butcher now occupied a small shack-like office down a long, unmarked, potholed dirt road on the same property as the water-filled oil tanks. We jounced and jolted along in an ancient oversized Cadillac too wide for the road, having grave misgivings as to how we would get out afterward. De Angelis, we knew, had gone into the fat-rendering business after prison, but we had no idea what this meant. He met us straight from the slaughterhouse floor, wearing a long white butcher's coat splattered with pork fat and blood and covered with flies.

In fact, he looked like an impostor. How could this chubby little man in the long stained smock have swindled banks and major commodities companies, not to mention American Express, for more than $100 million? With us he made no effort to hide what he'd done. He readily admitted having issued fraudulent and fictitious warehouse receipts, blaming it on the financial pressures he'd faced. He saw himself as a legitimate businessman who had built the international vegetable oil market and who'd been ruined when his rivals—the processors and Bunge Corporation—decided they wanted that business for themselves. He also blamed his troubles on the U.S. government's failure to process his export licenses quickly enough. Con men have a capacity—one that never fails to amaze me—to con themselves too, and Tino De Angelis was no exception.

Kaye and I did learn one critical fact from him that would shape our cross-examination in court—De Angelis had no animus against either of our clients, the Produce Exchange and Continental Grain, but he hated Bunge. Under questioning that day, he acknowledged that he'd kept his position in futures contracts secret from the Produce Exchange and its directors. He also admitted that all of his dealings with my client, Continental Grain, had been at arm's length. As a witness, we were sure he would hurt the Haupt trustee's case more than he would help it, and we could only hope that the lawyers wouldn't change their minds about calling him. They didn't disappoint us, and so, on October 6, 1975, I rose to cross-examine Tino De Angelis.

I immediately brought out that my client, Continental Grain, was one of his victims, not his collaborator.

"In any event, am I correct that you issued worthless warehouse receipts or procured the issuance of worthless warehouse receipts which you gave to many, many companies, am I correct?"

"I gave them to four or five companies."

"They lost millions of dollars in connection with it, am I correct?"

"Well, I will accept that. I will say yes."

"Will you also acknowledge that my client, Continental Grain Company, was one of your victims?"

"Yes, I will."

"Can you tell the jury how Continental Grain acted in the conduct of its business affairs with you?"

"I have the highest and utmost regard for the Continental Grain organization, and more particularly Mr. Totah, who administered that company in his dealings with me."

"They acted fairly?"

"Extremely fair."

"And in good faith as you saw it?"

"Absolutely."

"In giving them these warehouse receipts, whatever may have been the circumstances, you took advantage of them?"

"That is correct."

Next, I established that, although the plaintiff had named Continental Grain and Bunge as codefendants and plotters against Haupt, they were bitter rivals and enemies.

"You understood, sir, did you not, that Continental Grain Company and Bunge were competitors?"

"Yes, I did, Mr. Liman."

"Had you observed that there was no love lost between them?"

"They were two separate companies. There was no relationship between them, absolutely none that I know of. They were separate and apart, two different companies, each doing the same type business. They were competitors."

"You dealt with each separately, am I correct?"

"Absolutely."

"Would you describe your relationships with Continental Grain as an arm's-length type of relationship?"

"Always in every way they traded as a first-line company."

Then, from De Angelis's own lips came testimony that he had never disclosed to Continental any of his illicit activities.

"Did you ever say to Continental Grain that you were engaging in any of these transactions in order to support the market or manipulate the market?"

"No."

"Is it a fact that you never disclosed to my client, Continental Grain Company, that you were forging receipts?"

"That is correct."

"Or to the Produce Exchange?"

"Or to anyone else."

"And you never disclosed to my client, Continental Grain, that you had a shortage of oil against which American Express was issuing receipts; am I correct?"

"Never."

"And the same is true of the Produce Exchange?"

"That is correct."

"Is it true that you did not disclose to Continental Grain or the Produce Exchange what your strategy was in the futures market?"

"Well, the word *strategy*—there was no strategy."

"Your intentions. Did you tell them, 'I intend to buy contracts?'"

"No, I did not disclose that."

"You kept that a secret too?"

"My operations were kept within our organization."

"And you never disclosed to Continental Grain that you were acting to try to support the price of futures, am I correct?"

"That is correct."

"And you never disclosed that to the Produce Exchange, am I correct?"

"That is correct."

Then I brought out that Haupt had sought De Angelis's business, and that the son of the founder had met with him for that purpose.

"You were asked about your dealings with Haupt. Am I correct that it was Haupt & Company that solicited the business from you and not vice versa?"

"Yes."

"You testified that you met with a Mr. Ira Haupt, whether he was the second, third, or fourth, but he was the real thing, am I correct?"

"I met with Mr. Haupt."

"Did you find that Ira Haupt & Company was aggressive in going after your business?"

"That is correct."

"They wanted as much as you could give them, am I correct?"

"That is correct."

Haupt, in fact, had been content to hold eight thousand futures contracts for De Angelis until mid-November 1963.

"Did Haupt ever tell you that they didn't want to hold eight thousand contracts for you until the very last day?"

"They never contested the amount that they were holding."

Finally, I brought out that De Angelis, in the fateful days when Haupt ran out of money, had warned Haupt that, if it dumped the positions it held for De Angelis, the price of cottonseed oil and soybean oil would crash and Allied and Haupt would be ruined. De Angelis, Haupt's own witness, testified that Haupt had ruined itself. "You are ruining yourself and you are ruining everything," De Angelis said he had told Haupt.

De Angelis's testimony came as no surprise to Kaye or me; it was all based on our interview with him. But to the jury, we must have seemed like Perry Masons. As Haupt's trustee's own witness, De Angelis gave testimony on cross-examination that left Haupt's case in ruins.

Haupt also called as a witness an economics professor from Stanford University, Robert Gray, to testify, in the light of theories he'd devised, that Continental Grain was receiving a return of 150 percent on 600 warehouse receipts it had financed for De Angelis, which should have been a tip-off to Continental that De Angelis was going bankrupt. The professor arrived at this figure by assuming that Continental Grain borrowed 90 percent of the money it lent to Allied at low rates; he attributed Continental Grain's profit to the 10 percent that it did not borrow. I went to work, in cross-examination, on Professor Gray's analysis.

"You read off some figures today in which you computed that Continental Grain had gotten a 150 percent return on a 600–warehouse receipt transaction. You read those from a piece of paper, am I correct?"

"First, may I respond to your question. I did not testify that Continental Grain had gotten that return. I testified that under certain assumptions this would have been the return. Yes, I read those numbers from a piece of paper."

"Let's talk about the assumptions. You don't dispute, do you, that Continental Grain laid out $4,570,200 for 600 warehouse receipts; am I correct?"

"I don't dispute that fact."

"You have seen a copy of the check, in fact, to Allied?"

"Probably have. Yes, I have."

"You, in making this computation, assumed that Continental borrowed 90 percent of the value of that warehouse receipt from its bank?"

"That was one of the assumptions."

"You then assumed that Continental Grain's equity in this receipt was 10 percent, or $450,000, rather than the $4,570,000 that it issued to Allied?"

"I didn't assume that was Continental's equity in the receipt. I assumed that was the portion of Continental's own money that was used in paying for the receipt."

"You then assumed that Continental had borrowed from the bank on the 90 percent at a rate of 4 $\frac{1}{2}$ percent; am I correct?"

"That was the assumption, yes, sir."

"That was the assumption that was based on the assumption that it had borrowed 90 percent of the receipt; am I correct?"

"Yes, sir."

"So that we are piling assumptions on top of assumptions."

"We piled one on top of another so far."

"You made another assumption that Continental was charging itself 6 percent interest on the 10 percent it didn't borrow from the bank?"

"Correct."

"As a result of doing all of that arithmetic, you said that the profit after deducting all of this interest on the transaction was $53,311?"

"I said—I called it return."

"Okay. I'm not trying to argue with you about interest or profit . . . "

"I'm just trying to respond accurately."

"I think we can understand each other. What you did, you attributed all of that to this $457,000 rather than to the $4,570,000 that Continental paid out, right?"

"I did in my calculation, yes."

"That gives you 150 percent?"

"Yes."

"If Continental Grain, using its credit facilities, had borrowed all but one dollar of the amount it paid to Allied, you could have made another computation; am I correct?"

"I would have had much higher leverage then, yes."

"In fact, if we assume that Continental went to the bank and borrowed all but one dollar, then you would come to the conclusion, would you not, that its rate of return was some 650,000 percent?"

"I haven't made the computation, but that sounds like a reasonable order of magnitude."

"If we assume that Continental Grain borrowed 100 percent of the money it advanced to Allied, then its rate of return would be infinite?"

"On its own money."

"Infinite; am I correct?"

"Yes."

"You know that banks discount their loans at the Federal Reserve all the time?"

"Yes."

"And what you are saying is that on the assumption that the money it lends to me, Arthur Liman, is money that it borrowed at a lower rate from the Federal Reserve, then its rate of return on equity in that transaction is infinite?"

"If all of the money that it lends is borrowed money, then its rate of return on its own invested funds would be infinite in that calculation, yes."

I paused. I hoped the jury was getting it, the theater of the absurd.

"You are aware, aren't you, sir," I went on, "that if a bank or Continental Grain or any company that had a file with the SEC reported its rate of return by that kind of method, it would be sent to jail?"

"It would probably be investigated. No, let me back up on the answer to that question. If it reported its rate of return as being that high, it would probably invite some investigation."

"Now, sir, do you know any companies that report rates of return on transactions by engaging in this kind of accounting that you have done here?"

"Oh, I don't think they account for their returns in this manner. But I know many companies that are well aware of the leverage available through this sort of transaction."

"You have testified on many occasions, haven't you?"

"Several."

"Can you point to a single time when you have testified, or a single publication in which this kind of methodology has been used, sir?"

"I haven't had occasion to use that."

"Thank you."

———

No matter how well a case is going—and by the time we finished with Professor Gray we had the jury laughing aloud—the verdict remains unpredictable. I'd already had one case in which, near the end, the judge received a note from a juror saying that she could no longer be impartial because she liked and trusted one of the lawyers more than the other. I was convinced this was juror no. 6, who was always sneaking smiles at me when I asked a potent question or made some joke to lighten the courtroom. What I didn't realize, at the time, was that juror no. 6 was doing this to the other side also, and they were equally convinced that she was in their camp! But when the judge revealed the identity of the juror who'd sent him the note, it turned out to be yet another juror, no. 4, whose face was like a mask but who was an avowed admirer of the opposition!

In another case, a juror had waved to me every morning and every afternoon throughout the proceedings. But my client, apparently, was a different matter. When it came to the verdict, she had voted against him on every count.

In fact, the Haupt jury worried me in just this way. Haupt's lawyer was younger than me—the years do have a way of creeping up on you— and I was no longer the nice young man he was. The jury clearly liked him. Worse, we had the impression that they felt sorry for him when, on cross-examination, we turned one after another of his witnesses to our advantage. Would they be willing to disappoint him, possibly to hurt his career, by throwing the case out? Or would they, as juries sometimes do, try to please everyone by a compromise verdict?

Before the case even began, the other side had been talking to us about a settlement. In fact, our clients, collectively, had offered a seven-figure settlement, but Haupt's trustee had turned it down. Now, as the case was drawing to a conclusion, Haupt's senior lawyer, who had not been in the courtroom, called me and said he accepted our prior offer.

"What offer?" I said.

"The one before trial," he responded.

"But that offer's no longer there," I reminded him. "You rejected it because you wanted to gamble on how the trial went. Now you've lost that gamble."

The renewed opportunity to settle, though, led to divisions within our camp. Bunge's lawyer was for it, though at a slightly lower level than our original offer, but O'Donnell, Kaye, and I were more buoyant about our chances before the jury, and we opposed any offer. Besides, there were enough parties to the lawsuit that, even in a worst case, the jury delivering a compromise verdict—the proverbial half a loaf—our clients could well afford the risk. We huddled, separately, with our clients and finally agreed to let the jury decide.

In our summations, each of the defense lawyers stuck to the theme that I'd sounded in the opening: it was our clients who were victims, not Haupt; Haupt had been De Angelis's broker and accomplice. As I put it, "What killed Haupt was its own mismanagement and greed and internal deception. A greed that was so powerful because there were millions of dollars in commissions to be earned."

I also wanted to urge the jury not to compromise, always a risky move, but my instincts told me this time that if the jury could be made to choose between one party or the other, we would prevail. Compromise was our enemy.

"In my opening address," I told the jury, "I challenged plaintiff to bring on some of the partners of Haupt. He didn't, and now you can understand why. Because their words are in this record, and they are, I submit, a reproach to the claim that has been asserted. You will recall that on November 19, when the board of directors voted despite the threat of lawsuits by the shorts to close the market and give Haupt the $3 million necessary to save it, Mr. Kamerman, the head of Haupt, thanked each of those directors.

"And even after Haupt discovered that the warehouse receipts that it had taken from Allied as collateral were forged, weeks later Mr. Brenner, a partner of Haupt, wrote the board to express his views. And you will recall that Mr. Brenner was one of the men who was engaged in the efforts to liquidate Haupt's position.

"What did Mr. Brenner write? 'I would personally like to thank you for all your help and assistance during the recent catastrophic development at Ira Haupt & Company. I thought that the Produce Exchange upheld every good tradition of Wall Street and the investment community, and I personally would like to thank you.'

"That was the verdict, ladies and gentlemen, which the men who ran Haupt passed on these defendants at the time. And I am confident that, on the evidence that you have heard over the last seven weeks, your verdict can be no different."

Once again came the long wait. I know I've mentioned it before, but this limbo, when the jury is out, is one of the hardest passages we trial lawyers must endure. We try to distract ourselves, but how? We read books, but who can concentrate on the page? We tell each other jokes that have long since become stale. We pace, the superstitious among us searching for omens, most of them bad because, psychologically, we want to prepare ourselves for the worst. But mostly we just wait, and we grow more anxious as the time goes by.

But then the wait was over. Suddenly, the bailiff announced that there was a verdict. As the jurors filed in, we searched their faces, looking for some sign, some ray of light in their inscrutability.

"Has the jury reached a verdict?"

"We have, Your Honor."

"On liability, is your verdict for the plaintiff or the defendants?"

"For the defendants."

We'd won! Now came another wait, much shorter but just as excruciating, while the judge dismissed the jury. The moment he was done, we ran for the pay telephones—this was long before cellular phones—to tell our clients.

Today, in fact, I'm not at all sure a matter like this would be tried to verdict. The damages at stake would be much greater, enough probably to ruin the defendants, and juries nowadays are more inclined to impose liability even when the facts do not warrant it. For a defendant, therefore, going to trial could well mean betting the company on a jury's common sense. Rather than take such a risk, there would be a powerful incentive to settle. But in the 1960s and 1970s, we still had some sense of proportion in this regard, and a defendant who believed in his case could still afford to allow a jury to decide.

There were two bonuses for me in the salad oil case. The first was that, when the Haupt trustee appealed the verdict, I was able to name young Judith Kaye to argue the appeal on behalf of all the defendants. She did splendidly, as I knew she would (she has since gone on to become chief judge of New York), and we were finally able to close the case. The second was that my efforts cemented one of the great relationships of my professional career, that with Continental Grain Company and the Fribourg family, who own it. I will come back to them in due course, for I have counseled Continental and the Fribourgs ever since.

6

U.S. v. Wolfson:
My Introduction to Defending White-Collar Crime

J UST AFTER I'd finished the Birrell case for Bob Morgenthau and returned to Paul, Weiss in the summer of 1968, I tried my first white-collar criminal case as a defense lawyer. It involved a flamboyant corporate raider from Florida, Louis E. Wolfson, and some associates, among them a Boston businessman named Joseph Kosow, whom I represented. It ended happily, but only because we prevailed on appeal after Kosow was convicted at trial.

Actually, my first acquittal in a criminal case came for a client I didn't even represent!

The story was this. General Motors was under investigation by a grand jury and had hired Judge Rifkind. One day Rifkind asked me to accompany two GM executives who had been summoned to testify that day. To kill time as we waited for the grand jury, I suggested that we go watch what was happening in the courtroom next door.

Two men were on trial there for having taken part in a sham marriage scheme. One was a Greek seaman who'd married an American woman so that he could get a permanent visa. The other was accused of having arranged the marriage. He'd persuaded the woman to appear at City Hall for the wedding. No sooner was it over than she'd disappeared, never to see the Greek seaman again until this day in court.

The erstwhile wife was on the stand when the two GM executives and I sat down in the first row. After she'd described the phony marriage, the prosecutor asked her whether she could identify in the courtroom the man who arranged the marriage and the Greek seaman. She scanned the audience, and then—out of the blue—she pointed at my two clients, the GM executives!

One of them leaned over and asked me in a loud, somewhat panicky whisper what he should do. I suggested that he decide quickly whether he wanted to be the bigamist or the procurer. My clients got up and fled the courtroom, with me at their heels, amid laughter from everyone but the prosecutor.

And the defendants?

Yes, they were promptly acquitted.

In the Wolfson case, my client wasn't so lucky. Louis Elwood Wolfson was the son of a scrap-metal dealer who, in the 1950s, built one of the first conglomerates by ingesting whatever companies swam within his reach. His skill at identifying, buying, and dismembering badly managed and undervalued companies earned him the nickname of "the Junkman." Wolfson controlled a publicly held construction and marine salvage company called Merritt-Chapman & Scott, and onto it he'd grafted dozens of other companies, including the New York Shipbuilding Corporation, a streetcar and bus company in Washington, D.C., called Capital Transit, and Devoe & Raynolds, a paint company. Wolfson was one of the first to use proxy fights to attempt to take over control of companies from existing management. In 1955 he'd staged a bitter proxy fight for control of Montgomery Ward & Company of Chicago, then the nation's third-largest retail company, but he'd lost out. He also began breeding and racing horses in 1958, and twenty years later he raised and owned Affirmed, our last Triple Crown winner.

Wolfson, together with Joseph Kosow and others, was indicted in 1966 on charges of having orchestrated a fraudulent stock deal in 1963 and conspiring to lie about the transaction to the SEC. Only a month before, in an unrelated case, Wolfson had been convicted of selling unregistered stock. Kosow had retained Judge Rifkind to defend him. He had made his fortune in the luggage manufacturing business in Boston, principally during the war when he'd made duffel bags for the government.

When the case came up for trial that summer of 1968, Judge Rifkind delivered an opening statement to the jury but then handed Kosow's defense over to me. The facts of the case couldn't have been worse for us, and I was about to learn, the hard way, one unhappy fact of life for white-collar criminal defense lawyers: no matter how good you think you are, you have to be prepared to lose.

In 1963 the stock of Wolfson's company, Merritt-Chapman, had been selling for about eight dollars a share, but in Wolfson's own judgment it was worth a lot more. Naturally, Wolfson wanted his company to buy up as much of its own stock as it could when the price was so cheap, but Merritt-Chapman had already been forced to borrow money, and its loan agreements prevented it from using its cash to make stock purchases. Instead, Wolfson proposed a deal to Kosow, among others, to circumvent the loan agreements. Kosow would buy on the open market hundreds of thousands of Merritt-Chapman shares at the low price. Wolfson secretly agreed to then buy it all back from him later at higher prices, thereby guaranteeing Kosow a very substantial profit. The SEC asserted that Kosow had really been making an illegal loan to Wolfson's company. That was a crime, the government said, because Kosow and Wolfson were cheating the sellers who sold their stock to Kosow at low prices while being kept in the dark about the secret repurchase agreement.

The indictment also accused Wolfson, Kosow, and the others of conspiring beforehand to lie to the SEC if it ever asked them questions. The SEC did indeed ask them questions, and because the defendants were sure they had destroyed all copies of their repurchase agreements, they'd each testified that no such repurchase agreements ever existed. Unfortunately, Kosow had had a minor partner named Kleven to whom he'd given copies of the Wolfson repurchase agreements. Later he'd asked for them back, but in the meantime Kleven had made copies for himself, and eventually Kleven's copies had been turned over to the government. Wolfson was also charged with perjury.

Many defense lawyers, it should be said, make it a practice never to ask whether a client is guilty or innocent. If the client has confessed to them, it virtually prohibits them from putting him or her on the witness stand and running the additional risk of committing perjury. But a defense lawyer has to ask a client what other witnesses may say, in order to avoid being taken by surprise. That's a more subtle way of knowing whether the client actually committed the offense. In the Kosow case, we never asked Kosow whether he'd entered into the repurchase agreements. They were already in evidence. Besides, Kosow had made the mistake of denying their existence before the SEC and had no intention of repeating that mistake by taking the stand in the criminal case. But at the same time, he refused to plead guilty. He looked to us to find some way of getting him off that would not require him to deny the offense, although he knew this was a long shot.

A long shot it was, but trials always have unpredictable elements. The government's witnesses can die. Jurors are fully capable of despising plea-bargainers who testify for the government and sympathizing with the defendant. A single idiosyncratic juror can always deadlock a jury. In addition, convictions can be—and sometimes are—reversed because the prosecutor has made a mistake or violated the rules. These may be slim possibilities, but a defendant, even if guilty, has a right to put the government to its proof. And that is what we did in the Kosow case.

The reader may also ask why, knowing Kosow's guilt, we undertook his defense. It is not an unreasonable question, and there have been occasions in my career when I've turned down cases on personal or moral grounds. One of the major Watergate defendants, for instance, tried to hire me to represent him, and I declined. But our legal and constitutional system, which I wholeheartedly support, provides that every accused has the right to counsel. Kosow was hardly an ax murderer, although ax murderers also need to be defended. Besides, I liked him.

I would add that money was not, and is not, a factor. Kosow could afford our fee, yes, but Paul, Weiss has defended countless clients who couldn't, and we have defended them to the very best of our abilities and resources.

The trial lasted for seven weeks, with Judge Edmund Palmieri presiding. From the very first day, I learned another rude lesson about defending white-collar criminal cases: defense lawyers are never favorites of the court. As a young federal prosecutor, I'd tried several white-collar cases in Judge Palmieri's courtroom. He, like many of his peers, was a former federal prosecutor, and while always impartial, he'd also been unfailingly generous, gentle, and friendly whenever I appeared before him. Now, when I came into his courtroom as an advocate for a defendant rather than the United States, he treated me like a traitor. He ruled against me constantly and abruptly. (I wasn't alone either. Wolfson, too, was convinced that Palmieri was unfairly antagonistic, and his lawyers tried unsuccessfully, before and after the trial, to have the judge removed from the case.) During my summation to the jury, he accused me of usurping his role as judge to instruct the jury on the law, because I had simply asked the jurors to deliberate about my client's fate with the same sense of fairness they would want in a jury deciding their own fates!

At the next recess, I called Judge Rifkind.

"All I did was cite the Golden Rule," I told him, "and now I'm afraid Palmieri's going to jail me for contempt."

I wasn't to worry, Rifkind replied. He was always ready to bail me out.

For the first four weeks of the trial, the government's witnesses detailed the complex stock transactions among Wolfson and Kosow and the other defendants, which the government alleged were fraudulent. When the government rested, however, we won a huge victory in that Palmieri ruled that the stock deals, even the secret repurchase agreements, were not illegal in and of themselves. Twenty years later, as I will relate, government prosecutors would call similar arrangements "stock parking" and treat them as felonies—allegedly illegal "parking" was at the heart of the government's allegations against Michael Milken—but in 1968 Judge Palmieri ruled they didn't violate the securities laws.

That left only one allegation against Kosow, that he and the other defendants had agreed among themselves to lie to the SEC—but that was an extremely tricky charge both to prove and to defend against. Kosow couldn't deny the existence of the repurchase agreements. The courtroom, in fact, was littered with enlarged copies of them. Nor could he could deny that, like all the defendants, he had lied to the SEC about them. However, Kosow wasn't accused of lying. He was accused of *conspiring* to lie. So, conceding that Kosow had lied, we set out to convince the jury that he had lied on his own, not as part of a general conspiracy.

The government called several of Kosow's partners as witnesses. Up to that point, most of the testimony had been about Wolfson, not Kosow, so I'd tried as best I could to keep a low profile in the courtroom for me and my client, not the easiest task for me, as I'm quite tall, but virtually impossible for Kosow, who was a huge figure of a man. Now that the witnesses were some of Kosow's best friends, though, I could no longer pretend we weren't there, and so I rose to cross-examine them. I was able to bring out that Kosow had never asked them to destroy or withhold records, nor had he asked them to lie to the SEC. The inference I wanted the jurors to draw was that if Kosow had conspired with Wolfson to lie to the SEC, wouldn't he surely have instructed his partners to do likewise? Had the government's case against Kosow relied solely on the testimony of his partners, I think we might have had a good chance of prevailing. But the prosecutors were able to produce a much better witness, a man named Alexander Rittmaster.

Rittmaster had been indicted along with Kosow and Wolfson and the others, but he'd pleaded guilty two days before the trial began, and now he became the government's star witness. Rittmaster testified that the defendants had indeed conspired to destroy all copies of the repurchase agreement and to lie to the SEC about it. So crucial was his testimony that the prosecutor, in justifying the plea bargain with Rittmaster, admitted to the jury that he doubted whether the government could have convicted the defendants without it, and Judge Palmieri instructed the jury later that it could convict the defendants on Rittmaster's testimony alone.

Unlike my cross-examinations of Kosow's partners, I knew I had to attack Rittmaster's credibility head on. The easiest way to do that was to point out to the jury that, as he'd already admitted, he'd lied under oath before. And having done so once, how could anyone assume he wouldn't again? So Rittmaster was a liar. But I was hoping to find a way to suggest that he'd had a particular reason for lying in this case.

As it happened, I actually found one. But Judge Palmieri wouldn't let me pursue it.

While I was cross-examining Rittmaster, documents that we'd subpoenaed suddenly arrived in the courtroom. I continued to put questions to Rittmaster, but at the same time I was trying desperately to scan the newly arrived material. I saw immediately that it was highly significant, and I asked Palmieri for a brief recess to study it. The documents showed that Rittmaster had previously owned $500,000 worth of unregistered

Merritt-Chapman stock, which he'd wanted to sell publicly. In order to do this, he'd needed to obtain approval from the SEC, so he'd written the SEC, seeking its permission. At the time, he had yet to testify before the grand jury investigating Wolfson. The SEC replied that, in view of the ongoing investigation, it couldn't grant him permission at that time. Soon after that, Rittmaster did testify—favorably for the government—and the grand jury handed up its indictments. Almost immediately, the SEC reversed itself and permitted Rittmaster to sell his stock.

I was elated. I was sure I could use the documents to impugn Rittmaster's credibility. Without my even having to say it, it would become clear that the SEC's permission had been part and parcel of his plea bargain. But no sooner did I start to probe his motives in corroborating the government's allegations than the prosecutor objected.

Judge Palmieri sustained the objection, and when I started to argue with him, he cut me off abruptly. I pleaded with him to let me go on, but he adamantly refused. He said that what I was talking about was a side issue to the case and that going into it would only delay a trial that had already lasted for weeks.

I was effectively hamstrung and monumentally frustrated, but all that was left for me was to try, on summation, to convince the jury that, when Kosow lied to the SEC, he had done so on his own. The repurchase agreement between Kosow and Wolfson was private and confidential, and even though my client had been wrong not to tell the SEC about it, he hadn't conspired with Wolfson.

Summation is the most intimate encounter between advocate and jury. Unlike the opening statement, it takes place after the jury has heard all the evidence, and so the advocate is talking with a knowledgeable audience. Like most trial lawyers, I try, during my summations, to speak directly to each juror and to watch how their eyes react to my arguments. Some juries, granted, are hard to read, but this one was all too easy.

Nice try, Mr. Liman, they told me with their eyes, but we just don't buy it. Maybe people in law school would go for your distinguishing between lying and a conspiracy to lie, but not we laypeople. My head told me they were going to convict Joseph Kosow, but I was still, in my heart, hoping for a miracle.

No miracle occurred: the jury convicted all the defendants. Kosow was sentenced to a year in jail and a $10,000 fine, Wolfson to eighteen months in jail and $32,000 in fines. Case closed.

As I said, I genuinely liked my client. He'd hired Judge Rifkind but quickly accepted me as his trial lawyer. He'd never tried to fool me or dissemble, had shown great confidence in me throughout the trial, and, when the jury convicted him, felt as badly for me as I did for him. He wanted to appeal, yes, but he also wanted to serve his jail sentence without waiting, and it was only with great difficulty that I managed to persuade him to see how the appeal turned out first. I thought we had something going for us, not the least of which was Rifkind's plan to argue the appeal himself.

On appeal we contended that Kosow hadn't had a fair chance to cross-examine Rittmaster. No one, of course, could be sure how the jury would have reacted had they seen the Rittmaster documents, but Judge Palmieri had denied them that opportunity and they'd voted to convict Kosow of conspiracy largely on the basis of Rittmaster's testimony. In an autocratic state, the doubt we raised might have been resolved in the government's favor, but in our constitutional system, which protects individual rights above all, it had to be resolved in favor of the accused.

This time the Court of Appeals agreed with us, and two years later, it reversed the convictions of all the defendants. Although the government could subsequently have retried Kosow, Rittmaster had died while the appeal was still pending, and I was able to convince them to drop the case.

Wolfson was not as lucky. With the lawyer Edward Bennett Williams of Washington, D.C., representing him, he was retried twice; neither jury could reach a verdict, and eventually he pleaded nolo contendere (no contest) to a felony and was fined, but not sent to jail. On the other hand, he was convicted for selling unregistered stock and eventually served nine months in jail on that charge. Some twenty years later, he was still fighting his conviction.

There was a strange sequel to the story: Wolfson's troubles with the SEC also led to Abe Fortas's resignation from the Supreme Court. Lyndon Johnson had appointed Fortas to the Court in 1965. (Coincidentally, as I mentioned before, Fortas's wife, Carolyn Agger, had been Paul, Weiss's first woman partner.) The appointment was prestigious but, for the Fortases, costly. As successful Washington lawyers, they lived lavishly, but the Supreme Court job paid only $40,000 a year—a huge drop in their income. As a partial solution, Wolfson, a client of Fortas's law firm, suggested to Fortas that he become a consultant to his family's foundation devoted to race relations, with a $20,000 annual retainer payable for life, and subsequently to his widow for *her* life. Fortas agreed, and soon after he arrived at the Supreme Court, he'd received Wolfson's first check. But once Wolfson was indicted, Fortas thought better of the deal. He returned the check and canceled the arrangement.

When Richard Nixon took office in January 1969, he and his Attorney General, John Mitchell, were eager to replace Fortas with a more conservative justice. With quiet help from the Justice Department, *Life* magazine revealed in May 1969 that Fortas had accepted a $20,000 fee from Wolfson in 1966 while he was under investigation by the SEC. Impeachment talk began. Two days later, Wolfson surrendered to the Justice Department a document showing that the fee had not been a onetime payment but the first installment in a lifetime arrangement. The Justice Department, meanwhile, already had copies of the Wolfson-Fortas correspondence in which they had discussed the SEC case against Wolfson. Some of this had even been given to us under seal during the Kosow trial.

Abe Fortas resigned a few days later.

7

Charles Bluhdorn Awards Us the Gulf & Western Good-American Medal

V*anity Fair* magazine once called me a "big trouble" lawyer. I was flat-tered, in that the label suggested that people facing big legal trouble sought me out. But to the extent that it was true, it also meant that I was on call twenty-four hours a day and on the receiving end of urgent calls from clients in all sorts of distress—old clients, new clients, a sort of legal ER.

I exaggerate, of course, but a trial lawyer never knows where his next case is coming from. At the same time, in an era when many law firms routinely advertise and "market" themselves, I still subscribe to a suc-cinct dictum of Judge Rifkind's: the best advertisement for a lawyer is a satisfied client.

Herb Siegel proved both points. I represented Siegel and his com-pany, Chris-Craft, in their protracted, roller-coaster struggle to take over Piper Aircraft (I won a record judgment of $36 million on appeal, but lost it in the Supreme Court), and over the years of our professional association, Herb recommended me to any number of prospective clients. We also became good friends—to such an extent that I made the monumental mistake of introducing him to another good friend, Steve Ross. Herb first found me in the most coincidental of ways: he was sitting in the courtroom during the Wolfson-Kosow trial, a simple spectator to my performance.

Before I come to my next, one might say "big trouble" client, the unique and unforgettable Charles Bluhdorn, I need to digress for a moment to describe my relations with an agency that figured, now as an ally, now as an adversary, in so many of my most important cases. I'm referring to the Securities and Exchange Commission. It may be hard to imagine today, when the SEC is enormously powerful and has become, among other things, a career stepping-stone for many ambitious young lawyers, but before my days at the U.S. Attorney's Office, it had been a sleepy, even impotent agency. Funded largely by the registration fees it collected, the SEC had no building of its own in Washington but rented rather grungy offices in a downtown commercial building. It had an almost green-eyeshade accountant's mentality, and the staff spent most of its time verifying the filings of companies, as provided by law, and reviewing the books and records of brokerage firms.

With the coming of the Kennedy administration, though, and the appointment of William Casey as chairman, things began to change. For one thing, Casey put Irving Pollak in charge of enforcement. Pollak, a veteran at the agency, wanted compliance with SEC regulations, and despite the limited resources at his disposal, he set out aggressively to get it. In this, he was helped immeasurably by the redoubtable Stanley Sporkin, another Yale Law graduate who became, first Pollak's associate director, and later his replacement as director of the division. Sporkin, who came to be resented by Wall Street and was considered antibusiness, nonetheless became *the* major figure in law enforcement in the securities field—until, that is, the same William Casey, appointed director of the CIA under Reagan, recruited him to be counsel to the CIA.

Thanks in part to my Morgenthau experience, I knew virtually everyone in enforcement at the SEC. Although we were often adversaries, I think even Sporkin regarded me as more than just another advocate, and over the years there have been times when, in a quiet, behind-the-scenes way, I have been able to counsel the agency as to what it should be doing and what its priorities ought to be.

I recognize, in passing, that such counsel is a subject of ongoing debate within the legal profession and that some lawyers would accuse me of trading with the enemy, in addition to taking fees out of their pockets. But in fact, one of Paul, Weiss's founders, Randolph Paul, who was in his day the leader of the tax bar, regarded it as a key part of his responsibility as a lawyer to make recommendations on reforming the tax laws and so closing those very loopholes through which he had steered his clients. He was one of our role models, and the inspiration for another of the firm's traditions—contributing whenever and wherever we can to shaping and defining the law of the land and its enforcement.

As far back as I can remember, *Reader's Digest* has run a feature called "The Most Unforgettable Character I Ever Met." As a lawyer who has represented a great variety of clients, I could come up with any number of candidates, but none on a par with Charlie Bluhdorn.

Charles G. Bluhdorn was an Austrian refugee who came to the United States at sixteen in 1942, virtually penniless, and built an empire. Using stock or borrowed money, he bought and sold companies and, over time, assembled a great conglomerate called Gulf & Western. At its zenith, Gulf & Western had $5 billion in sales and, organized into eight operating divisions, included Paramount Pictures, Simon & Schuster Publishing, Madison Square Garden and its professional teams, the Knicks and the Rangers, Kayser Roth hosiery, a major sugar-producing and refining business, the largest zinc producer in the country, and a huge finance company.

Short, emotional, bold, impatient, and animated, Bluhdorn at his most flamboyant and outrageous was a virtual parody of the brash business genius. He spoke in loud, fiery bursts with a Viennese accent, and he usually kept two or three conversations going at once. He loved to talk and haggle, and probably he met his match only once, when he and Fidel Castro met for eight straight hours. He was overbearing and could rule by fear and fiat, but he was gracious to those whom he respected.

Bluhdorn was an aggressive and crafty entrepreneur, with a great talent for spotting and acquiring undervalued companies. In 1957, just past thirty, he bought control of an automobile parts manufacturing company called Michigan Bumper. In 1965 he borrowed $84 million and bought control of New Jersey Zinc Company. Then came dozens of other acquisitions, including Desilu Productions, South Puerto Rican Sugar, and Consolidated Cigar. Bluhdorn's rationale for diversifying so widely and wildly was simple: he wanted, he explained, to be in many different lines of business so that, when hard times fell on one or more of them, the others would serve as a counterbalance and pull the entire enterprise through.

He had another quality that distinguished him from the typical, hard-driving executive, and that was his unabashed and outspoken patriotism. America, for him, represented all the decent values known to man, and he saw it as one of his duties to disseminate his own brand of Americanism, however dogmatic and identified totally with his own ends. What, for example, could have been more patriotic than for Gulf & Western to sell short and thus end up controlling the entire Dominican Republic sugar supply (as the SEC once charged) as long as Gulf & Western then propped up the Dominican economy by selling at high prices?

Bluhdorn's acquisitions masterpiece was Paramount Pictures. The company had been in trouble, losing money on its feature films, wary of plunging too deeply into television production, and propping up its earnings by selling off assets. It appeared to be going broke. Bluhdorn, who had no experience in motion picture production or the entertainment industry, took over personally as president and hired Robert Evans, a good-looking actor with a sparse production background, to run the film studio. Evans promptly turned to Mario Puzo and Francis Ford Coppola and made what was, at the time, the most successful film in Hollywood history, *The Godfather.* In less than three years, Paramount became the hottest studio in Hollywood. Bluhdorn himself became an outspoken member of the motion picture industry and the author of some unfortunately memorable speeches. He could never, for example, accept the principle that refusing to license a blockbuster film unless a theater also took his losers was a violation of the antitrust laws, insisting instead that he needed his locomotive to pull his caboose. This was the kind of pronouncement that inevitably caused industry executives to duck their faces in their plates, hoping they'd misheard him, knowing they hadn't.

Even today there are those who say Bluhdorn agreed to *The Godfather* only because he saw in Vito Corleone someone who runs his organization the way Bluhdorn liked to run his. In fact, few executives ever lasted long at Paramount and Gulf & Western. The total opposite of a Steve Ross, who recognized that inside most moviemakers is an insecure little boy or girl who needs to be stroked and pampered even after a failure, Bluhdorn ruled by fear. Soon Robert Evans was gone; he was replaced by Barry Diller, who never hesitated to stand up to Bluhdorn and even shout him down. Richard Snyder, who ran Simon & Schuster, Gulf & Western's publishing company, was also from the tough-boy school. You had to be tough to survive in Bluhdorn's enterprise.

Above all, Bluhdorn loved to trade. In his twenties, he'd made his first million with a series of breathtaking gambles in the commodities market, dealing in cotton and coffee, and years later, when we met in his palatial offices in the Gulf & Western tower at Columbus Circle, he was still at it, constantly interrupting the discussions to trade sugar futures, yelling buy and sell orders into the phone.

When he first asked to see me, Bluhdorn was still furious because the Justice Department's Antitrust Division had blocked one of his most cherished dreams—buying the A&P supermarket chain. A&P, once the preeminent grocery chain in America, had become a troubled company, but to Bluhdorn it was somehow emblematic of free enterprise. He constantly recalled an A&P coffee buyer who, when Bluhdorn first came to America, had chastised him for referring to the company as A&P. "It is the Great Atlantic and Pacific Tea Company, Mr. Bluhdorn. Always remember that." And Bluhdorn had. He badly wanted to acquire A&P, and he'd launched a hostile tender offer for its shares. Gulf & Western, however, already owned a small paper company that sold bags to supermarkets. According to the government, if Gulf & Western controlled A&P, Brown Paper would have an unfair advantage over its competitors in the paper bag field, and it brought a lawsuit that effectively stopped the acquisition. Today the notion that ownership of such a company could create an antitrust violation in the acquisition of a supermarket chain would be laughable, but in 1972 antitrust law was at the crest of the flood.

When A&P's financial difficulties worsened and it was subsequently acquired by a German company, Bluhdorn's anger at the Antitrust Division turned to outrage. And when, following the Mideast war of 1973, the OPEC cartel dictated a huge increase in the price of oil, his outrage gave way to a cry for action. In June 1974, Bluhdorn approached me with an audacious, even madcap notion: we—that is, the United States—should bring an antitrust action against OPEC for illegally conspiring to fix oil prices.

Only Bluhdorn could have proposed such an idea, and only Bluhdorn could have championed it.

"Arthur?" he would thunder at me. "Tell me why the oil-producing states can get together and set the prices we pay for gasoline and crude, when Gulf & Western, with less than 5 percent of the packaging market for supermarkets, couldn't buy A&P?"

For Bluhdorn, the position of the Antitrust Division wasn't merely irrational. It was downright unpatriotic!

Why, he insisted, wasn't OPEC subject to the same antitrust laws as Gulf & Western? And if it was, why didn't the Justice Department enforce the law when the cartel quadrupled its prices?

It's easy now to call the question eccentric, and it seemed so at the time, but it also had the truth of babes. At Bluhdorn's request, I consulted with a leading professor at Yale Law School, who agreed with him in theory. After researching further, I told Bluhdorn that, in my view, OPEC's actions had a direct and substantial impact on American commerce and, as a matter of theory, yes, it certainly could be sued for violating our antitrust laws. But as a practical matter? Wouldn't the OPEC nations simply thumb their noses at any U.S. lawsuit?

Never one to take no for an answer, Bluhdorn asked me to meet with Attorney General Edward Levi and ask him to sue. In July 1975, Levi met with me and Whitney North Seymour of Simpson Thacher & Bartlett, Gulf & Western's regular law firm. Whitney, I should point out, wasn't just a member of the establishment, he *was* the establishment. Without him, I doubt I'd have even gotten through Levi's door, but he agreed that Bluhdorn's views were entitled to a hearing, and his endorsement lent them instant credibility. After hearing us out politely and engaging in scholarly debate (Levi had been dean of the University of Chicago Law School, and he pressed us on jurisdictional and sovereign-immunity issues), the Attorney General said the problem with the lawsuit Bluhdorn proposed was precisely that a court might entertain the case. What if we won, he asked? How was the Attorney General of the United States supposed to enforce an antitrust decree against, say, the king of Saudi Arabia, or the shah of Iran, or the ruler of Iraq—three of our staunchest allies at the time?

In the meantime, though, the irrepressible Bluhdorn had found a way to take matters into his own hands. Paramount was distributing *The Godfather* overseas. Puzo's novel had also been a great international best-seller, and foreign audiences were desperate to see the movie.

Bluhdorn took aim at one of OPEC's most influential members: Iran. He announced that Paramount would refuse to license *The Godfather* to Iranian movie theaters unless the shah, whose government set the prices of movie tickets, agreed to raise the price of tickets by the same percentage that OPEC had increased the price of oil. Bluhdorn wanted the Iranians to experience some of the pain that Americans were feeling from the oil price increase. It was a classic Bluhdorn act—dramatic, patriotic, impetuous, emotional, and certain to provoke controversy.

———

A few years later, Bluhdorn turned to me again, but this time on a very different matter. Joel Dolkart, Gulf & Western's longtime lawyer who joined Simpson, Thacher at the time of the Paramount acquisition, had been caught stealing fees that Gulf & Western paid to his law firm. Simpson, Thacher had advised Bluhdorn that it was reporting the theft to the Manhattan District Attorney. Bluhdorn had joined in the call for criminal prosecution. As one of my partners on the corporate side pointed out, there was a potential danger in this. After all, as Gulf & Western's lawyer from its founding, Dolkart knew all the company's secrets and confidences, and, despite the lawyer-client privilege, he might well try to use them to plea-bargain with a prosecutor. If he would steal fees, why would he be reluctant to misappropriate confidences for his own benefit?

To Bluhdorn, though, this was of no importance. "Isn't this America? Am I supposed to stand by for the felonies of a thief? Since when is this a country where the victim gets punished and not the villain?"

Dolkart had betrayed his trust and deserved to be prosecuted. He—Bluhdorn—would take the consequences. Not only did he want to join in the complaint to the District Attorney, but he wanted to testify personally before the grand jury. And he practically banished from his presence my unfortunate corporate partner, who had made the point about Dolkart's likely strategy.

My partner, however, was the more prophetic. To Stanley Sporkin and the SEC, Bluhdorn was a much bigger and more visible target than some crooked lawyer no one had ever heard of. Dolkart retained Bernard Nussbaum to plea-bargain for him, and together they got him the deal of the decade.

In exchange for Dolkart's cooperation with the SEC in a civil enforcement proceeding, claiming in the process that Gulf & Western and its chief financial officer had engaged in accounting irregularities, the SEC would recommend leniency—no jail for the thief. The prosecutor, in other words, did what prosecutors traditionally do. But in this instance, not realizing how little Dolkart had to offer, he traded an airtight felony case against the lawyer, involving the theft of millions of dollars, for a relatively minor accounting case against the lawyer's client.

Because Simpson, Thacher was both victim and witness, Bluhdorn hired us to investigate the facts and represent Gulf & Western. I, in turn, got my litigation partner, Max Gitter, to work with me on the case. No one at Gulf & Western, we discovered, had been aware of Dolkart's scheme. He had stolen the fees by sets of double bills. Gulf & Western would be billed, for example, for $300,000 in legal services, but the copy of the bill filed at Simpson, Thacher would reflect legal services billed, say, at $250,000, with $50,000 to be held in escrow for disbursement to another company. Sometime later the company in question would invoice Simpson, Thacher for the $50,000. Dolkart himself would pick up the check and deposit it in a dummy account, for the company itself was but a shell, of Dolkart's own invention. It was a clever scheme, and Dolkart had been caught only because of some nifty investigative work by Don Oresman, a Simpson, Thacher partner who later became general counsel and a high-ranking executive at Gulf & Western.

The accounting story that Dolkart then traded for a no-jail sentence involved Gulf & Western's method of writing off its loss on a movie called *Darling Lili*, which had been devised by the chief financial officer and passed unchallenged by the company's outside auditors. Directed by Blake Edwards, *Darling Lili*, starring Edwards's new wife, Julie Andrews, had been an expensive musical comedy about an American air ace during World War I who falls for a German lady spy. A flop, it had cost Paramount more than $25 million. The loss, written down in the normal way, would have substantially reduced Gulf & Western's earnings for the year.

Instead, Gulf & Western had traded its rights to *Darling Lili* to a company called Commonwealth United in exchange for Commonwealth United bonds. Soon after, however, Commonwealth United went bankrupt and the bonds became worthless. Gulf & Western thus still had a $25 million loss that it would have to write off as a loss, this time on the bonds.

So, Dolkart alleged, Gulf & Western arranged another sideways transaction to hide the $25 million loss. The company had recently agreed to buy sugar lands in Florida from a Cuban family for $6 million in cash. The seller, of course, knew nothing about Commonwealth United bonds. All he wanted was cash for his lands. But Gulf & Western insisted that, in order to get his cash, he would have to take something else too—the Commonwealth bonds—and who was he to look a gift horse in the mouth? Gulf & Western then added the $25 million in Commonwealth United bonds to the purchase price of the sugar lands and never took the $25 million loss. In the meantime, moreover, the price of sugar land in the booming Florida economy rose so steeply that the loss simply disappeared. Gulf & Western's chief financial officer insisted that the accounting treatment, though aggressive, was legitimate, but the SEC proposed to charge Gulf & Western, the financial officer, and Bluhdorn with fraudulently disguising the $25 million loss.

Many corporate leaders would have settled the SEC charges immediately, but not Bluhdorn. He was livid, as he had every right to be, and he was unwilling to settle even for minor civil sanctions.

"What kind of country is this," he vituperated to anyone within earshot, including waiters in restaurants, "where the thief gets off by blaming his victim?"

Stanley Sporkin, on the other hand, was a born settler, and he just couldn't see why Bluhdorn should care about whether Dolkart received sufficient punishment. For Sporkin, the sole issue was the accounting one, that is, the charges against Gulf & Western and Bluhdorn. Since both were accused and I couldn't represent both, I took Gulf & Western as my client, and Edward Bennett Williams agreed to represent Bluhdorn.

Williams was a brilliant trial lawyer, and over the years we became close friends. Although he was based in Washington, where his firm, Williams and Connolly, was one of the leaders of the bar, we would find ourselves collaborating in any number of cases. As brilliant as he was in court, though, he may have been even more skillful at lowering the temperature of a case. Most prosecutors are young and fervent, and criminal defense lawyers frequently provoke them into combativeness. Williams wanted to avoid any referral of the Gulf & Western case to the Justice Department for prosecution, and thus he worked to keep the atmosphere calm, almost somnolent, until both sides were sufficiently exhausted to settle.

I, on the other hand, believed that any settlement the SEC could accept would, of necessity, be humiliating to Bluhdorn, at least as long as the aroma of the Dolkart bargain was in the air. I kept sending the SEC letters reminding the agency that it had forfeited any right to injunctive relief when it questioned Gulf & Western's former attorney about the company's confidences in return for excusing him from punishment. After all, as a prosecutor, I had once fought for the proposition that crooked lawyers should be punished for their misdeeds. Where was this principle now when just the opposite had happened?

As a result, the SEC investigation into the accounting charges dragged on for four years, and then into a fifth, with nothing changing. We held desultory settlement negotiations with Sporkin and his colleagues, but Bluhdorn was still adamantly against any outcome short of an apology from the SEC, while Sporkin kept insisting on the conventional SEC injunction order. Our settlement meetings in Washington were memorable particularly for their discussion of baseball and the Baltimore Orioles, which Ed Williams owned. Sporkin and his colleagues were avid fans. After lengthy analyses—with the owner himself—of what the Orioles had to do to win the pennant, the talk would eventually turn to the Gulf & Western matter. But just about then, Ed Williams would notice that it was getting late in the afternoon. "Look, fellows," he would say, "Artie came all the way from New York, and he has to get home for dinner with his family. Why don't we break for now and get together again in a couple of weeks?"

And so it went. In winter the topic might turn to football, because Williams had once had an interest in the Washington Redskins.

As patient as Williams could be, though, Bluhdorn's manic garrulousness tested him. While Ed himself epitomized the adage that brevity is the soul of wit, Bluhdorn could talk for hours on the phone. Often when Williams and I called in to report on our latest negotiations with the SEC, Bluhdorn would take over the conversation, and as he went on and on, nonstop, Williams would simply lie down on his back, on the floor, to relax while he listened.

The case reached a turning point not just because of the passage of time but because of the depositions of Dolkart and Sporkin, which Gitter and I took. The issue of depositions brought into play the differences between my perspective, as primarily a civil lawyer, and Williams's as mainly a criminal defense lawyer. Williams didn't want any depositions whatsoever. They would just preserve testimony, in the event that anything happened to Dolkart later, and why did we want that? But Bluhdorn wanted Dolkart and Sporkin cross-examined, and Williams finally agreed to a short deposition, as long as he didn't have to take it himself.

Dolkart's deposition was indeed relatively short—perhaps two or three hours—but it turned out to be disastrous for the SEC. Gitter had the impression, as he confided to me later, that I was able to delve into Dolkart's mind and his guilt feelings and, in some quasi-telepathic way, communicate with him. I intuited very quickly that he despised his SEC handlers. He had spent dozens of briefing sessions with whole successions of them, at their beck and call, flying down to Washington whenever they needed him, going over the Gulf & Western material again and again. As SEC lawyers came and went, they seemed to him to understand the case less and less. Meanwhile, this once-prominent member of the corporate bar had lost his colleagues and many of his friends. It became very clear that he regretted everything he'd done, particularly what he'd done to Gulf & Western and Bluhdorn, and that if we ever ended up in court he would make a terrible witness for the government.

Gitter then took Stanley Sporkin's deposition. The case had, by this time, become an albatross for him. Gitter concentrated hard on the moral implications of the Dolkart plea bargain, how Dolkart had been allowed to avoid punishment in return for testifying against his own client, while Sporkin spent as much time as he could defending the proposition that the government sometimes has to make deals with unsavory defendants. But Sporkin also saw himself as a man of principles, and what had happened clearly embarrassed him.

When we were done with the depositions, it was evident to Gitter and me that the time was ripe to settle. Together with Williams and Oresman, now general counsel of Gulf & Western, we worked out a deal that involved virtually no penalty for the company, its chief financial officer, or Bluhdorn. Slow as the process had been, we had come a long way. Our best guess was that Bluhdorn would accept the settlement, however reluctantly, and recommend it to Gulf & Western's board of directors.

But even a best guess was worthless when it came to Charlie Bluhdorn. I was present at the board meeting at which he rose to describe the settlement. To my surprise and consternation, he grew angrier by the minute. The more he told the directors how tyrannical the SEC was, and un-American, the redder his face got. Settling with the SEC meant total capitulation. It would be another Munich—and so on until, by the time he was finished, he was telling the directors that whereas he himself was ready to sacrifice principle, he'd do it only to save the company. Therefore, only if the board itself didn't have the guts to fight and insisted on settling with the SEC—but only in those circumstances— would he sign the agreement.

Why he did it, I cannot begin to say, but his impassioned, patriotic, and self-serving rhetoric so inflamed and inspired the board, or so cowed it, that every director offered to join him as a defendant. Ed Williams and I, who had spent considerable time and effort, much earlier in the case, persuading the SEC *not* to sue the entire Gulf & Western board, sat there amazed. Williams turned to me and whispered, "Artie, we came in here with a settlement that let everyone off the hook, and we are leaving with the whole damn board as defendants!"

That was Charlie Bluhdorn. But it was also Charlie Bluhdorn, once he'd made us all, including his board of directors, jump through the hoops of his high principle, to lose interest in the entire affair. Sporkin and the SEC were as worn down as we were by the time Bluhdorn finally allowed us to settle—quietly, and for less than a slap on the wrist.

But there was one last twist in this quixotic story. Once the documents were signed and the settlement was complete, Bluhdorn announced that he would host a special ceremony at Casa de Campo, the lavish resort he'd built in the Dominican Republic, to honor . . . his lawyers!

As much as he loved America, Bluhdorn had adopted the Dominican Republic as his homeland after he bought a huge tract of sugar lands there, part of which he turned into Casa de Campo. At first, he had imagined re-creating a rustic colonial Dominican village, but when he learned that all the original Dominican villages, built of wood, had long since burned down, he settled for a Tuscan hilltown, built of stone. Instead of terraced vineyards, Casa de Campo was surrounded by three verdant golf courses. There was even a stone replica of the Roman Coliseum for outdoor concerts, and friends of Bluhdorn had built vacation homes there, among them Oscar de la Renta, Dino de Laurentis, and CBS's president, Tom Wyman.

The ceremony in which Bluhdorn awarded us his special medal, though deadly serious on his part, was straight out of Hapsburg imperial farce. Martin Davis, Gulf & Western's executive vice president and Bluhdorn's eventual successor, Don Oresman, Max Gitter, and I were the guests of honor at a long lunch in a tropical garden. After lunch, Bluhdorn rose and made a lengthy speech in the hot Caribbean sun. His topic was the spirit of Americanism, and he went on at length about the American dream and how a few great Americans had shaped the country. Enthusiasm radiated from his face as he extolled the United States.

Finally, he announced that he wanted to call upon those great Americans who'd fought the SEC as a matter of principle. Each of us rose, and we bowed our heads. Bluhdorn, solemn as an emperor, hung heavy medals suspended from blue silk ribbons around our necks and hugged and congratulated us. I kept worrying that there was something in the Constitution about not accepting honors from foreign princes and potentates, but then I remembered that Bluhdorn, after all, was a naturalized American citizen.

It is easy, of course, to make light of him from this distance. Undeniably, there was an opera buffa side to the man—one he, of course, learned to use to his own advantage. He had his flaws and his outlandish excesses, and virtually everyone who worked for him—or with him, or against him—came away with Charlie Bluhdorn stories.

America's robust economy, however, was built by freewheeling, risk-taking entrepreneurs like him. While he and his contemporaries are often mocked and vilified today, their nineteenth-century counterparts—the Vanderbilts, Rockefellers, and Morgans—are lionized, and how many remember that they themselves were once labeled "robber barons"? When Bluhdorn died, at only fifty-six, in 1983, something was lost in the conglomerate he had created. Parts of it were sold off in subsequent years, and its name was changed from Gulf & Western to Paramount. Still more recently, what remained of the company was merged into Viacom, itself the creation of another entrepreneur of our time, Sumner Redstone. But as for me, whenever I pass the building at the edge of Central Park that used to be Gulf & Western's headquarters, I can't help but hear the voice bellowing down at me. It is Charles Bluhdorn, master of all he surveyed.

8

Continental Grain Chases the Silver Sheiks

C ONTINENTAL GRAIN COMPANY has been a client of mine since the days of Tino De Angelis. Having served as trial lawyer and counselor as well as a member of the board of directors, I've come to feel not only part of the company but part of the family. I've handled Continental's litigations when it was in trouble—notably in the silver sheiks case I'm about to relate—but more important, I've tried to keep the company out of trouble, which is a complicated task for a truly multinational operation that has to comply with conflicting mores and regulations in more than fifty countries.

A privately owned family business, Continental Grain has always been virtually anonymous, yet it is one of two privately owned businesses that together dominate the $50 billion-a-year world grain trade. Operating in nearly every country in the world, Continental has to be as sensitive to geopolitical and economic considerations as any government. Everyone who works there, whether as an employee or as outside counsel, feels the importance of the company's business to the welfare of people around the globe.

Continental was founded more than 150 years ago as a grain-trading firm by two brothers named Fribourg in French Lorraine. As World War II began in Europe, the family escaped through France, over the Pyrenees to Portugal, and then on a freighter to the United States. The company moved its headquarters to the United States, the new home of the Fribourgs, who became American citizens. In 1944, when his father, Jules Fribourg, died, thirty-year-old Michel Fribourg, who had joined the U.S. Army, became the head of Continental.

Everyone in the organization now calls Michel Fribourg "MF," and if he is aristocratic, it is without a trace of arrogance or hauteur. He has a seemingly innate understanding and tolerance of the cultures and political systems of different countries. A firm believer in free trade, he is as at ease in dealing with the head of a Communist country as the leader of a Western democracy. He can at times seem painfully shy, but friends and associates are witnesses to his warmth and wit. He is above all a gentle person who never displays anger or impatience.

Whereas executives of public companies are driven to make each quarter's earnings exceed those of previous quarters and concentrate on short-term opportunities, MF, since he runs a privately held family business, has always been able to think about long-term possibilities for growth. When American companies were permitted to sell grain to the Soviet Union, Continental was the first to do so. It also was one of the first American companies to do business in China, and certainly, if life is ever found on a distant planet, MF would want to sell food there. The excitement of opening new markets has been as important to him as the economics of it. Under his direction, Continental has grown from a trader of grain to one of the largest exporters of commodities in the world, moving surpluses from countries like the United States, Canada, and Argentina to developing countries in Africa and Asia that have starving populations. Continental has invested in milling, feed, and poultry operations in China and other developing countries. In addition, in MF's regime, it has been a company deeply conscious of a responsibility to work for the public interest. In a letter to his employees, MF once wrote:

We at Continental have a vocation beyond that of making money. We are bringing to many of the developing countries badly needed technical expertise that we have acquired over the years. After World War II, the colonial powers were forced to abandon their comfortable old concepts and make concessions, usually under duress. This begrudging attitude is no longer appropriate. If the capitalist world is to survive, it must adopt an enlightened approach to solving the problems of poverty and malnutrition that still plague most of mankind and remain its most pressing problems.

It is a fact of life for lawyers that we usually become closest to our clients during moments of crisis, and Continental has had its share of these. No sooner had the company settled with American Express in the salad oil debacle than it had to decide whether to recognize the debt of a former subsidiary in which it now had only a minority interest.

Several years before, the banker MF had hired to run his Paris office persuaded him to establish a finance company in Geneva to take advantage of Europe's booming postwar economy. Thus was formed La Société Continental de Gestion Finantiçère, S.A.—or Fribgest, as it became known, short for Fribourg Gestion. Fribgest financed everything from apartment houses to a ski resort in Spain, but it was often in the position of borrowing short-term money to make long-term loans—a recipe for disaster in the event that interest rates rose. MF grew increasingly uncomfortable with the strategy and eventually instructed its head to find a buyer for Fribgest.

In 1967 Continental sold two-thirds of its stake to European banks, but the new owners kept the Fribgest name. One of these banks, Banque de l'Indochine, took over the management of the business, and Continental Grain essentially became a passive investor.

In late 1970, Fribourg learned that Fribgest's loans were not being repaid. Then Banque de l'Indochine asked Continental to put more money into its operation. MF was incensed. He had turned over a healthy company to Banque de l'Indochine just three years earlier, and why, now, should he have to invest more money in it? Banque de l'Indochine countered that Fribgest's problems were the fault of loans that were made before it had taken control and were therefore Continental's responsibility.

Meanwhile, Fribgest became insolvent. Although Continental was now only a minority shareholder, the company still bore the family name, and any scandal involving Fribgest was bound to reflect on Continental.

Judge Rifkind and I spent weeks in Paris advising MF on how to handle the situation. Continental, by this time, was in a game of poker. Banque de l'Indochine wanted Continental to pay Fribgest's creditors, while Fribourg believed that, because the bank ran Fribgest, it should pay. Continental had gifted European lawyers, but by tradition they confined themselves solely to legal questions, finding the answers by consulting a thick commercial code dating back to Napoleon. In this situation, Continental's problems crossed the boundaries of law, business, and public relations. MF and I spent days in Paris reviewing files, preparing papers on why Continental was not legally or morally liable for Fribgest's debt, and planning his next moves. At the same time, Judge Rifkind and I and Continental's banker, André Meyer of Lazard Frères, were all of the same mind. No matter how good a case Continental could make for not being liable for Fribgest's debts, it had to contribute to a settlement, in the interest of its reputation. But the bank had to pay its share too, and with outraged principle on his side, MF held his own in the negotiations. Finally he reached a settlement with the bank and Fribgest's creditors. It cost Continental $10 million over a ten-year period, but the bank paid out almost $30 million. The terms made it clear that it was the Banque de l'Indochine, not Continental Grain, that bore the principal responsibility for Fribgest's failure.

Let me turn now to the story of the silver sheiks.

While I have prosecuted stock manipulators, defended accused stock manipulators, and sued stock manipulators, I had never had a case in which the manipulator sued the victim until Mahmoud Fustok sued my client, ContiCommodity Services, Inc., in 1982. Fittingly, the suit arose out of one of the most flamboyant manipulations of all—the effort by a family of Texas oil multimillionaires, plus Fustok and a flock of rich Saudis, to corner the world's silver market.

Nelson Bunker Hunt and his younger brothers, William Herbert and Lamar, were heirs to an oil, sugar, and real estate fortune. In the 1970s, the Hunts turned their attention to silver. They knew that demand for silver—silver has many strategic and industrial uses—far exceeded the amount mined each year. So, in 1979, they set out deliberately to corner the market.

That July they began buying huge quantities of silver bullion, plus contracts to buy even more silver in the future. As rich as they were, though, they needed allies if they were going to succeed. The Hunts, especially Bunker, liked to race thoroughbred horses, and soon they were joined in their silver spree by rich young speculators they knew through horse racing circles—Naji Robert Nahas and Mahmoud Fustok.

Naji Robert Nahas, in 1979, was thirty-five years old, a Lebanese born in Egypt who had lived in Brazil since 1970, where he ran two dozen businesses, including a big insurance group, the world's largest rabbit farm, and property developments. Above all, Nahas loved speculating in stock options and commodities, which he had started doing as a boy in Egypt trading in Cairo's cotton futures market. He was reputed to have made millions speculating in coffee futures. Nahas also liked to gamble on horses, which is how he met Mahmoud Fustok. Born in Palestine and raised in Lebanon, Fustok was now a citizen of Saudi Arabia. One of his sisters was married to the crown prince of Saudi Arabia, Prince Abdullah. Fustok used his royal connections to create a fortune that enabled him, among other things, to build a worldwide horse-racing operation. He had a splendid racing stable in France, and a 500-acre horse-breeding farm in Kentucky.

Hoping to control the world's silver supply, Fustok, Nahas, the Hunts, and their associates set out to buy billions of dollars' worth of silver—in bullion and futures. Their buying had a predictable effect. The price of an ounce of silver skyrocketed from $6 in early 1979 to almost $50 in January 1980.

———

Continental Grain had formed ContiCommodity Services, Inc., a wholly owned subsidiary, in 1970. For years the parent company had bought and sold grain futures as a hedge against fluctuating grain prices. Futures contracts, which are traded on the nation's commodity exchanges, are agreements to deliver or accept a quantity of a raw material, such as corn or pork bellies or silver bullion, at a specified future date at a set price. In the 1970s, speculators began to flock to commodities and especially to novel forms of financial futures that moved with interest rates. Continental Grain decided to try to market its commodities trading expertise to these new investors, and so formed ContiCommodity. The new operation was based in Chicago, far from Continental's main office in New York. The distance was deliberate. From the outset, the two firms operated independently. Since Continental was a major trader on its own in the same commodities that ContiCommodity's customers were trading, neither could know what the other was doing.

For a time, ContiCommodity's customers were conservative midwestern farmers. Like Continental Grain, they were hedgers, not speculators, using futures contracts to protect themselves if prices dropped before their wheat or corn or soybeans were ready for market. To compete in the rapidly growing commodities business, however, ContiCommodity knew that it had to lure risk-taking speculators who hoped to make money by guessing which way commodities prices would move.

Speculating in commodities futures is risky. Commodity prices are subject to violent changes due to a multitude of unpredictable causes such as drought or frost or political tensions. But it is possible to make huge profits almost overnight with little or no cash by trading commodity futures because the cash margin—or down payment—required to buy a futures contract is so low, especially compared to stock purchases on securities exchanges.

ContiCommodity's business grew swiftly, and it soon had more than thirty offices around the world. Since commodities brokers are paid a set fee on every trade, their major interest is in promoting the volume of trading. ContiCommodity boasted that it valued customer profits more than its brokerage commissions. Through its in-house "Yacht Club," management gave a weeklong, expenses-paid trip to its top producers—not on the basis of how much they made over the year in commissions but how much they made for their customers. The "Yacht Club" name alluded to the old Wall Street joke about J. P. Morgan. When shown some stockbrokers' yachts, Morgan supposedly asked, "But where are the customers' yachts?"

In January 1979, Naji Robert Nahas was thinking about growing oranges, not silver. Nahas called a ContiCommodity broker he knew named Norton Waltuch, who had made a lot of money for his customers a few years earlier in orange juice futures. Waltuch didn't like orange juice futures just then, but he knew silver was about to jump. Nahas set up an account and began buying silver. Later that year, Nahas introduced Waltuch to a Swiss investment advisory company, with a roster of rich Saudi clients, called Advicorp Advisory and Financial Corporation. One of Advicorp's clients was Mahmoud Fustok.

In August 1979, Fustok instructed Advicorp to buy silver for him, and by the fall he already owned more than $300 million of silver bullion and futures contracts. In November, Advicorp opened an account for Fustok with ContiCommodity. Through his ContiCommodity account, Fustok acquired an additional $70 million in bullion and futures. As the price of silver climbed, Fustok and Nahas made spectacular profits. In the twenty-four hours between December 27 and 28, 1979, for example, the value of Nahas's silver holdings jumped by $30 million. Silver was then $30 an ounce. Less than a month later, on January 21, it had gone up to $47.80 an ounce.

If the Hunts and Nahas and Fustok had begun to sell out in January, they could have counted their profits in billions. At their height, they owned more than $3 billion in bullion and futures. But they were dreaming of *tens* of billions. When extensive futures purchases came due in a few weeks, the Hunts figured that anyone who had contracted to sell silver at a much lower price than the price at the due date would be hard-pressed to find enough silver to meet their commitments, and so they would find themselves at the mercy of the Hunts. That is the essence of a corner.

In the commodities markets, for every winner there is a loser, because every futures contract is a bet. If the price rises, those who bought long (like the Hunts, Nahas, and Fustok) win, but those who have sold short must pay up. If all had gone according to plan, by March 1980 the Hunt combine would have owned $14 billion worth of silver, representing spectacular losses by other silver traders. But all did not go according to plan. As silver prices rose, the losing silver traders panicked and pressured regulators to take action, and in late January, with silver at almost $50 an ounce and rising, the Commodities Exchange in New York, where the Hunts and their allies did most of their silver trading, moved to restrict silver speculation. On that news, silver prices promptly began to fall.

The first line of defense against a market manipulation comes not from regulators but from the commodities firms themselves. They keep books and records of their clients' positions, and they are supposed to collect margins promptly, thus limiting the exposure that any firm has if the market behaves erratically. But there is a flaw in this form of self-regulation. Many of the salespeople are not just paid commissions on customer trades but trade commodities themselves. They often, as a result, identify their interest more with the customer's than with their employer's. They have little interest in closing out an undermargined customer, not just because they've been receiving commissions on his trades but because they've been profiting from the very same price moves as the customer. Walter Goldschmidt, the soft-spoken, silver-haired president of ContiCommodity, had begun as a runner for Continental on the Chicago Board of Trade in 1939. While not himself a trader, he had founded ContiCommodity, had utmost trust in his salespeople, and was almost congenitally unable to force them to close out a customer. They were his "boys." Moreover, he believed that their customers would meet their commitments, a faith that has ruined many a commodities firm. Goldschmidt, in other words, was a thoroughly decent man in an industry, and at a moment, that demanded the toughness and ruthlessness of a Charlie Bluhdorn. When the Commodities Exchange moved to restrict trading, he became almost as firm an advocate of his customers as their own lawyers.

On just one day, January 22, the price of silver plunged by $10, to $34 an ounce. It dropped all through February and early March. When it came to imposing position limits on its customers, ContiCommodity equivocated. The principal salesman kept telling Goldschmidt everything would be okay, and Goldschmidt didn't have the skepticism to doubt or overrule him. Moreover, the ContiCommodity salespeople maintained that the interests of their customers had to take precedence over those of the house.

The Hunts, meanwhile, unable to find buyers for their prodigious holdings, unable even to borrow money against their bullion, faced huge margin calls. By March 26, silver had fallen to $15.80 an ounce. That evening the Hunts told their brokers they didn't have the cash to meet their margin calls.

The Hunts' brokerage firm, Bache & Company, was less indulgent. The next day, Thursday, March 27, became Silver Thursday. On that day, the Hunts' brokers sold all of the Hunts' silver positions. Because of the sudden flood of silver, the price of silver on Silver Thursday dropped to $10.80 an ounce. Fustok's and Nahas's spectacular profits at ContiCommodity were wiped out. Fustok's ContiCommodity account had in it some silver bullion that ContiCommodity could sell, but at the extremely low prices it wouldn't yield enough cash to pay for all of Fustok's losing futures contracts. The day before Silver Thursday, Conti-Commodity had made margin calls of tens of millions of dollars on Fustok's and Nahas's accounts, some of which were in the name of dummy corporations, but neither paid. If they failed to make up the losses in their accounts, ContiCommodity would be rendered insolvent—just as Haupt had been, years before, in the salad oil scandal.

The day after Silver Thursday, when I arrived at Continental Grain's offices in New York, all was chaos and desperation. Walter Goldschmidt was totally distraught. He clung to the hope that Nahas and Fustok might pay. Nahas, he said, had hinted to him that day in a phone call that the Hunts had promised to bail him out. I thought Goldschmidt was being unreasonably, perhaps even desperately, optimistic. The Hunts, my own sources on Wall Street had told me, had lost a billion dollars. They were broke, and they'd nearly ruined Bache & Company in the process.

Though he faced the loss of millions, MF was a realist. He had dealt before with men like Naji Robert Nahas and Mahmoud Fustok—vain, spoiled men with vast fortunes who proved to be charlatans. Nahas and Fustok had always made Fribourg uneasy. Though bold and unafraid of risk, he himself was scarcely a reckless gambler. On the other hand, Fustok and Nahas were customers of ContiCommodity, which had to keep its distance from the parent company, so Fribourg had never interfered with their accounts. But now, with the crisis upon us, there was no longer room for distance or procrastination. MF ordered Goldschmidt to go to Paris to talk directly to Nahas and Fustok, and he asked me to go with him.

———

It may have been April in Paris, but there was little romance to our task. We found Nahas scrambling to borrow money to try to boost the price of silver. He and the Hunts also were trying to market bonds backed by their silver bullion. Nahas tried to charm us, and he pleaded for time. He would pay ContiCommodity everything he owed, he said, he just needed more time. Meanwhile, Fustok was ducking our phone calls.

After several days, Goldschmidt and I were fed up with waiting. We met with Nahas and told him that if he didn't pay ContiCommodity immediately, we would go back to New York, sell off his and Fustok's silver, and sue for the rest of what they owed. The meeting grew heated. Nahas looked desperate, wild-eyed, like a man who was only a half-step ahead of his creditors and had run out of "the check is in the mail" excuses to stave them off. For the first time, he said point-blank that he couldn't pay. The best he could offer was two freighters he owned, which we could sell, plus Fustok's promise to pay the $20 million he would still owe ContiCommodity. It was an unacceptable offer: it left us with not just the debt from Nahas but those of Fustok and the dummy corporations as well. Our only alternative, however, was forcing Nahas into bankruptcy, with no assurance that we would get anything. We agreed to settle, but we made Nahas promise to help us get a written guaranty from Fustok that he would pay ContiCommodity what he and Nahas owed.

Our next stop was to see Fustok. Because he'd refused to take our phone calls, Goldschmidt, Continental's general counsel, myself, and Nahas took the train to Chantilly, about thirty minutes north of Paris, where Fustok maintained his stable. Chantilly has a beautiful chateau and a splendid racetrack, bordered with immense, baroque stables, where the French Derby is run each spring. Fustok's stable turned out to be a lavish compound. There were air-conditioned horse stables alongside a private racetrack, and a large modern mansion. The horses lived better than kings.

Greeting us affably, Fustok led us on a long tour, showing us his prize thoroughbreds. They were handsome, expensive-looking steeds, and I wondered how much we could collect if the horses were sold to satisfy a judgment. Unlike Nahas, Fustok didn't seem to have lost any sleep over what he owed, nor did he appear to expect to be pressed to pay. After the tour, he led us into his home, which was opulently decorated with rich fabrics, thick carpets, and erotic statuary. It looked like some debauched seraglio. We settled into plump cushions. Half-naked Arab boys came out of the servants' kitchen and served us delicacies and teas. Fustok was gracious and chatty and made it clear that he wanted to avoid unpleasant topics, such as his debt to ContiCommodity. Leaning back in his pleasure palace, sipping my tea, nibbling on a biscuit, listening to Fustok prattle on, I composed in my head a cable to Michel Fribourg, who was waiting back in New York: "Entertained lavishly in Fustok's chateau. Had a wonderful day. Improved my knowledge of horses. Payment not discussed. Your former lawyer, Arthur."

Finally, as the soft daylight outside began to fade, it fell to me to be the spoilsport. The Continental executives were enjoying Fustok's show of wealth. Rousing myself, I told Fustok that Goldschmidt and I were not going back to Paris until he told us when he would pay us. Fustok bristled. My tone, he said, was insulting. Of course he planned to pay Conti-Commodity whatever he owed. From there, though, the meeting went downhill. Fustok said he couldn't pay just then because his own records were in disarray and he didn't know exactly how much he owed. He blamed his losses on Advicorp, which he said had betrayed him, buying silver without his knowledge or permission. Seeing his own hard-won settlement falling apart, Nahas began to panic. He leaned over and spoke to Fustok in Arabic. Fustok, prompted by Nahas, then told us that it would be a simple matter for him to guarantee Nahas's debt to ContiCommodity, but he had an even better idea. Rather than sell the silver bullion in his account, Fustok said, ContiCommodity should let him keep it and also lend him cash to buy *more* silver. When the price of silver went up, as Fustok was sure it would, he would make huge profits, enough for him and Nahas to pay back ContiCommodity, and everyone would be happy.

I couldn't believe my ears. It was like someone who owed money to a bank asking the bank for a loan to buy a lottery ticket. But Fustok seemed serious.

"Why," I asked, "would ContiCommodity throw good money after bad? Lending you *more* money to speculate? What if the market goes down further, are you going to guarantee *that* loss? Let me assure you that if ContiCommodity wants to speculate in silver, it's capable of doing so on its own account."

But Fustok turned imperious.

"You're only a lawyer," he said, "not a businessman, like me. I, Mahmoud Fustok, *know* silver will go back up."

He said, further, that he would honor his debt, and Nahas's as well, but on *his* terms, not mine.

I told him that his proposal was unacceptable, and that I would never take it to Michel Fribourg. We had come to France to find out when we would be paid, not to risk losing even more money.

With that, we got up, bid farewell to Fustok, his scantily clad waiters, and his beautiful horses, and returned to the real world.

This was my introduction to the art of Middle Eastern negotiations, a subject I would learn more about years later during the Iran-Contra investigation. Alternately charming and threatening, Fustok's words seemed filled with nuance and special meaning, but I had trouble figuring out exactly what these were. On the train back to Paris, Nahas assured us that we had misunderstood his friend. He intended to pay, but we had to be patient. In the Middle East, Nahas said, friendship was the key to business. We had to be Fustok's friend. Years later, Reagan's national security adviser, Robert McFarlane, would be given the same advice: don't press the Iranians too hard on getting the hostages back. Let trust and friendship develop.

We telephoned MF as soon as we got back to Paris. Still optimistic, Goldschmidt told him that he thought Fustok might pay, as Nahas kept saying he would, but I told Fribourg I thought our chance of getting anything besides Fustok's silver bullion was slim. MF agreed, and Goldschmidt and I returned to New York.

ContiCommodity sold Fustok's silver bullion for about $2 million, less than the account owed. Fustok lost $68 million in his ContiCommodity account as well as related dummy accounts he controlled.

Mahmoud Fustok had studied petroleum engineering at the University of Oklahoma and spent his summers at horse tracks in New York and Chicago. Whatever else he may have learned in the United States, he'd learned how to sue. He sued everyone, everywhere. He sued Advicorp and his Swiss bankers, and he received a settlement after threatening the bank that Saudi Arabia would withdraw its deposits. He sued Nahas. In 1982, amazingly, he sued ContiCommodity, its officers, and Continental Grain in federal court in New York.

His trial lawyer was an old friend of mine, Peter Fleming, one of the best trial lawyers in the country. Fleming and I had gone to law school together, and we'd both worked for Bob Morgenthau as federal prosecutors. Fleming is tall and lanky, with silver hair and a disarming charm. Envious colleagues in Morgenthau's office used to think Fleming won more than a few of his cases only because women jurors got crushes on him. We had worked together on many cases, but never on opposite sides.

Fustok's claim was simple but bold: ContiCommodity owed him $68 million, the amount of futures his accounts at ContiCommodity had lost, plus interest, because he had not authorized any trading whatsoever in the account in his name. Advicorp, he claimed, had betrayed him. Advicorp had had his permission to manage only his Swiss bank account and to buy only silver bullion, not futures contracts.

At first it seemed to be an easy case for ContiCommodity. After all, Advicorp was Fustok's agent, and Advicorp had placed the orders for silver bullion and futures contracts in Fustok's account. Plus, ContiCommodity had mailed a confirmation to Fustok's office in London each time it purchased silver, and monthly statements recapitulating the activity in the account. Fustok had never objected to any of those trades.

On these bases, we asked the judge to dismiss the case.

Fustok, however, had a document, never sent to ContiCommodity, showing that he had authorized Advicorp to buy only $30–40 million worth of silver, and only silver bullion, not silver futures. ContiCommodity had an early record that showed that only Fustok himself, not Advicorp, was authorized to trade the account in his name at Conti-Commodity. So the paperwork never caught up with the practice. At the same time, ContiCommodity could document having sent Fustok countless confirmations of futures contracts acquired, without any protest from Fustok and with acknowledgment by his office.

I have rarely seen a case of this kind where there weren't imperfections in the brokerage's paperwork, particularly when thousands of confirmations and payments have been sent. Some judges, even while realizing that clerical error is inevitable, hold a brokerage firm to a high standard, thus leaving the issue of whether a customer was or was not ignorant of his trading to a jury. And that, in denying our motion to dismiss, was what the judge did here.

In a discovery where there are tens of thousands of documents, the process is almost always a two-way street, with both disappointments and pleasant surprises. After the judge's ruling, Fustok turned over to us several extraordinary documents that put the lie to his claim that he was ignorant of Advicorp's silver purchases in his name at ContiCommodity. One document showed that when Fustok opened his ContiCommodity account, in November 1979, he already owned $325 million in silver, and much of it was in the form of futures contracts. The documents also showed that Fustok's relationship with Advicorp was much closer than we had suspected. He'd helped form Advicorp in the first place and was its first and biggest customer. Finally, we discovered that ContiCommodity was just one of Fustok's silver brokers. Fustok had bought silver through many other intermediaries. Altogether, he'd bought $1 billion worth of silver, and only $70 million of it was through ContiCommodity.

But Fustok, in discovery, also got his share of favorable documents, including ones that showed that in March 1980, as the silver market slumped, ContiCommodity salespeople, on Advicorp's instructions, had moved losing silver contracts from Fustok's securities accounts into dummy accounts, thus compounding an already deteriorating situation. These and other documents made it possible for Fustok to portray himself as an ingenue who'd dealt only in limited quantities of silver through a broker who was supposed to accumulate only a limited amount in his account. If our salespeople, in turn, had relied on instructions from Advicorp, only a few of those documents had been signed by Fustok himself. In the intelligence world, this is referred to as deniability.

In short, a case that had appeared simple at first became overwhelmed by documents. It abounded in unpredictable elements, and both Fleming and I had material to work with. But there were also the stakes to be kept in mind: because any judgment against Fustok was presumably uncollectible, all Fustok was risking was Fleming's fee; if Continental Grain lost the case, it stood to lose almost $100 million.

———————

The trial began in March 1986, six years after Silver Thursday. The large courtroom was jammed with lawyers and trial buffs. During jury selection, Fleming asked each prospective juror if he or she might be prejudiced against Fustok because he was a rich Saudi Arabian seeking millions from Americans, and each said no. When my turn came, I assured the jurors that ContiCommodity was not, for its part, seeking a verdict based on attitudes toward the Middle East. I then concentrated on drawing out any biases a prospective juror might have against brokers, or any misconceptions that brokers were responsible for the losses of customers. Did they understand that investing in stocks and commodities wasn't risk-free? And on a still simpler level, did they understand that just asking for money didn't entitle one party or the other to get it?

Though I reassured myself on this score, I did strike one prospective juror. He was the chef in one of my favorite neighborhood restaurants, and I knew they would never serve me again if I kept their chef tied up for more than a month!

In his opening statement, Fleming focused on ContiCommodity's inept failures to follow its own guidelines and the rules of the commodities exchanges. In mine, the longest I've ever delivered, I wanted the jury to focus on Fustok. I observed that Fleming was not only an extraordinary lawyer but a master magician: he'd made disappear all the evidence that was damning to Fustok's case. Fustok, I told the jury, was one of the largest speculators in the silver market in 1979 and 1980. He could have made an $800 million profit if he'd sold in January 1980, but he was simply too greedy.

I promised to show that, far from being a poor, unsophisticated little boy who was so preoccupied with racing his thoroughbreds that he could be taken advantage of, Fustok was a sophisticated, international businessman who loved profits and didn't like to take losses. He'd been accumulating the precious metal at such a rate, I said, that he'd been obliged to charter 747 cargo planes to transport it from New York to Geneva, where not even his Swiss bank's vaults were big enough to hold his silver. I likened him to the gold-loving criminal in Ian Fleming's *Goldfinger*—he was a man in love with silver, and he'd grabbed all that he could.

The case, I said, would boil down to one fundamental issue. Was Fustok responsible for his own acts, for his own decisions, for the documents and agreements that he'd signed, for the transactions that his hand-picked agents had entered into operating under his power of attorney, and for the investment risks he took? Or could he renege on those agreements—relying on boilerplate disclaimers that he was responsible only for limited amounts of physical silver while buying more—disown his agents as if they didn't exist when trades turned out poorly, walk away from his losses, and claim he'd never read any of the documents, confirmations, or agreements? And could he lie to avoid the consequences of his own trading strategy?

There were no surprises in the testimony. Fleming and I and our teams had taken the depositions of each other's witnesses and knew what to expect. Fleming first called ContiCommodity's managers and salespeople and made them admit every deviation from the rules. They made unconvincing and unsympathetic witnesses, as I'd known they would, and when I cross-examined them, I brought out only that they'd relied exclusively on Advicorp and that their reliance had cost Conti-Commodity a great deal of money.

But I kept weighing another factor. I was reasonably sure the jury would find Fustok disdainful of the truth. In one of the first questions of his deposition, I asked him how old he was, and he answered emphatically that he was thirty-eight. When I then showed him his own passport and asked whether it would surprise him to find out he was forty-four, he simply shrugged, dismissing the question as though a few years here or there were of no importance. The truth, in other words, was a relative matter for him, and I was convinced I could easily catch him in lies during cross-examination. But on the other hand, if I embarrassed him too much in open court, I was afraid he would refuse to settle. I came to the unavoidable conclusion that if we were going to settle, it would have to happen before Fustok took the stand.

Fleming and I had talked settlement before, but we were too far apart. For Fustok, as I've mentioned, the lawsuit was like a lottery ticket—he had nothing to lose—but losing could be a disaster for Continental Grain. Knowing this, Fustok had made exorbitant demands, and MF, convinced that his company had done nothing wrong, had refused them.

But nothing forces litigants to reassess settlement like the uncertainties of a jury trial. My ego and competitive instincts had been engaged the moment the trial started, and for days I'd been plotting exactly how I would attack Fustok's credibility on the stand. But I was Michel Fribourg's counselor, not just his advocate. I had to separate my ego from my assessment of the risk. Given a lean cycle in the grain industry, what effect would a negative verdict have, not only on the company's balance sheet but on its very credibility?

Some trial lawyers, I know, are disdainful of settlers. I myself know that there are so-called trial lawyers—I prefer to think of them as litigators—who are afraid to go to court and would rather settle at any price. In my case, settling has often gone against my own convictions as well as my sense of justice, but there are times when the stakes are simply too high. Even if Fustok's odds of winning were only one in ten, MF had to be willing to gamble, and that gamble could involve severe damage to what he and his family had worked to build over generations. The day came when I felt I had to reopen the question. We reviewed the pros and cons together, and I reminded MF that, of course, whether to settle or not was the client's decision.

"But what would you do in my place?" MF asked, fixing me with his intelligent gaze.

"I have mixed feelings," I answered, hating what I was about to say. "But if you're asking me whether we could lose, the answer is yes. I think we should see whether we can get a reasonable settlement."

Fustok was scheduled to begin testifying on Wednesday, March 19.

The night before, after a series of phone calls back and forth, Peter Fleming and I worked out a settlement. ContiCommodity agreed to pay Fustok $15 million.

The decision still rankles—in a sense, we had been blackmailed—and later events have made me even more ambivalent. Several years after we settled with Fustok, Nahas turned over to Continental Grain, during a lawsuit in Brazil, a document, signed by Fustok, guaranteeing Nahas's and his silver debts to ContiCommodity. It was the very same guarantee Nahas had promised us in Paris, and it would have constituted a complete defense for us, in and of itself. But Nahas and Fustok had hidden it from their lawyers, and Fustok had lied and denied ever having signing such a document. By then, it was too late to try to reopen the settlement. Moreover, federal regulators, in a separate investigation, had accused ContiCommodity's salespeople of improperly handling silver trades for customers when the silver market was collapsing. If the jury in the Fustok case had reached the same conclusion, Fustok might have won.

Meanwhile, Continental Grain has flourished. Varied and far-flung as its interests are, there have always been new problems, and many of them have required more than simple legal advice. Some years ago, one of its huge grain elevators in New Orleans exploded and employees were killed. Once again, the issue was moral as well as legal, and we quickly settled with the families of the victims. Another time, some Continental employees tinkered with scales to short-weigh grain bought from suppliers to make up for shrinkage in the handling of the grain. We settled with government regulators and then worked to build safeguards so that it wouldn't happen again. When Continental became one of the first exporters to sell grain to the Soviet Union under an agreement first reached during the Kennedy administration (it later made large sales during Nixon's), angry American farmers filed antitrust lawsuits against us, alleging that they'd sold Continental their grain at prices much lower than they would have demanded if they'd known the Soviet Union was buying.

I also handled legal planning for the Fribourg family. The company had been privately held since the time of Napoleon, and the Fribourgs wanted to keep it that way, a goal we helped them achieve. Similarly, there was the problem of succession. When MF reached an age when he wanted to pass on management responsibilities to the next generation, no one in the family was ready. We arranged for the first nonfamily manager, Donald Staheli, to become CEO. Having led the company through a prosperous interim period, Staheli is now passing the CEO position to Paul Fribourg, MF's son.

Over time, I became the eyes and ears of the company, learning of problems from employees and counseling management on how to solve them. There were decisions about whether to sell businesses or to close treasured but unprofitable operations, and questions raised by operating in countries with very different cultures. As I mentioned, I also served as a director, but most of my counseling has taken place between formal board meetings. I regard Continental in an almost paternal way. I feel responsible for guiding and nurturing it, for keeping it out of trouble, for preserving its reputation. To this day, I take great pride in the company's achievements, and if, for whatever reason, my practice had not allowed for this sort of relationship, I would have lost something of enduring value.

9

The Rise and Rise of Steve Ross and the Mega Merger of Time and Warner

STEVE ROSS AND his companies, first Warner Communications and then Time Warner, were clients of mine for nearly twenty-five years, yet I never tried a single case for him. My relationship with Ross was as a counselor and as a friend.

Many lawyers for the major entertainment companies have become powerful figures within those companies, and some of them do lead the glamorous lives the public likes to imagine all Hollywood executives enjoy. But this wasn't what I wanted, nor did Ross really, although he went through a phase of trying to hire me. On my trips to California, I never stayed in a bungalow at the Beverly Hills Hotel, and if my life depended on it, I couldn't have gotten a reservation in my own name in the "power" restaurants where the celebrities dine. What counted was that I kept my independence and that I was thereby able to give the disinterested, sometimes tough-minded advice that became the hallmark of our relationship. Over the years, as Ross, beginning with limited assets, wheeled and dealed to create, in Time Warner, the largest media company in the world, any number of lawyers obviously served him, many of them my own partners at Paul, Weiss. I played a different role. It was my task to keep Ross and the company out of trouble when I could, to plunge into the breach whenever crises struck, and, in certain key situations to serve as a combination *éminence grise* and intermediary between Ross and the outside world.

He was just forty when I met him in 1968, a strikingly handsome man, tall, athletic, and boundlessly energetic and charming—and boundlessly attractive to women too. Perhaps because of a hearing impairment, he spoke so softly that you had to bend forward to hear him, but when he held forth at a conference table or simply walked into a room, he became the center attraction, the immediate and commanding presence. He carried himself like an emperor, yet he had what in Yiddish are called *hamisher* qualities. He also had some of the Jewish mother in him. If he learned that you had a toothache or a back pain, there was a fair chance he would make you open your mouth or take off your shirt and you'd be sent to see one of his doctors on the spot. I was present once when he interrupted a business meeting to call an orthopedist—this for someone he hardly knew. His close relationships were never just professional; they quickly became personal. An integral part of knowing Steve was never wanting to let him down, and I think both his employees and his outside advisers, myself included, were motivated to try harder to achieve results simply in order to please him.

At the time we met, he was running a company called Kinney National Service. He had started in his father-in-law's funeral parlor business in New York, where his genuine affinity for people, particularly people in distress, made him stand out in what must have seemed otherwise a dreary, if profitable, business. But Ross was ever restless and an incorrigible deal-maker; it was just a matter of time before he began, piece by piece, to build a corporate empire. Noticing that the funeral parlor's limousines were being used for mourners only during the day, he hit on the idea of renting them to a limousine company in the evening. Meanwhile, his father-in-law's company also owned a small and unsuccessful rental car business, which was having trouble competing with the big operators. Looking for an edge, Ross struck a deal with a company called Kinney that operated dozens of parking lots in New York City—anyone who rented a car from Ross could park free in any Kinney lot. His advertisements, announcing that there were only three ways to park free in New York City, pictured three license plates: an MD for doctors, a DPL for diplomats, and a Kinney. Ross knew that most people who rented cars in New York did it to *leave* the city, not to park in its lots, and that few would ever take advantage of the free offer, but the gimmick gave the company the edge it needed, and business boomed.

The two companies merged. There followed a series of mergers and acquisitions, including an office cleaning company, National Cleaning Contractors, and DC Comics. Along the way, Ross took Kinney public and got it listed on the New York Stock Exchange. Then, in 1967, he bought a talent agency called Ashley Famous. Run by Ted Ashley, Ashley Famous was the second-largest agency in the country; its clients included Burt Lancaster, Ingrid Bergman, and Sean Connery. With Ashley as his guide, Ross was now ready to move into the entertainment industry.

Kinney National's outside counsel at the time was a Paul, Weiss corporate lawyer and colleague of mine named Allan Ecker, who first introduced me to Ross. We hit it off immediately, and I quickly became a member of his kitchen cabinet of advisers, which included Ecker, my tax partner Alan Cohen, and the young but already prominent investment banker Felix Rohatyn of Lazard Frères. Felix was five years my senior. I found that I shared his values, particularly his commitment to public service, and more important, I admired his independence. Lazard was run by André Meyer, a client of Judge Rifkind's who could be imperious, even with presidents, but Felix had his own style. He always spoke his mind, no matter how powerful the client, and I never once saw him fawn. I aspired to be a Felix Rohatyn of the law.

We could be frank with Ross, and we were, sometimes bluntly so. He delighted in it. He was in his element in the midst of a small group of trusted people, a kind of rump board of directors, with yellow pads and pencils on the table. Later on, Jay Emmett would be in those meetings, and Martin Payson, Warner's general counsel who became closer to me than to many of the partners at Paul, Weiss, and Oded Aboodi, who became Ross's fellow wizard of the deal. Often Ross would announce a new idea by saying he'd had this stupid or crazy notion he wanted to try out on us, but something, somewhere, was wrong with it. Where was the flaw? And off we'd go, criticizing and debating in a spirited exchange. Or he'd say, there's got to be a creative solution here somewhere, come on, we're missing it, what's wrong with us?—meanwhile jotting down numbers as fast as his pencil would travel in those calculator-free, mathematical gyrations he was famous for. As often as not, it was his own ideas that proved both brilliant and novel. The Warner–Seven Arts deal, as it unfolded, contained several prime examples.

In fact, Warner–Seven Arts demanded all of Ross's skills as a deal-maker and strategist. The company's main record labels—Warner Brothers and Atlantic—were highly successful, but its film company, Warner Brothers Studio, had lost money for years. Ted Ashley advised Ross that if he could acquire Warner–Seven Arts for a price that was no more than the value of the two record companies, there was no way he could lose. If the movie studio kept losing money, they could simply shut it down and still come out on top because of the record companies. On the other hand, if Ross could make the film studio work—and Ashley thought there was a shot—he would have acquired a moneymaking business for nothing.

Most of the other potential buyers, because they focused on the unprofitable studio, failed to see the opportunity. But not everyone. In January 1969, another conglomerate called Commonwealth United announced its offer to buy Warner–Seven Arts in exchange for stock, not cash. A few hours later, Steve Ross's Kinney National announced that it too would make an exchange offer for Warner–Seven Arts. The battle was joined.

Kinney's offices at the time were at 10 Rockefeller Plaza, and its conference room quickly became our headquarters. Based on Commonwealth United's stock price at that particular moment, its bid was higher than what we were prepared to pay, but Ross smelled a rat. He was willing to bet that Commonwealth United, which owned insurance companies, a jukebox company, and real estate, had used "creative" accounting gimmicks in order to boost its stock price—a common enough practice at the time. And it turned out he was absolutely right.

Analyzing Commonwealth's numbers, we discovered that its strong earnings for 1968, on which its stock price was hanging, had come from a single year-end transaction, the purchase and then virtually immediate resale—at an enormous markup—of real estate in Hawaii. Not only was this, in and of itself, a suspicious event, but on closer examination, we found that the buyers of the real estate had paid not cash but a nonrecourse note, payable over a number of years. To make matters even worse, the buyers, it turned out, were partners of Commonwealth United's own financial adviser!

The plot, as they say, had thickened. Commonwealth United's earnings, we now knew, were phony, but it nevertheless propped up its stock price on Wall Street and that gave it a distinct advantage over us.

Our ace in the hole, though, was Ross. As I said, he disdained calculators, managing the most complex computations in his head, and habitually solved mathematical business problems with only yellow pad and pencil, which he often used as props. Similarly, although he'd had no formal training in either domain, he had a quasi-intuitive grasp of accounting and tax law and, with technical help, devised brand-new securities with tax and accounting features that, time and again, enabled both buyer and seller to come out winners. In fact, simple deals tended to bore him. In later years, I sometimes had to urge him to prune and untwist deals he had shaped into elaborate Rube Goldberg–like contraptions, all because of small and inconsequential savings.

But Warner–Seven Arts was my first exposure. Working at a blackboard in the Kinney conference room, with the rest of us gathered around him, Ross devised and laid out a three-part strategy to outwit our competition.

Step one, without which nothing else would work, was to stall Commonwealth United's exchange offer. We had to report to the SEC exactly what we'd learned about Commonwealth United's phony earnings. This job fell naturally to me, since I'd just come from being an SEC prosecutor and since those same SEC analysts who would have to review Commonwealth's prospectus had been, in effect, my clients. I had help from Ecker and an outside financial analyst Ross used, Emanuel Gerard. But if Commonwealth United's accounting practices troubled the SEC—and I was sure they would—there was no way the SEC would actually bring suit in time to help Kinney. We debated the issue and came up with a different tack. In order to go forward with its exchange-of-stock offer, Commonwealth United was going to have to file and clear its registration statement with the SEC. The SEC can delay the clearing of registration statements for months, sometimes even years, and it's happened often enough that securities lawyers even have a name for it—the "deep freeze." If we could get Commonwealth United's proposed new securities entombed in the deep freeze at the SEC, then the Warner–Seven Arts board would have to choose between

Kinney's unencumbered offer and Commonwealth United's, which, though higher on paper, might never be permitted to happen.

I was convinced that the skeptical lawyers I'd dealt with before at the SEC would do what they could to keep the Commonwealth United prospectus from emerging from their review, if only they knew the right questions to ask. At the same time, having been in their position, I knew how busy they were. Accordingly, Ecker and I quickly prepared a questionnaire for them to use in interviewing Commonwealth United about its year-end accounts. It would take months to probe and answer, we thought, and we were convinced that Commonwealth United would only get itself in deeper by trying to explain its earnings.

Ross, meanwhile, knew he would have to woo some key shareholders of Warner–Seven Arts, but before he did, he wanted some unique kind of security in his arsenal, an enticement he could use as part of his offer. A form of warrant maybe? This was my partner Alan Cohen's territory. Together with Ross and their accountants, Alan developed an instrument that would qualify for tax purposes as a preferred stock but for accounting purposes would be treated as a warrant.

That was step two.

And then there were the shareholders. Several of them I had last seen in the U.S. Attorney's Office. One of them, Mac Schwebel, who in the course of the negotiations became a strong supporter of Ross, had been represented by Judge Rifkind in settling a securities case. Another was Bernard Cornfeld, a flamboyant investor and expatriate whose international mutual fund, Investors Overseas Services, had substantial holdings in both Warner–Seven Arts and Commonwealth United. Rohatyn called on Cornfeld to explain the risks inherent in Commonwealth's balance sheet and urge him to cast his vote with us.

Then Ross and Rohatyn met with Carroll Rosenbloom, who, among other investments, owned the Baltimore Colts. They won him over too, and without, in the end, having to compromise themselves. When Rosenbloom complained to them that he was suffering from a distracting headache because he wasn't getting enough sex, Rohatyn said, "Sorry, Mr. Rosenbloom, the most we can offer you is aspirin."

Last, but far from least, was another player in the Warner–Seven Arts picture who had to be courted—for a different reason. And that was Frank Sinatra.

Some years before, Sinatra had merged his own record company, Reprise, into Warner Bros. Records. It turned out that, in making the deal with Jack Warner, Sinatra's longtime lawyer and manager, Milton "Mickey" Rudin, had gotten his client not only a one-third interest in the new company, Warner Reprise, but full veto power over any deal Warner–Seven Arts might make to sell off its interest in Warner Reprise.

Ross's last stop, therefore, was a meeting—actually a series of meet-ings—with Mickey Rudin.

Rudin was quick to realize that Commonwealth United's earnings were indeed phony—possibly he'd known it all along—and finally, con-vinced by Ross, he persuaded Sinatra to side with us too. That negoti-ation was one between two masters. Rudin, among other things, was an expert on the values of the record industry, and Ross was Ross. Each liked to say, afterward, that the other might have outdone him, but they ultimately reached terms, and after the acquisition, Rudin became Ross's legal adviser on Warner's record business.

The deal was now as good as done. Schwebel and Rosenbloom had fallen into line, as well as Sinatra, and the Commonwealth United offer remained in the SEC's deep freeze. The Warner–Seven Arts board voted to recommend the Kinney offer to the shareholders, and in July 1969, the deal went through.

It was a spectacular acquisition for Ross and became, quicker than anyone had expected, an equally spectacular success. In order to clear the decks for the future, Ross immediately wrote down the inventory of the films that Warner Brothers owned, which had been carried on the books at an inflated value. The losses were thus pushed into the past and no longer weighed on the future of the new company. Then he installed Ted Ashley as head of the movie studio—fulfilling an old dream of Ashley's—and John Calley as creative head, and soon there were several unexpected hits, including *Woodstock*, which cost almost nothing to make, followed later by *The Exorcist*. To top it off, the record labels turned out to be even more profitable than Ashley had predicted.

Almost overnight Ross found himself running one of the growth companies in the entertainment industry. He changed the name to Warner Communications, and its stock rose year after year. Ross, it turned out, was a natural for the new business. He had long been a movie buff. Charismatic and charming, he bonded easily with Hollywood peo-ple—directors, actors, musicians. He also hired well, paid well, and gave his division heads and creative executives virtual autonomy. He rarely second-guessed them, never criticized their creative decisions, and when they made mistakes—there is no industry quite as mistake-prone as entertainment—he encouraged them and spurred them on.

In fact, I can think of only one exception, offhand, and that was myself. Very early in our relationship, Ross decided that my opinion on the merits of a movie was the proverbial kiss of death. He used to say, with a great guffaw, "If Arthur likes it, we *know* it's going to bomb."

Although the Warner acquisition came early in our relationship, my work on it brought me into Ross's circle, and he sought my advice more and more on problems ranging from legal issues to personal ones. Except when I was on trial for another client or engaged in public service, Warner became my most active client.

The relationship showed how a lawyer can be a friend and adviser of a CEO and yet remain independent. Ross himself, after all, was already a celebrity—a power in the business world, in the entertainment community, and in Democratic politics—when I was still a $100,000-a-year partner at Paul, Weiss, yet I can't remember an instance when he treated me as less than an equal. Close as we became later on—I performed the ceremony at his wedding to Courtney and am the godfather of their daughter Nicole—he trusted me never to pull my punches and always to give him independent advice. Never once did he ask me to soften an opinion, nor did he ever, as he might have, ask me to circumscribe my list of clients. At various times, I represented Paramount and Columbia, among others, but Ross was in fact proud that his own lawyer was also sought after by his competitors. He always delighted in my successes in the courtroom and in my public assignments, such as the Attica and Iran-Contra investigations. In a way, we played older brother to each other, Ross seeking to promote my career, and I to steer him through company and personal crises.

Ross entered the entertainment industry at a time when it was nearly being strangled by legal problems and restrictions that affected its ability to distribute films and records and to provide programming for the television networks. For example, the government had grown suspicious of movie distributors gaining control of theaters, or chains of theaters, as they once had, thereby preventing competitors' products from being shown. There were now elaborate auction rules to ensure an even playing field. The networks, meanwhile, had started making their own films for prime-time showing, a practice that gave them enormous power and began to limit film studios' sales to them and other markets. On our side, the studios couldn't buy a network, nor could we own theaters. In the end, we filed suit against the networks and succeeded in limiting their ability to make prime-time films for their own stations.

In the record industry, meanwhile, we tackled the payola problem—with only partial success. Airtime was the way to success for a record, usually the only way. Record promoters would sometimes bribe the disc jockeys for airtime. The record promoters, in turn, shook down the record companies for payments in exchange for their services. Ross and Mickey Rudin hated the practice, deeming it bad business as well as bad ethics. Ross asked Rudin and me to try to break the promoters' stranglehold. Rudin felt that Warner Records was being hurt by the willingness of other record companies to make payoffs, and he wanted me to try to stir up a prosecution. We tried—we made a presentation to the U.S. Attorney's Office in New Jersey, and later there were indictments in California—but the effort didn't stop the practice. All we could do was institute a strong policy at Warner prohibiting our record subsidiaries from using the crooked promotion agents, and despite protests from some of the recording groups, who feared it would hurt their records, we stuck to it. But there was no way, other than moral persuasion, we could prevent some of them from using their own advertising money to pay off the same people.

I had better luck in one of my first matters for Ross, which came about when *Forbes* magazine, in June 1970, published a story about Kinney. According to the piece, the father of Caesar Kimmel—the largest Kinney stockholder when Ross acquired it and now a member of the Warner board—had been a gambler and bootlegger. Not Caesar Kimmel himself, mind you, but his father. No evidence whatsoever existed to connect Kimmel's father to Ross or to the company, as the article acknowledged, or, for that matter, to connect Kinney to organized crime, but the implications were clear, and they did damage to Kinney. Ross was hopping mad and turned to me. I was also offended. The article was sheer innuendo and, for Kinney, guilt by association twice removed.

On the other hand, as I pointed out to Ross, libel litigation is difficult to win, particularly when the libel is by innuendo, and it is costly too. Furthermore, while our case languished in the courts, *Forbes*, simply by reporting on the lawsuit, could retaliate with additional articles that could be harmful to Ross and Warner. As the old expression goes, never fight with anyone who buys printer's ink by the barrel.

We decided to ask *Forbes* to retract the story and print an apology. This I did—nicely but firmly, as I recall—but *Forbes*, in its wisdom, refused. I reported this to Ross. We looked each other in the eye, and though I don't remember his actual words, the message was clear: let's go for it. Thereupon, we initiated a lawsuit. Libel actions rarely end with apologies, but lo and behold, this one did, and quickly. *Forbes*, embarrassed and obviously in the wrong, offered to settle, with the apology we wanted.

Ross's relations with the media were often difficult, and at one point, I brought in Gershon Kekst, a corporate public relations expert, who recommended that Ross make himself more accessible to the press. But this proved a hellish task for Steve. If he gave an interview to one reporter, it meant he'd have to face demands from others. If he gave interviews to all, he would be criticized for not giving an exclusive. Moreover, even aside from the two scandals that were to rock the company, the media often made Ross a target. His high compensation was a frequent source of attack, and so was his lifestyle.

Ross always lived well, spending freely and generously. After his marriage to Courtney, and relying on her taste and guidance, he became an avid art collector. As with anything Steve tackled, collecting became a passion, and wheeling and dealing in the art world a source of enormous pride and pleasure. Works by de Kooning, Gorki, and Pollock hung on the walls of their Park Avenue and East Hampton homes, and he and Courtney began collecting other things as well, from Viennese art deco furniture to Bordeaux wine. In fact, as we used to joke, if Ross had invested Warner's assets in the works of art that Courtney identified for him, the return on investment would have been even higher than that reflected by the rising price of the company's stock.

For all his high living, Ross could also share someone else's more plebeian tastes. He and I often sneaked out of Warner's headquarters on Sixth Avenue to munch Nathan's hot dogs on the sidewalk while we weighed the pros and cons of one of his enormously complicated deals.

I always steered clear of any formal involvement in Ross's compensation negotiations with the Warner board, for obvious conflict-of-interest reasons, but I knew Ross believed in incentive compensation, and so, for that matter, did I. As Warner's earnings exploded and its stock rose steadily, Ross's bonuses did too, as well as the value of his stock and his stock options, making him, in time, one of the highest-paid CEOs in America. But as he put it, in the entertainment industry, as in securities trading, your principal asset walks out the door every night, meaning that your principal asset in those fields is people, the key people who, because of their relationships, their creative talent, and their managerial skills, make the business happen. Warner, under Ross, always took good care of its top management team and had a record unequaled by any of its competitors in keeping them together.

This is not to say that it was always easy, or that there was never internal strife. Ross's hands-off and laissez-faire style of management aroused criticism among some of his executives, who felt that he failed to pay enough attention to the details of the business. His free-spending ways came under attack too, particularly in an off year, and what company in entertainment doesn't experience them? To a degree, Ross was stuck in a catch-22 situation: either he didn't delegate enough or he delegated too much, depending on whom you talked to, but the company came close at one point to a palace revolution against the too-benevolent leader. Ted Ashley and Felix Rohatyn learned of it before I did, but neither of them wanted to be the one to tell Ross what was going on, and so I was nominated to intercede.

We all knew how he prized loyalty above all. When I'd finished reporting the situation to him that day, he grew, predictably enough, very angry. But I was ready for him. I pointed out that, before contemplating mayhem against the insurgents, he should stop to think. Among other things, what would it do to his ability to lead in the future? Not to mention the bad publicity—for him personally as well as Warner's. Instead of punishing the plotters, I urged him to give his executives what they wanted—taking on the active and direct management of the company and meeting with them on a regular and organized basis—and to get Warner moving again toward greater profitability and higher stock prices. This would be the tangible and irrefutable proof of his leadership. In other words, I took their side, and I doubt that anyone, certainly no one inside Warner, could have spoken to Steve that way and lived to tell about it!

For a time, in fact, Ross confused my ability to give him independent advice with a supposed knack for management, and on several occasions he put out feelers to me about joining Warner. He knew perfectly well how deeply committed I was to the practice of law, and so he tried a very Ross-like maneuver, end-running me by dropping broad hints to Ellen about how great life would be if I became his president. "Arthur," he would say to her, "cuts through business problems with such quick solutions, he really ought to think about it." I pretended, for a time, not to know what was going on, but finally I had to call him out on it. I told him I was no manager of other people and hated administration. Besides, I was so lousy at numbers and details involving numbers that I was always way behind preparing my bills to clients at Paul, Weiss. If I couldn't do that, how could I manage a whole company? Moreover, if I accepted his offer, it would mean the end of my independence. How could I ever give him frank counsel, especially when I knew it went counter to his instincts? He would lose a counselor and get a lousy manager.

He took some convincing—he always did when an idea grabbed him—but at the same time he knew I was right. And that was that. My advice, I'm sure, saved Warner from a disaster and also, I like to think, served Paul, Weiss.

In 1976 Warner acquired a small video game company in Sunnyvale, California, called Atari for about $20 million. It was a highly speculative investment—the video game industry hardly existed at the time—but one of Ross's top executives, Emanuel Gerard, once a securities analyst in the entertainment field and, since the Warner–Seven Arts acquisition, a member of Ross's top team, waxed enthusiastic about the opportunity. Ross, being Ross, went along with him.

Within four years, Atari's sales had exceeded those of all other Warner divisions combined, and its profits skyrocketed.

Consumers, it turned out, loved video games with a passion, and for several, astonishingly profitable years, Atari had the industry almost to itself. But even in Atari's heyday of 1981, Ross worried that video games might prove to be a passing fad, a high-tech version of the hula hoop, and he wanted to explore the possibility of cashing in by selling at least part of Warner's interest.

Accordingly, Ross and I met with Felix Rohatyn, whom Ross had asked to evaluate the situation. Rohatyn now delivered the good news and the bad news. The good news was that Atari had been so spectacularly successful—its pretax operating profits were about $500 million—that it was now, conservatively, worth more than $2 billion, and probably a lot more. The bad news was that few companies in the country could afford it. Maybe GE? Or IBM? Neither of these, though, was likely to be interested. It was a case of too much success, too quickly.

But how quickly fortunes change!

While Atari continued to reap record profits through the third quarter of 1982, there were some signs that its growth was slowing, and its budgets had to be revised downward. But Gerard, always an optimist by nature, remained enthusiastic, and Ross, while more restrained, nevertheless made a multimillion-dollar deal with Steven Spielberg, in the summer of 1982, to produce a video game of the movie *ET* in time for Christmas release.

December 7, of course, is a particularly memorable day for any American who was alive in 1941, when the Japanese bombed Pearl Harbor. But for us December 7, 1982, became memorable for another reason. Ross called me that morning and asked me to drop everything and rush to his office. He had never made such an urgent request before. Nor had I ever heard him so upset.

When I arrived, he said he'd just learned from Gerard, who in turn had just heard it from Atari's management in California, that Atari's sales had stopped cold, plummeting like a stone, along with sales of competitors like Mattel and Coleco. The stores and distribution networks were glutted with games, and since Thanksgiving, major retailers were refusing to take any new shipments. Worse, they were insisting that Atari take back the old unsold ones. In other words, shipments of Atari games that Atari had booked as sales could now turn out to be no better than consignments. Among other things, this meant that Warner's earnings, once adjusted to account for the change, would fall far, far below the estimates of Wall Street analysts.

Virtually overnight the phenomenal success had become a phenomenal, and disastrous, liability.

On my advice, Warner immediately put out a press release revealing the bad news, and as we expected, the price of Warner stock collapsed. At the same time, things took an even uglier turn. As Ross, Gerard, and I were drafting the press release, panicked Atari managers had begun selling their own Warner stock. When we learned of it, Ross went totally ballistic, and he ordered the individuals in question to nullify their sales. But now we had two legal crises on our hands: the Atari sales figures that Warner had reported to the public in its filings with the SEC were wide open to question, and Atari's top executives had sold their Warner stock before the public knew about the trouble. Ross himself had sold some Warner stock months earlier, and now he was concerned that the financial community would become suspicious of him too.

While Ross contended with Atari's business problems, my immediate job was to restore Warner's credibility. With Ross's blessing, I reported what had happened to the SEC and pledged Warner's cooperation. I was confident that an SEC investigation into who had known what when Atari's sales collapsed would exonerate top management. Ross, I was sure, had known nothing before the morning he called me— I had witnessed his shock and anger at the events of that day—but what *I* was sure of was of no importance. What mattered was whether Wall Street and the investing public would retain their trust in Warner's management. Only an SEC investigation and clearance would be credited, and this, as I insisted when the question was raised, was no time to take a stonewalling or adversarial position. On the contrary, I advised Ross that our goal should be to make sure the SEC investigated as promptly and thoroughly as possible.

Ross was despondent about Atari, the value of which had just fallen through the floor. I told him that Warner could survive the loss, that it could survive whatever sanctions the SEC might impose on Atari's management, and that it could even survive class action lawsuits. But it could not survive if Ross and Warner's top management lost their credibility in the financial community. Wall Street had to be convinced that Ross was as surprised by the sales collapse as Wall Street itself had been.

So intent was I on getting the SEC investigation behind us, and certain that its outcome would be favorable, that that winter, when the SEC lawyers were questioning a group of Warner executives in Washington, and despite the groans of the participants—particularly the lawyers and the court reporter—I insisted we keep going in spite of the fact that the city's worst blizzard in decades was raging outside. Everyone was anxious to leave, but I promised that I'd hire some four-wheel drive vehicles to take the SEC people home afterward. And so I did. It was late in the evening when we finally finished. I think I must have taken care of everyone except *myself* and Les Fagen, my partner, for I remember the two of us trudging the many blocks to our hotel, exhausted but satisfied, through three-foot-deep snowdrifts that came up past our waists.

While I was taking care of the SEC side, my in-house "partner," Martin Payson, was working to reorganize Atari. The SEC investigation ended with two Atari executives, who'd actually sold Warner stock before the press release, accepting consent decrees, but no charges were filed against Warner or Ross or any member of Warner's senior management. That people in the Atari division had known the extent of Atari's troubles and acted on that knowledge was embarrassing enough, but, as I'd anticipated, the SEC concluded that no Warner executive had shared in that knowledge.

Afterward, Warner was able to reorganize Atari and absorb its enormous write-offs; Ross even found a buyer who was willing to take control of the game company, though for a modest price. The buyer was Jack Tramiel, a Holocaust survivor who had owned and then sold Commodore Computer. The billions that Atari seemed to have been worth the previous year proved illusory, needless to say, but Ross and Warner survived the debacle, and as Warner's film, record, and cable divisions prospered, its stock price began climbing again.

There was another reason why the Atari crisis shook Ross so badly, and why we were so eager to get it behind us. It had broken just as Ross and Warner were beginning to recover from an even more serious scandal—the Westchester Premier Theatre affair.

In 1972 a stockbroker named Leonard Horwitz had helped raise money to build a theater in Tarrytown, New York, that would book big-name recording artists. Horwitz approached his friend Jay Emmett, who bought some of the stock. Emmett was then a member of Warner's Office of the President, as well as Ross's closest aide and probably at the time his closest friend—the prototype of Ross's tendency to mix the professional and the personal. The next year, Westchester Premier had a public stock offering, and at Emmett's urging, Warner bought $250,000 of stock. It was a small investment; although Ross was aware of it, no one at Warner told me, and there was no reason anyone should have.

Westchester Premier Theatre, a cash business, was soon dominated by the mob. A "gang that couldn't shoot straight" mob, I should add, for by 1977 the business was bankrupt and the FBI and the U.S. Attorney's Office in Manhattan were investigating its finances. In the course of the investigation, the FBI discovered that Horwitz, the original promoter, had made a secret $50,000 cash payment to Warner's assistant treasurer, Solomon Weiss, at the same time that Warner agreed to buy Westchester Premier Theatre stock. Eventually, Horwitz, Jay Emmett, and Weiss were indicted for defrauding Warner. They were accused of arranging the $50,000 payment to Weiss as a kickback for Warner's $250,000 investment. Emmett and Horwitz pleaded guilty, and neither was given a prison sentence. Weiss, however, went to trial and was convicted.

I first learned of the investigation in early April 1978, when Emmett and Weiss were served with subpoenas to testify before a grand jury, and Warner itself was subpoenaed to produce documents. Emmett and Weiss asked me and my partner, Max Gitter, to represent them. We informed them that our first obligation, as Warner's lawyers, was to Warner, and we could represent them only if they were going to testify for and cooperate with the government. If they had anything to hide, or if they wanted to invoke their Fifth Amendment privilege against self-incrimination, they needed their own lawyer. Emmett and Weiss both assured us they'd done nothing wrong and were eager to testify.

Certainly I wanted to believe them. I knew both men and liked them both. Furthermore, they were trusted Warner's employees, and it was hard for me to believe that one or both of them would have taken a personal kickback on the company's investment. But I was not so naive as to accept their declarations of innocence at face value. At the same time, the prosecutor assured us that neither Emmett nor Weiss was a "target" of the investigation. He'd have no objection, he said, if we represented them as well as Warner. That gave us comfort. But there is naive and then there's naive, I suppose. What we didn't know was that the prosecutor, not wanting to tip his hand, was relying on new Justice Department guidelines that narrowly defined "target" so as to include only persons whom he was actually about to indict.

Two months after Emmett and Weiss testified before the grand jury, in June 1978, Leonard Horwitz and several others who ran the theater were indicted. The indictment charged Horwitz with defrauding the theater's investors, skimming funds, and obstructing justice. Though Horwitz wasn't charged with bribery, the indictment also noted that he had paid two "unnamed executives" at Warner a $50,000 kickback for influencing Warner to buy the theater's stock.

This was the first time I'd heard such an allegation. But then, that September, the government publicly identified Emmett and Weiss as the two executives in question, while still not charging them with any crime.

If these disclosures were personally painful for me, they were devastating to Ross. He and Jay Emmett had been very, very close. Of course I asked Ross what he knew, and he knew nothing of the kickback, but for reasons I will come to, we both understood that we were dealing with a very serious situation, one fraught with danger.

The first thing I did was tell Emmett and Weiss that they needed to hire their own lawyers. Then I turned to how Warner could handle the accusations against two of its top officers. Since neither was charged with a crime, firing them on the spot would have been both unfair and inconsistent with due process. Moreover, since Paul, Weiss had represented Emmett and Weiss, we could not be involved in any decision concerning their future. Yet it was essential that there be no cover-up, or any appearance of one. As would happen with Atari, the company had to be cooperative with any and all investigations into the matter, not go into a defensive crouch.

I took four steps.

First, I instructed Ross not to discuss the matter with Emmett and Weiss. Not a word to either, however tempted he might be. Even efforts to sympathize with friends have been known to lead to charges of perjury and obstruction of justice.

Second, I had Warner disclose in its SEC filing that two corporate officers had been named as unindicted coconspirators. Warner Communications was a public company, and its shareholders were entitled to know.

Third, on my recommendation, Warner's audit committee, made up exclusively of outside directors, resolved to conduct its own investigation. It hired as its counsel Michael Armstrong, a good friend of mine from our days together at the U.S. Attorney's Office. Armstrong had had nothing to do with Warner before. He had served as counsel to the Knapp Commission's wide-ranging and highly regarded investigation of New York City police corruption, and when the District Attorney of Queens was removed from office, Governor Rockefeller had appointed Armstrong to replace him. I could think of no lawyer who would have greater credibility in looking into Westchester Premier Theatre—and letting the chips fall where they might.

Armstrong was to report only to the audit committee. Not even I was to receive that report.

Finally, to my very considerable consternation, I had to decide what Warner should do with Leonard Horwitz. I was amazed, and dismayed, to learn that in January 1978, just a month after the FBI first approached Horwitz, he had been given a job—at Warner! And once indicted, he began demanding that Warner pay his legal fees. He'd even insinuated that, if it did not, he would turn government's witness.

I was adamant that Warner refuse.

Emmett, however, who had separate counsel, could not resist Horwitz's pressure. He paid Horwitz's legal fees personally, and though he did so under an agreement that made it clear that he did not control Horwitz's defense, it still gave the appearance of collusion. But once Emmett had separate counsel, I was helpless to intervene.

Before I go on, I have two things I want to say.

First, I don't to this day know what actually happened. This has always baffled journalists who've investigated the story—how could Arthur Liman not know?—but it is the absolute and unvarnished truth. In the course of the criminal investigations and trials, witnesses and defendants told self-serving stories, whether to protect themselves or to win leniency, and their accounts were often sharply in conflict. Although, in the light of the guilty pleas and the outcome of Solomon Weiss's trial, it seems indisputable that $50,000 was paid, to whom it was paid and for what purpose and what happened to it remain mysteries and probably always will.

Second, I don't believe Steve Ross had anything to do with it. I say this not only because I know what the man told me but because he was interviewed, in detail, by three separate bodies on the subject of Westchester. One was the SEC, to which agency he gave a deposition in September 1979. The second was Rudolph Giuliani, who, as U.S.

Attorney in overall charge of the Westchester Premier Theatre investigation, wanted to interview Ross. This was a transcribed interview, under oath. Although I was present, because I represented Warner, I could not also serve as Ross's personal lawyer, so I advised him to hire Peter Fleming. I admit that, like any defense attorney, I had second thoughts about going through with the proceeding, but I was outvoted. Ross, affirming his innocence, insisted on going, and Fleming agreed.

Both the SEC and Giuliani concluded that no charges against Ross were warranted. Because Ross and Warner had been so damaged by the bad publicity, I wanted to take the unusual step of getting this conclusion in writing. I persevered, making a pest of myself over several years, and finally, in February 1985 after repeated efforts, I persuaded Giuliani to issue me a letter to that effect.

Was this prescience on my part? Hardly. It simply reflected a conscientious attorney's wish to dot the i's and cross the t's. But this letter was to become very valuable to us, for reasons I will come to.

Finally, there was Michael Armstrong's investigation for the outside directors of the Warner board's auditing committee. It lasted more than eight years, partly because Armstrong didn't want to be accused of having missed any possible shred of evidence, and partly because he wanted to see what evidence Giuliani's people, with all the investigative power of the federal government behind them, might develop. In the course of his work, Armstrong interviewed Ross several times. Finally, in 1986, in a 663-page report, Armstrong reached the same conclusion as the earlier investigators: Ross was not involved with kickbacks. He neither received them nor knew of them, although the report did criticize him for providing inconsistent explanations of his gambling winnings and uses of cash.

I emphasize Ross's exoneration not in special pleading, and not even because my good friend is no longer here to defend himself, but because over the years journalists of various stripes and talents have had a field day with the Westchester Premier Theatre story. I suppose, in a way, this was inevitable. Ross, for one thing, was a public figure and a charismatic one. For another, he was a high-stakes player, with far more than his share of wins, but some losses too. And Hollywood—the entertainment industry in general—has been a perennial media target, one joined during the go-go 1980s by Wall Street. Add to this the whiff of mob involvement, and for certain writers and their readers the mix became as irresistible as catnip to the cat, whatever the facts. Whence the idea that Steve Ross kept a briefcase stuffed with cash in his office—for girlfriends perhaps? Or for gambling? I called this idea ridiculous then, as I do now. And whence the innuendo, equally foolish, that somehow Steve Ross, the highly visible CEO of a major and highly visible American company, must have been a bagman for the mob.

Let me return, though, to the money. That corporations have always created and maintained secret cash funds, for uses that cannot be disclosed and may well be illegal, is nothing new. We live, for better or worse, in an imperfect world. Companies that do business abroad, for example, have often had to make under-the-table payments to foreign officials. In the domestic sphere, corrupt union leaders have extorted payoffs without which businesses in certain industries wouldn't have been able to function. Typically, in the past, when government prosecutors learned of such payments, they settled for consent decrees and testimony against the extorters. Moreover, while the Westchester Premier case was going on, almost one hundred American companies reported to the SEC, as they were legally obliged to, that they had entered into cash funds for payments abroad.

In this light, the $50,000 Westchester Premier Theatre payment certainly looked like corporate slush-fund money. While at his trial Solomon Weiss steadfastly denied having received the money, he later acknowledged on appeal and sentencing that that was its purpose. Emmett also claimed that there was a secret corporate cash fund. The government prosecutor himself subscribed to that theory, but no evidence was ever produced in court to support it, and if the money was indeed intended for some clandestine corporate purpose, it was a purpose of which I—and Ross—were unaware.

Instead, we were left with a mystery.

Hurt by the Atari losses and the Westchester Premier Theatre scandal, Warner became a takeover target. Perhaps it would have happened anyway. During the 1980s, every company was fair game. We began to hear rumors regularly about one purported buyer or another. At one point, they came so thick and fast that I asked Rudy Giuliani to investigate whether stock manipulators were deliberately putting out false rumors and then trading on them.

Finally, in December 1983, Rupert Murdoch, the Australian publisher who controlled Independent News Corporation, made an unsolicited bid for the company. At first, he said he would buy no more than 49.9 percent of Warner, but within a few weeks he said he would mount a proxy fight if necessary to gain control. Ross, in fact, might have brought this on himself. The two men had met in August 1983, and Murdoch had asked whether Ross would object if he bought some Warner stock. "Be my guest," Steve had replied cavalierly, adding, of course, that Warner was a public company and anyone was free to buy its shares. Now he regretted his largesse, for Murdoch had the resources to take over Warner.

Years before, I had introduced Ross to Herb Siegel of Chris-Craft Industries. I had represented Herb in two trials and two appeals in litigation over the control of Piper Aircraft and had argued for Herb in the U.S. Supreme Court in defense of a $36 million judgment that I had won for him in that case. Ross had testified on Herb's behalf as an expert witness during that case. Although Chris-Craft had begun as a boat manufacturer, by 1983 its principal business was operating television stations.

Ross now turned to Herb Siegel for help, using me as an intermediary and adviser. I helped to broker a transaction in which Warner swapped Chris-Craft 19 percent of its stock in exchange for a large stake in Chris-Craft's television stations. With Warner now in the broadcast television business, Murdoch was effectively thwarted. Federal regulations restrict foreigners from owning television stations, and Murdoch was an Australian. Murdoch sued, but a few months later Warner was able to buy back his stock—giving him a huge profit in the bargain.

Besides blocking Murdoch, the deal between Ross and Siegel seemed to me a natural. Herb had once run a Hollywood talent agency; then he'd bought a major stake in Paramount Pictures, and later in 20th Century–Fox. Having made a great deal of money in both transactions, he nonetheless wanted in the worst way to have equity in a movie studio. Conversely, Warner could well benefit from owning the broadcast properties.

But did I learn a lesson from this! *Never* bring two friends and clients together in a business venture, no matter how apparently beneficial to both parties. (I didn't adhere to the lesson very long, I confess. Perhaps the matchmaking instinct was too strong. A few years later, I introduced Bill Paley to Lawrence Tisch, and they formed an alliance that allowed Tisch to become CEO of CBS.) While Warner kept its independence and prospered, and Chris-Craft's investment multiplied in value, Siegel and Ross turned out to be a disaster as partners. Their business philosophies thrashed and clashed. Siegel was economical and hard-headed; he detested extravagance. Ross believed that in the entertainment business you spend money to make money, and Warner's own success seemed to validate his philosophy. Before the deal was completed, I tried to show Siegel the difference between him and Ross, to give him a kind of Miranda rights warning. I took him on a tour of Warner's headquarters and showed him the utterly lavish and high-tech office that had recently been renovated for one of Ross's deputies. "Look around, Herb," I said to Siegel. "This isn't even Ross's office. It's for the man who runs the record business. If that bothers you, please don't do the deal." By this point, though, it was too late to budge him. Siegel said he was betting on Ross and trusted his judgment.

Companies have, of course, succeeded in the entertainment industry following these two very different philosophies, but never by following the two at the same time. It was personally painful to me to see my two friends and clients feuding and battling in a transaction I'd helped engineer, and enormously frustrating that I could do nothing about it except duck when the skirmishing broke into open warfare at board meetings and the blood flowed. Oddly, though, there were ways in which Siegel's opposition helped Warner. Ross hated confrontations and never could bring himself to fire people, but Siegel's provocations became a pretext for corporate streamlining. The executive vice presidents went. Robert Morgado, Governor Carey's chief of staff, was brought in to trim the staff. Waste was hunted down.

On the other hand, one of their biggest clashes was over the cable joint venture that Warner owned with American Express. When American Express wanted out, Warner had to agree to buy American Express out or sell part of what they owned jointly, meaning the cable divisions, Nickelodeon and MTV. Ross, inevitably, wanted to keep it all, or at least the cable and Nickelodeon, because he was convinced that the world population of children viewers made Nickelodeon an undervalued asset. But

Siegel was adamantly convinced that the company could not take on the added debt, and so both MTV and Nickelodeon were divested.

For some years, there seemed to be no solution to their feuding, but once one presented itself and their business interests were separated, the two men became friends. And that solution came in 1989, when Ross decided to merge Warner with Time Inc.

I first heard that Ross was discussing some kind of combination with Time while I was in Washington, completing my Iran-Contra assignment. The initial impetus, he told me, had come because of the cable business. Ross loved being in cable and had believed in it early, but Warner's own operations were stagnant—they were large enough that the investment mattered but too small to have sufficient market power. Time's were in the same position. By combining their cable systems, Ross explained, Time and Warner would instantly become the second-largest player in the cable industry.

Ross told me that he and Warner's financial adviser, Oded Aboodi, were meeting with Time's management to discuss merging their cable businesses, or perhaps even their cable and entertainment businesses, in a joint venture. Aboodi, originally an accountant and tax specialist for Arthur Young, had handled first the Kinney and then the Warner Communications account, set up his own small business in 1980, with offices inside Warner, and become a key figure in Ross's inner circle. He had a keen and highly creative financial mind, and Ross's confidence in him was amply borne out in the weeks and months ahead.

By the time I returned from the Iran-Contra investigation, in December 1987, the talks were still in their initial stages. Ross and Aboodi scarcely needed my counsel just then. They were both geniuses at developing a deal, and Aboodi and Time's Gerald Levin were expert negotiators. Little by little, though, the idea of the joint venture expanded, and the more it expanded, the more the players realized that there was no reason not to go further. Indeed, I'm quite sure that Ross had this in mind from the very beginning.

But then the negotiations ran into a stumbling block, namely, Time's anxiety about Ross's background.

Felix Rohatyn and his partner at Lazard, Jon O'Herron—both respected by Time—gave Ross unqualified references, but a few Time directors were skittish because of Westchester Premier Theatre. It wasn't that they believed that Ross had been personally involved, but Time was fiercely proud and protective of its corporate integrity. The company had never been involved in any sort of scandal, and its directors were unwilling to let it go into business with another company if the ethics of its management were at all in question.

Ross, needless to say, was offended by this development, but Rohatyn proposed to him that I talk to Time's top officers, Richard Munro and Nicholas Nicholas, and Time's counsel, Sam Butler, from Cravath, Swaine and Moore. I didn't know Munro or Nicholas, but I'd represented Time in an acrimonious and difficult libel litigation in which *Time* magazine had been accused of suggesting that the head of the Schiavone Construction Company, a friend of Nixon's secretary of labor, Ray Donovan, was involved in Jimmy Hoffa's disappearance. Based on that experience, Munro and Nicholas knew that I would be the last person to misstate the facts to them. Sam Butler, in fact, already knew a great deal about Westchester Premier, for he'd represented Herb Siegel in connection with his disputes with Warner, and at one point, Herb, as a major stockholder, had gone to court in order to get to read the Armstrong report. I knew Butler liked Ross. I knew, further, that he was aware of all of the investigations and their results. Above all, he was a lawyer of great practical wisdom, one who would recognize that Westchester Premier was behind us and should not be permitted to block any deal between the two companies if the deal made business sense.

Before I met with Munro and Nicholas, Ross freed me from any attorney-client privilege, even though I knew no more about Westchester Premier than was a matter of public record. Besides, the Giuliani letter, which I took with me, was far more credible than anything I could say. I led Munro and Nicholas through the various steps we'd taken during the crisis, including the Armstrong investigation; I described how I'd accompanied Ross and his counsel when Ross was interrogated by the U.S. Attorney's Office; I pointed out that Giuliani had issued his letter because there was no doubt that his office believed Ross. I told them of Ross's earlier actions with regard to the record industry's payola practices and of my experiences with him during the Atari crisis. All that was left for me to say, in the end, was that, in all my years of representing Warner, Ross had never once asked me to do anything that crossed the line of legality or ethics. And this I did say, wholeheartedly.

As it happened, I had my own concerns about a merger between Time and Warner, and I gave my own form of Miranda warning to both Ross and Time's management. I pointed out that Warner's corporate culture was very different from Time's and that of most other public companies. Ross ran Warner like a family business in which virtually any employee, including those in the mailroom, could call him with a complaint or a problem. Hundreds of employees still received turkeys from Ross at Thanksgiving. He was "Steve" to everyone, never "Mr. Ross."

Time, on the other hand, had a far more traditional and formal hierarchical structure. It operated on formal plans and budgets, not on intuition, as Ross did. But Warner's strength was Ross's sometimes intuitive feel for the businesses he was in, and if Time couldn't accept that, no merger would work.

By this time, though, the negotiators on both sides had come to believe that the combined company could accommodate the different styles. Both sides wanted the deal, believing strongly that the sum of the two companies was greater than its parts.

There was, however, one issue on which the negotiations finally ran aground. Early in their discussions, Ross and the Time management had agreed on the principle that the merger would be one of equals and that the new board would be equally divided between Warner and Time directors. They also agreed that Nicholas and Ross would serve as co-chief executive officers. But Time wanted ironclad assurances that Ross would retire as CEO after five years and that Nicholas would then, automatically, become the sole leader. Ross was amenable to the concept of the succession, but he was unalterably opposed to carving it into stone, regardless of what might happen in between or what the circumstances might be after the five years had elapsed.

Essentially, Ross wanted some measure of flexibility; Time wanted the future spelled out, in detail, as part of the merger agreement. With the two sides deadlocked, Ross called off the discussions in August 1988. He then proceeded to the friendly acquisition of Lorimar Telepictures Corporation, a major producer of television series. Combined with Warner's own productions, the Lorimar acquisition made Warner the largest single supplier of television programming.

The Lorimar deal, however, almost didn't happen. The negotiations dragged on and on, while Ross and Aboodi proposed additional refinements. In fact, while Ross had called off the Time negotiations, the merger was clearly still on his mind, and he didn't want a Lorimar deal to foreclose the possibility. Then too, he was under pressure from his studio heads, who believed that he was overpaying for Lorimar and that he should try to get it at a lower price. Finally Felix Rohatyn called me in exasperation. He was afraid Lorimar might do a deal with a competitor unless we pushed to close. When Felix spoke in those tones, I realized it was time to intervene. I told Ross essentially that, while I myself couldn't judge what the right price for Lorimar might be, he'd soon forget having paid the extra nickel, if that's what he was doing, as long as the deal made business sense. But on the contrary, if Lorimar got away, he would always remember and regret it. Finally, at a meeting at Rohatyn's apartment, Ross decided that he wanted the deal. He and Merv Adelson of Lorimar shook hands on it, and it turned out to be one of the best acquisitions Warner ever made.

Once Lorimar was done, Ross and Time quickly resumed their mating dance. Perhaps the delay had helped clear the air. In addition, the Lorimar acquisition was well received by Time's executives. Both sides now discovered that their ardor for a merger was undiminished, and Levin, representing Nicholas and Munro, and Aboodi, representing Ross, sat down to negotiate the financial terms.

By March 1989, the conditions of the deal were set. Warner shareholders would receive shares of Time in the merger. Neither side would incur any debt. The result would be the creation of the most important media company in the world. In a lifetime of making deals, this was to be Ross's masterpiece.

Board meetings at both companies were called to approve the merger, and the plan was to make a public announcement almost immediately afterward. But then, at the eleventh hour, that same, never-quite-resolved issue of management succession raised its head again. Time was now insisting on a provision in the new company's bylaws that would oblige Ross to resign as co-CEO in five years and leave Nicholas alone in the role.

For the Time board, the bylaw provision seemed to be an imperative. Perhaps its members—that is, those who were most rigid on the issue—thought they were acting in the spirit of the founder? From the beginning, Henry Luce had imbued the company with a strong sense of independence. Perhaps, too, they were apprehensive lest the more entre-preneurial Warner executives overwhelm the Time culture. Certainly, in the long run, they wanted Time to emerge the dominant partner.

But the bylaw provision—that the succession question actually be inscribed in the company bylaws—was too much for Ross to swallow. Ironically, Luce's son, Hank, didn't share the view that a bylaw provision was required. He agreed that Ross's word should suffice, but he was overruled. Ross, in turn, took this as a sign that the Time directors didn't believe him when he said he planned to retire in five years. Also, he feared that, with such a provision inscribed in stone, he would be regarded as a powerless lame duck for the five years of his reign, and he, in turn, worried that the executives who ran the Warner divisions would feel abandoned if they were committed contractually to Nicholas's succession. Who was to say that there might not be an obviously better choice than Nicholas when the time came for Ross to retire?

Ross was used to a board that treated his word as his bond. If the Time directors weren't willing to accept his oral statement that he intended to retire in five years, then, in Ross's mind, the merger would never work. There had to be trust.

So, just when the press release was ready to go, Ross called off the merger. The disappointment on his face was unmistakable and matched only by that on the faces of Munro, Nicholas, and Levin. It was at this point that I told Ross I had a solution that might be acceptable to both sides.

A counselor has to know when to set aside legal formalities. All of us lawyers are trained to protect our clients by drawing unambiguous, air-tight contractual provisions—such as those very bylaws Time was insisting on. Still, it is just as important for us to know the limits of con-tracts, that is, to recognize the point beyond which relationships cannot be reduced to formal legal documents and must depend instead on trust between the parties. It was plain to me that we had reached that point.

With the two boards in recess, I invited Levin to my office. Writing in pencil on a legal pad, I set out a statement of the principles on man-agement succession that both sides had agreed on. I proposed to Levin that Ross would sign it as a good-faith statement of his intentions. It would be neither a formal bylaw nor a binding, legally enforceable con-tract, but it would enable Ross to maintain his pride. Levin edited my handwritten draft, I edited his changes, and within an hour we had mutually acceptable language. The letter read:

The merger is a true combination of two great companies. For either company to be looked upon as anything but an equal partner in this transaction would sap that company of its vitality and destroy the very benefits and synergy that the combination is intended to achieve. It was not a condition of the negotiations that [Ross] retire at the end of five years. . . . When [Ross] resigns as co-CEO in 1994, [Nicholas] will become sole CEO and [Ross] will remain as sole Chairman of the Board of the combined companies and will continue to have an active role and provide leadership and guidance to the businesses that he helped build.

The Time people dubbed this "the Liman letter." We agreed that only the two boards would see it so as to avoid upsetting the management of either company. Since it had no legal status, each side would have to trust the other to live by it. But there was no other choice. Even apart from Ross's objections to a bylaw provision, no active company can be governed by a binding legal contract. The boards of the two companies would have to become one, and executives would have to start thinking of themselves as Time Warner executives, not Time or Warner employees. Ross signed the Liman letter, and the Time board accepted it. Common sense had prevailed, and the merger passed.

I had never seen Ross as happy as when we announced the Time Warner merger. It was his ultimate deal. It would be tax-free; Warner's shareholders would receive a premium for their shares; because the consideration would be Time stock, no new debt would be involved; Ross would be co-CEO until he retired; and Warner would have equal representation on the new company's board. Furthermore, when Ross did retire, he could do so with pride, not because a bylaw required it.

But the terms of the deal, alas, were too good to survive. The 1980s, it must be remembered, were a time of frenzied takeover activity. No sooner would a merger be announced than a third party would enter its own bid for one of the companies involved. Investment bankers, lured by the huge fees paid in mergers, would actively solicit new players to bid for one of the companies in a proposed merger.

Both Time and Warner were well aware of this risk. By agreeing to merge, they had put themselves in play, and every investment banker *not* in on the Time Warner deal could earn a fee of $10-20 million for finding a new partner. Ross, well aware of this possibility early on, and fearing it, had set out to tie up every banker of substance with a piece of the deal. He almost succeeded. But he had only a little part of the transaction left for Morgan Stanley, and Robert Greenhill, the head of investment banking there, chose to stay on the sidelines and see what happened. When I, as Ross's emissary, told Greenhill that Ross had a role for him in the deal, he simply laughed at me.

In June 1989, while I was in the middle of the Harvard graduation ceremonies as a member of Harvard's board of overseers, my cellular telephone started ringing. It was Ross. Morgan Stanley had found a bidder for Time. Paramount, which that same week had changed its corporate name from Gulf & Western, had just announced an all-cash offer for Time, at a price of more than $50 a share above where Time's stock was then selling.

For Ross, it was like someone throwing ink at his Mona Lisa. Time's management, for their part, reacted with outrage. In a letter to Martin Davis, who had replaced Charles Bluhdorn as Paramount's CEO, Richard Munro wrote, "You've changed the name of your corporation but not its character. It's still 'engulf and devour.'" But we all knew that, with such an offer on the table, even though it was conditioned on financing, it was unlikely that Time's shareholders would approve the Warner merger.

Ross and the Time people were determined to fight back. The merger between Time and Warner had now to be restructured so as to avoid the necessity of Time shareholders' approval. The best way to accomplish this was to have Time make a tender offer to buy half of Warner's stock with cash and the rest with some type of debt security. This meant, unfortunately, that the Ross-Aboodi-Time dream of a debt-free merger had to be abandoned. In fact, the combined company—Time Warner, Inc.—would begin its new life owing a huge debt to pay for the Warner shares.

Aboodi and Levin negotiated the new terms. In one sense it was an odd negotiation. Ross hated debt because it interfered with what a company could do. He now urged that the debt securities Warner's shareholders would receive for the last 50 percent of their stock carry an even lower interest rate than what Time's own bankers recommended. This was the first time in Ross's deal-making career, needless to say, that he ever insisted on *less* for his shareholders than the other side was willing to pay! But he was already thinking in Time Warner terms, and he feared that, in the long run, massive interest costs could ruin the combined company.

As soon as the new plan was announced, Paramount sued both Time and Warner. Because, back in Bluhdorn's regime, I had represented Paramount (Gulf & Western) in the SEC matter, Paul, Weiss was disqualified from handling the litigation for Warner. Herbert Wachtell of Wachtell Lipton and Charles Richards of Richards, Layton and Finger took our place, arguing alongside Cravath Swaine and Moore for Time in Delaware's famous Court of Chancery. We prevailed there, and two weeks later, the Delaware Supreme Court gave short shrift to Paramount's attempted appeal. The deal was finally done. Time Inc. and Warner Communications, Inc. became Time Warner, Inc.

The victory came at a price, though, for Ross's fears about debt proved unfortunately sound. The perfect transaction was no longer quite so perfect, and although, in the intervening years, the merged company has performed reasonably well in operating terms, the debt that Paramount's intervention forced upon it has served as a giant undertow, pulling down the Time Warner stock price.

After the merger was consummated, Ross invited Aboodi and me and our wives, along with the Dustin Hoffmans, Barbra Streisand, Faye Dunaway, and assorted other luminaries, to celebrate with him on a cruise off the island of Sardinia on the *Klementine*, an enormous and sumptuously appointed yacht he had chartered. He had Warner Brothers duffel bags for each of his guests, stuffed with "party favors" like leather jackets, T-shirts, hats, and watches—so typical of him, for he was ever on the alert for ways to be generous. (Once he ordered bathing suits from a catalog and, while he was at it, bought six for me, in assorted colors!) One day, on the beach, we encountered a peddler selling plastic bracelets for a few cents a bracelet. Ross was intrigued, and he couldn't resist. Having just completed the largest media merger in history, there he was, on that island beach, negotiating with the peddler for a volume discount. News of the American buyer soon spread, and new peddlers showed up from all over Sardinia. Ross bargained with them, in a hodgepodge of languages and gesturings, with all the intensity and cunning I had experienced in him when he was negotiating deals involving billions of dollars. Sure enough, he ended up with thousands of bracelets at less than two cents a piece, and like the proverbial kid in the candy store, he couldn't have been more proud.

It was a grand and carefree moment—one of the last such, alas, that I spent with him. The peddlers got the best of the deal. The bracelets were worthless; my parents wouldn't even have deigned to call them *tchotchkes*. I've no idea what became of them, but I do know we had to hide them from Courtney, Steve's wife, who'd threatened to throw them overboard.

But the period following the merger was a most difficult one for Ross and his new colleagues. Not only did the "true combination of two great companies" create myriad daily problems and challenges—enough, certainly, to occupy the time and ingenuity of the most talented corporate executives—but the shadow of the debt, and the pressure it put on corporate earnings, hung over them all. Ross, Aboodi, Nicholas, and Levin pursued deal after deal, trying to reduce it, and the effort led eventually to a clash between the co-CEOs, Nicholas and Ross. Nicholas favored selling some of Time Warner's assets, including some cable franchises, to reduce the debt. Ross, a believer in cable, did not want to sell. He preferred other means of raising capital, including an ill-fated "rights" offering and, later, the sale of a minority interest in Time Warner's entertainment business to Toshiba and another Japanese company. Nicholas deferred to Ross on the rights offering, which almost brought on a shareholders' rebellion, but he remained adamantly opposed to the sale to Toshiba.

The rupture between Nicholas and Ross, inevitable though it may have been, was painful to both men. While it came about because of the Toshiba deal, it reflected the basic differences on matters of corporate policy that neither was prepared to compromise. Ross wanted Time Warner to "grow" its way out of debt, through a series of strategic alliances with international companies. Nicholas, more conservative, wanted to shrink the company to its core businesses. Gerald Levin favored the Ross policy.

More important, Ross realized that the company could not continue to function with the two co-CEOs feuding. In addition, running the combined company was less fun for him now than in the more free-wheeling days at Warner. He'd always hated confrontations, and having just emerged from the long-standing feud with Siegel, he didn't want to spend his energy on another fight. So he sent me as an emissary to Nicholas to make peace, and I took with me an extraordinary concession. I told Nicholas that if the Toshiba transaction went through, with his support, Ross would then resign as co-CEO and leave that position solely to Nicholas, remaining only as nonexecutive chairman and running an investment fund for the company. Ross would consider his work at Time Warner finished. But Nicholas either did not believe the message or was incapable of yielding on what he considered a matter of principle. He may even have thought his position was stronger than it was. He counterproposed that the decision on Toshiba be left to the board, which, he believed (wrongly), would oppose the transaction. And he turned down Ross's resignation offer.

Ironically, when Nicholas finally realized that the board supported the Toshiba transaction, he cast his own vote in favor of it, but it was too late. The relationship between the two men deteriorated even further. In February 1992, Ross proposed that Levin replace Nicholas as his co-CEO and his successor, and the board agreed.

The rest is very sad.

Back in the mid-1980s, Ross had suffered from prostatic cancer. He recovered from it and plunged back into life. The greatest single adventure of his career, the creation of Time Warner, was still in front of him. But late in 1991, the disease struck him again, and although he struggled on for a little over a year, on December 20, 1992, he finally succumbed.

Steve was buried three days later, in a private funeral, in East Hampton, Long Island. Ellen and I flew out in the cold and the rain in Warner's helicopter, as we had numerous times before to visit Steve and Courtney, and despite the proximity of Christmas, people who'd been close to Steve managed to fly in from all over the world. Perhaps a hundred of us—friends and relatives—crowded into a gallery of the Guild Hall in East Hampton for the ceremony; in this spare but elegant setting, Courtney had had hung one of Steve's favorite paintings, a spectacular, large-scale de Kooning. Although there were memorial services to follow, one in Carnegie Hall and another at the Warner Studio in California, this was the service I cherish. Quincy Jones spoke, and Steven Spielberg, with whom Ross had developed a close bond in his last years, and Beverly Sills. Steve's children spoke, as did other members of his family. Paul Simon sang "Bridge over Troubled Water," and Barbra Streisand, memorably, "Papa, Can You Hear Me?" Afterwards, at the cemetery, we were all handed long-stemmed roses to place on the casket. I spoke too, and in quoting part of what I said, I hasten to add that I do so not because I'm enamored of my own eloquence, or lack thereof, but because the words seem to me as true today as they were then.

"Steve was a giant of a man," I said,

giant in his accomplishments, giant in his vision, giant in his capacity for love, giant in his loyalty and concern toward others, giant in his energy, whether in business, on the tennis court or on the dance floor, giant in his philanthropy and giant in his generosity of spirit. He gave more to every friendship than he took. He made all of us feel important and good. He was a man from whom you sought advice on your own troubles, not one who burdened you with his. When Steve asked you how you were, it was not polite conversation but genuine interest. He considered nothing impossible. He inspired us to perform beyond the limits of our abilities and made us better than we were.

I cannot imagine him at rest. I only hope, therefore, that you, Dear God, have plenty of yellow pads and pencils, for if you do and can understand his math, Steve will show you how to make heaven a better place, as he did every institution he touched.

I concluded, then as now, "Steve ended all of his letters with the words, 'much love.' With that understated emotion, on behalf of all of us, I bid you good-bye, dearest friend."

———

The statement of principles that Levin and I had drafted, that day in my office, worked.

On Ross's death, Levin became Time Warner's sole CEO. Ross kept his word: a Time executive would run the company after him.

Paul, Weiss continued to represent Time Warner, along with Cravath Swain and Moore, but I faded out of the relationship. It was best for the company and me, once Steve was gone, because that relationship—founded on independence and mutual experience and that special kind of brotherly give-and-take I've tried to describe—could not be transferred to Levin. One day, when I urged him to delay slightly putting new directors on the board to replace Ross appointees, he asked me, in all earnestness, whom I thought I represented, Ross or the company. I told him the question had never come up with Ross, because Ross had expected me to advise on what was best for the company, even when I knew it was something he didn't want.

It was time. I knew it at that moment. My last advice to Levin was to suggest, with equal earnestness, that he get his own Arthur Liman.

Keeping the Eye was Bill Paley's Prize

No ACCOUNT OF people with whom I have played the counselor's role would be complete without William S. Paley, the legendary founder and longtime leader of CBS. Even though he was eighty-three years old when I met him, he still had a boyish grin and mischievous eyes. Clearly, he was up to mischief when he called me in the spring of 1985.

At the time, Paley was still CBS's largest single shareholder, with some 8 percent of the outstanding shares, but he had been forced to step down as chairman of the board in 1983 and was left with only the vague title of founder chairman. His replacement was Thomas H. Wyman, whom Paley had himself installed as president of CBS in 1980.

Paley's call to me came shortly after Ted Turner, the head of Turner Broadcasting, announced in April, after weeks of rumors, that he was seeking control of CBS by offering to buy two-thirds of its stock. Turner was offering CBS shareholders a package of securities in exchange, which he claimed was worth $175 a share, almost double CBS's then-current price. Paley hated to see his company, which he had built from a tiny network of radio stations in 1928 into a billion-dollar news and entertainment company, go up for grabs.

CBS vowed to fight off Turner's bid. In July, it announced that it would borrow almost $1 billion in order to buy back 20 percent of the outstanding shares at $150 a share, creating a premium of $32 a share over the market price. Faced with Turner's offer and the CBS stock buyback plan, Paley needed independent advice. His regular lawyers, because they represented the company as well as Paley, had been obliged to step aside.

We met in Paley's lavish Fifth Avenue apartment overlooking Central Park. By that time, I'd represented many wealthy and powerful clients, but Paley's apartment was absolutely stunning. It was filled with valuable antique furniture and his truly magnificent art collection; started in the 1930s, it now included paintings, sculptures, prints, and drawings by Cézanne, Dégas, Gauguin, Matisse, Picasso, Renoir, and many other masters. One of the first sights one saw on entering was Picasso's *Boy Leading a Horse*. Having grown up myself in a home where the living room furniture was covered with plastic, I felt whenever I was at Paley's apartment as if I were visiting the royal apartments at Windsor Castle.

Paley said that as much as he admired Ted Turner's daring, he wanted CBS to remain independent and so supported the board's effort to fend off Turner's bid. The buyback plan, though, presented him with a unique problem. He had acquired his own CBS stock for pennies. If he sold 20 percent of it back to the company now, at $150 a share, he would make a whopping profit, which the government would tax as a capital gain. My first task for Paley, then, was to negotiate an agreement with CBS that would allow him up to ten years to sell back his stock under the buyback arrangement. Paley, typically, had only one question later when I explained it to him. Ever the optimist, he wanted to know why I'd limited the selling period to only ten years. What on earth was he going to do when he was ninety-five?

As it turned out, though, he had much more on his mind, that afternoon in 1985, than just his personal finances. He confided that he was growing more and more unhappy with Wyman's leadership. Though Paley had personally selected Wyman just five years before, he said he'd quickly lost confidence in the man. For one thing, the network was clearly in trouble. Its entertainment programming was sagging in the ratings, and many of its shows were aging hits like *Dallas*. Its TV stations' profits lagged behind those of the other networks. Furthermore, Wyman's strategy of diversifying CBS into other businesses like publishing and toys was failing, and to top it off, he complained, Wyman had no flair for the news or entertainment business. He was a professional manager who'd spent years at Polaroid and then at various food companies like Green Giant and Pillsbury. For all his refined tastes in art, Paley himself was a born showman, with an undeniable and intuitive grasp of how to entertain and inform the public. He was also a perfectionist. When he donated a park to New York City to honor his father—the pocket-sized Paley Park, just east of Fifth Avenue on Fifty-third Street—he even chose the hot dogs for the concession stand. He tasted dozens of different varieties and finally asked Sabrett to manufacture a special one, slightly fatter than average. In addition, he developed the cooking method: the hot dog was steamed first, then grilled, and served on a toasted and lightly buttered roll.

Above all, though, Paley loved the details of programming. He spent hours watching his network's shows—except those with high ratings, which didn't need his help—and talking about scheduling, or the development of characters in certain shows, or new shows the network had in the works. His closest relationships at CBS were with the programming executives. When Wyman took over, though, he'd stopped asking Paley for his advice and had made a point of keeping him away from people in the network's news and entertainment hierarchy.

CBS succeeded in fending off Turner, but Paley was nervous about its future. To buy back its stock, CBS was taking on millions of dollars in debt. Paley worried that the company, his company, was undervalued and poorly run and would remain a takeover target unless a new management team was brought in. He wanted to assemble a group of his billionaire friends to do a leveraged buyout (LBO) of CBS and restore him as chairman. He recalled that, in 1968, he and several other wealthy art collectors had formed a syndicate, each putting up $1 million, to buy Gertrude Stein's collection of thirty-eight postimpressionist paintings, most of them by Picasso, and now, on a larger scale, he wanted to do the same thing with CBS.

Skeptical though I may have been at first, I sat with Paley in the coming months as, one by one, a parade of investment bankers he'd summoned gave him advice on whether he could organize such a group of investors to purchase CBS. Many of them were his friends, yet none took him seriously. They all advised him that his plan was hopeless. I, on the contrary, began to take Paley seriously. Despite his years, he had an indomitable will, and I became convinced he would keep trying until he found a way to replace Wyman. At the same time, I made it clear to him that, in my view, the bankers were right: he had no chance of organizing a buyout on his own. Even if a group of investors could be found, they would insist on a much younger figure in the entertainment industry, such as Barry Diller, to run the company.

But Paley persisted. What if he could persuade the CBS board to oust Wyman—wouldn't the board have to make him chairman again?

I had to say no. The board, I told Paley, might give him back his old title, but it was not going to oust Wyman and install Paley alone in his place to run the company.

———

There was a solution to Paley's hopes and aspirations, but it came, as far as he was concerned, from an unexpected quarter. That July of 1985, when CBS announced its stock buyback plan, Laurence A. Tisch, through the company he heads, the Loews Corporation, had begun buying CBS and quickly accumulated 5 percent of the outstanding shares. Although Tisch phoned Tom Wyman at that time and told him he had no plans to seek control, he continued to buy CBS stock, and by the fall Loews had replaced Paley as the single largest shareholder, with some 12 percent of the shares. Then, in October 1985, CBS invited Tisch to join its board.

Tisch and his younger brother, Bob, had started in the hotel business after World War II and had gone on to acquire Loews, which owned real estate, MGM, and a chain of movie theaters, then the Lorillard Corporation, a large tobacco company, and the CNA insurance company. As shrewd an investor as Larry Tisch was—and he and Bob had accumulated enormous wealth over the years—he had an even greater talent for setting struggling companies back on their feet. Judge Rifkind had represented Loews for years, and Larry and his wife, Billie, and I were close friends. Larry and I often ate lunch on Saturdays. Although I had misgivings about it, and although I'd sworn to myself after the Ross-Siegel fiasco that my days as a matchmaker were over, within a few days of Larry's acceptance of CBS's offer to join its board, I arranged for him and Paley to meet.

I was unsure at first whether the two men could get along. They were an odd pair. Tisch, for all his wealth, led a quiet, comparatively modest life and worked out of an unpretentious office at 666 Fifth Avenue. Paley had a sumptuous and elegant lifestyle, at home and at work. CBS's headquarters, a black granite modernist skyscraper on the Avenue of the Americas known as Black Rock, was designed at Paley's direction by Eero Saarinen, and Paley's office on the thirty-fifth floor was richly paneled and filled with antiques, among them a beautiful, circular nineteenth-century chemin-de-fer table inlaid with pearl numerals that he used as a desk, and more of his art collection, including paintings by Rouault, Picasso, and Franz Kline. Paley liked to say that more money was wagered on programming at that table in his office than had been wagered in all its years in the casino. Tisch is a devout Jew, and a very substantial backer of Jewish philanthropies. Paley, though the son of a Russian Jewish cigar manufacturer, was often accused, however unfairly, of repudiating his Jewishness. Tisch was a brilliant, hard-nosed investor; Paley, although he could be ruthless, was a romantic at heart. Tisch was a private man who surrounded himself with family and a close circle of old friends. Paley had been on stage for more than fifty years, ever since he founded CBS.

One afternoon in November, I accompanied Larry and Billie to Paley's apartment. To my vast relief, the two men hit it off immediately. Tisch was forceful and direct. As much as he respected CBS's tradition and its independence, he told Paley he believed the company was adrift and not achieving its potential. At the same time, he flattered Paley by encouraging him to speak candidly about CBS's management, its programming, and its prospects for the future. He listened attentively. Wary of Paley's dominance, Wyman had always treated him like a fossil, but Paley now had someone who thought his views, especially about programming, were important. By the end of the meeting, Paley was even using the few Yiddish phrases he had at his command. Telling Tisch about how Teddy Kollek, the mayor of Jerusalem, had convinced him to build an art museum in Israel, Paley described Kollek as the best *schnorrer* he'd ever known.

In the months after that first meeting, Paley and Tisch continued talking, sometimes face to face but often using me as an intermediary.

Cautious as I might have been before, I began to see that, despite their considerable personal differences, they shared two fundamental goals. Both were firmly resolved that CBS not be sold, and both were deeply unhappy with Wyman.

At the same time, I also began to see how each could help the other.

To begin with, Loews continued to accumulate CBS stock, announcing in August 1986 that it owned 24.9 percent of the shares. With Paley's 8 percent and the support of some lesser investors, the two owned enough to block anyone else from acquiring CBS, since a merger under the law now required approval of two-thirds of the outstanding shares. In addition, they could now present the board with a practicable alternative to Wyman—Tisch was fully capable of overseeing the company's day-to-day operations as president, and Paley could resume his position as chairman. Arriving with Paley's blessing, Tisch would be regarded as a legitimate heir to the CBS tradition, not as some corporate raider.

At first, Wyman had welcomed Tisch's investment in CBS. Tisch had said in the beginning that he was not seeking control of the company, and he'd repeated that statement several times. Wyman took Tisch to mean that he was content to be a passive and supportive investor, even as Tisch's ownership of CBS continued to grow. But Wyman never understood Tisch, and he missed one salient fact. Loews is a publicly traded company, and Tisch owed a fiduciary duty to his shareholders. He could support Wyman only if CBS prospered. CBS's continued decline in the ratings and the continued failure of Wyman's efforts at diversification made it inevitable that Tisch and Paley would join to oust him.

By early 1986, Tisch had lost confidence in Wyman and thought he should be replaced, and by May, Wyman had decided that Tisch was his enemy, someone trying to gain control of CBS without paying a premium. Wyman, together with several friendly board members, tried to persuade Tisch to sign a standstill agreement promising not to buy more than 25 percent of CBS stock. Tisch refused. He was insulted by the request, having already given his word not to. Then, at a stormy board meeting in July, it came out that the company's results were falling well short of its own projections. Meanwhile, Wyman had begun looking on his own for a friendly buyer.

The pivotal confrontation finally came in September 1986. The night before their scheduled board meeting of Wednesday the tenth, CBS's outside directors held a dinner meeting in a private room at the Ritz-Carlton. Neither Wyman nor Tisch was present. Paley asked me to come with him. Although the main topic of the dinner was CBS's independence, it became quickly apparent that at least some of the directors wanted to find out whether Paley could be persuaded to support the sale of the company to an outside merger partner. Paley told the directors that he preferred that CBS stay independent with a principal shareholder such as Tisch, rather than go the way of NBC and ABC, which had been taken over by General Electric and Capital Cities. Some of the directors worried out loud that their fiduciary duty to the shareholders might require them to put the company up for sale. I argued that the combined size of Tisch's stake and Paley's eliminated the option of selling the company and so they had no fiduciary duty to try. Sam Butler of Cravath, CBS's outside counsel, agreed with me. But privately, I told the directors that Paley was adamant and that selling CBS wasn't an option.

The next day, at 9:00 A.M., the full board met on the thirty-fifth floor of Black Rock and didn't adjourn until after six o'clock that evening. Included in their number were Michel Bergerac, formerly of Revlon; Harold Brown, formerly secretary of defense; Walter Cronkite, the only CBS member besides Wyman; Roswell Gilpatric; Newton Minow, ex-chairman of the FCC; Franklin Thomas of the Ford Foundation; and Marietta Tree.

I attended as Paley's counsel, and I heard Tom Wyman address the board, asking them to support him in selling the company. In fact, he disclosed, he was already holding secret preliminary negotiations with Coca-Cola.

Some of the directors had to have known this was coming, but the news stunned others. Among them were Tisch and Paley. Rumors had abounded in recent weeks—Phillip Morris and Disney among them—but neither Tisch nor Paley had known anything about discussions with Coca-Cola, and both were incensed. Both refused categorically to sell. Tisch then moved formally to remove Wyman as president and chairman and to affirm that CBS was not for sale, a position that Paley supported.

The board asked Wyman to leave the room.

It adopted the Tisch-Paley motion. Tisch and Paley then proposed a joint arrangement under which Tisch would replace Wyman as president and CEO and Paley would resume his position as chairman. Both appointments, however, would be temporary. A search committee would be named to look for a permanent president with an entertainment industry background.

The board then asked Tisch and Paley and me to leave.

We huddled in Paley's office, around his beloved chemin-de-fer table. All we knew was that Wyman was out—he was gone from the building that same day—but there was no predicting what the board members might decide about the company's future.

After a while, a delegation arrived from the board with the results of its deliberations. The board had agreed to make Tisch temporary president and CEO, but it refused to name Paley chairman. Whether this decision came about because some of the members already felt remorse about firing Wyman, or blamed Paley for having brought on the crisis or for other grievances and concerns, old or new, I couldn't say. But I saw the hurt and the anger on Paley's countenance, and I wasn't prepared to let it happen.

We didn't even have to dismiss the delegation. A man of his word, Tisch said he would never allow the board to humiliate Paley. Instead, he insisted that Paley be made temporary chairman. Otherwise, the company would be thrown into chaos.

But anyone who knew Larry Tisch would have realized that such a warning was entirely unnecessary.

I don't think Paley ever fully accepted the fact that, although he'd won back his title as chairman of the board, the company was no longer his to run. Unlike Wyman, however, Tisch consulted frequently with him and especially about programming. Tisch deferred to Paley, for example, when Paley initially opposed the sale of CBS Records. Acquired by Paley in 1938 for $700,000, the record company now posted profits of $75 million. CBS Records was eventually sold to Sony, but by then it was with Paley's support. Key figures in CBS's programming and news divisions once again called on Paley for advice and treated him with respect. Paley retained until the end his love of programming and his attention to detail. He called me many times to ask me to convey messages to Larry Tisch that the camera angle on such and such an anchor person was not right or that some other detail was wrong. He also was constantly suggesting changes in the programming lineup, although few of his ideas were in fact adopted. Tisch came under a great deal of fire as he led CBS through a period of divestiture and cost-cutting, but the company's balance sheet took on a much healthier look, and eventually CBS stock soared on Wall Street. The company was later sold to Westinghouse, but not until several years after Paley died.

Paley and I became good friends. After the palace revolution at CBS, he asked me to join the board of the William Paley Foundation, which, after his death, would receive the bulk of his estate, and much of his last four years were devoted to another obsession—a museum to gather the artifacts of broadcasting and give them the status already accorded to theater and film. The Museum of Broadcasting had first opened in 1976 in a small building on Fifty-third Street but had quickly outgrown the space. In 1986 Paley bought a new site, on Fifty-second Street, and began raising money to build a new and larger building. He hired Philip Johnson to design it, and as he had thirty years earlier with Black Rock, he spent countless hours working with Johnson, even debating the location of the restrooms and the choice of faucets for the sinks. Paley's new museum— now called the Museum of Television and Radio—opened in September 1991, a year after his death, in a beautiful and dignified limestone tower.

In February 1988, a little over a year after he was restored as chairman, Paley became gravely ill, and his doctors were sure he wouldn't live through the week. He summoned me to his sprawling suite at New York Hospital—the Niarchos suite. Propped up in his hospital bed, with tubes running everywhere, he asked me to come close enough to hear his words. I expected some last instructions. Instead, Bill, whose eyesight was impaired by glaucoma, whispered in my ear that he knew he wasn't actually in the Niarchos suite because the room was filled with cheap reproduction furniture, not the original eighteenth-century antiques!

Just as I was leaving, I bumped into Paley's doctor and told him what his patient had said. He seemed to be hallucinating, I reported. Not at all, the doctor said. Just a month before, he explained, the hospital had thrown out the old junk furniture in the suite and replaced it with brand-new chairs.

At that point, I was convinced Paley would recover. He had no intention of dying in anyplace so commonly and poorly furnished. Sure enough, after a month in the hospital, he returned home and resumed his active social and business schedule. When he died, in October 1990, it was in his own apartment, surrounded by his priceless art collection.

III

Public Service

As Natural as Breathing

I WAS BORN just three days before Franklin D. Roosevelt was elected to his first term as president, and I have been a Democrat all my life. Except for Eisenhower in the 1950s, a Democrat was in the White House until I was thirty-six years old, and we Democrats thought of Eisenhower as a fluke, in that he won election less as a Republican than as a war hero. So, when I left the U.S. Attorney's Office in late 1963 and returned to Paul, Weiss, I was sure that after a few years in private practice I would leave again for stints of public service, most likely with a Democratic administration in Washington.

It didn't turn out that way. Nixon was elected in 1968, and again in 1972. Jimmy Carter won in 1976, but he brought his own people with him from Georgia. Early in the Carter presidency, I met with Griffin Bell, the Georgia lawyer whom Carter made his Attorney General, to talk about a position in the Justice Department. Nothing came of it, though, possibly because we didn't understand each other. Bell's thick southern accent was impenetrable to me, and he probably found my New York accent equally tough. Four years later, in 1980, there was some talk that President Carter might appoint me to be the U.S. Attorney for the Southern District of New York, Morgenthau's old job. It was a job I wanted, but only a few months were left in Carter's presidency, and I was skeptical about his chances of reelection. I didn't want to take it on only to be forced out before I was able to get anything done. Besides, I thought a Democrat would be back in the White House soon enough.

After Carter, of course, came twelve years of Republicans in the White House, first Ronald Reagan and then George Bush. In the federal government run by Reagan and Bush, there was no place whatsoever for a liberal Democrat from New York.

My public service, then, has turned out to be very different from the model of the lawyer-statesman like Dean Acheson, whom I so admired in law school and who moved easily from private practice to the federal government and back again. Instead of high government office or the federal bench, my work has largely been done from outside of government, either prodding government to meet its obligations of fairness or advising government officials on how to reform and improve the criminal justice system—or even, as in the R-46 case I'll describe later, defending government in court. But I also served as the chair for the Commission on Mayoral Appointments for New York City's former mayor, David Dinkins, an experience that convinced me more than ever that affirmative action, used fairly and well, can help overcome decades of exclusion. First formed by Ed Koch to protect him from the pressure of friends and political allies seeking jobs, the commission was used by Dinkins to serve as a talent scout for talented racial and ethnic minorities. By aggressively scouting for qualified candidates from all of New York's minority communities, we were able to introduce fresh faces into city government, particularly into its regulatory commissions.

I have represented the poor and disadvantaged too, as founding chairman of a public-interest law firm, the Legal Action Center (a twenty-five year affiliation), and later as president of the Legal Aid Society in New York City. Most recently, I have served as chair of the Capital Defender Office in New York.

My most challenging stints of public service have been the several independent investigations I was asked to conduct. They were very different—from Attica in 1971 to the alleged cover-ups of police violence by the New York City medical examiner's office in 1985, to the Iran-Contra investigation in 1987. Yet each involved the same fundamental task. In each instance, government officials and institutions, either through ineptitude or deceit, had lost the trust of the governed.

Younger lawyers sometimes tell me that lawyers of my generation had more chances to do worthy public service. I don't agree. Opportunities abound today, and in addition, there is always a huge demand for pro bono work. History tells us that no invisible hand looks after the disadvantaged and the persecuted. Laissez-faire theories were correctly discredited in the first part of this century, and we hardly need another depression or fires in our ghettos to teach us that they're no more valid today. Young lawyers took trains and buses to Washington to protest the Vietnam War. They went into the deep South to register voters. Where have they been in more recent years, when, quite clearly and in so many ways, the pendulum of justice has swung toward law enforcement and away from civil liberties, and when government budgets to help the have-nots of our society have been slashed?

I can't speak for other firms, but our commitment at Paul, Weiss to public service and pro bono cases has never been a subject of debate. On the pro bono side, we've handled civil rights and criminal cases, and we've been leaders in representing death row inmates in habeas corpus petitions. In two such cases, we've won the defendants new trials.

Our boldest pro bono assignment came when we agreed to take on the docket of cases brought by prisoners in the U.S. district court in Manhattan—cases in which the prisoners were complaining of violations of their constitutional rights by the correctional institutions where they were incarcerated. Most of the complaints were handwritten and hard to understand, but the federal judges often detected in them descriptions of behavior on the part of correction officials that disturbed them, and as a result, they sought law firms to handle the complaints. We decided to take them all. In one case, a Black Muslim minister was shunted from prison to prison because he was seen as an agitator. He was virtually serving his time in shackles on buses between prisons. In another, an inmate was unlawfully denied the right to wear religious beads. Still others complained of inadequate medical treatment. The lion's share of the work in these cases was done by Paul, Weiss associates, under partner supervision, and they took them on with zeal, honing their skills and achieving some spectacular victories, including the case of the Black Muslim minister.

Much of the work that has to be done, though, in the public-service sector is unglamorous, time-consuming, and underpublicized. Some years ago, for instance, I was on a committee that commented on new legislation passed by the New York State Legislature and waited for the governor's approval or veto. Most of the bills were obscure and little noticed, though there was one that would have made the toll collectors on the Triboro Bridge peace officers and thus authorized them to carry guns.

Public service also has its risks. It often brings criticism, sometimes from a lawyer's own clients. But if we care about society, we must be willing to take those risks. Public service, in my view, is a lawyer's privilege, one of the rewards of the profession. It is not an act of duty or charity. For a lawyer, public service is as natural as breathing. It is what we do when we're at our best.

1 2

The Attica Uprising: Investigation and Implications

On Christmas Day 1971, three months after forty-three men died at the Attica Correctional Facility, I marched into the Attica mess hall with five hundred maximum-security inmates and ate Christmas dinner with a plastic spoon. We sat at metal tables on metal stools bolted to the floor. Talking was forbidden. Overhead, guards with tear-gas guns watched us eat. We had been given plastic spoons only, no forks or knives. The only noises were the spoons scraping on the plates and men chewing.

I was there for the special commission investigating the events of those bloody September days and why they happened. On September 9, during a riot, three inmates and a guard had been killed. Inmates soon seized forty hostages and took over an outside exercise yard called D yard. The governor, Nelson Rockefeller, wanted to retake Attica by force, but his corrections commissioner hoped to avoid bloodshed through negotiations, and so Rockefeller waited. Negotiations went on for four tense days, with observers like Tom Wicker of the *New York Times* serving as intermediaries. But when the inmates demanded that Rockefeller come personally to Attica, the governor refused, and the negotiating ended. On Monday morning, September 13, Rockefeller ordered the state police to retake the prison.

The assault was a catastrophe. It was led by state police troopers, some with rifles, others with shotguns. They were joined by angry Attica prison guards. The inmates had no guns, and a helicopter dropped tear gas into D yard just before the assault. Seeing inmates making what they took to be hostile gestures toward the hostages, sharpshooters with rifles began shooting, and then others, firing buckshot from shotguns, began a sustained barrage. Six minutes later, when the shooting stopped, nine hostages and twenty-six inmates were dead, and another hostage and three inmates died in the next few days. More than eighty others were seriously wounded. Save for the Wounded Knee massacre, the assault at Attica was the bloodiest one-day encounter between Americans since the Civil War.

State officials claimed that inmates executed the hostages by cutting their throats, and that one hostage was castrated. Those were short-lived lies. Autopsies proved that no hostage had been killed by knife wounds. None were castrated or mutilated. All were killed by bullets or buckshot. Prison officials, the state police, and, above all, Rockefeller lost all credibility.

Someone had to investigate what had happened, but the public would mistrust any investigation conducted by the state. Rockefeller therefore called for an independent fact-finding commission, chosen by New York's senior judges, and promised it full access to the prison and all the inmates. The judges picked nine members, none with any official ties to the state government. Officially, it was called the New York State Special Commission on Attica, but soon it became just the McKay Commission, after its chair, Robert P. McKay. McKay was dean of the New York University Law School, a Quaker, and a man of unbending principle. He asked me to serve as his chief counsel, and I accepted. The bishop of the Roman Catholic Diocese of Albany was a member of the commission, and so was Burke Marshall, the Yale Law School professor who had run the Civil Rights Division of the Justice Department under Kennedy. All the members, save one, had one thing in common—none had ever been inside a prison or knew anything about prison life. The sole exception was Amos Henix, who had done time in prison and now ran Reality House, a drug rehabilitation program.

To explain what happened at Attica, we would need to persuade the inmates to talk to us freely, not only about the rebellion but about prison life. In the beginning, most inmates were highly, and understandably, skeptical of the commission, so when I learned that no outsider had ever eaten in the mess hall with inmates, I thought that might be one good way to gain acceptance. I asked permission. Prison officials refused. They feared that inmates would seize us as hostages and that they would be held responsible. They relented only after we promised, in writing, not to sue if we were killed or injured.

Dean McKay himself joined me that Christmas Day. Along with the inmates, we were lined up outside the mess hall in single file, by height, and now, inside the mess hall, we sat silently eating the tasteless prison food.

After a few minutes, I could keep still no longer. Turning to the man next to me, I asked him whether this was a typical meal in Attica, and we began to talk. Seeing us talking, several guards moved to silence us or throw me out. As they came nearer, a few inmates started to bang their hands and their spoons on the table, and others picked it up, and soon the whole mess hall was chanting, "Let the man alone. Let the man alone."

The guards backed off, and I suddenly began to hope that we might actually be able to learn what had happened at Attica.

Judge Rifkind had advised me not to take the Attica assignment. Attica polarized people, he said; everyone sided automatically either with the inmates or with Rockefeller. No matter what we reported, Rifkind believed, it would just confirm people's preconceptions, and nothing would be gained. His advice was sobering, but I didn't follow it. I think I sensed how fed up the public was with government institutions. I felt then— as I do now—that the most corrosive threat to democracy is cynicism and resignation. I hoped that an honest, independent, and credible account of what had happened at Attica might not only improve prison conditions but also mend, in a small way, the public's fraying trust in its government.

Some, I'm sure, regarded me as a liberal Pollyanna, but I looked to the Triangle Shirtwaist fire as a hopeful precedent. In 1911, 141 people, mostly young girls, died when a fire spread through the Triangle Shirt-waist Company's crowded workshop on several high floors of a building in New York. Exits were inadequate, and the doors to many locked. Dozens of terrified girls were crushed to death; others suffocated in the heavy smoke; still others leaped to their deaths. The horror of the fire led to a statewide investigating commission—its members included Robert J. Wagner, then a state legislator, and Bob Morgenthau's grand-father—that exposed the lethal conditions in the New York sweatshops and stirred a public outcry that led the way to reform.

What I didn't expect when I joined the investigation—what I surely could not have been prepared for—was what I would see and hear at Attica about institutionalized racism, degradation, and inhumanity. Nor did I anticipate how its searing effect would stay with me forever.

The commission resolved to finish its report in just one year. It was a daunting task. Maximum-security prisons are forbidding institutions—closed, mysterious, and dangerous. They are usually built far from cities, and Attica was no exception. The bureaucrats who run them mistrust out-siders. The McKay Commission was the first group of outsiders to study an American maximum-security prison from the inside.

In addition, there were thousands of witnesses to the events of those terrible September days, and from the outset, I vowed that we would talk to each and every one of them. The result was more than 3,000 interviews—2,000 inmates who'd been at Attica, 450 prison guards, 550 state troopers, 200 National Guard soldiers called in after the assault, the observers, and others. And not a one of them wanted to talk to us. The inmates naturally were suspicious that we wanted to protect the prison officials and the governor. Guards and state troopers regarded us as liberal do-gooders. Meanwhile, the governor himself appointed a special prosecutor to investigate crimes that might have been commit-ted during the uprising. Already reluctant to talk freely to us, inmates and even the guards and state troopers now had to worry that what they told us might be used to convict them of crimes. In addition, most of the witnesses were now spread across the state, including many of the inmates, who had been transferred to other prisons.

I visited Attica for the first time in late November 1971, along with the full commission. It was a raw and overcast day. The road to Attica from Rochester, New York, passed through rolling fields and grim small towns. Suddenly, in the distance, rising above the land, was the Gothic hulk of the prison, which had been built in 1931.

Though I'd prosecuted men who'd gone to prison, I had never actually been inside one until that day. The Attica superintendent, Vincent Mancusi, took us on a tour. He showed us the tunnel leading to A block, where the riot had begun, and D yard, where the inmates had held the hostages and where the assault took place. We didn't ask to tour the cells, thinking that, given our numbers, it would be too much like visiting a zoo and observing animals in cages. Mancusi showed us the gate at "Times Square"—Attica's strategic center where the tunnels connecting the A, B, C, and D cell blocks intersected—the same gate that had given way when a cracked bolt snapped and where William Quinn, who was guarding the gate, was killed.

"One good thing that's come out of the events," Mancusi commented, "is that all the prisons have reexamined their gates." I found the observation astonishing, the more so since, even on that first visit, it was obvious that gates and walls, no matter how strong, cannot forever contain angry and desperate men. All over Attica I saw iron bars severed with acetylene torches, heavy metal gates knocked down with forklifts, and smashed windows. Confronted by a mass of unarmed inmates, the prison's security had collapsed in an instant. Yet the principal lesson the superintendent appeared to have derived from this explosive rage was that the locks on the gates had come from the factory with a defect in their casting. In that moment, even before our investigation had started, I think we had a vision of what had gone wrong at Attica.

My first task was to assemble a staff. I needed able lawyers with investigative experience, willing to interrupt their careers to work day and night under sometimes difficult conditions. That was the easy part. I also wanted African American and Hispanic lawyers on the staff, to help ensure that the entire community would have confidence in our findings and recommendations. Fortunately, that too was easier than I'd feared. We recruited Milton Williams, a black lawyer who later became an appeals court judge in New York, and Charles Willis, a black lawyer and a former police officer from Rochester, and a former judge who ran our office in Rochester near Attica. I also found two exceptional Hispanic lawyers, Oscar Garcia-Rivera and Robert Sackett, who is also now a judge.

I had, surprisingly, a more difficult time at the law schools, where I hoped to recruit volunteers to help us with the thousands of interviews. Students innately mistrust authority, and during the Vietnam War this mistrust grew exponentially. One day I met with skeptical members of the Black Law Students Association at Yale. I made a point of telling them that the commission included Burke Marshall. Describing the investigation, I used words like *pragmatic* and *objective* and *impartial*. I assured them that the investigation would not be a whitewash and told them that if they did not believe me, they should join our staff and see for themselves. Later the friend who'd arranged the meeting gently told me that everything I'd said was wrong. He said the students regarded Burke Marshall—who had become general counsel of IBM after leaving the Justice Department—as a sellout, and they'd mistrusted my moderate language. In the end, somehow, maybe as a result of my assurances, we recruited four of them as part-time interviewers, including Harlon Dalton, who later became a professor at Yale Law School.

The Attica investigation was especially difficult for the black and Hispanic lawyers on my staff. Attica is located in a small, white, rural town in upstate New York. They faced serious and ugly racism both inside and outside the prison walls. Even more troubling, at least for some, was that they'd grown up on the same streets and gone to the same schools as some of the inmates. Why had they managed to emerge from the poverty, drugs, and violence of the ghetto that had claimed the inmates' lives? Now that they had escaped, what responsibility did they owe to those left behind?

One day I visited Attica with several of the black law students. Most wore jackets and ties, but one had on a turtleneck sweater and a Muslim pendant. As we walked through the prison, the inmates gave him Black Power salutes and quietly called him "soul brother," but inside the interview room it was a different story. The inmates were among the most politically sophisticated people I have ever met. Sizing up the earnest and naive law student in the turtleneck sweater, they shrewdly concluded that he was not going to be able to change or influence how the elites who controlled the state's coffers treated them. Students dressed in vests and ties, who looked like they were headed for Wall Street firms, got more respect, and their interviews were more successful.

We also had several women on the staff, and they too had difficulties, especially in the beginning. I guessed that some inmates might talk more openly to a woman interviewer than to a man, but the prison officials at first refused to let a woman be alone with an inmate. If many of the guards assumed that the men on the commission staff would be raped by inmates during interviews, many more were positive that women staffers would be attacked. But we insisted, and we never had a single incident.

Women did create a controversy within our staff, however. Whenever we were at Attica, we ate at a private club near the prison called the Batavia Club. The Batavia Club had only recently permitted blacks and women to enter, and it still forbade women to stand at the bar. They could sit at tables but not drink at the bar. One night the Yale students, all men, announced that we shouldn't patronize a club that discriminated against women. At the time, I was enjoying a steak dinner with our two female secretaries. Both said the club's rule didn't bother them, and they kept eating. Jokingly, I said that I was a man of modest goals: reforming the state's prisons was enough for me, without also toppling sexual barriers at the Batavia Club. Besides, I pointed out, the private dining room was a comfortable place to talk without being overheard. But this was 1972, and the students were inflamed with principle. To them, I was an appeaser who lacked convictions. I relented finally, and the next evening dinner was sandwiches in our cramped office across the street from the Batavia Club. The sandwiches were tasteless and cost more than dinner at the club, and the two secretaries, I noticed, in whose name but without whose support the men had vetoed the Batavia Club, wound up as waitresses for the students, pouring coffee and cleaning up when they were done.

Gaining the confidence of the inmates and the guards was our most important task, and the toughest. Each group mistrusted us, though for different reasons, and each was quick to see evidence of bias and favoritism. Reports of the most innocuous gestures—saying hello to a guard in front of an inmate, or to an inmate in front of a guard—spread swiftly through the ranks of either side as proof of the commission's bias.

The last thing I wanted was for the guards to regard us as naive, opinionated do-gooders who sided automatically with the inmates. If that was their perception, neither they nor the state troopers would ever speak honestly to us. Besides, I sympathized with the guards. They were in many ways prisoners too, trapped in the same brutal institution. In rural western New York, the job at Attica for most of them was one of the few jobs available. Many had wanted to join the state police and took jobs at Attica only because the state police had no openings. Others were the second and third generation in their families to hold the job. They were all white, and the inmates were almost all black or Hispanic, and nearly all from the New York City area. The keepers and the kept shared nothing in common, and there was no communication or rapport between them. One inmate told me about a prison guard, a decent man bothered by prison conditions, who tried vainly to strike up some small talk with him. All the guard could think to talk about was fly fishing, which was something the inmate from New York City could not even picture, let alone talk about.

We spent hours trying to convince the prison guards that we were fair and impartial. With some, we struck out. They saw us as downstate liberal—some Jewish—lawyers. Others, however, confided in us, and we got inside the minds of men who held one of society's worst jobs.

The inmates were even more wary of us. They feared that what they told us would be used to prosecute them and other inmates. Beyond that, they doubted that a group of educated lawyers, members of the establishment, no matter how sympathetic, could truly understand life in Attica or do anything to make it better.

To begin with, we assured them that whatever they told us about what happened during the riot would remain confidential, that we would never turn them over to the special prosecutor. As to their other concerns, we told them they would have to trust us, and gradually, I think we did win their trust. Predictably, the leaders of the uprising were the least cooperative. Militant and suspicious, isolated in segregation, aware that they were particular targets of the special prosecutor, most of them refused to talk to us. Many worried too that if they spoke to us, the others would think they were snitching.

Early on we met with several groups of inmates. Predictably, prison officials were reluctant to let this happen. Prison rules forbade large gatherings, and the officials were particularly fearful of any meeting of inmates who'd taken part in the uprising. But we insisted. At one meeting, in A block, I spoke with an inmate named Richard X Clark, also called Brother Richard. Clark was a Navy veteran and a drug abuser. He had joined the Nation of Islam at Auburn, another state prison, and was moved to Attica because he was regarded as a revolutionary. In D yard, Clark emerged as a leader. Clark told me that he arranged to observe, in November, the Islamic holiday of Ramadan—the month-long period when only one meal a day is permitted and must be eaten before dark. Then he'd learned that the Nation of Islam actually observes Ramadan in December, but now the guards refused to let him observe Ramadan a second time. When I spoke to the Attica superintendent later, he readily agreed to let Clark observe the holiday again, but this was another example, a small one among many, of how the keepers and the kept at Attica couldn't talk to each other.

In addition to the details of the events of those four days in September, the commission wanted to learn about life inside Attica. We heard the same story over and over, one that few people outside prison had ever heard, or ever listened to if they did hear it. The inmates maintained that the prison guards consistently degraded them and humiliated them, often in small ways, and made them feel not like men but like children, or even animals. Early on, I came to believe that it was the complex psychology of this relationship between guards and inmates that had led to the fury of the riot and the savagery of the assault, but how to understand that relationship? We recruited a psychiatrist named Robert Gould, and he spoke to many of the inmates, including some of the suspected leaders of the uprising who had refused to talk to anyone else. Even Gould found it wrenching to face the brutality of daily life in Attica. He spent several long evenings on the couch in my living room afterward, trying to make sense of it, while I listened.

The interviews were the heart of the investigation, and they were tricky. Whether talking to inmates or guards, we could be skeptical, but never hostile. At the same time, we had to separate advocacy and fabrication from the truth. Early on, I divided the staff into two groups for the interviews—one to interview the guards and staff at Attica and the state police troopers, the other to interview inmates, the observers, and the media people who'd covered the event. This put added pressure on me. Each group, in subtle ways and without even realizing it, began to identify with its interviewees, and over time each developed a wary caution toward the other. I had to get the story without biases, and so I became the filter through which every fact was passed.

Dean McKay believed that television could best convey to the public what we were learning about the causes of the uprising, the failure of the negotiations, and the retaking of the prison, so he pushed for televised public hearings. The hearings, we agreed, were not to be inquisitions. Instead, we tried to present a balanced picture—inmates, correction officials, prison guards, state troopers, National Guard soldiers, all testified, as did observers who were present during the siege. We wanted to let them tell the story as they'd experienced it, or rationalized it, and let the public draw its own conclusions.

Others might have done it differently. For example, Superintendent Mancusi had been asked, shortly after the uprising, to testify before a congressional committee; he'd stated that the uprising was the work of Communist conspirators inside the prison. Charles Rangel, a congressman from New York and a former Morgenthau assistant (I had supervised his first trial as a prosecutor), questioned Mancusi adroitly and made him look totally foolish. When he returned from Washington, I went to visit Mancusi at Attica and told him that no matter how critical the commission's report might be of his actions, I would not use the public hearings to attack or humiliate him. After he testified, the public might indeed denounce every decision he'd made, but in no way would we make a spectacle of him, or of any other witness.

The hearings, as we presented them, did much to explain why the uprising took place. They showed clearly that there had been no revolutionary plot. Like maximum-security prisons throughout America, Attica had been ready to explode. In that respect, it was far from unique. "The Attica Correctional Facility in September 1971 was not perceptibly better or worse than the other maximum-security prisons in the state system," Dean McKay observed in the introduction to the commission's report. "That the explosion occurred first at Attica was probably chance, but the elements for replication are all around us. Attica is every prison and every prison is Attica." The state had created a prison system that methodically and relentlessly stripped away any vestige of dignity or self-respect and denied inmates the chance to make any decisions about their daily lives. It was an organized and deliberate effort to demean and degrade. Inmates were locked in cells that were six feet wide by nine feet deep. Idleness was their principal occupation. They worked a few hours a day at jobs that were often make-work and were paid as little as 25¢ a day. They had little exercise. Their uniforms were old and baggy. They were permitted one shower a week, and given one roll of toilet paper and a bar of soap once a month. Their food was poor. Medical facilities were inadequate, and the doctors callous and inattentive. Their mail was read, censored, and sometimes withheld, and reading material and radio programs were restricted. Visitors, even family members, were separated from inmates by a screen. Inmates were strip-searched before and after every visit. Twenty years after the Supreme Court had outlawed segregation, the prison still had "black" and "white" ice buckets and segregated sports teams. What good jobs there were went to white inmates. Most of the inmate population was black and Hispanic and urban, but the white prison guards were untrained in how to talk with them and regarded the issue as of no importance. The prison guards were commonly called "keepers," and that is what they did. The inmates were the kept. Prison discipline was often arbitrary. Inmates regarded parole hearings, the only way out for most of them, as unfair. In fact, the average parole hearing lasted only five minutes. Job training was almost nonexistent. The equipment in the shops was obsolete and, in some cases, unusable. The auto mechanics instructor, for example, had waited two years to get gasoline for the engine used for instruction.

The negotiations that had been held in an effort to end the siege peacefully became an inseparable part of the story. Public opinion was polarized. Some faulted the state for not conceding enough, though it had offered everything but amnesty. Some accused the inmates of being interested only in getting on the evening news, not in ending the crisis. Both groups missed the point. The negotiations between the inmates and the state, with observers looking on, were unique, and probably hopeless. For the first time in their lives, the inmates had an audience to listen to their stories. Because they are so powerless, prisoners learn an intuitive understanding of power. They knew that once they returned to their cells, they would not be heard from again. They were in no hurry to end the negotiations, though by the end of the fourth day the majority were hungry and tired and wanted, most of all, to return safely to their cells. It was then, however, that they found out that Officer Quinn, the young correction officer who had been hit by a two-by-four when the inmates initially stormed the gate, was dead.

When Officer Quinn died, the chance of a negotiated outcome ended. The jailhouse lawyers were convinced that every inmate who participated in the uprising could be indicted on a felony murder charge as an accessory to Quinn's murder. Consequently, they were not prepared to surrender without amnesty. Although the District Attorney was a practical and decent man, he would not offer blanket immunity for murder, nor would inmates trust his statement of his intention not to charge felony murder. So there was an inexorable movement of events toward a violent and bloody climax.

But it needn't have gone that way. In an untold part of the Attica story, we became convinced that Quinn's death had been the result of malpractice. The seriousness of his injury was misdiagnosed, and procedures to relieve pressure on his brain had been done too late. The neurological surgeon in the case took a reporter for a bizarre ride on the Thruway several days later and confided that birds talked to him!

Before we concluded the investigation, I felt a duty to tell the Quinn family that they might have a malpractice claim. But this was Attica, and the family became bitter at the suggestion that blame for Quinn's death should be shifted from the inmates to a doctor.

The hearings brought out why the assault had been so savage and deadly. State troopers themselves had filmed it, and that film, which we broadcast, provided vivid and damning evidence. It lasted just a few minutes, but the noise of continuous, indiscriminate gunfire was unmistakable—a sound that, for me, is a haunting memory of Attica.

We found that one out of every ten persons who was in D yard had been shot. The state police are not a paramilitary force, nor are they trained or equipped for such a mission. The troopers carried shotguns loaded with buckshot, which killed and seriously wounded not just their targets but those around them. Although the governor had ordered prison guards not to take part in the assault, no one conveyed his message, and state officials took no precautions to reduce the loss of life. Prison guards and state troopers for days had heard rumors that the inmates were sodomizing and castrating the hostages. Self-restraint under these conditions was impossible. Revenge was the mood of the day, and some of the attacking force had talked openly about going on a "coon hunt."

As bloody and inept as the assault was, even more horrifying was what came next. After the state troopers retook D yard, they had to get the inmates back in their cells. State officials, we discovered, had been warned of possible reprisals by correction officers, but they did nothing to stop them. By their inaction, they became accomplices and then conspirators in a cover-up. From D yard, the inmates were herded first into A yard, where they were stripped and searched. Then, one by one, they were taken through A tunnel to A block. The tunnel was a gauntlet of guards and troopers who cursed them, called them names, kicked them, and beat them savagely with clubs. A National Guard surgeon who was present described it best:

> As we sit here today in a well-lit, reasonably well-appointed room with suits and ties on, objectively performing an autopsy on this day, yet we cannot get to the absolute horror of the situation. To people, be they black, yellow, orange, spotted, whatever, whatever uniform they wear, that day took from them the shreds of their humanity. The veneer of civilization was penetrated.

Thus did a prison rebellion sparked by dehumanizing prison conditions end in even more brutality.

On April 5, a Saturday, in Rockefeller's Manhattan townhouse, I questioned the governor about Attica. Rockefeller didn't want to testify publicly, but after protracted negotiations, he had agreed to a private session, and we later released a transcript of it. In fact, he thought it degrading for a governor to be questioned by a young staff lawyer like me, and he proposed instead a discussion with commission members. But the commission said no: the commission's counsel would question the governor, with follow-up questions from the commission.

Whatever I thought of his imperiousness, I sought to be respectful of the governor during my examination, partly to show respect for his office, but also to avoid a confrontation, which would have been pointless. As with the witnesses at the public hearing, I wanted Rockefeller to tell his own story, to explain why he had refused the inmates' demand that he come to Attica and why he had authorized the assault to retake the prison.

His testimony, though, was disheartening. He had genuinely and firmly believed that negotiating over hostages would encourage more hostage-taking, but it was also clear that he and other state officials completely failed to grasp the lethal consequences of racism when they ordered white state troopers to assault black and Hispanic inmates. Worse, it was clear that, even afterward, Rockefeller had either failed or refused to understand the danger. I asked him whether he'd ever considered ordering black troopers to join the assault force. He said he didn't see what difference that would have made. After all, he said, the troopers all wore gas masks during the assault, and so the inmates would not have been able to see the color of their faces! In other words, he missed the point completely. I doubt the man was a bigot, but he seemed oblivious to the possibility that white state troopers and guards, in a state of fear and anger, would turn the assault into a terrible and needless slaughter.

I approached the governor's testimony as a chance to prod him into reexamining his own views and behavior in the light of what happened, but Rockefeller simply wasn't interested. He, in turn, was out to defend his position against negotiating with hostage-takers and his decision to commence the assault. With all of the other witnesses, inmates, and correction officers, we got beyond their prepared speeches and saw how their minds worked. But the governor wore his mask more tightly than any trooper, and we could never see who he really was.

Besides a full written report, the McKay Commission wanted to prepare a televised version of its report. Fred Friendly, the former CBS producer who now worked with the Ford Foundation and the American Bar Association, generously agreed to provide the funding, and millions saw the broadcast, adding to the impact of our conclusions. When Dean McKay and I first approached Friendly, we thought he was enthusiastic because of the balance we'd achieved, or the general excellence of our presentation, but he had something more specific in mind. For years, he said, he'd wanted to have people speak in news broadcasts just as they did naturally, without bleeping out the profanity. At our hearings, when we asked an inmate what the trooper said who was beating him, he was allowed to reply, without censorship, "Take that, you black motherfucker." To Fred Friendly, that was the high point of the Attica investigation!

Just as we released our report, on September 13, 1972—one year to the day after the assault at Attica—we found ourselves in a confrontation with the special prosecutor, Deputy Attorney General Richard Fischer, who was bringing criminal charges against inmates. He subpoenaed our files, including the records of the more than three thousand confidential interviews of inmates.

Governor Rockefeller had appointed Fischer just two days after Attica was retaken and asked him to conduct a "broad investigation" of the rebellion and to prosecute any crimes committed during it. From the beginning, relations between the special prosecutor and the commission were chilly because we had such different tasks.

For one thing, the special prosecutor was investigating possible criminal cases, which might take years to complete. A criminal case, by its nature, does not present the full picture, and is not supposed to. Its sole purpose is to adjudicate individual guilt or innocence, not the conditions that produced the crime.

The McKay Commission had a very different mandate. We wanted to get all of the facts out to the public as promptly as possible. We were dealing with systemic issues, not the guilt or innocence of any individual. To discharge our responsibilities, we interviewed everyone who was at Attica those four September days. Predictably, the special prosecutor regarded this as interference: prosecutors always prefer that witnesses speak only to them. In fact, he angrily accused us of discouraging inmates from talking to him.

Fischer's effort to subpoena the Attica files was one of the most difficult moments in my life as a lawyer. During the investigation, inmate after inmate had asked me why they should trust me. We had little common ground, but slowly I was able to win them over by giving them my absolute assurances that they could speak to us freely without fear of punishment. The commission had authorized me to promise full confidentiality to every person who agreed to be interviewed, and I had made that promise repeatedly. It was solely on that basis that many of the inmates and correction officers had been willing to talk so frankly to us.

Now the state was telling me to repudiate our promises and betray that trust. The special prosecutor wanted to use the McKay Commission as a Trojan horse, to get at all the inmates who'd refused to talk to him, people to whom I'd given my word and the commission's word. Just when I expected to feel relief, now that our difficult work was done, I found myself faced with a deeply upsetting possibility: that public service might be no place for a man of conscience.

We had some legal basis to resist the special prosecutor's subpoena, but the moral grounds were overwhelming. I decided that under no circumstances would I break my promise of confidentiality. I'd go to jail before I would turn the records over to anyone outside the commission. To their everlasting credit, Dean McKay and the other commissioners never wavered. McKay told the media that the commission's position was firm and inflexible: not only the commission's counsel but the commissioners themselves would go to jail for contempt rather than turn over our files. He meant it too. If the courts ruled in favor of the special prosecutor, they would have to send not only me to jail but also the dean of the New York University Law School, the bishop of Albany, and the rest of the commission. While the legal issues on the subpoena were close, it was unthinkable to me that a court would jail us for honoring our pledge of confidentiality.

After the McKay Commission issued its report, Burke Marshall sent me a hacksaw with an inscription pledging the commission's support. As it happened, I never had a chance to use it, for the courts upheld our position and quashed the special prosecutor's subpoena.

The McKay Commission investigation, hearings, and report had an immediate impact and also, I hope, some lasting effect. Published in book form, our report caused something of a sensation and was nominated for a National Book Award. The investigation helped start the prisoners' rights movement. The riot, and the hearings, opened up prisons to public view for the first time. Until Attica, lawyers who worked for prisoners' rights were seen as left-wing revolutionaries, and prisoners' complaints were largely ignored. Afterward, courts recognized the rights of prisoners to freedom of speech, to receive mail, to practice their religion freely, to medical treatment, to fair disciplinary procedures, to representation at parole hearings, and to the ability to seek vindication of their rights in federal court.

The report also put the lie to the prevailing myth that jail sentences could rehabilitate or correct criminals. After Attica, judges could no longer send convicted criminals to prison thinking it would be good for them, and that, at least theoretically, made for more realistic sentencing.

In fact, there was a time when it looked as if Attica might lead to more fundamental sentencing reform. That it didn't illustrates the law of unintended consequences, of a good ideal going bad.

The McKay Commission in its report noted that the randomness of sentencing was a major cause of anger inside Attica. Swapping histories, inmates convicted of similar offenses found that they'd received very different sentences, depending on the judge, the county where the offense was committed, and the defense lawyer. Parole hearings only added to the sense of arbitrariness. At the same time, judges and others had begun to criticize the same inequities in our system. Under existing law in New York and most states, a judge sentenced an offender to an indeterminate sentence, with a minimum term and a maximum term, say five to fifteen years. After the minimum sentence was served, it was up to a parole board to decide how much longer the person had to serve before being released on parole. Judges had wide latitude on what minimum and maximum sentence to impose, and the parole board had similar latitude on when to release the offender.

Attica stimulated interest in the fairness of sentencing and parole procedures. Federal Judge Marvin Frankel wrote an influential book charging that sentences were arbitrary and urging a system of sentencing guidelines to ensure consistency. In Minnesota and Florida, legislatures enacted such guidelines. In New York, Governor Hugh Carey appointed a commission to consider sentencing reforms. Robert Morgenthau chaired it, and I was asked to serve on it. After lengthy study, we recommended that New York also adopt a system of sentencing guidelines and abolish parole entirely. We recommended that an independent commission, not elected legislators, prepare those guidelines. A commission, we believed, would be immune to the political pressure to adopt longer sentences and able to establish rational sentences for offenses based on the gravity of the offense and the record of the offender.

When Mario Cuomo became governor, he supported Morgenthau's recommendations, and the legislature created an independent commission. I was selected as one of the members. Joseph Bellacosa, now a court of appeals judge, was the chair. But the simple idea, once we began to consider its applications, suddenly seemed overwhelming. How did you decide, in advance, what was an appropriate sentence for a given offense and a given offender? First we looked at the record: the average sentence actually given in the past for each offense. We knew that if the guidelines raised the average sentence length, the state would need more prison capacity. Then we compared the sentences that were given for different offenses, since a fair and rational system of justice cannot impose longer sentences for less serious offenses. We then attempted to apply the most intangible of qualities—good judgment and common sense. Should the punishment for particular offenses be greater? Should a court be allowed to give nonjail sentences for particular offenses, such as probation or community service?

In theory, if the process worked, we should have been able to form guidelines that ensured that sentences were proportionate to the gravity of the offense and the criminal history of the offender. Where existing sentences were too low, we would raise them; where they were too high, we would lower them. But it didn't work that way. Deciding on the length of a sentence is inherently subjective, as much for a sentencing commission as for sentencing judges. No principle exists that dictates that three years is the appropriate sentence for a given crime and five years is wrong. Different people will reach different conclusions. But the pressure on a sentencing commission, more than on a judge, who for the most part deals in cases not worthy of newspaper notice, is to make sentences more severe. Though we worked behind closed doors and didn't pander to public opinion, members of the commission had their own biases and constituencies. Some felt sex crimes were underpunished. Others felt that way about narcotic offenses and white-collar crime. The result was a form of log-rolling more subtle than the kind that takes place in a legislature, but nevertheless a kind necessary to reach consensus. Almost all of the compromises we reached resulted in *higher* sentences. I suspect that no one member of the commission would have drawn guidelines with the sentence ranges we proposed, but collectively we produced an escalation virtually across the board.

Having been involved in the process, I am convinced the whole concept is unsound. Sentencing cannot be reduced mechanically to the nature of the offense and the criminal history of the offender. It is too human a process. Each sentence requires a court to evaluate the distinctive qualities of the offense and the offender, as well as those qualities common to the offense. Every prosecutor and defense lawyer recognizes that there are distinctive factors that can make computerized sentencing unjust. The federal courts have finally begun to recognize this. In 1996 the Supreme Court, while generally tough on crime, decided that district courts had discretion even under the federal sentencing guidelines to give lesser sentences than the guidelines recommended if the circumstances warranted a departure (a lower sentence than the guidelines otherwise dictated).

New York still has a sentencing system with discretion given to the judges and parole boards. Efforts to adopt guidelines have been abandoned, and that is for the best. No politician who wants to get elected can run on a platform of moderating our sentences. We therefore persist in the false belief that longer sentences lead to less crime, and we shy away from programs that might make a difference, such as drug treatment and inner-city job creation. I have never met a client who considered the length of sentence before deciding to commit a crime. It doesn't work that way. Offenders, particularly in the white-collar area, may weigh the risk of being caught, but increasing sentences appears to make little difference in the crime rate.

Our mandatory sentences for drug offenses defy rationality. I once argued a case for the Legal Action Center in which the defendant received a maximum life sentence under the Rockefeller drug laws for possessing a $20 bag of cocaine. We claimed that the sentence was cruel and inhuman and unconstitutional. We won in the district court but lost by a two-to-one vote in the Second Circuit Court of Appeals because the majority there felt that the defendant would be paroled earlier than the full sentence. Perhaps if the judges in the majority had been prosecutors and knew how arbitrary and unfair prosecutors can be when they charge crimes that carry severe mandatory sentences, they would have favored giving trial judges more flexibility in sentencing. Having once been a prosecutor didn't harden my heart. Instead, the experience made me more aware of the inequities in our system.

As for Attica, conditions in many prisons did improve after the McKay Commission report. Prisoners were no longer locked up for sixteen hours a day. Educational and training programs were begun. Family visiting conditions were improved, and contact visits were introduced. New prisons were built closer to cities, in part to make visits less of a burden. Minority corrections officers were hired, and training in talking to inmates was adopted for all corrections officers. Prison officials—at least some of them—recognized that most inmates would one day return to the community, and while prisons were not country clubs, they saw it as their responsibility not to make inmates more anti-social. Moreover, more minimum-security prisons were built. Nonviolent offenders no longer have to be housed in fortresses like Attica. Still, twenty-five years later, it seems that the bitter lessons of the uprising are once again being forgotten. Prison populations are growing, and our prisons are more crowded than ever.

Personally, the Attica investigation was searing, unsettling, and unforgettable. I had encountered anti-Semitism in my time, and I'd read about racism, but Attica made me feel in my gut the racism that was tearing out the soul of America. Attica was jammed with young men whose lives were destroyed by the effects of poverty and racism—alcohol and drug dependency, illiteracy, fatherless homes, child abuse. I never had to ask an inmate about his background. Attica took these young black and Hispanic men, systematically degraded and brutalized them, and then sent them back to the same communities and their same desperate lives, only now filled with the fury that had expressed itself in unspeakable violence during the Attica uprising. I was never the same after Attica. I returned to Paul, Weiss and private practice, but the call to community and public service has had, ever since, a different urgency.

The Case of New York's Collapsing Subway Cars

I n 1979 the bottom fell out of the New York City subway system, literally.

Seven years before, the city's Transit Authority had ordered a new fleet of subway cars from Pullman, Inc. Dubbed R-46, the new cars were state-of-the-art, and they cost a fortune—more than $200 million for a fleet of 754 cars. The undercarriage of a subway car is called a truck, and there are two per car; the R-46s had newly designed, lightweight trucks, built for Pullman under subcontract by Rockwell International. Unfortunately, no sooner did the Transit Authority put the new R-46 cars into use on its IND line, in early 1976, than the trucks that Rockwell designed, tested, and built began to crack; the bottoms of the subway cars fell apart. The Transit Authority blamed the cracks on Rockwell's faulty design and testing. Rockwell, in turn, said that Transit Authority engineers had okayed the design, and although it offered by way of a settlement to repair—or "retrofit"—the trucks, the company insisted that it was the Transit Authority's failure to maintain its subway tracks during the city's fiscal crisis that had caused the trucks to crack.

The dispute was complex and highly technical, and it could have lasted for years. By keeping the case narrow, limiting discovery, and focusing on a simple, commonsense theme, we tried it in less than a year, the jury made a reasoned decision on the merits, and New York City and the Transit Authority won a $72 million verdict. It was one of my most satisfying cases.

Although the city's contract was with Pullman, Rockwell had indemnified Pullman, and so, in June 1979, the city and the Transit Authority sued Rockwell in federal court, asking for the $100 million the Transit Authority would have to pay to repair the R-46 subway cars by replacing the Rockwell trucks. The prior MTA and city administrations had wanted to accept Rockwell's proposed retrofit and settle the case, but MTA engineers were convinced that the defects in the undercarriages could not be remedied and that this would be just one more case of the city letting a contractor walk away from its warranties.

For Mayor Ed Koch, the case represented an important test of New York City's willingness to change its ways. Koch was feisty. Having pushed residents and unions to make sacrifices to bring the city, when it was near bankruptcy, back to its glory, he now wanted to show that the city itself would hold all parties to their contracts and the days when the city would roll over and play dead were finished. The R-46 case presented just that opportunity.

Koch had been my congressman, but I'd known him only slightly before he became mayor. He was a good friend of one of my best clients, David Margolis of Colt Industries, for whom I had handled a number of litigations. Alan Schwartz, the counsel for the city under Koch, had tried a case with me, and early in Koch's first term, I helped the city negotiate a reduced settlement in a suit brought against it by contractors in the abandoned multimillion-dollar water tunnel project. When it came to Rockwell and the R-46s, Koch and Schwartz concluded that the city did not have the requisite legal staff for what promised to be a stiff legal battle, and they asked me and the firm to handle the case at a reduced rate. We agreed. Given the city's financial condition, it seemed inappropriate to make money from it. I tried the case with Leslie Fagen, then a young and eager Paul, Weiss associate and now one of the best trial lawyers in New York. Typically, such a complex case with so much money at stake would have begun with extensive discovery and pretrial motions and might not have been tried for years. But the city was anxious to have the dispute resolved, and I was not looking forward to protracted, costly, and tediously technical discovery.

So it was an enormous relief when the Transit Authority's lawsuit was assigned to U.S. District Judge Edward Weinfeld, who was strictly no-nonsense when it came to managing a trial in his courtroom. In the midst of all the usual pretrial wrangling and the vituperative letter-writing back and forth between the lawyers on both sides, Weinfeld set a trial date of November 1980, some six months after the Transit Authority asked Paul, Weiss to handle the case. Six months gave both sides a reasonable amount of time to conduct discovery, but it was short enough to prevent discovery from becoming a litigation weapon. Still, by the time we were ready to go to trial, both sides together, in pretrial discovery, had questioned more than 160 witnesses, resulting in about 30,000 pages of deposition transcripts. We had more than 1,000 documents as trial exhibits.

With the November trial date approaching, I struggled to find our theme. An effective trial theme, I have always held, is more than just an organizing, unifying device for the facts, it is a powerful persuasive tool. It should be announced in the opening statement to the jury, and each witness and every piece of evidence should in some way fit it and reflect it. A good theme shapes the jurors' view of the facts, telling them which ones are important and what they signify, so that by the end of the case only one interpretation seems possible, and any alternative explanation unlikely and illogical.

Obviously, themes aren't made from whole cloth. They emerge out of preparation, that is, out of the facts and out of the trial lawyer's mastery of those facts. But there is also the element of inspiration—the discovery, in the welter of evidence and testimony that make up a case, of the single idea that will most influence the jurors.

In a case like the R-46, I knew that, no matter how methodically and clearly we presented the technical engineering facts, no juror could understand them, let alone remember them, unless they were made part of a theme. In fact, the issues were so complex that about a month before the trial was to start, Rockwell's lawyers made a motion that the case be heard without a jury, just the judge. In their motion, they said it would be constitutionally unfair to Rockwell to allow a jury to decide, because "the scientific and engineering testimony which must be presented is so technical and sophisticated that it will be beyond the capacity of the average juror to understand."

I, on the contrary, believed that, provided we found the right theme, the jury could understand even the most complicated of facts and make a sound, reasoned decision on the merits of the case. But it was up to us to make an otherwise complex case simple.

I kept going over the elements. The city and the Transit Authority were suing Rockwell for breach of contract and breach of warranty. These were straightforward legal claims, relatively easy to explain, but in order to prove them, we would have to deal with highly technical material, and the key witnesses would be engineers using the arcane language of subway technology. How could we make sure that the jurors brought their commonsense notions of fairness to bear?

Another problem was that Rockwell—a highly regarded aerospace company with hundreds, indeed thousands, of skilled engineers and computer experts—had offered to retrofit the subway cars if we dropped our lawsuit. In fact, one of the Transit Authority's own top executives had felt that the MTA should accept Rockwell's offer. But having lost confidence in Rockwell's design, the MTA now wanted to replace the trucks with their older, time-tested design and so had rejected Rockwell's offer. It would be up to me, in court, to convince the jury that the Transit Authority was justified in spurning Rockwell. (Rockwell, it should be remembered, was the same company that had designed and built the Apollo spacecraft.)

Furthermore, at the time of the trial, we were only a few years removed from the city's disastrous flirtation with bankruptcy. Most New Yorkers held the Transit Authority in low regard. The subway system it operated was considered unreliable and dangerous, and its subway cars were dirty, noisy, and covered with graffiti. There was one last problem: Transit Authority engineers had been involved, from time to time, in the trucks' design. Rockwell, we knew, was going to claim that the Transit Authority had provided the design specifications, and therefore that the faulty design was the Transit Authority's mistake, not Rockwell's.

The theme, when I found it, was going to have to convince the jury of the opposite. It would also have to match my own courtroom style, which is simple, unadorned, and devoid of histrionics. I've never believed that showmanship decides cases. If it did, then the best-looking, best-tailored, and most grandiloquent lawyers would always win, and I would have long since been obliged to take up plumbing. More often, though, in my experience, it is the young, unprepossessing prosecutor, dressed in a cheap, ill-fitting polyester suit, who talks to the jury in a halting but sincere manner, who has the advantage, and in civil cases, especially in complex commercial litigations, jurors tend to respond to appeals to their reason and common sense, not their emotions.

In R-46, I had, I think, one additional advantage. I never even took a high school course in physics. I figured that if I could understand what was wrong with Rockwell's design and manufacture, then any juror would.

But where was my theme? Finally, about ten days before the trial, it came to me—on a plane ride home from California, where I'd been on another matter—and as with all good themes, it was very simple. Rockwell, the company that put a man on the moon, that had lured the city into a contract with its boasts of engineering prowess, had nonetheless produced a lemon. Its R-46 subway car was a lemon. Wouldn't any juror who had ever bought a car and then had to deal with constant repair bills know exactly what a lemon was? Wouldn't anyone who had ever heard of the Edsel?

Opening statements, I believe, should be brief and uncomplicated, and yet they are supremely important, for they are the trial lawyer's first and best opportunity to establish his theme.

In the R-46 case, my opening took less than an hour.

After introducing myself and the other lawyers, I told the jury, "This is a case, as the court indicated, of breach of contract and breach of warranty. The term 'warranty' is familiar to anyone who has ever bought a refrigerator or a television set. Here we are dealing with warranties on a different type of product and a different consumer. Here the consumer was the city of New York and the Transit Authority, and the product was subway cars. . . .

"To give you the case in a nutshell, the proof here will show that when the defendants were selling and promoting the R-46 to the city, they promoted it as if it were a Rolls-Royce of the subway industry, fast, safe, quiet and long-lasting.

"We will show you that they didn't deliver a Rolls-Royce. They delivered an Edsel, a lemon, a car whose undercarriage is disintegrating, literally."

I described for the jury how two-thirds of the trucks in question—that is, more than a thousand out of fifteen hundred—had cracks in their cross-beams, and how they vibrated so violently that equipment mounted on them, including safety equipment, was shaken loose. I told the jury that I could turn the courtroom into a junkyard by bringing in samples of parts that had fallen off R-46 cars and been found along the subway tracks.

"The only way that the city and the Transit Authority have of salvaging this fleet," I concluded, "for which they paid Pullman $200 million, is to replace these cracking and vibrating trucks with another truck, tested in service, a reliable truck, and we will prove to you that the cost of substituting this new truck for the defective R-46 trucks, as well as the costs of repairing them and inspecting them to date, is in the neighborhood of $100 million, and those are the damages that we are seeking."

Our first witness was the former chairman of the MTA, who testified that, among other things, in ordering modern cars for its subway system the city had left their design to the manufacturer. Because I wanted the jury to bear Rockwell's engineering sophistication in mind, I'd decided to use only a midlevel Transit Authority manager, Joe Sebastiano, to describe the R-46 contract for them. In contrast to Rockwell and its aura of high-tech genius, the Transit Authority, as I brought out in questioning Sebastiano, was composed of hardworking ordinary civil service employees trying to do their jobs. All they needed, Sebastiano affirmed, was equipment that worked. We then called just two expert witnesses, one a professor of engineering at Princeton, and the other from the University of Connecticut, using them to explain why the Transit Authority had rejected Rockwell's offer to retrofit the subway cars. In the words of the first, Dr. Robert Scanlan, the design of the trucks "was fraught with difficulties from the very beginning and still is."

Equally important to our case, though, was the chance, once we'd finished our presentation, to cross-examine Rockwell's witnesses. One of their first was Richard Bruggen, a manager at its manufacturing plant in Kansas where Rockwell had built the R-46 trucks. Through Bruggen, I was able to establish that New York City wasn't the first Rockwell customer to have had a problem with the trucks.

"Mr. Bruggen," I began, "you testified that before 1972 you had provided trucks for the Chicago Transit System, am I correct?"

"Yes, sir."

"And you testified that you had some cracking in the Chicago system before you contracted to make the trucks for New York, is that correct?"

"Yes, it is."

"And you testified that you proposed a fix for that cracking, am I correct?"

"Yes."

"And that fix was adopted, am I correct?"

"Yes."

"And you testified . . . that the Rockwell trucks are still operating in Chicago, am I correct?"

"Yes."

"Did you neglect to mention that those trucks have continued to crack since your fix?"

"I didn't neglect to mention it. In 1972 they had not cracked again. We have learned subsequent to that that they have cracked, yes."

In fact, as I was able to bring out, the crossbeams in the Chicago trucks were still cracking in 1980.

The question of what Rockwell knew, and what its customers were told, would come up again. I pursued it further with Bruggen and got from him what I thought was a telling admission, confirming Dr. Scanlan's earlier testimony: neither the people at Rockwell nor anyone else knew for sure why the trucks kept cracking.

But sometimes cross-examinations take an unforeseen turn. I've made it a general rule not to attack witnesses in the courtroom, in part because browbeating and sarcasm don't come naturally to me, but also because it's all too easy for jurors to develop sympathy for people on the witness stand. I'd rather try to turn a witness to my advantage or deflect his testimony. But Bruggen, without the slightest anticipation on my part, did my job for me.

I'd asked him, innocently enough, about a Transit Authority design specification that apparently hadn't reached him before Rockwell signed its contract with Pullman to produce the R-46 trucks. He replied that, while the meeting in question at the Transit Authority had taken place on December 20, the minutes hadn't come to his attention until after the holidays, which was why the letter he'd written, confirming all the understandings between the parties, had been dated December 27.

"So that was just another failure of communication within Rockwell?" I suggested. "Is that what you are saying?"

His reply to this otherwise innocuous question stunned me, and stunned the courtroom.

"No, it had to do with the Christmas holidays," Bruggen said. Then he paused momentarily, before adding, "Which *we* at Rockwell celebrate."

Whether Bruggen was aware that I was a Jew, or that the two top Transit Authority engineers responsible for recommending rejection of the proposed retrofit were also Jews, or that New York City is home to hundreds of thousands of Jews, I cannot say, but there was an unmistakable anti-Semitic slur in his tone, and I was far from alone in hearing it.

I said nothing. I simply stared at him for a minute, while his answer hung there in the courtroom. This was purely a reflex on my part, not a calculated reaction, yet it was far more effective than if I'd asked more questions to drive home the point. His ugly remark shocked the jury, and I had nothing more to say to Mr. Bruggen.

━━━━━

Expert witnesses in particular, I should point out, are hard to attack directly, and Rockwell brought its share into the courtroom. Experts are, after all, just that, masters of complex subjects, and it is unlikely that a lawyer is going to catch them in an error or, more important, be able to make that error understandable to the jury. Experts are paid for their testimony, of course, but that fact alone is insufficient to make a jury disregard an expert's testimony. Besides, when the other side calls an expert witness, you will probably be calling your own, and yours too are being paid to testify.

Once, though—if I digress to tell the story, it is because it was one of my better moments in the courtroom—I had to cross-examine a Nobel Prize–winning physicist who had testified against my client, Bell & Howell, in a case brought by an inventor named DeDavega. DeDavega had licensed a patented idea to Consolidated Electronics Corporation, a company later acquired by Bell & Howell. His patent had to do with something called process control, which was used to monitor and automatically control industrial processes. Consolidated Electronics promised to pay DeDavega's royalties on all process control equipment that it (or any affiliate) produced, even if DeDavega's patent proved invalid. But since Consolidated Electronics never produced any such equipment, DeDavega had never received any royalties.

Bell & Howell, however, pioneered the use of electronic eyes in cameras, and after Bell & Howell acquired Consolidated Electronics, DeDavega demanded royalties under his old agreement and sued to get them, claiming that Bell & Howell's electronic eye equipment was a process control device in that it controlled the process of light hitting the film in a camera. No matter that his so-called invention had nothing to do with Bell & Howell's camera, or that Bell & Howell had been producing the camera long before it acquired Consolidated Electronics and even before DeDavega had licensed his patent, DeDavega claimed his contract entitled him to royalties on all process control equipment, period.

Electronic eyes? Process control? These matters were gibberish to me. Still, I knew instinctively that DeDavega's claim was preposterous.

At trial, the Nobel Prize winner testified that a camera's electronic eye controls a process and thus can be deemed a piece of process control equipment. There was no way I could challenge the witness's expertise in optical principles, so I tried a different tack.

Was a light switch a process control device, I asked?

Yes, the witness agreed, because it controlled the process of electricity flowing to the lightbulb.

How about the tip of a ballpoint pen?

That too, he conceded, was a process control device that controlled the flow of ink.

Finally, I asked him whether the judge himself, who controlled what was happening in the courtroom, wasn't in fact controlling a process.

Yes, the expert was obliged to answer.

His testimony in DeDavega's behalf was suddenly worthless—not because I'd attacked his credibility or his credentials, but because the whole suit was based on an absurd literalism. For if a camera's electronic eye can be said to control a process, then virtually every item in our daily lives controls *some* process, and if that were so, then DeDavega was entitled to royalties on every item that Bell & Howell produced!

Case closed? Not quite. In fact, we ended up settling for a nominal amount because of another, most unfortunate process, one over which none of us has any control. The judge in the case died before he could issue a decision.

Rockwell's best witness, it turned out, wasn't an expert, but its chairman and chief executive officer, Robert Anderson. The defense lawyers brought him to the stand, not because he'd been involved in the R-46 contract—of course he hadn't been—but to attest to his company's engineering skill and high standards. Rockwell's engineers, he boasted, were "as good as there are in the free world," and he professed to have been "shocked" when their retrofit solution was rejected by the city.

Handsome, sincere, articulate, and obviously a decent man, Anderson made a strong impression on the jury. Now I had to cross-examine him.

When it comes to cross-examining a strong witness, a lawyer has three choices: he can pass entirely, try to discredit the witness, or, if he can find a way, use him to score some points. Discrediting Anderson was out. The jury liked Anderson; so, for that matter, did I. On the other hand, his testimony could help Rockwell unless we did something.

The one thing I'd realized, listening to his direct examination, was that Anderson was essentially unfamiliar with the facts relating to the city's claims of defects. There was no reason he should have been familiar with them either, as the CEO of a Fortune 500 company with many thousands of employees in a number of divisions, any more than the chairman of a large car manufacturer knows when a consumer drives a lemon out of a dealer's showroom. But I still thought I saw a chance of making him endorse my theme—by contrasting his own high standards for his company with its actual performance on the R-46 contract.

Together, we reviewed things he'd already covered on direct examination: his pride in his company, the high caliber of the engineers and scientists Rockwell employed and his confidence in them, the fact that companywide neither he nor the people who worked for him would tolerate shoddy work. He was careful in his responses. When, for instance, I asked him whether Rockwell would tolerate castings that were replete with anomalies, he answered that, as far as he knew, all castings contained anomalies, leaving me only a technical argument I chose not to pursue. But then I began to show him documents I knew he hadn't seen before—photographs of broken welds, for instance, and internal Rockwell reports concerning quality lapses.

We reviewed them, one by one. I asked him, each time, whether the shoddy practices reflected in the documents also reflected the standards of Robert Anderson's Rockwell. Of course they didn't, and he was obliged to say so.

One of the key documents was a memo from a Rockwell employee concerning "Troy." Troy, New York, was the headquarters of the Rockwell division responsible for the R-46 trucks. Anderson testified that he'd never seen it before, but that didn't stop me from quoting it: "Troy wants to keep failure quiet until after their presentation to the TA board."

The "failure" in question, I was able to establish, was the failure of the *retrofitted* truck to pass performance tests, and the "presentation" was Rockwell's pitch to the Transit Authority to be allowed to repair the trucks. In other words, even as Rockwell tried to resolve the dispute with its retrofitting plan, some of its own employees knew the plan might fail and had sought to conceal that knowledge from the MTA.

I established, carefully, that Anderson had no knowledge of any of this. But I also established, piece by piece, that it reflected behavior he, as CEO, could not condone. I wanted the jury to remember the refrain: "The Rockwell that Robert Anderson represents would not do that," while reminding them, over and over, that that was precisely what Rockwell had done.

Called by Rockwell as a kind of "character witness" for the company, Robert Anderson ended up as one of our own best witnesses.

———

In my closing argument, I wanted to remind the jury that despite Rockwell's excuses, the fundamental issue was simple: the company had broken its promise to deliver subway cars that worked. Using an easel with a large artist's pad, I outlined what Rockwell had promised to build and what they'd actually built. They might have built a vehicle that could travel to the moon, I said, but all that we'd asked for was a subway car that could go from Forty-second Street to Thirty-fourth Street without cracking, and in that they'd failed.

As I usually do for the closing argument in a big and highly technical case, I wanted supporting documents at hand, and I'd asked Leslie Fagen to organize and handle them for me, as I once had for Judge Rifkind. I remember, that morning before we started, Fagen lugging a battered old Heineken beer carton into the courtroom. Inside the carton were piles of individual file folders containing the documents we would need. Fagen started arranging them in "birdcages," those accordion-like filing devices that he already had organized according to some carefully devised system.

I asked him what he was doing. He started explaining his system to me.

"Fine," I said, "only don't put them in the birdcages. Just leave them in that carton and put the carton on the counsel table."

Fagen looked at me, I remember, as though maybe the pressure had gotten to me at last. But then he grinned at me, and I at him, and I think we understood each other. What I wanted was for the jury to see us as unadorned, unflashy lawyers, the opposite of the white-shoe crowd that represented Rockwell. Our client, after all, was the city of New York, and the taxpayers who rode its subways.

So, with Leslie handing me documents from the Heineken carton, I talked on, and as I talked, I began to draw crude stick-figure rabbits on the easel pad, but I didn't tell the jury what they were or why I was drawing them. I'm not much of an artist, even though my wife Ellen, who is an accomplished painter, had coached me the night before on how to draw rabbits. A generous critic—a very generous critic—might say my rabbits had a folk-arty feel to them. I knew the jury would start speculating about what I was doing, or thought I was doing, and I could almost feel the desire of some of the jurors to come up and help me with some of my lines.

I let them puzzle over my artwork for a few moments. Then I explained what they were. The rabbits, I said, stood for Rockwell's excuses.

"I call them rabbits," I went on, "because they remind me of the mechanical rabbits they have in tracks where they hold dog races, and the dogs are let loose and they chase after the mechanical rabbit and they expend a lot of energy, and of course, they never catch it, and they come away very, very confused. And they have set a lot of rabbits loose in this courtroom, and I intend now to deal with them and show that they are nothing more than that. They are nothing but phony alibis."

One by one, I went through my "rabbits" with them, and as I neared the end of my argument, I could sense from their eyes and posture that they were with me. So I gambled and went for broke. I asked the jury not to compromise in its verdict, but to award the city the full $100 million of our suit—the $72 million it would take to replace all the R-46 trucks and another $28 million to pay for an interim inspection and repair program while waiting for the trucks to be removed. Either that, or nothing at all.

"Ladies and gentlemen," I concluded, "I don't want you to compromise. I want you to vote your convictions. New York isn't here asking for mercy or charity or anything like that. If you were to vote to compromise and the city didn't get what it was entitled to, then it's at the mercy of every purveyor of merchandise. If you think we are wrong, then vote against us, but please, the principle here of integrity of contract is too important to be bargained away. . . . Let your verdict speak the truth for both sides."

The jury was out for ten and a half hours. This was late in December; it was dark out and snowing, and still they deliberated. As we waited nervously, I got up and, so to speak, worked the room, shaking hands with every member of our trial team, because, whatever the outcome, I knew we'd all done our jobs well, and I wanted to share that knowledge with every last one of us.

But then they came back—juries always do, after all—and they had a verdict, and that verdict, announced aloud in court, awarded $72 million to the city of New York. Not quite the whole loaf, but a lot more than half! And I remember the general jubilation, the noise, the excitement. Together, Les Fagen and I had the pleasure of delivering the news to Mayor Ed Koch, who was on a trip to Egypt. Because of the time change, it was the middle of the night in the Middle East, and we woke him up at his Cairo hotel. Normally, he told us, a call like that meant either a police officer had been shot or a fireman killed in the line of duty, but our happy news elated him.

When we finally got outside, in the dark and snow, some of our team was in the midst of a snowball fight, and they were shouting about their plans for libations and celebrations, but I managed to duck away and head off for home. It is what I always want to do, win, lose, or draw, but I was particularly satisfied and proud that night. Among other things, we had shown the world that New York City, which had almost declared bankruptcy a few years earlier, was capable of fighting back. In that earlier, bleaker period, the city would never have dared sue Rockwell; helpless and hapless, it would have compromised for a next-to-nothing settlement. Now we had left a clear message: New York could, and would, hold its suppliers to their contracts and would never again be afraid to take them into court.

For all of us, it was a privilege to be able to represent the city where we lived and practiced our profession. For that reason alone, R-46 remains my favorite case.

14

Representing the Unrepresented: The Legal Action Center,
the Legal Aid Society, and the Capital Defender Office

MOST OF MY public service has not been conducted in front of
television cameras. Much of it has been on behalf of poor men and
women accused of crimes, and through these experiences, several of
which I am about to describe, I have come to believe very firmly that we
delude ourselves if we believe that criminal law and criminal prosecution can of themselves stamp out crime. This is not an issue of ideology—of whether one is "soft" or "hard" on crime—but of whether we,
as a society, are ready to approach our problems more realistically than
we have to date.

Criminal law is based on the premise that an individual is responsible
for his or her own conduct and can be deterred from criminal acts by the
prospect of punishment. But there are reasons why an individual's ability
to assert self-control may be impaired, among them drug addiction and
alcoholism, which are not, however, allowed as defenses in court. Impos-

ing a severe sentence on an addict for possessing the drug he is going to use is not as useful as probation together with supervised treatment. Addicts who receive only prison terms are far more likely to commit more crime than those who also get treatment in jail. My experience at Attica alone taught me that those who leave prison illiterate and unemployable are more likely to resume careers of crime then those who have job opportunities. Yet we, as a society, persist in doing what we've always done: we brand offenders as outlaws not worthy of employment, thereby forcing them into the only jobs that require no prescreening—street crime.

I have no doubt, myself, that in the white-collar area criminal prosecution and the prospect of imprisonment form an effective deterrent. Telling a client that he can land in prison for five years if he fixes prices or breaks the securities laws has a far more traumatic effect than telling him he might be sued or fined. But outside of white-collar crimes, fear of imprisonment is often not a factor in behavior, particularly in the inner cities, where a high percentage of the residents will serve or have served time in prison. Consequently, social programs that develop self-respect and dignity must be considered as much a part of our crime budget as they are of our social welfare programs. Providing job training, improving the schools, creating incentives for affordable housing, battling racism, punishing and trying to prevent spousal and child abuse, promoting drug and alcohol treatment—all these are anticrime measures.

I emphasize that I am no bleeding heart. My wife and I ourselves have been victims of violent crime, assaulted in our own home by a deranged neighbor armed with an ax and saved only because I was up at 6:00 A.M. making telephone calls to clients. On the enforcement side, I also chaired a commission for Governor Carey on improving the effectiveness of the police and the criminal courts. But having experienced our criminal justice system as a prosecutor, a defense lawyer, and even a victim, I believe I know its limitations well, and the frustrations they cause.

Soon after the Attica investigation was finished, I was recruited by the Vera Institute of Justice, a highly regarded "think tank" in New York City that develops and operates innovative criminal justice programs. I was asked to run a new public-interest law firm, called the Legal Action Center, which planned to use class action lawsuits to force public employers, such as the New York City Transit Authority, to hire former convicts and recovering drug and alcohol abusers. Although I had just returned to private practice, which I had neglected while I was busy with the Attica investigation, how could I say no when our own Attica report had been so sharply critical of the state for failing to help inmates cope with their lives after release from prison?

At the time, class actions were an innovation, and many lawyers in private practice were skeptical of, and even hostile toward, lawyers who purported to litigate in the public interest. Before class actions, there had been test cases, but these usually were filed on behalf of a particular person, and then only to challenge the constitutionality of an important new law. Even Rifkind, who was firmly committed to civil rights, was wary of the new breed of lawyer who claimed to represent the public interest, or an entire class of persons. In Rifkind's view, a lawyer's job was to represent an individual client with a particular problem, and he could not identify with these lawyers who litigated without clients.

I had a different view. I believed that class actions brought on behalf of broad groups of disadvantaged persons were often the only way to achieve social justice. Rifkind, a New Deal lawyer in background, had more faith than I did in the legislative and executive branches of government, but I believed that, while much of the legislation was already in place, federal, state, and local governments were unwilling to carry out the law, and that it was up to the courts to force them to do so.

Under its first executive director, Elizabeth Bartholet, who is now a chaired professor at Harvard Law School, the Legal Action Center successfully litigated important cases against public agencies that refused to employ former drug and alcohol abusers. It brought cases challenging zoning restrictions against drug treatment clinics. It forced the New York City Transit Authority to abandon its practice of discriminating against persons who enrolled in the methadone program, taking the case all the way to the Supreme Court, where it established an important precedent. The case permitted persons who needed methadone treatment to receive it without fear that they would lose their jobs.

We sued the Veterans Administration for denying extended educational benefits to GIs who suffered from alcohol or drug abuse, habits that had often been formed during military service. That case also went to the Supreme Court, where we lost on technical grounds, but the result led Congress to change the law. We sued the Postal Service for firing, and refusing to employ, qualified people who were in methadone programs or had arrest records, and the Postal Service dropped the prohibition. In another case, a zoning board in White Plains, New York, refused permission for a drug treatment center to open in its downtown area—against the advice of the city's counsel. We sued and won a decision, the first in the Northeast, that such discrimination violated the Americans with Disabilities Act.

Drawing on these experiences, we broadened our mandate to include persons infected with HIV and suffering from AIDS who faced egregious discrimination—in employment, housing, education for children—because of the general ignorance about how AIDS is contracted. Today, little known though we still are to the general public, we provide legal counseling to thousands of clients a year, but unlike most advocacy groups, we also combine litigation with programs of public education and cooperation with government agencies. We have even helped draft legislation and regulations. Our philosophy is to try to work out the problems we take on through ingenuity and persuasive reasoning, but if that fails, to litigate.

My private practice is obviously a world apart from that in which the Legal Action Center's clients live and struggle, and it has given me no exposure to the acute problems people with drug or alcohol histories or HIV-AIDS face every day. So I've given the center my time and help over the years with an enthusiasm tempered by the realization that the law and lawyers can bring about change only in small increments, and that there will always be far more to do than has already been done.

Another great institution in the service of the poor is the Legal Aid Society of New York, the country's oldest legal aid organization. To describe Legal Aid's clients as underprivileged is a gentle euphemism. These people seek basic human rights, not privileges. Organized by lawyers in 1876, Legal Aid originally provided free legal services to new immigrants in civil cases, but later, when the courts decreed that every criminal defendant, no matter how poor, was constitutionally entitled to a lawyer, it became the leading criminal defense organization for the poor in New York City, representing tens of thousands of clients each year. Its civil work is funded primarily from donations by the bar, especially the city's major law firms, while its criminal defense work is done under contract with the city.

Legal Aid is the largest criminal-defense law firm in the United States. It is a nonprofit corporation run by a board of directors, most of whom are picked from the ranks of the city's major law firms. The board hires management, sets overall policy, and responds to crises, like strikes or threats of inadequate funding by the city. Although I had served on the board for years, I'd never sought the job of president because I hated administration. In late 1983, however, I accepted a two-year term because I believed the society was at a very critical juncture in its history. Its workload had surged, morale among its lawyers had sunk, and public support for its clients was drying up.

Legal Aid's most serious problem at the time was labor relations. It desperately needed to restore its relations with the union that represented its employees—the lawyers who handled its caseload.

The society had a staff of hundreds of lawyers, most of them in the Criminal Division. Compared to lawyers in private practice, they were grossly underpaid and they carried huge caseloads. In the previous few years, their union had called four strikes over working conditions and wages. The most recent had lasted ten weeks and left the courts and jails jammed and in chaos. The city was enraged that lawyers would strike, leaving clients undefended. Mayor Koch responded to the walkout with a threat to cancel the city's contract with the society and replace it with a public defender's office. The courts and the bar also were angry, and disciplinary action was threatened against the Legal Aid lawyers. But the lawyers were protected by federal labor law, and the strikes were settled. Still, the labor disputes left a bad aftertaste, not only with the administrators of the justice system but among Legal Aid's own board of directors.

I dedicated my two-year term as president to improving relations with the union and also trying to improve Legal Aid's reputation for effective and zealous advocacy. Legal Aid lawyers, I believed, felt pushed to strike because they were frustrated at being treated like second-class lawyers who couldn't get jobs elsewhere. I personally have tremendous admiration for Legal Aid lawyers. Underpaid and unappreciated, they represent clients accused of heinous crimes. They work in run-down, dreary courtrooms lacking all dignity. While I couldn't raise their wages or better their conditions, I tried to find ways to let them know how much we respected them.

In the past, Legal Aid's management had shared little information with the union, especially about finances. Every year, in fact, was a struggle to avoid deficits. If the union understood our financial problems, I believed, some of the mistrust that had erupted into the recent strikes would be eliminated.

My work as president led me into a dispute, the first I can recall, with my old boss, Bob Morgenthau, who had become the District Attorney of New York County. The Criminal Division was in the process of implementing a court order, one Legal Aid had pushed for, that every defendant be arraigned within twenty-four hours of his or her arrest. At arraignment, a defendant goes before a judge, hears the charges read, is appointed counsel, and has bail set.

New York's criminal justice system, however, wasn't organized for swift arraignments. After their arrests, defendants were housed in police precincts all over the city and sometimes literally lost. We proposed twenty-four-hour-a-day arraignments. Morgenthau strenuously opposed the idea. He argued that we would accomplish nothing in the middle of the night and that the inability of the police department to verify fingerprints and other logistical problems were beyond his control. He was probably not wrong, but at the same time, Legal Aid had to stand up for its clients' rights. In the end, Morgenthau prevailed, but as a result, the arraignment process in Manhattan was streamlined.

If our Criminal Division required most of my attention, the Civil Division was closest to my heart. In a civilized society, it is simply unacceptable that the only time a poor person can get into court is when he commits a crime. Those who look upon free legal services for the poor as a luxury we can't afford don't have the slightest understanding of what it means to be a member of the profession of law. It means insisting on the independence of the bar and the bench. It means defending the rights of the helpless, not just the mighty. It means sometimes taking on the government—not just for a giant corporation, which is deemed acceptable, but for the economically disadvantaged, which arouses controversy. And it means having the courage to take on cases that may not be popular and having the courage to plead them with all one's skill. The Civil Division of the Legal Aid Society measures up to all of these standards.

The poor have legal problems of the most urgent nature. True, lawyers can't solve the underlying social and economic ills and inequities that have created a virtually permanent underclass. But when heat or hot water is not provided in a tenement, some of them city-owned; when Social Security, welfare, Medicare, or unemployment benefits are arbitrarily and erroneously denied, as was too often the case during the Reagan administration; when deportation proceedings are threatened against somebody who has a right to be in the country; when the elderly are confronted with mazes of forms to fill out; when the homeless face discrimination and obstacles even in the education of their children—people need a lawyer, and the Legal Aid Society, Civil or Volunteer Division, is that lawyer.

The Civil and Volunteer Divisions—the latter composed of associates from the city's law firms—depend on the bar and the business community for most of their support. This is a burden that we willingly bear, yet, for want of resources, these divisions must turn down three clients for each one they accept. Indeed, we as a society seem to have reached that paradoxical point at which we are lampooned for producing more lawyers per population than any country in history, while fewer and fewer people each year can afford a lawyer—unless they have a whiplash injury. In the long run, no society can claim to practice equal justice when it grants its citizens rights and entitlements by legislation, only to withhold from them the resources to enforce those rights through the legal system.

During my presidency, we were deluged with two other classes of cases. First, New York faced a crisis of homelessness, not just for single people but for whole families. Litigation became necessary to press the city to provide housing, food, and education for the homeless. Second, the Reagan administration adopted a policy of cutting back on Social Security disability payments. Even when the courts held the policy unlawful, the administration chose a policy of nonacquiescence, forcing the same type of case to be litigated over and over again. The Legal Aid Society brought case after case for the disabled, while I, as president, tried to raise community consciousness of what was happening and went begging for private funds to support our activities.

After my two-year term, I felt I hadn't accomplished all I'd hoped to, and I was right. For one thing, management was as entrenched as it had been when I arrived, for neither the board nor I had had the stomach to remove longtime managers. This contributed to the ongoing estrangement between younger, more zealous lawyers and tired supervisors they didn't respect. Years later, there would be changes, but other problems would surface, and ironically, Legal Aid lawyers of this later period romanticized the years when I had headed the organization as an era of good feeling. Still, the organization continues to this day to provide the poor with legal services comparable to those they would receive from the private bar—and better services in many cases.

When I was a young lawyer, I attended a speech by Robert Kennedy, then Attorney General. Kennedy told an apocryphal story about visiting a fraternity house at an urban university that looked out on a slum.

"What," Kennedy asked the fraternity brothers, pointing out the window, "are you going to do about that?"

The next day, the fraternity bought curtains.

That was not Kennedy's answer to the problem. Nor can it be the bar's. Nor ours.

Much more recently, I've become involved in another public-service organization that, though too young to have flavorsome stories in its archives, is nevertheless a critical addition in the struggle to protect human rights.

Although I've never handled a death penalty case, I've thought a great deal about capital punishment, and I oppose it. Its proponents often argue that it deters murder; the assumption is that, before pulling the trigger, a killer calculates that he or she will risk life imprisonment but not death. That is not how murderers think. In addition, many of those who support capital punishment believe—wrongly—that prison life is like a country club. Life in prison without the possibility of parole is slow death.

I am a pragmatist, even on such an emotional issue. For me, the death penalty is wrong because it cannot be imposed fairly and without discrimination. Many opponents, myself among them, would have absolutely no objection to capital punishment if it could be reserved for Adolf Hitler and other perpetrators of genocide who have truly put themselves outside the law. But that's not what the debate is about, at least not in our country. Years of experience in the United States have shown that the death penalty is most often imposed when the defendant is black, and still more often when the victim is white. The plain and ugly truth is that juries, and some judges, tend to value black lives less than white lives. Courts have tended to rationalize and ignore these statistics, but as Felix Frankfurter said, "We cannot be blind as judges to what we know as men."

For most of my career, New York State had no death penalty, except for very rare cases. We had none at all during the sixteen years Hugh Carey and Mario Cuomo governed the state. Each year, the legislature passed a bill reinstating the penalty, and each year Carey, and then Cuomo, vetoed it. But in 1994, George Pataki, who had pledged to reimpose capital punishment, ousted Cuomo, and less than three months after he took office, the bill was passed and signed into law.

With other New York lawyers, I had previously formed a committee to oppose the penalty. After Pataki's election, it would have been easy to continue in opposition, but futile too, and we would probably have ended up with the worst of laws, one with few safeguards. Regardless of which side one takes in the debate, everyone agrees that defendants facing death must be effectively represented. Death is final, there can be no mistakes, and no New Yorker wants the slipshod defense systems that have prevailed in other parts of the country, where superannuated lawyers or absolute novices take on the defense of the cases to make a few dollars and often make hashes of them. Though many of these are overturned on appeal, men and women have been put to death without the benefit of a fair trial and an adequate defense. Thus, we proposed amendments to the governor's bill. The most important of these required the state to establish and fund an office dedicated to defending persons accused of crimes punishable by death who otherwise couldn't afford to hire effective lawyers.

Furthermore, in capital cases where the defendant is convicted of murder, there is a second trial in which the defendant is given the chance to tell all of the facts and circumstances of his or her background. Some people misunderstand this part of the death penalty procedure, claiming that murderers simply blame their parents or someone else for their crimes. But imagine yourself in the place of a juror in a death penalty case, faced with this awesome decision. Surely you would want to know as much as you could about the defendant, and about what led him to commit murder. To deal with this aspect of their work, lawyers, accustomed to thinking in terms of innocence and guilt, have to become sociologists and theologians, and since we hadn't had a real death penalty in more than thirty years, few of us in the New York bar were prepared to try such cases.

For these reasons, the legislature created a special Capital Defender Office and made it responsible for ensuring that capital defendants who couldn't afford counsel were adequately represented at trial and on appeal. Judge Judith Kaye, my old friend from the Tino De Angelis days, asked me to serve as chair of the board of directors of the Capital Defender Office. She feared there could be conflict between the private bar, eager to handle high-profile cases, and the Capital Defender Office, which would be establishing qualifying standards for lawyers, and she looked to me to help unite the bar in developing a system for effective representation.

Joining me on the board were Chris Stone, who runs the Vera Institute and was appointed by the Democratic speaker of the Assembly, and Senator John Dunne, a former state senator from suburban Nassau County on Long Island who, under President Bush, ran the Civil Rights Division of the Justice Department with great distinction. As directors, we have no role in actually defending capital cases, nor do we select the cases the office will take. We set policy and act as intermediaries between the office, the state, and the private bar. This can be a difficult job. We had to make it clear from the beginning that, although the Capital Defender Office is funded by the state, it serves only its clients' interests. We may take the king's shilling, but we do not do his bidding. As noted, the history of capital punishment in many other states has been an embarrassment to the bar, and it has been left to volunteer lawyers—many from New York firms, I'm proud to say, such as Paul, Weiss—to seek redress for botched defenses in federal court, through writs of habeas corpus. But the Supreme Court has become hostile to habeas corpus, and the Congress has sharply curtailed its use in death cases. Thus, it has become more and more important for defense lawyers to get it right the first time, and the Capital Defender Office board has had the responsibility not just for recruiting our own legal staff but for establishing standards and training for the private lawyers who supplement our staff.

As I write, it has been two years since New York reinstated the death penalty. More than a dozen defendants have faced it, but as I write, not one capital case has gone to trial, owing in part to our efforts. Our lawyers toil long hours to develop ahead of time psychological profiles and social histories of the accused, in order to persuade prosecutors to seek life without parole, not the death penalty. In cases where the prosecutor has persisted, we have filed numerous motions to protect the rights of our clients. Prosecutors aren't used to lawyers who are so well prepared and who spend so much time in the pretrial stages. Some have complained that we are making it nearly impossible and too costly to take death cases to trial. But this, after all, is part of our mission.

John Dunne, Chris Stone, and I have used our standing in the legal and political communities to protect the office from reprisals in funding, not by restraining its advocacy but by making clear that we will denounce any effort to interfere with its independent work on behalf of its clients. We have also stood our ground against some criminal defense lawyers, who resent the fact that we now have the responsibility of determining which lawyers, including experienced ones, are qualified to be appointed and who must now attend classes, sponsored by the Capital Defender Office, on how to defend a capital case. We have selected young, tough lawyers to work in the office, including Kevin Doyle—a Bronx native and son of a New York City cop—who prior to his selection as capital defender spent five years in Alabama defending capital cases, and Peter Sistrom, who formerly worked for me at Paul, Weiss.

The new capital defense system is now up and running. If the day ever comes when one of our clients is executed, I will grieve along with the whole staff, but I will know, at the same time, that even the poorest of defendants will have received representation as effective as any he would have received as a wealthy client of Paul, Weiss. And that is saying a lot.

15

Was the New York City Medical Examiner Covering up Police Brutality?

IN 1985 front-page *New York Times* articles charged New York City's medical examiner, Dr. Elliott M. Gross, with covering up the cause of deaths of persons who had died in police custody. The articles examined several incidents in which the medical examiner had ruled that he could not classify the cause of death of someone who died during an arrest or while in police custody. The *Times* suggested that the medical examiner was protecting the police from charges of excessive force. Since the dead were either black or Hispanic, and the cops typically were white, the ugly odor of racism inevitably permeated the issue.

The mayor, Ed Koch, realizing that, by their implications, the *Times* charges could ignite the city, asked me to head an investigation. He was well aware that the investigation must be truly independent. Otherwise, no one—neither those who blamed the cops and suspected Dr. Gross nor those who backed the cops—would take its findings seriously.

One difficulty in investigating dramatic, highly publicized allegations against a public official is the enormous pressure on the investigator to choose sides—either to confirm the allegations or, equally electric, to refute them completely. When the accusations are made in a prominent and respected newspaper, the pressure to confirm them becomes dominant. This is part of the reason the Whitewater independent prosecutor cannot easily close any part of his investigation: to do so would invite the inference, and accusation, of cover-up. This is also why Edward Bennett Williams would one day warn me that, if I took on the Iran-Contra investigation, I would probably become one of the villains. The investigator who, because of his objective findings, must exonerate a public official inevitably becomes a target himself. This is why, finally, I consider it an act of high public service when the investigator finds that he must do precisely that.

The key to any investigation of this kind is assembling an able and fair-minded staff, and to convince it that an independent inquiry is not, and cannot be, the same as litigation. Our goal was not to "win," but to bring out all of the relevant facts as promptly and completely as possible. As my second-in-command, I chose my partner, Max Gitter, and I insisted that he be named my co-counsel in the mayoral order that empowered me. We, in turn, found lawyers in other firms, including blacks and women; our group, for the several months of the investigation, became its own little law firm—some twelve lawyers assisted by five expert pathologists. We met for an hour and a half every morning, starting at seven-thirty, and we bonded through the heat of intensive work. Our report itself, once we got to it, was written in just ten days, but some of those days, for some of us, lasted twenty-four hours.

In some ways, the medical examiner investigation resembled my Attica experience almost fifteen years before. Like a maximum-security prison, a medical examiner's office is a closed and impenetrable world that the public knows little about. This, in and of itself, contributes to a lack of public understanding of the function and importance of the office—unless there is a scandal or charges of misfeasance. Before our investigation, in fact, there had never been an independent investigation of the city medical examiner's office.

By law, the medical examiner is charged with determining not only the actual cause but also the manner of death. This is not strictly, or solely, a medical judgment. For instance, a man is found dead, crushed under the wheels of a subway car. The literal cause of death is simple, but what really happened? Was he pushed, did he jump, or did he fall? A push means that the medical examiner should classify the death as homicide. A jump means a suicide, and a fall an accident. Families often pressure the medical examiner's office for a determination, whether it be for insurance reasons, religious ones, or other personal motives. The medical examiner cannot just perform an autopsy. He must also interview witnesses. In difficult cases, the medical examiner's classification of death becomes a matter of judgment, or, as we said, "more of an art than a science." When the medical examiner cannot determine the circumstances of a death, he lists its cause as "unclassified."

At the same time, the medical examiner is under particularly strong pressure whenever someone dies in police custody or during an altercation with police. Classifying the death as a homicide suggests that the police used excessive force. There have been instances, usually involving a shooting, when a finding of homicide cannot be avoided. Often, though, the proper classification is not at all evident, such as when a choke hold is used to subdue the subject.

As with Attica, we found that the medical examiner's office was a highly troubled institution. Some of the cases referred to in the *New York Times* articles had already inflamed the public's consciousness—particularly that of Michael Stewart, the graffiti vandal who, after transit officers arrested him in a subway station on September 15, 1983, never regained consciousness and died thirteen days later. As we wrote in our report,

> The greatest challenge for a Chief Medical Examiner is not how he handles the administration of the seven thousand cases a year autopsied by his office, or even how he handles the deaths resulting from police action, but how he acquits himself in the occasional big and controversial ones—where the cause of death cannot be determined in the autopsy room, where the eyewitnesses, instead of providing reliable information, engage in a cover-up and where the media put a spotlight on the Medical Examiner's office and demand answers.

Dr. Gross's policy when someone died in police custody was to classify the death as "unclassified." He simply couldn't bring himself to use the term "homicide"; he felt that it automatically accused the cops of an intentional killing and that, he believed, was a judgment for grand juries and prosecutors to make. Dr. Gross, we discovered, was not the only medical examiner who followed this practice. Others, including one of his immediate predecessors, Dr. Dominick Di Maio, had classified deaths in police custody as homicides only if they were certain that undue force had been used. Nonetheless, it could be argued that the broad use of "unclassifiable" was not really neutral, as Dr. Gross maintained it was, since it implied, at least to those unaware of the policy, that the person had not died violently. This was the very policy, in fact, that had led some of Dr. Gross's subordinates to accuse him of a cover-up on behalf of the police, accusations that, in turn, had led to the *New York Times* articles.

Our investigation took almost three months. We reviewed thousands of documents, questioned fifteen members of the medical examiner's office under oath—Dr. Gross's examination alone lasted nine days—and interviewed scores of others. I insisted that two members of the staff be present at each interview so that witnesses whose testimony was not transcribed could not change their stories. Of the five pathologists we hired, four were from other jurisdictions (Florida, Massachusetts, Minnesota, and Washington, D.C.) so that when they questioned witnesses and gave us their expert opinions, there would be no hint of political axes to grind.

At the end of the process, while we described him as a terrible and terribly sloppy administrator, we concluded that the charges of a cover-up by Dr. Gross were unfounded. Yes, he'd found it difficult to apply a loaded term like "homicide" to deaths in custody, but in each such instance, he had referred the case to the District Attorney for investigation. Although Dr. Gross himself might have left the cause of death unclassified, this had never, we discovered, affected the District Attorney's decision about whether to prosecute the police for undue force.

Moreover, we found that some of the allegations by Dr. Gross's staff were untrue. Once, according to an assistant, Gross had pointed out a neck fracture to her—a sign of strangulation—but had omitted this detail from his autopsy report. The neck specimen, however, had been preserved. It revealed no such fracture. The assistant's story had clearly been fabricated. Indeed, while all of us came to the conclusion that Gross did not belong in his job, many staff members wanted to criticize the *New York Times* too for its sloppy reportage. In the end, I was able to defuse their anger. The *Times* had brought the story to light, and now our mission was to deliver a neutral, fact-finding report on the specific charges against Gross, not to pass judgment on the performance of the press.

At the same time, however, we had a lot more to say about Dr. Gross. We criticized him specifically for the Michael Stewart case. Despite obstacles put in his path by the transit police and the investigating authorities, and even a faulty diagnosis on the part of his own consultant in neuropathology, his handling of the case had been "flawed in material respects." More generally, we expressed dismay at how poorly he ran his office. The fact that so many of his staff were willing to make accusations against him, and that their accusations initially appeared credible, we attributed to the following:

1. An office plagued by mutual mistrust and factionalism;

2. an unwise (and insufficiently publicized and explained) practice and policy in custodial cases that antedates Dr. Gross's tenure;

3. Dr. Gross's confused handling of at least one very significant case (Michael Stewart);

4. a conservatism and cautiousness on the part of Dr. Gross that, while not ill-intentioned, can be so excessive as to undermine credibility rather than enhance it; and

5. the public's understandable frustration over how police brutality cases are investigated and prosecuted.

The way Gross ran the office, we concluded, reflected his lack of leadership and his inability to inspire collegiality on his staff. We also recommended that the police department and district attorneys establish special units capable of investigating allegations of brutality, and, finally, that in order to maintain public trust, particularly in the light of racial tensions in the city, there had to be a "single standard of classification applicable to all cases of alleged justifiable homicide, whether the person responsible was an officer or an ordinary citizen." In other words, the rule of law had to be applicable to all persons, including those in authority.

The Gross investigation was concluded more than ten years ago—after receiving our report, Mayor Koch replaced the medical examiner with a more capable administrator—and having since moved on to other cases and other investigations, I have no knowledge of the office as it may be today. Probably, like so many other little understood and socially sensitive functions in the city, it needs periodic, and objective, review. But one thing our investigation couldn't end, I imagine, was the public's tendency to equate every case of official sloppiness with cover-ups and obstruction. More citizens than I'd realized seem to live in a world in which all errors are intentional and no one makes a mistake because of sloppiness or poor judgment or simply the day-to-day pressures of his tasks.

The truth was that Dr. Gross was no villain, simply the wrong man for his job.

IV

A Thumb on the Scale of Justice

16

The Runaway Prosecutors

I F THE EPITHET has been written that fully captures the 1980s, I've
yet to read it. For my profession, it was a time when the government,
as litigant, demonstrated a seemingly irresistible and, some might say,
irresponsible propensity for putting its thumb on the scales of justice.
Of course, the Milken case looms over the period for me, and the threat
of RICO prosecutions that characterized it, but in that instance the
government had help, for it was the media that made of Michael Milken
a symbol of all the perceived excesses of an era and a whipping boy for
all that had gone wrong. A purer example would be the GAF case,
which I will also describe; the government prosecutors, after committing themselves, mistakenly, to a criminal proceeding, simply couldn't,
or wouldn't, let go.

In these cases and others like them, I would say the government was
acting not so much out of malice as out of frustration, a frustration born

of trying to control and regulate an economic and technological world that was changing too fast, and in too many unforeseen ways, for the laws and regulations we ourselves had devised. Whole new industries had sprung up out of nowhere, and new ways of financing them were being invented by fast-stepping entrepreneurs who didn't always play by the old establishment rules. There were casualties, to be sure, and dislocations. People did lose their jobs; companies did go bankrupt; and a whole national industry, the savings and loans, had to be bailed out by the taxpayers. But looking at the period from this vantage point, that is, in the light of the economic situation of the late 1990s, gives a rather different perspective.

Of graver consequence to the society, in my view, and greater danger, was a different kind of government excess. I'm referring to what we would uncover in the Iran-Contra investigation. The disdain expressed by members of the Reagan administration for the rules of law and constitutional procedure during this sorry affair may well have encouraged the widespread disdain for government that has become fashionable in the 1990s. Since, in many ways, I regard my role in the Iran-Contra investigation as the high point of my career, I will save it for last, but putting Iran-Contra into the context of the 1980s, as I experienced them, I can't but observe that we have trodden the same path before. As Justice Brandeis wrote more than fifty years ago: "Men born to freedom are naturally alert to repel invasion of their liberty by evil-minded rulers. The greatest dangers to liberty lurk in insidious encroachment by men of zeal, well-meaning but without understanding."

The temper of the times in the 1980s also made a lawyer nostalgic for an era of more civilized and, I think, more fitting prosecutions. A case in point involved my first "insider trading" case back in 1973, that now-antediluvian era, when the SEC brought charges against the chairman of Bausch & Lomb, a man named Daniel Schuman. Schuman was new to the position in March 1972, when he was called upon to respond to persistent questioning by a group of securities analysts about how the company was doing. Using an old ploy, the analysts told him they were about to publish grossly inaccurate earnings estimates. A more sophisticated corporate executive would have warned them that they were on their own, but Schuman, upset that wrong information would be disseminated, revealed to them more than he should have, namely, that the company was going to fail to meet its projections. The analysts proceeded to sell Bausch & Lomb stock, and the SEC brought a civil action in federal court in 1973, claiming that Schuman and Bausch & Lomb had violated the securities laws by giving the analysts advance notice of a downturn in sales.

I remember consulting with my partner, Lewis Kaplan, on how to defend the case, which would be tried by a judge without a jury. We could have challenged the tactics and credibility of the analysts (some of whom had already entered into consent decrees with the SEC), but we concluded that our best chance was to defend on the willfulness issue alone, for the SEC had to prove not just that Schuman had disclosed inside information, which he had, but that he had done so willfully. We would argue that Schuman had acted spontaneously and impulsively, had regretted it immediately, and would never make the same mistake again.

Schuman, in addition, was a natural on the witness stand. We took him through his background, which included service as a gunnery officer during World War II on destroyers hunting Japanese submarines. When he came to his conversations with the analysts, he broke down. In the midst of telling the judge, Robert Ward, how, under threats by the analysts to publish the wrong earnings, the correct information had just "popped out of him," he suddenly burst into tears.

His contrition was genuine, and Judge Ward saw it. It didn't hurt that the judge had himself been a gunnery officer in World War II. In sympathy with Schuman, he observed that when you see a periscope, you instinctively shoot. That, he concluded, was what had happened here. He thereupon dismissed the SEC's case, a decision the federal appeals court quickly affirmed.

What a contrast to *U.S. v. GAF* and *U.S. v. Milken.* Not to mention the proceedings brought in 1992 by the Office of Thrift Supervision (OTS) against the New York law firm Kaye Scholer Fierman Hays & Handler, which I represented.

In that instance, Kaye Scholer had for several years represented the Lincoln Savings Bank, which had been controlled by Charles Keating and had failed, largely as a result of the collapse of real estate values in Arizona. To the OTS, egged on by the media, Keating and Lincoln Savings were evil, wicked, and anybody who'd represented them was tarred with the same brush. The OTS claimed that Kaye Scholer had kept its bank examiners at bay during their investigation of Lincoln Savings, thus aggravating the losses of the bank.

My point isn't to argue the merits of the case. Sometimes, under the guise of zealous reputation, lawyers do overstep the bounds, although the government's main gripe against Kaye Scholer was that the firm had maintained the confidences of its client rather than revealing them to the regulators. But what was so disturbing was what the Office of Thrift Supervision did about it. Using a procedure that the Congress had added to the banking laws in 1990 to prevent dishonest bankers from running off with assets, the OTS simply issued an executive freeze order, freezing Kaye Scholer's assets and the assets of its partners. Without appearing before a court to obtain a restraining order or even to demonstrate probable cause, it served as prosecutor and judge at once, much like the king's agents Jefferson had denounced in his remarkable declaration, who had only to sign their own royal search warrants.

The OTS couldn't seriously have believed that Kaye Scholer's partners would en masse flee in the middle of the night with their assets. They all had spouses, children, and homes, and their only means of support was to practice law in New York City. If they hid assets, they would face immediate and certain disbarment. But with its assets frozen, Kaye Scholer couldn't continue to practice—a fact of which the OTS was certainly aware—and its only choice was surrender. Within seventy-two hours, the firm capitulated, and we agreed to a multimillion-dollar settlement.

I use the term loosely. We normally don't equate ransom with settlement.

———

The practice of law itself changed in many ways in the 1980s, and so did Paul, Weiss. When I entered the firm in 1957, it was as part of a "class" of five associates, four of whom became partners. Today, out of an incoming class of between thirty and forty associates, only five will become partners. Paul, Weiss, when I arrived, had twenty or so partners and fifty lawyers all told, and even the heavyweight downtown firms had no more than one hundred lawyers. We now have between three and four hundred, of whom more than one hundred are partners, and where we once all fit into 575 Madison Avenue, we now have offices in Washington too, as well as Tokyo, Beijing, Hong Kong, and Paris.

Some of the changes have clearly been for the better. There were, as I recall, three or four women in my law school class. Paul, Weiss had just one woman associate in New York in 1957, and she was also the firm's only African American lawyer. Morgenthau's office, in the early 1960s, had only one woman and a couple of African Americans. Today well over one-third of all law students are women. Paul, Weiss now has nine female partners and more than seventy-five female associates—not a perfect ratio, but better than where we were.

Traditionally, a law partner in a law firm was expected to be available to work around the clock. Clients demanded that, even if it meant the sacrifice of a family life. But the addition of women to law firms raised new issues. When a partner is a woman with children to bring up, or a man, also with children, whose wife has a grueling work schedule, the firm cannot demand such rigor. Yet many of our new women partners have resisted flexible hours, in the fear of being stigmatized for it and held back. Those of us who wanted more flexible schedules for women lawyers were deemed old-fashioned, not to say sexist.

I had the pleasure of telling our first female litigation partner, Colleen McMahon, that she was going to become a partner. The occasion was during my visit to the hospital, shortly after Colleen had given birth to her first child. She knew she was being considered that year, and she worried terribly lest her pregnancy hurt her chances. I told her she was going to be elected. It's a secret we don't normally share until the formal vote has been taken, but what better baby present could I bring? In the end, Colleen found it nearly impossible to juggle the demands of practice and those of her growing family, left us to take on an important assignment from the chief judge, and ended up herself a distinguished judge. The loss was ours, and the lesson clear that we had to find better ways to enable lawyers, men as well as women, to have a family life.

Law firms, like businesses, also found that it wasn't enough to preach nondiscrimination. We had to back up our high-sounding ideals by recruiting minority law students, giving them mentors to help them in a practice where almost all the clients were white, and making sure we had enough of them so that, in due course, members of minorities would join our partnership. Our efforts, to our own continued frustration, have never been wholly satisfactory, and the same is true of the bar in general. I once served on a bar association committee of all the major law firms in which each of us pledged to try to achieve a meaningful percentage of minority associates and partners. But the pool of minority law students on which we all drew didn't increase fast enough, and if our good intentions remained intact, our goals were unattained.

We must keep trying. Despite what has just happened in 1997 to affirmative action in Texas and California, and the resulting diminution of the number of minority students in the leading public law schools of those states, I continue to believe that, over time, affirmative action—in our schools as in our workplaces—will prove one very important remedy to our social ills. In fact, as a member of a group of people whom, as Justice Frankfurter noted, once formed "the most despised minority of history," I believe the health of our society depends on it, as does the health of our profession.

In other respects, changes in the practice have, in my opinion, been for the worse. For one thing, litigation has become so expensive that, as I've taken to saying, I couldn't afford to hire myself as a lawyer. Studies have shown that the middle class very often depends for legal services on family members or friends who will take on a matter at cut rates as a favor. Class actions, in which plaintiffs' lawyers act for a contingent fee awarded by the court, too often provide mainly illusory relief. There have been notable cases in which victims of discrimination in employment situations or business frauds have received some compensation through a class action settlement or judgment, but in many instances most of the money awarded goes for expenses and legal fees, and the clients receive what amounts to no more than a tip—a check for $20 or so in the mail, *if* they fill out the forms. Class actions also cannot provide legal assistance for the middle class in the most pressing crises most people face, such as divorce or disputes over child custody.

There are numerous reasons for the high cost of legal services, not the least of which is the misuse and abuse of discovery, that process by which lawyers learn the facts from the opposing party and other witnesses in preparing for trial. Adopted in the federal system in 1938 as a well-intentioned and sensible reform, discovery became in my time a weapon lawyers wielded to harass and bludgeon adversaries into submission or settlement. In some cases, wave upon wave of written inter-rogatories were served. In complex cases, litigants and their lawyers spent days and weeks and sometimes years searching for and copying documents, producing—I am not exaggerating—hundreds of thousands of pages of documents and making the other side spend endless hours reviewing them. Depositions went on endlessly and aimlessly. We once took over a case shortly before trial from a big firm that had deposed a single witness for more than one hundred days! No wonder litigation is now possible only for the wealthy—or the very poor.

There are, of course, cases in which discovery is essential, when all the essential documentation, for instance, is in the hands of the other side and going into court without it would be going into, as it was once called, trial by ambush. But even lawyers who practice with the best of intentions have been guilty of overblown discovery, much as doctors who, with the specter of malpractice hanging over their heads, can't resist ordering every lab test for a common cold. To use a hypothetical example: if thirty bystanders saw an automobile collision and one video-taped it, an insecure lawyer would feel the need to depose all thirty wit-nesses, even if the first five told a story consistent with the tape. Thorough, yes, but prohibitively expensive.

In 1980 Chief Justice Warren Burger appointed me to an advisory committee of lawyers, judges, and professors to recommend to the Supreme Court changes in the rules of federal court procedures. Among our recommendations were changes to curb discovery abuses, including giving federal judges the authority to impose stiff monetary penalties on lawyers who used discovery for harassment or in bad faith. Other reforms have followed. But the high costs remain, and conse-quently the immense pressure to settle.

There are other reasons—obviously—for those costs. In almost all my cases, I was used to working with just one other partner and one or more associates. Rifkind-trained, I rarely saw the need for more, and we could practice this way because of the nature of our partnership—a series of constant collaborations among partners and associates that cut right across departmental demarcations. Nothing prepared me for what I would think of as the armies of legal talent arrayed on the battlefield of the Michael Milken case, although one unfortunate truth of the pro-fession in the 1980s was that litigations of any size became staffed by teams of lawyers. I use the word *unfortunate* advisedly, in that young lawyers tend now to be assigned to just one aspect of a litigation, and so cannot grasp the whole. Similarly, young corporate lawyers are given a discrete task and cannot understand the entire transaction or be privy to the overall legal strategy of a matter. The hierarchy of lawyers working on a large matter will often mean that younger lawyers will be working for associates but a few years older than themselves and not for the senior partner—and thus both lawyers, the junior and the senior, are deprived of the benefit of each other's insights. As a result, young lawyers often feel they are exploited and not performing meaningful work. At Paul, Weiss, as hard as we have tried to preserve the collegial atmosphere that has been one of our greatest strengths, that give-and-take between all levels of age and experience and rank, a young associate did say in a recent *American Lawyer* survey, "I would rather be a shoe salesman."

That still hurts.

Mirroring the rest of society, the profession also became more materialistic. Young lawyers, all during the 1980s, saw their classmates enter investment banking firms and make fortunes in mergers and acquisitions. Why shouldn't the lawyers who structured those transactions make the same money? Again, *American Lawyer* published a scorecard of how much different law firms made. Lawyers in firms at the bottom of the list, dissatisfied, left to join more profitable ones—something that never would have happened in the past—while some firms increased their profitability by going in for wholesale firings. I attended a conference on law firm management in this period in which I was actually ridiculed for boasting that Paul, Weiss still maintained its democratic, collegial traditions.

In my own primary field, litigation, the winds of change have already started blowing. Virtually every bar group is proposing reforms so that controversies can be decided promptly and on the merits, not by which side can wear the other out first. At the same time, the size of firms has probably peaked. Indeed, the very largest firms are finding themselves increasingly in conflict-of-interest dilemmas. It has even happened at Paul, Weiss.

For years, going back to the days of its founder, Charles Revson, Judge Rifkind had represented Revlon. He had taken the company public, sat on its board of directors, and was Revson's executor and the chairman of the large foundation Revson started. Always interested in arranging succession for his clients at the firm, Rifkind had introduced me to Michel Bergerac, the aristocratic CEO of Revlon, and I became Bergerac's adviser on various corporate matters, including fending off takeovers, for after Charles Revson's death, rumors flew and various takeover combines started to form. Then, in 1984, a credible takeover candidate appeared, Ronald Perelman, a very 1980s entrepreneur who had built his own mini-conglomerate. The problem for Paul, Weiss was that Judge Rifkind also served on Perelman's board and had advised him as he built his company. We were therefore disqualified from participating in the ensuing litigation. At one point, Bergerac and Perelman did ask me to try to bring them together. Given my spotty record as a matchmaker, I ought to have refused, but in any event, I knew the chemistry was wrong from the baleful look on Bergerac's face the moment the irrepressible Perelman, lit cigar in hand, stepped across the priceless Oriental rugs with which Bergerac had decorated his office.

The forum shifted quickly from settlement talks to the courts.

From the 1980s to the present was, all in all, the period of my most exciting and challenging work. Although I participated in the first case I will describe, *Pennzoil v. Texaco*, only as a counselor and a witness, the others all found me at work on the courtroom floor. The only generalization I can make about them, and about practicing in the 1980s, is that, as time went on and my reputation as a trial lawyer grew, the stakes kept getting higher and the cases harder. To some degree, this reflected the lesson I'd learned early from Sam Silverman and the *Diary of Anne Frank* case—that a trial lawyer has to learn to lose. Two stories come to mind that illustrate aspects of the theme.

In 1989 John Kluge of Metromedia hired me to argue his appeal in a dispute with one of his partners in the cellular telephone business, the Lin Broadcasting Corporation. Kluge had been an early investor in cellular telephones and become one of the richest men in America. Still, more than $2 billion was at stake, and Kluge had lost in the lower court.

I thought we had a strong case, and the Appellate Division—the first level of appeal in New York State—agreed with us. But then Lin Broadcasting appealed to the New York Court of Appeals, the state's highest court.

Normally, I would point out, cases like this are settled. There is simply too much money at stake, and the risk of losing everything usually encourages the warring parties to split the difference. But John Kluge hadn't made his fortune by avoiding risk, and after all, hadn't the Appellate Division found for us?

All he did, before we went into that lovely courtroom in Albany, was ask me whether I was still confident.

Like every advocate preparing for argument, I had by this time completely convinced myself. With an inner gulp, I told Kluge I was sure we'd win.

"I'm pleased to hear that, Arthur," he said mildly, "because I've just turned down a huge settlement offer."

We did prevail, thank God. But what if we'd lost? $2 billion! I could hardly comprehend that number.

And then this flavorsome story, which my friend Edward Bennett Williams used to tell with great gusto. It concerned his retention by Bernard Goldfine, who'd become famous in the 1950s for giving President Eisenhower's chief of staff, Sherman Adams, a vicuña coat. Goldfine, as Williams told it, had been indicted for failing to report on his income tax return dozens of interest-paying savings accounts. At Goldfine's insistence, his local lawyer, a man named Slobotnik, brought Williams in to represent him. Williams puzzled with his new client over what their defense might be.

"I've got it," he said finally. "While you were away on business in Washington, the 1099s from the banks arrived at home and they got mislaid, that's all."

"No, Mr. Williams," Goldfine apparently responded, "I saw every one of them."

"Oh?" Williams said. "Well, then here's what obviously must have happened. You gave them to your accountant, and he inadvertently left them off your return."

"No," Goldfine corrected, "I withheld them from my accountant."

Williams always paused for effect, at this point, in telling the story.

"Well, frankly, Mr. Goldfine," he said next, "I'm not seeing what your defense is."

"If I had a defense," Goldfine replied, "I'd use Slobotnik."

17

Pennzoil v. Texaco: The $10 Billion Handshake

D URING THE 1980s, a time of unparalleled hostile corporate takeovers, we were involved in any number of mergers and acquisitions, representing both raiders and targets. As I've mentioned, though, in one of the most dramatic of those battles—between Texaco and Pennzoil for control of Getty Oil—I ended up in a highly unlikely role, as a witness.

In December 1983, Felix Rohatyn asked me to represent Lazard Frères, which was in turn advising the Pennzoil Company in connection with a possible acquisition of Getty Oil. Counsel to an investment bank acting as a financial adviser usually has a limited role, since Pennzoil's own lawyers would normally have handled the transaction. Pennzoil is based in Houston, however, and it had no regular New York lawyer. As my relationship with Pennzoil's chief executive officer, Hugh Liedtke, developed, and my New York accent became familiar to his ears, I found myself first in the role of deal-maker and then as a witness in the case in which a Texas jury . . . well, let me start at the beginning.

Getty Oil was a public company, but Gordon Getty, grandson of Getty Oil's founder and the fourth of J. Paul Getty's five sons, controlled about 40 percent of Getty's stock through the family trust that he served as trustee. The Getty Museum owned another 11.8 percent of the stock, and the public approximately 48 percent.

Together, therefore, the trust and the museum owned a majority of Getty's stock, enough to control the board of directors and to sell to any buyer they could agree on. By mid-1983, Gordon Getty had become openly unhappy with the company's management, and the company, meanwhile, led by CEO Sidney Peterson, was seeking ways to dilute the stock in order to prevent the museum and the trust from together owning 50 percent. The museum was headed by Harold Williams, one-time chairman of Norton Simon and, more recently, chairman of the SEC under Jimmy Carter. As the maneuvering and skirmishing threatened to break into open warfare, the museum hired Martin Lipton of Wachtell Lipton as its lawyer and strategist, and the trust—that is, Gordon Getty—hired Martin Siegel of Kidder Peabody as investment counselor. Lipton and Siegel had already invented the poison pill together, the controversial device that, in a variety of forms, had become one of the most potent anti-takeover measures of the 1980s.

One of the first things Lipton, always inventive, tried to do was to broker a one-year truce between the trust, the museum, and the company, a so-called standstill agreement during which none of the parties would take any aggressive action against any of the others. But, as in a matrimonial dispute, emotions were already running too high for such an agreement to be honored. In November 1983, at a Getty board meeting, Gordon Getty was asked to leave while the board discussed the standstill agreement, for as trustee of the trust as well as a director of the company, he had a conflict of interest. The moment Getty stepped out of the room, however, the company's lawyers, led by Barton Winokur of Dechert, Price & Rhoads—"Back Door Bart," as he would later be dubbed—came in a side door and convinced the board to allow the company to join in litigation to force a coventure on Gordon Getty. This duplicitous action, when it was discovered, ended the truce, and although peace was temporarily obtained when it was agreed that Gordon Getty and the museum could add new directors to the company's board—these included Larry Tisch; Al Taubman, a billionaire real estate developer from Detroit and owner of Sotheby's; and Harold Williams—it would be short-lived.

———————

Hugh Liedtke had been dreaming about Getty Oil and its rich hoard of oil reserves for a long time. Liedtke's company, Pennzoil, had few oil reserves. So when Liedtke heard that there was a fight between Gordon Getty and Getty Oil, he sensed a chance to get in the middle.

As convincing as Liedtke was in the role of the Texas "good ol' boy" oilman, he was also a graduate of Amherst College and Harvard Business School, as well as Texas Law. A friend and business partner of George Bush, he had even had business dealings with J. Paul Getty, Gordon's father. Liedtke—that is, Pennzoil—set out to accumulate Getty stock. He'd bought about 8 percent of the outstanding shares when, on December 28, 1983, he announced a tender offer for 20 percent more, at $100 a share. A stake of 28 percent would make Pennzoil a serious player, since those shares, combined with the 40 percent held by the trust, would mean control.

I flew back from Christmas vacation to advise Liedtke and James Glanville of Lazard. I wasn't a corporate lawyer—my partner Seymour Hertz and Pennzoil's regular counsel, Moulton Gorham, fulfilled that role—but given the other players already on stage, what Pennzoil most needed was strategic counseling.

Liedtke's first step was obvious enough: to try to sew up a deal with Gordon Getty. They met on New Year's Day 1984, at the Pierre Hotel, and within hours they had formed a plan to take the company private. The museum's interest and all of Getty's public shareholders would be bought out at a price of $110 a share—a premium of $30 above where Getty Oil was trading before the Pennzoil tender and $10 a share more than Pennzoil's original offer. Pennzoil and Gordon Getty would then run the company as a joint venture, with Getty as chairman and Liedtke as president and CEO. The trust would own four-sevenths of the stock, and Pennzoil three-sevenths. If the two men didn't get along, they would be "divorced" and the assets divided in the same proportions. Either way, Liedtke would get what he wanted, a large percentage of Getty's oil reserves. The deal was conditioned on the approval of the Getty board and the museum.

Although Lipton had previously had other ideas for defeating Pennzoil's tender at $110 a share, he recommended that the museum accept. Just before the company's board met in New York the next afternoon, January 2, Harold Williams arrived in New York from California and signed the memorandum of agreement, which was then presented to the board with the proviso that it would expire if the board failed to approve it at this meeting. Meanwhile, in a side letter with Pennzoil, Gordon Getty pledged to try to remove the recalcitrant directors, consistent with his fiduciary duty, if they did not approve the deal.

The Getty board met at the Intercontinental Hotel, but Liedtke refused to be in the hotel because he hadn't been invited to the board meeting. Instead, he sent me to wait in Gordon Getty's suite, next door to the room where the board was convened. There I received reports from Lipton and Gordon Getty's representatives on what turned out to be a long, long meeting.

After several hours of discussion, the Pennzoil proposal was finally put to a vote. All of Getty's old directors, who were still in the majority, voted against it. The new directors voted for it. There followed another lengthy debate on what to do next. Some of the directors feared the possibility of shareholder suits unless there was an alternative to the Pennzoil bid, but no one budged until Gordon Getty disclosed his pledge to Liedtke—to remove the recalcitrant directors. This created a veritable explosion. Finally, after all advisers were asked to leave the room, the board came up with a counterproposal: they would accept Pennzoil, but only if Pennzoil increased the $110 tender price by another $10.

At 2:30 A.M., the meeting was recessed until the next afternoon, to await Pennzoil's reply.

Liedtke was enraged. He had already, on his own, raised his offer from the original $100. Was the board now asking him to bid against himself? And why hadn't Gordon Getty tried to remove the directors, as he'd promised in the side letter?

The answer to this last was simple: Getty didn't have enough votes. The vote in favor of the additional $10 had been 14–1. Even the newly appointed directors had been for it. The only vote against had been Gordon Getty's.

By the next day, January 3, I was convinced that if Liedtke made no countermove, the deal would be dead. But then, reviewing what appeared to be an impasse, I came up with a possibility. The company owned an insurance company, part of a diversification program undertaken by Sidney Peterson, that neither Liedtke nor Gordon Getty wanted to keep. Why not sell it? We worked the numbers around. I suggested to Liedtke that he offer to sell the insurance company within five years and guarantee the Getty shareholders an additional $3 out of the proceeds. Liedtke agreed, and when the Getty board reconvened at the hotel later that day I was ready with that sweetener.

Then I waited and waited, in Gordon Getty's suite, for the board's response. It seemed to take forever. Finally, Marty Lipton emerged from the boardroom. He told me that if I would raise the guarantee on the insurance company proceeds—which we called the stub—to $5 from $3, we would have a firm final deal approved by the board at this meeting. Without it, we didn't have the votes.

I telephoned Liedtke. He caucused with his other advisers. Some of them didn't want to increase the offer even by this small sum, but Liedtke recognized it as his last opportunity to get a deal. He asked whether Lipton would represent that the $5 stub would do it.

I said I would insist on it.

This I did. Lipton agreed. He said that if Pennzoil raised the stub price to $5, we had the deal. He carefully wrote down the proposal, including the condition that the deal was final, and he read it back to me for verification.

Then he took the proposal into the board, and the board approved it with only one dissent. The agreement was recorded in its minutes, and within moments I was on the phone to Liedtke to tell him that he now owned three-sevenths of Getty Oil.

A year and a half later, Joseph Jamail, Pennzoil's Houston lawyer, argued to a jury in Texas that I shook hands with Getty's board on the acquisition that night, and that in Texas a handshake means a deal. But there was far more than a handshake. The board minutes recorded that the board approved the agreement. Lipton had a note of my counterproposal that stipulated the final price, which is what he read to me, and there were other documents that made it clear there was an agreement.

And yes, there was a handshake too, but it wasn't really to seal the deal. It was to assuage my hunger!

By this time, I'd been sitting outside the boardroom for hours, waiting for the Getty board to act, and I'd eaten nothing. Inside the boardroom, I knew, the board had big platters of sandwiches; I'd seen them being carried in. After that last vote and my phone call to Liedtke, I'd asked Marty whether I could grab a leftover sandwich in the boardroom. When I walked in, the board meeting had adjourned, but the directors were still milling around talking. Naturally, I shook hands with them and congratulated them before eating. And that became the $10 billion handshake.

The Getty board's agreement should have ended the matter, but it didn't. Just after the announcement was made, Wall Street got busy, and even as we were drafting the final merger papers, two of the stars of the mergers and acquisitions world, Joseph Perella and Bruce Wasserstein, then of First Boston, made a sudden bid for Getty Oil, $125 a share, on behalf of Texaco.

Marty Lipton, a superb lawyer, wasn't prepared to let his client, the museum, accept Texaco's offer of $125 unless it was indemnified by Texaco against any claims Pennzoil might make for breach of contract. Normally, in such an agreement, the seller represents that it is free to sell and has no prior commitments that would be inconsistent with a sale. But because Lipton specifically carved the Pennzoil deal out of the sellers' representation, thus putting Texaco on notice that there was another contract, Texaco's bankers knew exactly what they were doing. They penciled a note that they had to "stop the train"—meaning that they had to stop Getty from signing the formal merger agreement with Pennzoil.

Sure enough, although we didn't understand why, Getty's lawyers began stalling. At the same time, a senior Texaco executive wrote, in a document that later came to light, that Pennzoil had only an oral agreement with Getty—suggesting that Texaco was free to interfere with it.

Then, on the morning of January 6, a press release announced that the museum had agreed to a merger with Texaco at $125 a share, and that, in a special meeting that same afternoon, the Getty board would do likewise.

For Hugh Liedtke, it wasn't just like getting jilted at the altar. It was like a new husband taking over the wedding ceremony and reception. Pennzoil's Houston law firm rushed into Delaware court to stop the Texaco merger. The court refused to grant an injunction, saying

Pennzoil had an adequate remedy in damages, but Pennzoil won a moral victory nonetheless: the Delaware judge, who devoted much of his opinion to the question of the contract, wrote, "I can only conclude that on the present record Pennzoil has made a sufficient preliminary showing that in all probability a contract did come into being between the four partners."

This from the most sophisticated commercial court in the country.

While corporate lawyers still debate whether Pennzoil did or didn't have a contract—because no formal merger agreement had been signed—the facts pointing toward a contract were both unique and compelling, and every court that considered the issue so found. I myself had no doubt that I had made a contract with the Getty board, and that it was so recorded in the board's minutes.

Following the Delaware decisions, Pennzoil sued Texaco for contractual interference in the Texas state court in Houston. Liedtke's friend Joseph Jamail, the most successful tort lawyer in the country, was the principal trial lawyer for Pennzoil and the only Pennzoil representative who dealt directly with the Getty representatives. I was his principal witness.

I was called early in the case, and I narrated in a straightforward way the details of the negotiations with the trust, the museum, and the board. I emphasized that Liedtke was reluctant to raise his price on the stub from $3 to $5 and did so only after Lipton had told me we had a final deal at that price, an agreement the Getty board would—and did—confirm in its minutes. There was a firm agreement, I testified, and I had made it with Lipton. Having seen many juries, although none in Texas, I sensed this one liked me and appreciated my presenting what had happened in simple terms.

Texaco's lawyer then, in my judgment, made a huge mistake—perhaps because lawyers, as a rule, make poor witnesses. They tend to ramble on. Texaco's lawyer invited me to do just that, not simply to answer a question yes or no but to provide a complete explanation. Even appellate courts had never been so indulgent with me. Under cross-examination, I became not just a witness but an advocate, and I made the most of it.

Moreover, Texaco's strategy was to try to pit me against Lipton by demanding that I give him a character reference. If I did, they seem to have convinced themselves, I would be conceding the case. But as a witness, I saw it differently. It was precisely *because* of my admiration for Lipton's integrity that I'd trusted him when he said we had a done deal. Lipton's integrity, I was sure, was a pivotal part of Pennzoil's case, not Texaco's.

Given free rein by Texaco's lawyer, I testified as follows:

"I think that Marty Lipton was my friend, still is my friend, and my opinion of him and respect for him is undiminished.

"Martin Lipton was presented by Texaco with an offer he couldn't refuse. What do I mean by that?

"His client was a seller. He was offered a substantial premium over what we offered.

"Everybody who is a party to a contract has a right to either perform or to pay damages. You could always breach and pay damages, and he was offered in this case an indemnity so his client wouldn't have to pay damages. . . . His client was getting more money, and instead of having any kind of risk of damages for walking out of the contract, the buyer, Texaco, was going to pick that up.

"I don't see how Martin, given the fact that he was trying to get as much as he could for the museum, could have turned down the offer that was made to him. And when I ultimately saw the document he drew with Texaco, he specifically refused to represent that he didn't have a contract with Pennzoil. He excluded that and got an indemnity from them, so I think that Martin put his interest in getting as much for his client above any kind of obligation that his client had to Pennzoil and said Pennzoil could resolve that with Texaco since they gave the indemnity.

"That's how I feel. It does not in any way reflect on Martin's integrity. I think he did an extraordinary job for his client in getting them the highest price *and* the indemnity. An extraordinary job."

I managed finally to escape from Texas in August and get back to work. Joe Jamail told me later that, after my testimony, the defense spent the rest of the case trying to undercut me but that they failed. I'd relied on uncontestable documents: Lipton's memo confirming the deal, the board minutes, Lipton's representation in his agreement with Texaco, and Texaco's indemnification of the museum.

Jamail concluded his case with experts who testified that, if Getty had honored the deal with Pennzoil, Pennzoil would now own three-sevenths of Getty's oil reserves at a price well below market. By their testimony, Texaco had appropriated $10 billion that properly belonged to Pennzoil.

On this issue of damages, Texaco's lawyers had an expert who was prepared to tell the jury that Pennzoil's actual loss was much less—about $1 billion—but they worried that the mere mention of the lower damage figure might be regarded by the jury as a concession that Texaco was liable. So they kept the expert off the stand and offered no damage testimony whatsoever. They rested their case entirely on the claim that Texaco wasn't liable because there'd been no signed agreement. Years before, in fact, I had counseled a client, who wanted to back out of an acquisition deal that was not fully formalized, to pay the other side for a release. I didn't want to take the very risk that Texaco had taken in the Getty transaction. Juries, in my experience, will punish a party they feel has acted improperly. Legal technicalities—for example, when does a contact become a contract?—tend not to provide a safe haven for unequitable conduct.

Jamail's summation picked up on this theme. He threw the words of Texaco's witnesses back at them. He reminded the jury of all the documents that hurt Texaco, down to the executive's note saying Texaco could upend Pennzoil's deal with Getty because it was just oral. And he concluded, a Texan speaking to Texans:

> I ask you to remember that you are in a once-in-a-lifetime situation. You have a chance to right a wrong, a grievous wrong, a serious wrong. It's going to take some courage. You got that. It's going to take a logical examination of what went on. . . . If you come to the conclusion, as I hope and believe that you will, that a grievous wrong has been done to Pennzoil . . . then no verdict less than $7.5 billion actual and $7.5 billion punitive is enough. . . . I know you are going to do the right thing. You are people of morality and conscience and strength.

About a month later, I received a telephone message from Jamail. It was terse, but not cryptic: "$10 billion compensatory and $3 billion punitives."

———

After the verdict, Texaco changed its team. Since New York law governed, the contract having been made in New York, it hired David

Boies of Cravath Swaine and Moore to argue the appeal, and Linda Robinson to wage a public relations campaign against the verdict. Hardly a day went by when, thanks to Robinson's efforts, there wasn't another *Wall Street Journal* editorial denouncing Texas justice.

But we had our ace in the hole. As I mentioned before, the Pennzoil people were incredulous when I recommended Judge Rifkind to argue the appeal. He was eighty-five years old, they protested. Yes, I agreed, he was eighty-five years old. But after they'd met him and heard him speak, they hired him on the spot.

I went with Judge Rifkind to Texas, not to speak myself but for the pleasure of witnessing his performance. The argument was held in the auditorium of a law school in downtown Houston, where the demand for seats was so great that tickets had to be printed and parts of the overflow audience watched the proceedings on closed-circuit TV.

Needless to say, not only did Judge Rifkind know New York law, he had helped shape it. Directing his attention to Texaco's appellate brief and Boies's argument, he said he was "a stranger" to the version of New York law they'd offered. He then proceeded to lecture the Texas judges, but not at all in a condescending way, on New York's law of contracts and interference with contracts, calling Texaco's interference the most brazen he had ever encountered. He was masterfully persuasive, and the court loved it. In their judgment, handed down in February 1987, they upheld the compensatory damages but reduced the punitive damages to $1 billion—for a total verdict of more than $10 billion.

Texaco immediately tried to settle the case for $2 billion, but Pennzoil refused, whereupon Texaco, that April, filed for bankruptcy. Carl Icahn, the sometime raider, then bought a significant block of Texaco stock. I knew Icahn well; I had represented him when he made a takeover bid for Phillips Oil and also defended a textile company against one of his raids.

One day, he called me. He said, in his blunt way, that a settlement was in everyone's interest, and he asked me to produce Joe Jamail. This I was able to do, not long after. Jamail, ever filled with machismo, immediately challenged Icahn to a drinking bout. Three hours later, with their voices slurred but their minds still sober, they reached a settlement figure—$3 billion—and the Texaco-Pennzoil struggle came finally to an end.

18

U.S. v. GAF: Good Things Don't Always Come in Threes

W HEN IT FIRST started, *U.S. v. GAF* looked like a kind of warm-up, on the government's part, for the more complex case against Michael Milken it was then preparing. Aspects of the two cases were certainly similar, and they eventually overlapped in time. *GAF* illustrated, perhaps even more clearly than Milken, what happened during the 1980s when, as I put it earlier, the government tried to put its thumb on the scale of justice. To put it another way, if trying a case for a second time, after a mistrial, is as unpleasant as putting on a wet bathing suit, I have yet to come up with a simile to describe accurately what it is like the *third* time.

Let me explain.

GAF Corporation was a chemical and building-materials conglomerate controlled by a smart and witty former federal prosecutor named Samuel Heyman. In late 1987, the company and one of its top executives were indicted for violating the federal securities laws. I had represented GAF before, and the company asked me to defend it again.

After leaving the U.S. Attorney's Office years before, Sam Heyman had run his family's real estate business for several years, but when his father died, he began buying GAF stock and then waged a proxy fight to oust GAF's management in the annual election. Poorly run, GAF was ripe for change. It was a bitter fight, though, and as often happens in such situations, each side sued the other in the midst of it. Heyman approached me at the time, but I told him he'd be wasting his money if he hired me. The lawsuits, I said, were but sideshows to the main event. His money would be better spent persuading GAF's shareholders to vote for his slate, because if he won the election, the court would never overturn the results and he would control the company.

I was wrong.

Heyman won the vote handily, but then a federal judge voided the election, ruling that Heyman had failed to disclose to GAF's shareholders during the proxy fight that his sister had accused him of mishandling family trusts he'd run since their father died. The trusts had in fact multiplied in value under his administration, and the sister's allegations were all too typical of family disputes.

This time I agreed that Heyman might need my services. Among other things, the court's decision set a terrible precedent. If it ever stood up, it would mean that the officers of publicly held companies faced the same loss of privacy as candidates for public office. Everything, from their marriages to their family relationships, would be subject to disclosure to the shareholders. Fortunately, on appeal, the decision was reversed, and Heyman was reinstated as GAF's chief executive officer.

In December 1985, GAF had asked my advice in connection with a bid for Union Carbide, the giant chemical company. Union Carbide had been a component of the Dow Jones average, but its stock price plummeted because of a disastrous explosion at its plant in Bhopal, India, which killed hundreds of workers. Union Carbide's management opposed GAF's acquisition, and after a difficult battle, GAF gave up the struggle. By this time, though, it had acquired millions of shares of Union Carbide stock, and these turned out to be a spectacular investment. In 1986, when GAF began selling its Union Carbide stock, it made a profit of more than $250 million.

Two years later, however, federal prosecutors charged that just before GAF began to sell its holdings, James Sherwin, the GAF vice-chairman, had illegally manipulated the price of Union Carbide stock—from $21.87 a share to $22 a share—to increase its profit. Heyman himself was not accused of a crime, but his company and Sherwin were both named as defendants.

The government claimed that GAF wanted to sell ten million shares of its Union Carbide stock for at least $22 a share. But in October 1986, when it wanted to sell, Union Carbide was trading at only $21.87. According to the government, Sherwin asked a broker he knew, Boyd Jefferies, to buy Union Carbide at the very end of the day so that its closing price for that day, which is the price of the last trade, would be $22.

Boyd Jefferies's company specialized in trading large blocks of stock. After Jefferies agreed to buy the shares, the government alleged, Sherwin phoned James Melton, Jefferies's chief trader, and told him to proceed. Melton then bought Union Carbide stock, on behalf of Jefferies & Company, on two afternoons in October 1986, and again on two days in November. He then immediately sold the stock. Several days later, Union Carbide rose to $23 a share, the price at which GAF actually sold the ten million shares, retaining other shares for a later sale.

The government's charges were based on the testimony of Boyd Jefferies himself, who also told the government that Sherwin had promised to reimburse him for his losses in the event the price of Union Carbide dropped. He claimed that a $40,000 bill Jefferies & Company had sent to GAF, which appeared to be for a consulting fee, was actually to cover losses he'd incurred buying and selling Union Carbide stock.

The case, with its eighth-of-a-point manipulation—or $40,000—on a transaction in which GAF made a total of $250 million, had, if it was to be believed, the character of a misdemeanor. What it was doing in a criminal proceeding is a question only the innermost circles of the SEC and the Department of Justice could have tried to answer. But even believability came with difficulty. A former U.S. Open champion and a grandmaster in chess, James Sherwin had been trained as a lawyer and was deeply involved in public and charitable affairs, including the International Rescue Committee. He had taught underprivileged kids. The idea that he would commit a felony to save the company $40,000 on a $250 million transaction defied all logic.

Moreover, Jefferies was a flawed witness, caught in Ivan Boesky's web. Boesky, whom we will meet again in the Milken case, was the leading insider trader and securities law-breaker of the 1980s. Among other things, Jefferies had been secretly taped by federal investigators arranging illegal stock-parking transactions with Boesky. To avoid a jail sentence, Jefferies had agreed to plead guilty and to cooperate by helping the government bring cases against others. His accusations against Sherwin and GAF were a crucial part of that deal. But Jefferies himself didn't believe that he and Sherwin had done anything wrong or illegal. In a magazine interview, he himself pronounced the government's case against Sherwin "chickenshit."

Our defense strategy would be simple. We would attack Jefferies's credibility. Then we would point out to the jury how absurd it was to suggest that GAF had tried to manipulate Union Carbide's stock price by one-eighth of a point—12¢—when it was already sure of more than a $200 million profit. Jefferies & Company was a block trader, so its purchase and sale of Union Carbide stock on its own was unremarkable. Finally, we would have James Sherwin himself—a most unlikely white-collar criminal.

The case went to trial in late 1988.

Choosing a jury, I should say, has become one of the great sports of our judicial system. It is neither an intellectual nor a scientific activity, although the court and the opposing lawyers question prospective jurors closely, searching for causes for dismissal, and in the exercise of peremptories—the right to challenge a set number of jurors without cause—the lawyer is looked upon as a mind-reader who, by his powers of intuition, can divine hidden prejudices. Many of us hire jury consultants for the purpose, often psychologists and sociologists who have studied community dynamics, conducted focus groups, and taken polls and advise on types of jurors to avoid in particular cases. In one famous criminal case, the consultant concluded that a naturalized Chinese American citizen, employed by a bank, might give the benefit of the doubt to a public official accused of breach of the public trust!

Each lawyer's experience is different. I, for instance, have never knowingly encountered the race factor in jury selection. But then, I have never been called upon to defend Rodney King or O. J. Simpson.

Choosing a jury in a white-collar criminal case is always difficult because the facts are complex and the defendants are usually well off. In the GAF case, I had an even harder time. For one thing, the Wall Street insider-trading scandals were at their height, and prospective jurors had tended to form strong, unfavorable opinions about people accused of financial wheeling and dealing. In addition, there was my own new and, to me, unfortunate celebrity. Many of the prospective jurors had seen me on television the summer before, during the Iran-Contra hearings. Some may have liked me, but others, I'm sure, thought I'd tormented Oliver North and the other witnesses.

Still, we got through the jury selection process before the defense used up all its peremptories, and the government's first witnesses, as the trial began, were the sort that defense lawyers love to see on the stand. Called to give the jury general background, they are viewed as harmless, but often the defense can use them, on cross-examination, to bring out favorable facts.

One of them was the trader from Salomon Brothers who'd bought GAF's Union Carbide at $23 a share. He was anything but the victim-witness that one expects in a case of this kind, and on cross-examination, we got him to poke a hole in the government's theory. He told the jury that traders pay attention not to the closing price of a stock but to the prices it was trading at during the day. The government, remember, was claiming that Sherwin had specifically asked Jefferies to manipulate Union Carbide's closing price. Better still, he said that Salomon Brothers had been happy to buy GAF's Union Carbide stock at $23 a share and made a nice profit when it resold it at an even higher price. That contradicted the government's theory that Salomon Brothers had been the unsuspecting victim of a market manipulation.

Boyd Jefferies himself took the stand one day in early January 1989. In his daylong testimony, he confirmed the story in the government's indictment. Sherwin had called him and asked him to make sure Union Carbide closed at $22 a share. Jefferies said he'd directed his chief trader, Melton, to buy Union Carbide, and then had sent Sherwin an invoice to cover his losses, when he later sold the shares at a loss.

That evening, after court, I huddled with my colleagues—my partner Max Gitter and Steve Kaufman, with whom I'd been friends since we were federal prosecutors together and who was representing Sherwin—and talked about how to cross-examine him. Jefferies, we agreed, had been uncomfortable on the witness stand and visibly disliked testifying. Kaufman predicted that he would become peevish and unlikable on cross-examination, as long as I pushed him. Knowing that my cross-examination style is usually low-key, Kaufman urged me to go right after him.

I took his advice with gusto. Jefferies, trying to convince the jury of his humble background in his direct testimony, had testified that he'd worked as a cowhand after he graduated from business school in 1952. Only afterward did the significance of that detail strike me. In 1952 we were fighting the Korean War—the Vietnam of my generation—and Jefferies must have been busy evading the draft!

This is how my cross-examination began.

"You told the folks on the jury that you graduated from UCLA Business School in 1952."

"Yes, sir."

"And then, as I recall it, you went to work on a ranch."

"Yes, sir."

"You made a point of telling us that it was hard work. Do you remember that?"

"Yes, sir."

"And you said it was good experience, correct?"

"Yes, sir."

"It was a character-building experience?"

"I don't believe I said that."

"Was it?"

"Yes."

"Is it a fact, sir, that when you chose to work on that ranch in 1952, that the regulations provided for an exemption from military service in the Korean War for working on a ranch? Yes or no."

"I don't know what the regulations were."

"Did you know that the exemption was provided, sir?"

"Absolutely not."

"Did you serve?"

"No."

One of the jurors, I'd noticed, was wearing a service ribbon, and as Jefferies squirmed, I saw him smile.

Next, I wanted to show the jury that Jefferies was a man who lied even to his friends and customers.

I asked him, "Is it a fact, sir, that in October and November of 1986, your firm, Jefferies & Company, was having capital problems?"

"Absolutely not."

"Did you ever tell Mr. Boesky that your firm was having capital problems?"

"Yes."

"And that was just a lie?"

"Yes."

When it came to his key conversation with Sherwin, Jefferies had to rely on his memory—or his imagination. As it happened, he often took notes of his conversations on yellow legal pads, but he had thrown out all his notes pertaining to Sherwin—*after* he'd begun cooperating with the government. Of course, the government hadn't mentioned the yellow pads in its direct examination, and as I now questioned Jefferies about them, I could tell the jury was listening intently.

"Is it a fact, Mr. Jefferies," I asked him, "that you destroyed yellow pads and other notes that you took after you began cooperating with the government?"

"Yellow . . . ?"

"Yes or no."

"Yes. They were thrown out."

"Well, that's in what we call the passive tense: 'They were thrown out.' Who threw them out?"

"My secretary cleaned out my office on March 30, 1987."

"Did you, when you cleaned out that office, throw out a yellow pad with information on it?"

"I threw out many yellow pads, yes."

"Was it your decision to throw them out or your secretary's?"

"We cleaned out my office together."

"But who made the decision to throw out the yellow pads?"

"I did."

The more we went on, the more I was able to weaken Jefferies's credibility. Now I began to attack his claim that Sherwin had asked him to buy Union Carbide and guaranteed him against loss. Well before the trial, Jefferies had made a written presentation to the SEC about his dealings with Sherwin, but he'd made no mention of the alleged guarantee in it. Now he claimed that the guarantee was "implicit."

But what did "implicit" mean?

Jefferies agreed that it meant "not spoken."

I was also able to make good use of notes the SEC lawyers had taken during their interviews with Jefferies. Jefferies had told them he bought more Union Carbide in November in an effort to recover his losses on the October purchases. But now, in court, the government was alleging that Jefferies's November purchases were also part of the illegal manipulation scheme with GAF. If GAF had guaranteed Jefferies against his October losses, as he now testified, and if he had already billed GAF for them, as he now testified, why would he have risked his own capital in order to make up those losses on his own?

Or could it be that he'd lied to the SEC? Or had the SEC lawyers misunderstood?

Moreover, Jefferies claimed that Sherwin asked that the price be closed at $22 a share, but he also admitted now that Sherwin had turned down his offer of $22 a share for the whole block of Union Carbide owned by GAF. If that were the case, then why would Sherwin have been so interested in a $22 closing price?

Before I was done, I wanted to show the jury that Jefferies had made a sweetheart deal with the government in exchange for his testimony against GAF and Sherwin. In most cases, I would have brought this out at the beginning of my cross-examination, but I'd decided to give the jury a good taste of Jefferies first. By this point, I hoped, they would have developed a sufficient dislike for the man that they would seethe with anger at the prosecutors for having let him off the hook.

Jefferies, I established, had been permitted to plead guilty to technical record-keeping offenses, not market manipulation, a much more serious charge. He had been allowed to keep his stock in Jefferies & Company, and the company itself was not prosecuted. In five years, according to his deal, he could be back in the securities business. He had yet to be sentenced, but he knew the prosecutors would tell the judge how much he'd cooperated.

Normally, government witnesses are coached to testify that, while they hope they won't receive a jail sentence, they know the judge might still imprison them. I had a hunch Jefferies could be led to answer differently, so I ended my cross-examination with some loaded questions.

"You live in Aspen?" I asked him. "And in a resort community in California? Two homes?"

"Yes."

"And you understood, sir, that one of the things that a court looks upon in passing sentence is community service, what someone has done for the community?"

The prosecutor objected, so I asked the question another way.

"Mr. Jefferies, are you so confident that you will not be sentenced to a term of imprisonment and is your idea of community service to run a golf clinic in Aspen for children? Yes or no?"

"Yes."

With that, I sat down, and the trial adjourned for the weekend.

We on the defense team were almost giddy. We were positive the jury disliked Jefferies and that, by now, they doubted his story.

Trials, though, are as unpredictable as March weather.

One day that next week, the prosecutors came into court and handed us a report by a typewriter expert who had examined the consulting-fee invoice that Jefferies & Company had sent to GAF, the one Jefferies claimed was actually a bill for the losses he'd suffered. The expert claimed that Sherwin had altered his copy of the document. Clearly, the government should have given us the expert's report before the trial began, and the judge now ruled that we could have a mistrial if we wanted it, meaning that the case would start all over with a new jury— *if*, that is, the government decided to retry it.

It was a hard call. We were all sure the trial was going well for us, that Jefferies was a discredited witness, and we were hopeful of a complete acquittal on all counts. At the same time, it is axiomatic, virtually a rule, that a prudent defense lawyer never turns down a mistrial. Often the other side will decide to drop the case, particularly if the tide has turned against them. We debated over lunch, all the pros, all the cons, but in the end prudence won out over our instincts.

We decided to ask the judge to declare a mistrial.

And we were wrong.

When we spoke to some of the jurors afterward, they told us, just as we'd thought, that they'd been leaning toward acquittal.

The government, meanwhile, announced that it was going to retry the case. And this time they knew our strategy in advance.

Just twenty days later, we gathered in court to begin the second GAF trial. This time around, we all knew what to expect, and the tense uncertainty of facing witnesses for the first time was gone. Still, it was a criminal case, and our client's liberty was at stake, so I was as anxious and edgy as ever.

As in the first trial, the government's case was based on Boyd Jefferies's testimony and on the $40,000 consulting-fee invoice that Jefferies claimed was meant to reimburse him for his losses on the Union Carbide stock. This time, the government also relied on the testimony of Jefferies's chief trader, James Melton.

Melton testified that he had executed the manipulative trades in October 1986, and then, using Jefferies's WATS line telephone service, had called Sherwin twice at GAF's headquarters in New Jersey to thank him for the purchase order and to confirm that it had been done. Sherwin, however, was insistent that he'd received no calls from Melton, and so Melton's testimony stood uncorroborated.

Also, at the second trial, the government called the typewriter expert whose report had led to the first mistrial. The government had two copies of the $40,000 invoice—one from Jefferies & Company and one from GAF—and they were not the same. The Jefferies & Company copy bore a notation that the invoice was for Jefferies & Company's consulting services on an investment GAF had allegedly made in a British company. That notation was missing from GAF's copy of the invoice, and the typewriter expert told the jury that he could tell that it had been deleted, but he wasn't sure how. The government was suggesting to the jury that someone at GAF, possibly Sherwin himself, had tampered with the evidence.

It is always damning when a criminal defendant is charged with covering up or destroying evidence. We had to explain what had happened to that invoice. Consequently, I turned to the same typewriter expert who had testified for me at the Gulf Coast Leaseholds trial almost three decades before. She demonstrated to the jury that on GAF's copy of the invoice the missing notation had been removed by the erasing feature of an IBM Quietwriter, a then state-of-the-art typewriter. We were able to prove that Jefferies & Company used such typewriters but that GAF did not. The change, therefore, had to have been made at Jefferies, not at GAF. The invoice backfired on the government.

This left Melton's testimony about his two long-distance, California-to-New Jersey, WATS line phone conversations with Sherwin about the Union Carbide purchases. Since WATS line bills do not separately identify each call, the government had no way of corroborating Melton's testimony. Furthermore, Melton's and Jefferies's accounts were at odds with each other. Jefferies testified that Sherwin had first asked him whether he could close Union Carbide at a certain price, then that Sherwin had given Melton specific instructions on the two days in October to close it at $22 a share. According to Melton, though, the instructions had come from Jefferies, not Sherwin. One of the government witnesses was lying, and if it was Jefferies, then he, not GAF, was responsible for the manipulation. Similarly, whereas Jefferies originally claimed that the November purchases had been made for Sherwin as part of the manipulation, he now testified that he had made the November purchases on his own, without any request from GAF. Needless to say, this is the stuff out of which reasonable doubt emerges.

The government rested its case, and now we had to decide whether to have Sherwin testify. Putting the defendant on the stand is the most difficult decision in every criminal case. Once a defendant testifies, the rest of the trial becomes largely irrelevant—the verdict will turn on the jury's reaction to him. But on the other hand, if the defendant is not called, the jury may infer he is guilty, even though the court will instruct it to draw no such inference.

The government had interviewed Sherwin during its investigation. Then as now, he'd asserted his innocence, but his recollection of some unimportant background facts had been faulty. We knew the prosecutor would use these inconsistencies in an effort to impeach him, and while we had every confidence in Sherwin, we worried about the effect this might have on the jury. So, once again, we went by the book. In other words, if the defense is winning on the government's case and still calls the defendant as a witness, then the case will turn not on reasonable doubt but on how well the jury reacts to the defendant's testimony.

After calling our own typewriting expert and some character witnesses for Sherwin, we chose instead to rest.

In my summation to the jury, I borrowed from an Edward Bennett Williams story about an English courthouse. I told the jury that on the walls in one of the oldest courthouses in America was the following statement: "In this hallowed place of justice, the government never loses. When the rights of a citizen are protected against false witness, the people win." That principle, I said, could have been written for this case.

When I finished, Steve Kaufman asked me whether the story was true. I admitted that I'd made it up. But it *ought* to be written on the courthouse walls, I told him, and if we won, I'd see to it that it was.

That second GAF jury deliberated for twelve days, the longest I've ever had a jury out. In the beginning, we were most hopeful and optimistic. The jurors' expressions had seemed friendly and sympathetic to us. After all, it isn't every case in which you can show that the prosecution's expert was dead wrong, or in which the star witness's credibility is as shaky as Jefferies's had been. But as the days dragged on, we realized that the jury must be sharply divided. From time to time, we could hear raised voices coming from the jury room. As tough as the waiting was for the lawyers, though, we had at least gone through it before. But Sherwin, though outwardly his usual good-natured self, began to agonize.

Finally, on the twelfth day, the jury reported that it was deadlocked, and it had failed to reach a decision. Once again, the judge had no choice but to declare a mistrial. Once again, we spoke to the jurors afterward. We learned that most of them had wanted to acquit GAF and Sherwin, but a few had held out for conviction and they could not be convinced. They'd kept returning to Melton's testimony about his phone calls with Sherwin. The fact that there were no phone records for the WATS line calls hadn't bothered them. They'd also been puzzled, they told us, and some of them troubled, by the fact that Sherwin hadn't testified.

It seemed as though there was just no way we were going to get a unanimous verdict, no matter how many of the government's theories we managed to disprove. All we could do was hope—once more—that the government would drop the case. Having gone this far, however, the government was determined to pursue it through to a verdict.

The third GAF trial began on October 24, 1989. The prosecutors now knew our entire strategy and shaped their case around it. This time, they would neither call a typewriter expert nor contend that GAF had tampered with the $40,000 invoice. Nor would they try to prove that Jefferies & Company's November purchases were part of the manipulation scheme.

Once again, I listened to the answers of potential jurors during their questioning. Our jury consultant had told us to avoid candidates who were anti–Wall Street, but at the same time, according to his polls, most members of the community believed that Wall Streeters were greedy and willing to break the law to make a profit. There were other generalizations to keep in mind: artists and Jews allegedly tended to be more sympathetic to defendants; Irish and persons in bureaucratic or government jobs—such as workers for the post office, the telephone company, or city agencies—were supposedly more willing to credit the government. On the other hand, most of the people who are willing to serve as jurors in a long trial do work in jobs for the city or the utilities.

So we had to choose, based not on stereotypes but on our impression of individual jurors. Would we be able to relate to them? Did they seem open-minded? Intelligent enough to follow our arguments? Or were they maybe too eager to serve? Did that mean they had their own agenda?

Having tried many cases, Kaufman and I had given up trying to read jurors. We would have been willing to take our chances on the first twelve jurors called to the box as long as they didn't seem prejudiced. But we went along with the game, making decisions based not on wisdom but on guesses and intuition.

Sherwin, as the individual defendant, had the final say, and he and his family did have opinions. His wife thought a particular juror seemed kind, even though every one of her relatives, for generations, had worked for the police department. So, to the surprise of the prosecutors, we kept that juror and hoped that our action would be interpreted as showing that we had total confidence in our case.

"The jury is acceptable," we said, the final formality, and we said our prayers.

The third trial began.

Jefferies, after two dress rehearsals, made a much better witness. The jury was worse. Each time we'd started to try the case, the trial judge had told us that jurors were growing more hostile to defendants in Wall Street cases and suggested that we work out a plea bargain. But each time Sherwin had refused. He wouldn't admit guilt for something he vehemently denied having done.

We knew that the second jury had deadlocked, in part, because of Melton's testimony about his two long-distance phone calls with Sherwin. While the diehards had accepted that there could be no corroboration because of the WATS lines, others, who favored the defense, had the feeling that the calls had never been made.

I believed Sherwin. He, in turn, kept pressing us to check the WATS line story.

We had hired Kroll International, the investigative firm, to try to find the WATS line phone records, but to no avail. According to Kroll, there were no such records. Either they'd never existed or, if they did, the phone company had discarded them.

Then, on a Monday afternoon near the end of the trial, the government turned over pretrial material for a surprise witness—Melton's secretary. In her deposition, she had told the government that one day in October 1986 she had "overheard" Melton on a telephone call to Sherwin, thus corroborating Melton's story. It would now be two witnesses, Melton and his secretary, against one, Sherwin, on the matter of the telephone calls. After the day's session ended, the defense team gathered in my conference room. Every last one of us was despondent. How could we possibly cross-examine the secretary unless we found the phone records?

Suddenly, Max Gitter had an inspiration. His brother worked for AT&T. He called him on the off-chance that he might know something and discovered that, some time before, his brother had in fact sold WATS line service for the company. Gitter's brother was sure AT&T kept WATS line records separately, identifying each call, but he didn't know exactly where. He believed records might be kept at one of three or possibly four regional offices—in Colorado, San Francisco, Atlanta, or New Jersey.

At least we now knew, which the prosecution didn't, that we could subpoena the records and get our hands on them. At the same time, we had to have them in the next forty-eight hours; Melton's secretary was scheduled to take the stand on Thursday.

The next day, Tuesday, we had Kroll flood AT&T with subpoenas and send investigators to each regional office to talk to the record-keepers. AT&T was cooperative and promised a response within twenty-four hours.

But as of that night—Tuesday—no records had been found. The same thing on Wednesday.

Melton's secretary testified Thursday morning, corroborating what her boss had said about the phone calls. But Max Gitter, after court that day, stayed behind to arrange some scheduling matters, and while he was still in court, his brother called to tell him that he personally had found out where the records were kept.

It turned out that AT&T did indeed have them. They weren't in any of the regional offices, but in a deep underground repository—safe, apparently, from nuclear attack—in Bedford, New York. Each call, according to Gitter's brother, was separately identified. By 6:30 P.M., subpoenas had been served at the Bedford facility and at AT&T headquarters. Although most employees had gone home by that hour, AT&T called in a special overtime staff to track down the codes so that the particular records could be found.

At 1:00 A.M., Friday morning, Gitter got a call from AT&T. They'd found the records.

So now the records did exist, but no one knew what they would reveal—whether they would confirm or refute Melton's story.

The next morning, Gitter sent John Gevertz, a Paul, Weiss associate, out to examine them. Gevertz called Gitter every five minutes to report on what he'd found. Or hadn't found. Before the day was over, it was clear to Gevertz that there was no record whatsoever of any call made to Sherwin's office. We then spent the entire weekend tracking down the other calls made on that line to make sure Sherwin couldn't possibly have been at any of the numbers in question. He hadn't been. On Sunday, I sat with our chart-maker, putting together a dramatic exhibit for court the next day, and, still on Sunday, we delivered it to the prosecutor for his review.

We thought this eleventh-hour discovery would end the case. Even though we could tell nothing from the jury's impassive reaction when we introduced the chart, Melton's story of the calls, and his secretary's, could not possibly be true.

The prosecutors clearly felt the same way. Just after the case went to the jury, they offered to drop the case against Sherwin if he would just admit that he'd manipulated the stock and if GAF would plead guilty. Sam Heyman himself was willing to accept the deal just to get the case over with, even though it would have meant a plea by his company. But Sherwin flatly refused. He wouldn't confess to something he hadn't done, not even to save his own skin.

Whereas the second jury had stayed out for twelve days, this one came back after just a few hours.

As the jurors filed into court, I had that sinking feeling in my stomach. Somehow I knew.

The verdict was guilty. After three trials, GAF and Sherwin were both convicted. The judge sentenced Sherwin to six months in jail. She said, at the sentencing, that she had never been so anguished by that aspect of her job.

There was, however, one twist left to this bizarre case. Criminal convictions resulting from a jury verdict are particularly difficult to overturn on appeal. Appellate courts usually defer to a jury's deliberations. But the GAF case was different. The government got its convictions only after three trials. The theories and proofs it offered in court had kept changing from trial to trial. The November purchases that, for a time, had allegedly been part of the manipulation scheme, suddenly turned out not to have been. Sherwin had allegedly tampered with an invoice to cover up the scheme; then he hadn't. WATS line records didn't exist, according to AT&T and the government, but when they appeared at the last minute, they proved Melton had never made the calls. Jefferies had bought blocks of Union Carbide stock supposedly to raise the price at which GAF could sell its own block, but had sold his shares before GAF did, thus depressing the price. Even with the deference an appellate court traditionally shows to a jury, there is a limit to what a court can swallow.

In our brief to the federal appeals court, written by Max Gitter, and in the oral arguments that Kaufman and I made, we emphasized these shifting inconsistencies in the government's case. One thrust of our argument was that whoever had been responsible for Jefferies & Company's November purchases of Union Carbide must also have been responsible for the October purchases, only a few days before, and for the same motives. Therefore, it had been unfair when the government, after two trials, had suddenly dropped the November purchases, and the court had simultaneously refused to allow us to inform the jury that, in the earlier trials, the government had claimed they were manipulative too. This, we contended, had deprived us of a key element in our defense.

In the end, we found justice. The court agreed with our arguments. It vacated the convictions of GAF and Sherwin.

Today no case involving a disputed charge of an eighth-of-a-point manipulation would even be prosecuted. But in the 1980s, the government was convinced that it could police Wall Street only by bringing criminal cases, no matter how minor the alleged offense, and as we will now see again in the case of Michael Milken, having made questionable bargains with witnesses, the government was bound and determined to prove itself right.

Age 8 with double-cousin
Joan Hamburg, age 5.

At graduation from
Lawrence High School, 1950.

A favorite portrait by Ellen, 1964.

From left to right: Donald Arnold, Doug, Yale President Richard Levin, Ellen, Arthur, Yale Law School Dean
Anthony Kronman, Emily, and Lewis, at the fall 1996 dinner to announce the Arthur Liman Chair in Public
Service and the Liman Fellowship and Fund for Public Service at Yale Law School.

Harvard Overseer (1988–1994) and Executive Committee member (1991–1994).

A playing card from the Liman 19th century game collection.

Fishing on Long Island Sound.
Inset: With Steve Ross (left) in Lyford Cay, Bahamas.

Clockwise from top left: Simon H. Rifkind, in his office at Paul, Weiss; Receiving the UJA Judge Proskauer Award from Robert Morgenthau, 1987; With William Paley, 1986. Arthur was a board member of the Paley Foundation and The Museum of Radio and Television founded by Paley.

A Continental Grain board meeting in Caneel Bay, BWI, 1983. From left to right: Donald Staheli, Henry Kissinger, Arthur, CEO Michel Fribourg, Morton Sosland, Walter Goldschmidt, and Olivier Wormser.

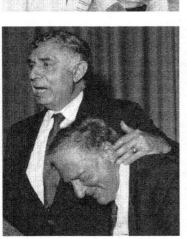

Clockwise from top left: With John Kluge of Metromedia, 1994. In 1989, Arthur won a $2 billion settlement for Metromedia against LIN Broadcasting; Presenting a birthday gift to Steve Ross, 1980s; New York Observer, 1990; With Joe Jamail, 1993. Arthur had a "hand" in Pennzoil's historic $13 billion judgment against Texaco. With Charles Bluhdorn of Gulf & Western (center), and Donald Oresman, Casa de Campo Beach, Dominican Republic, 1981, where the "Good-American Medal" was awarded.

The Complete Story of the
Events Leading to the Bloodiest
One-Day Encounter Between
Americans in This Century

ATTICA

The Official Report
of the New York State Special
Commission on Attica
Plus 64 pages of
on-the-scene photographs

*Clockwise from top left: Pass for Attica Correc-
tional Facility; The shocking cover, showing
inmates forced to march naked in the prison
yard, from the official report on Attica written
by Arthur, one of the first "instant" books and
nominated for a National Book Award—a rarity for a government report; Eating Christmas
dinner with Attica inmates; Attica commission
staff meeting, photographed by Cornell Capa, a
good friend.*

Morgan Guaranty Trust Company OF NEW YORK

1-120
210

CT 01649

New York March 8, 1982

EXACTLY= $80206,380&52

Dollars

THE NEW YORK CITY TRANSIT AUTHORITY

Reserve Bank OF NEW YORK

Authorized Signature

⑈0000 1649⑈ ⑆02 100 1⑊08⑈

From top to bottom: Former Governor Hugh L. Carey, signing the proclamation creating the Liman Advisory Commission on the Administration of Justice in 1981; With former Mayor Ed Koch and an $80 million settlement check from Rockwell International to the New York City Transit Authority as payment for 754 faulty subway cars; With former Governor Mario Cuomo, who appointed Arthur to the New York State Executive Advisory committee on Sentencing Reform from 1983–1985.

Clockwise from top left: Giving President Bill Clinton advice on his golf game at a White House dinner, 1995; Meeting Nelson Mandela with Heinz CEO and client Anthony O'Reilly at Paul, Weiss, 1993; (left to right) Legal Action Center directors Herbert Sturz, Professor Elizabeth Bartholet, Lewis Liman, and President Paul Samuels in 1997, celebrating Arthur's twenty-five years as founding chairman of a public interest law firm dedicated to protecting the rights of ex-offenders, former drug addicts, and people with AIDS; Former Mayor David Dinkins appointed Arthur the chairman of the New York City Commission on Mayoral Appointments in 1990, an experience that convinced him that affirmative action if used fairly and well can overcome decades of exclusion.

An informal committee meeting with Senators William Cohen and George Mitchell, where Arthur is holding Evan Morgan, son of Press Officer Lance Morgan.

Arthur was Chief Counsel to the U.S. Senate Select Committee on Secret Military Assistance to Iran and the Nicaraguan Opposition. The hearings, held from May 5 to August 6, 1987, included 28 witnesses, 262 hours of testimony, 40 days of public hearings, and over a million pages of documents. Bottom photo: The swearing-in of Oliver North.

19

Michael Milken: The Demon of Wall Street

MY BLACKEST moment as a lawyer came on November 21, 1990, in room 318 of the federal courthouse building downtown on Foley Square, when Federal Judge Kimba Wood, in a calm, measured voice, sentenced Michael Milken to ten years in prison.

Never had I felt that I'd so badly let a client down.

Milken and I had little enough in common. We were from different generations, different backgrounds. He was born in 1946, the son of an accountant, and grew up in California. He came of age in the 1960s and went to college at Berkeley, the seat of student radicalism. The radicalism suited Milken fine, but he had always marched to a different drummer, and his own radicalism wasn't political but economic, taking the form of an almost evangelical conviction that the country needed deep and rapid economic reform in order to achieve social change. While still at Berkeley, he wrote a paper on high-yield bonds, which became the cornerstone of his business.

As Milken pointed out, when corporations have needed to borrow for growth, they have had, historically, only two choices. They can float public bonds, but to do so they need what is known as an investment-grade rating from a rating agency such as Moody's or Standard and Poor's, which base their evaluations largely on historic earnings and corporate balance sheets—in other words, the past. Or they can borrow from the banks, which generally saddle their short-term loans with conditions, for banks also look to the past, not the future. Growing up at a time when the computer was creating whole new industries, Milken saw an urgent need to create a market in which newer companies not eligible for investment grade could issue bonds based on their prospects, bonds that would carry higher rates of interest to reflect the greater risk.

After Berkeley, Milken did his graduate work at the Wharton School of Business of the University of Pennsylvania. Along the way, he wrote an extraordinary letter to the *New York Times;* though never published, it expressed very clearly where he was going:

> Unlike other crusaders from Berkeley, I have chosen Wall Street as my battleground for improving society because it is here that government institutions and industries are financed. While the Wall Street community, surrounded by stacks of stocks, certainly seems a long way from the egregious gutters of California ghettoes, the future of both are highly dependent on common factors.

While still a student at Wharton, he went to work summers for Drexel Burnham and Lambert in New York, commuting from Philadelphia by train or bus. There he began promoting and selling high-yield bonds. Overnight, and almost single-handedly, he transformed Drexel Burnham, a second-line Wall Street firm, into the financial powerhouse of the 1980s. Potential customers, like Larry Tisch, remember receiving phone calls from him in which, in almost academic style, he described the merits of high-yield bonds, pointing out that investment-grade bonds could always lose their rating because of downturns in the company's business, while high-yield bonds typically had nowhere to fall to. In those days, in fact, high-yield bonds, often called "fallen angels," were issued by companies that had started with an investment grading and been downgraded because of poor performance. But Milken, over the phone, would discuss the merits of a particular issue of high-yield bonds, analyzing in almost clinical detail the performance of the company and the reasons he believed in the investment. He had always done his homework. He would also go into the advantages that the customer might achieve by issuing high-yield bonds in his own business, a discussion that would reveal the thoroughness of Milken's knowledge of the company he was approaching.

He was as different from the normal Wall Street salesman as night from day, and also from his clients. He had a prodigious memory, an overwhelming intellect, and he relied not on instinct or hunch but on research, research, and research. He was particularly interested, early, in the companies that were then flourishing in his native California in the telecommunications, entertainment, leisure, and nursing-home industries. In fact, he was never at home on Wall Street and quickly moved his high-yield bond operation from New York to Beverly Hills. He could have been chairman of Drexel anytime he wanted to, but he preferred the less pretentious title of vice president.

In some ways, he could be said to have lived the American dream, but an exaggerated, distorted version of it. A millionaire while still in his twenties, he was considered to have become a billionaire in his thirties, yet money, for Michael, was never more than a gauge by which to measure the success of his ideas. He was, in his private life, a paragon of family values. He married his high school sweetheart, and they lived within walking distance of where Michael had grown up. By the standards of his personal wealth and his era, he lived modestly. In his heyday, in his offices across from the Beverly Wilshire Hotel in Beverly Hills, he was at work before five in the morning, day in, day out. He had meals for himself and his staff catered so that the work would flow uninterrupted until well into the evening. While he made huge sums, based on a percentage of what Drexel made on the business he brought in, he gave prodigiously to charity. By his early forties, he had funded his own foundation with almost $400 million.

But no one could be as successful as Michael Milken and remain unknown. He became, for many, the embodiment of all that was wrong with America in the 1980s, its materialism, its rampant greed. Established firms on Wall Street didn't like him. For one thing, he was a loner. His Rolodexes contained the names of thousands of clients but probably not one head of a Wall Street firm. They regarded him as an arrogant kid who insisted on creating his own securities and markets, while he saw them as wedded to the ways of the past. Besides, since he was capable of underwriting high-yield issues on his own, why should he share his clients with them? And so he became a threat to their business, and its club-like conventions. As one veteran banker on Wall Street once observed to me, "Milken just didn't play by our rules."

To some extent, it could be said, Milken brought about his own downfall. Some of it was even simple semantics. He himself called his new instruments high-yield bonds, because they paid higher interest rates than other corporate bonds. Others quickly dubbed them junk bonds, a catchy phrase, which Milken naively accepted, but a misnomer. (Corporate bonds of any kind stand higher in balance-sheet ranking than common stock. If a company's junk bonds were to become valueless, so would its common stock. Yet, does anyone call common stock junk stock?) And then there was the annual conference Drexel hosted, at which Drexel clients held forums about their businesses to raise money; because some in attendance were well known as corporate raiders, though most were not, the media dubbed it the Predators' Ball. So Milken became, for the media, the purveyor of junk and the predators' predator.

Moreover, while Milken rarely gave a press interview, some of his clients were brash and openly hostile toward established companies. They bragged of their takeover victories—and layoffs—while Milken was giving lectures on job creation. But he was blamed for their attitudes. In the eyes of some, he and his clients became one, and even his peers in the industry, who made huge fees representing clients who were threatened with takeovers by Milken's clients, were hoping he'd fall.

And finally there was the money. Because of Milken's celebrity, or notoriety, and because, in the single year of 1986, his Drexel bonus alone paid him the staggering sum of $550 million, he became the regulators' and prosecutors' ultimate prize. Nothing in his experience had prepared him for the anti–Wall Street hysteria that gripped government regulators and the media alike in the late 1980s and early 1990s, but when the dominos began to fall, one Wall Street operative turning in another in what became a virtual parade of plea-bargainers, it was almost inevitable that the last one standing would be Michael.

I was in at the beginning of the parade when, one afternoon in May 1986, Fred Joseph, the head of Drexel Burnham, called me. He asked me to represent one of his firm's young investment bankers, Dennis Levine, in what Joseph believed would be an SEC civil investigation. I spoke to Levine, and we arranged to meet the next morning, but before that could even happen, I had a distress call from him from an unusual venue, the U.S. Attorney's Office. He had just been arrested and was being held pending a detention hearing. The charges against him were not civil but criminal. He was accused of insider-trading through a Bahamian bank and then ordering the bank to destroy his records. By the next afternoon, I had arranged for Levine to be released on $5 million bail. By that time, federal investigators had shown us copies of the account at the Bahamas branch of a Swiss bank he'd used to trade the stock of companies about which he had secret information.

Normally, prosecutors aren't eager to share incriminating evidence with a defendant. I knew Levine was caught red-handed the minute he told me that the prosecutors couldn't have been more cooperative and had even given him files of documents to read overnight. Even my Paul, Weiss partner Martin Flumenbaum, who was generally a fighter to the end, couldn't figure out a defense. Instead, Flumenbaum and I opened negotiations in Levine's behalf with the government, principally with Charles Carberry, who headed the fraud unit in Rudolph Giuliani's U.S. Attorney's Office. Within a few weeks, in exchange for leniency, Levine agreed to plead guilty and to cooperate with Carberry and his staff. He revealed to them that he was part of a group of young investment bankers trading on insider information, and that he'd sold insider information about impending deals to Ivan Boesky.

Boesky was a famous "arb," or arbitrageur—arbitrageurs, historically, were hit-and-run investors who profited from very slight discrepancies between markets—and one of the most notorious and flamboyant figures on Wall Street. Sometimes he plunged heavily on stocks that were the subject of announced takeover bids, betting that the deals would go through. More often, he speculated on stocks that might be the targets of takeovers. If he guessed right, of course, the profits were enormous. Boesky, ever vain and self-promoting, boasted continually of his genius and his aggressive, bold hunches, but it turned out he'd simply been paying Levine and another investment banker for insider information.

The government, of course, asked Levine about Milken, but Levine told them Milken was clean. Why would Boesky have needed him as a source if he'd had Milken?

Boesky in turn agreed to plead guilty, in September 1986, and to cooperate, secretly at first, with the SEC and the U.S. Attorney's Office. He told the government that, besides Levine, one of his principal sources was another Drexel investment banker, Martin Siegel, whom Fred Joseph had wooed away from Kidder Peabody at the beginning of the year. Boesky revealed that Siegel had tipped him on deals, and that he delivered Siegel his share of the proceeds in briefcases stuffed with cash. But what Boesky said next was even more exciting to his interrogators.

He started talking about Milken. As prominent a catch as Siegel was for them, delivering Milken would earn Boesky the greatest reduction in sentence.

The charges Boesky leveled against Milken were many, and they ranged from insider trading to parking: he claimed that Milken had parked stocks for him and that he had done the same for Milken. The insider-trading allegations were strained and, as I will explain, never stood up. But they were important to Boesky. Psychologically, Boesky wanted to leave the impression that insider trading wasn't at all unusual. After all, hadn't the most famous investment banker of the day given him information? And insider trading, if it had occurred, was all-important to the prosecutors. It is a most serious offense, a fraud on the trading public by which individual investors are invariably victimized and the integrity of the market as a level playing field is destroyed. But until the Wall Street prosecutions of the last decade, the kind of stock-parking arrangement that Boesky told the government he and Milken had made was much more minor. Parking often involves violations of record-keeping or disclosure rules, but for many years the SEC treated it as a technical violation. Parking is what Joseph Kosow had done for Louis Wolfson, more than twenty years before, and Judge Palmieri had actually dismissed the criminal parking charge in that case, ruling that parking wasn't a crime! Furthermore, another defendant with whom Boesky claimed he had parked stocks, Princeton-Newport Partners, was exonerated, and two others, Boyd Jefferies and Sandy Lewis, received no prison sentences.

By the mid-1980s, though, the distinction between criminal and civil law had become increasingly blurred, in part because prosecutors were convinced that the securities industry was willing to evade regulation as long as the risk was only civil injunction against doing it again, not prison time. In this respect, they may not have been wrong. Meanwhile, the SEC announced, very publicly, that it was its *policy* to define offenses vaguely in its regulations—so that the securities industry would not know when the line was crossed.

Ever naive about how he was viewed by the outside world, Milken didn't see danger coming. He kept doing business as usual, and as much of it as possible. Many experienced bankers know that controversial clients can get them into trouble, but Milken had less of a sense of it than anyone I ever represented. As long as a company had prospects worth financing, he plowed ahead. Most investment banking firms also have large compliance departments to instruct the bankers on the more complex SEC regulations and to keep them out of trouble. Drexel in California had only one compliance lawyer, and most of the legal work was done by lawyers not familiar with SEC rules. There was an air of invincibility, of untouchability, about Drexel, particularly in its California operations. As it happened, I'd had experience of this several years before the Milken investigation when I was representing a Drexel client in private litigation and the other side subpoenaed Milken. I tried to schedule Milken's deposition but received only an angry protest from one of Drexel's executives.

Didn't I know who Milken was? He does not give depositions, I was firmly told.

That attitude, which pervaded Drexel, always leads to trouble.

On November 14, 1986, just after the close of the markets and just before the government's agreement with Boesky was made public in a press release, subpoenas were issued to both Milken and Drexel Burnham. It became a page-one story, a national sensation. The government's announcement was augmented with leaks from the SEC and the Boesky camp, both of whom wanted to stress his importance as a cooperator. Literally hundreds of thousands of documents were subpoenaed from Milken and Drexel. Plaintiffs' lawyers also brought lawsuits, an inevitability when there is publicized litigation. The SEC filed its civil lawsuit first, but it was stayed pending the criminal proceedings. And those proceedings were now out in the open.

That November, when the case started, Milken hired Edward Bennett Williams as his lead lawyer and at the same time asked Paul, Weiss to collaborate in his defense. We could provide experience in securities law as well as manpower. From the very beginning, Ed Williams was haunted by the money, by that $550 million bonus. He worried that no jury could ignore Milken's extraordinary wealth and would vote to convict not because of what he had or had not done, but simply because he'd made too much money. Ivan Boesky could easily be discredited on the stand, but Milken's earnings could never be erased. Williams accurately foresaw that the media and the government would turn Milken into an all-purpose symbol of discontent about Wall Street; Williams also made the prediction, although it was much more difficult to perceive in the beginning, that the solidarity between Milken and Drexel Burnham, which was targeted in the same investigation, might turn out to be tenuous.

When it came to the staffing, the Milken case, as I've mentioned, was like the beginning of a new era for me. I had just finished trying the GAF matter with one partner and one associate—a small enough group that I was on top of every fact. But the Milken case was like the plant in *The Little Shop of Horrors*—the staffing just kept growing and growing. In addition to Ed Williams, two other partners from Williams & Connolly, Vincent Fuller and Robert Litt, were working on the case, as well as some associates. Michael's personal lawyer, Richard Sandler, functioned as his general counsel and was involved in all aspects of the defense. Representing Drexel were my old friend, Peter Fleming, and the firm's corporate counsel, Cahill Gordon and Reindel. There was another friend, Michael Armstrong, and his team representing Michael's brother Lowell (also a Drexel employee), and the lawyers for the other defendants too. Since Milken was the principal defendant, though, we served as a clearinghouse for all facts and for strategy.

At Paul, Weiss, Martin Flumenbaum acted as my alter ego and chief of staff, aided principally by a soon-to-be-partner, Eric Goldstein, but four other partners and at least half a dozen associates also participated. The size and structure of the defense team meant that, for the first time in my career, I didn't have a collegial relationship with the associates. By and large, they communicated with me indirectly, either up through the hierarchy or by memorandum. One day, for instance, one of them, Peter Sistrom, came to visit me in the country to discuss a new transaction the government was planning to add to the indictment. He briefed me on all the facts. At the end, I asked him, as was my custom, what he thought our best defense was. I saw him hesitate. Then he admitted that, while he had been charged to learn all the facts of the transaction, no one had asked him that question before!

Welcome to big litigation practice, in which the division of labor destroys initiative among the youngest lawyers and denies the senior lawyers the benefit of their minds.

In fact, the defense, in its organization, resembled the way Michael ran his business. Drexel specialized in researching every security it traded. Its traders read prospectuses about the securities in which they dealt and other documents down to the finest of the fine print. Michael wanted his defense lawyers to be as knowledgeable as his traders, to have specific assignments, and to fit into a hierarchy controlled by their supervisors. The casualness, indeed the chaos, of normal defense preparation, in which ideas are put forward by any lawyer on the team, was inconsistent with the way Milken worked.

Arrayed against us, meanwhile, as leaders of a sizable government team, were three smart and tough young prosecutors, John Carroll, Jess Fardella, and Reid Figel, who served first under Carberry and then, after Carberry left the U.S. Attorney's Office, his successor, Bruce Baird. Rudolph Giuliani, of course, was in charge until he left to run for mayor of New York, in 1988, and also Gary Lynch, chief of enforcement at the SEC. I think none of us could have guessed, at the time, that it would be more than three years before Drexel finally broke ranks, and almost four before our own black day in court, in November 1990, or finally, that Carroll and Fardella would still be traveling to California, in 1992, in the company of Martin Flumenbaum and myself, to meet with Michael. Along the way, Ed Williams died—a terrible loss to the case, but even more so to the profession. Later my friend Stephen Kaufman joined us for the defense.

For a time, after the initial crisis, the U.S. Attorney's investigation appeared to move slowly, while the SEC investigation involved an almost unending production of documents and witnesses. We appeared, at times, to be virtually at a standstill, and it became clear that, without corroboration for most of Boesky's charges, Carroll and Fardella were reluctant to proceed to trial. God knows what we might do to their protégé before a jury. On Milken's and Drexel's side, it was, at least outwardly, business as usual. Despite the cloud over their heads, the annual "Predators' Ball" continued to be held, if in a more subdued way, and Milken presided in Beverly Hills. In 1988 Drexel even became involved in the biggest single deal in its history, acting as banker to Kohlberg Kravis Roberts in its takeover of RJR Nabisco, although Milken spent little or no time on the matter. Indeed, it may well have been RJR Nabisco that first gave Drexel the idea that perhaps Milken wasn't indispensable after all and, possibly, that it could settle its case on its own.

We had, of course, represented unpopular clients before. Ed Williams, in his time, had defended not only organized crime bosses but even Joe McCarthy. None of us, however, had ever seen anything like the reckless anti-Milken mania that the media, fed largely by leaks from the SEC, indulged in. Michael was blamed, at one time or another, for virtually everything that was wrong in the economy and society. He was deemed responsible for the failure of the savings and loan industry that cost the taxpayers billions of dollars, even though the principal villain there was clearly the government's own regulatory agency, aided and abetted in its laxity by certain members of Congress. He was accused of masterminding the takeover movement that led to layoffs in acquired companies, even though the other major Wall Street firms represented far more takeover promoters than Milken ever did. He was vilified as the symbol of greedy and uncaring capitalism despite the fact that, in addition to his charitable work, he provided more financing than any prior banker to enterprises owned or run by women and blacks. He did so not as a matter of social conscience but in the belief that financing shouldn't be based on color or ancestry but on the ideas and prospects of the borrower. In fact, when it came to pleading in court, he specifically asked me not to mention the race or sex of his clients, seeking no credit for what he considered proper business practice.

But even in the domain of social conscience, Milken was an iconoclast. He was convinced, for instance, that if the economic oligarchy in Mexico could be eliminated and access to capital provided more freely, Mexico would become a significant economic power. That in and of itself would alleviate the problem of illegal immigration. To back up his belief, he formed a Mexico Fund in which he and his clients invested. To many of them, his speeches on the subject were like pitches for his pet charity, and they "gave" because Michael was asking. But to Milken, the Mexico Fund, like everything else, was a matter of conviction.

Similarly, during the 1980s, a number of investment bankers took up an idea promoted by the businessman Eugene Lang and began "adopting" public schools, agreeing to serve as role models for the children and, later on, to pay their tuition to public universities. But this was too conventional an approach for Milken. He went into the Los Angeles ghetto and began teaching himself. He actually taught grade-school children algebra, using games of his own invention.

Nevertheless, Ed Williams turned out to be right. In the end, maybe nothing could have saved the image of a man with $550 million dollars on his W-2.

———

Over time, the government slowly began to increase the pressure. Carroll, Fardella, and company began offering immunity to Milken's coworkers at Drexel and menacing them with indictments, under RICO, if they failed to cooperate. The RICO (Racketeer-Influenced and Corrupt Organizations) Act was a statute originally designed as a weapon against organized crime. In RICO, all of an accused's assets can be confiscated if he is convicted. Under this pressure, colleagues and customers, many of whom owed their success and their wealth to Milken, suddenly began to develop amnesia on facts helpful to him. Drexel itself was threatened with indictments. The government let it be known that the investigation would continue until they found charges that would stick, and that there would be as many trials as were required to secure Milken's conviction. (The GAF case, literally a penny-ante manipulation in comparison, was already sending out the same message.)

This campaign of intimidation left Drexel employees, and finally Drexel itself, literally terrified. Drexel's business was carried out amid virtual thickets of regulations that few of its employees understood. Drexel bankers, sellers, and traders had created and sold whole new forms of securities, and not always with the benefit of the most conservative counsel. I'm sure many Drexel executives had no idea whether they'd broken the law or not. What they did know was that they were living a nightmare—fabulously wealthy one moment and, because of RICO's confiscatory provisions, potentially broke the next.

For potential white-collar defendants, it takes strong character and courage to stand up to that kind of pressure. Every transaction, every possible misdeed, is summoned back to mind, brooded over, suffered over. If most criminal defendants engage in denial, blotting out whatever they did wrong, in white-collar RICO cases the effect is often just the opposite. As we know from the psychological study of show trials in other countries, it is not unheard of for a defendant to convince himself of his own guilt. We members of the Milken team were quite aware of this risk, to the point of wondering which of the Drexel executives would break ranks first.

Milken, as it happened, had little doubt who this might be. Milken's Drexel, it should be noted, was a remarkable exception to the prevailing "good ol' boy" macho atmosphere of Wall Street, and Milken himself, for instance, was embarrassed by off-color jokes. He was sure it would be one of his high-powered salesman types, someone who womanized and/or did drugs, the kind his wife Lori was always urging him to get rid of, just as she'd urged him to stop doing business with Boesky. The most likely candidates, he thought, were James Dahl, who did business with the savings and loans, selling them high-yield securities, and Cary Maultasch, rumored to be the office's skirt-chaser, who had left First Boston to come to Drexel because Drexel was a faster track. Dahl, who as part of Milken's group at Drexel had been represented by Robert Litt of Williams and Connolly, began sending out the message that Milken had become a liability and that he, Dahl, should be made head of Drexel's high-yield department. Maultasch, meanwhile, had begun telling other employees that, at the beginning of the investigation, Milken asked him not to reveal the existence of a ledger book containing transactions with a Drexel customer. Then Dahl began to drop hints that he, not Boesky, was Milken's real problem and that he could provide incriminating evidence that Milken had parked securities with some savings and loans. As for Maultasch, I myself had interviewed him at the beginning of the investigation and asked him directly whether he knew of any improper conduct at Drexel. He had looked me square in the eye and said no.

Then, in September 1988, Dahl dropped the Williams office as his lawyers and began cooperating with the government. Maultasch did likewise. And finally, perhaps inevitably, Drexel itself lost its nerve.

The cause related, in part, to Drexel's much vaunted compensation scheme. The company was able to attract salesmen not just because of the bonuses it paid but because it gave them the opportunity to receive warrants—options to buy—on leveraged buyout transactions that

Drexel was financing through high-yield bonds. The Congress, that is, the House Oversight and Investigations subcommittee, had held hearings in the spring of 1988 in which the amount of warrants being given to Drexel employees and, in some instances, the executives of favored Drexel customers, was featured. Fred Joseph and Drexel's corporate lawyers denied knowing the magnitude of the warrants Milken and his employees were getting. In one instance in which executives of a Drexel customer had shared in the warrants, Joseph and the lawyers denied knowing that fact too, although a Drexel lawyer employed on the West Coast had set up the transaction.

Then, that September, the SEC filed its own civil suit, naming Drexel, Michael Milken, Lowell Milken (Michael's brother and a Drexel employee), and assorted others, and in November, the Justice Department approved the RICO charges. The next step would be criminal indictment under RICO. Finally, in December, I had a phone call from Fred Joseph. In the belief, mistaken as it turned out, that an indictment would surely destroy his company and a plea bargain would save it, he told me Drexel was about to sign a plea agreement.

A little over a year later, Drexel would file for bankruptcy. Meanwhile, we were burdened not just with the notoriety of Milken's compensation but with the fact that his own employer had pleaded guilty to acts that Milken himself had allegedly committed.

The government had succeeded in isolating us. The noose had tightened.

Milken was as difficult a client as I have ever represented. He hovered over us all like a hawk, questioning us constantly, exploring this, then that scenario, making up his mind only to change it. It was like having a good lawyer for a client. A perfectionist in his own business, he tried to be one in ours. When I got to my office in the morning, normally a little before eight, I knew my first call would already be waiting for me and I knew who it would be—at five o'clock California time. At all times, he seemed confident that he'd done nothing wrong—nothing, that is, that everyone else on Wall Street didn't do. Milken was confident, too, that he was vastly misunderstood, that someday he would be appreciated, and that meanwhile no one could touch him.

There had, of course, been pressure on both sides, earlier, to reach a settlement, and differences of opinion on both sides too. While I'm well aware that some lawyers specialize in plea negotiations, I find them virtually the most painful part of the criminal side of the practice. I may have this attitude in part because of the empathy I feel for my clients, and in part as the result of experience. I have rarely known a client who, over the years, did not come to regret his plea, even if the sentence was lenient. (Dennis Levine was a notable exception.) The plea makes it impossible for clients to deny the offense. They read of others who got off, and they tend to blame the lawyer for not fighting hard enough for them. Knowing how persecuted Milken felt, I knew he would always be unhappy about a plea, no matter how stoical he was about it.

On the government's side, Giuliani had pushed for resolution before he left office, but below him there were differences of opinion. Some, perhaps knowing that the successful prosecution of a Michael Milken would be the open sesame to future careers, wanted to stay the course, continuing, meanwhile, to gather evidence. Others preferred the certainty of a guilty plea to the hazards and unknowns of a jury trial. Early in 1989, when we were the last of the dominos, the grand jury was sitting, and the indictments would soon be handed down, we did come close to a deal. There were items still open, problems that hadn't been resolved, including such basic issues as the degree of exposure to prison and the status of Lowell Milken, whom the government was still threatening to indict. But even as the government, now impatient with the delays, was preparing to file its indictments, it was Michael who had to look at himself in the mirror and see whether he could utter the word *guilty*. At the eleventh hour—I should say the eleventh hour and fifty-ninth minute—he refused. Shortly thereafter, a grab bag of indictments was filed, and in March 1989, in a packed courtroom in the federal courthouse, Michael pleaded not guilty.

The government's indictment consisted of ninety-eight counts, and it was filed against Michael Milken, Lowell Milken, and a Drexel salesman, Bruce Newberg. The first illegality charged was an arrangement between Boesky and Milken in which they each parked shares for the other and under which Boesky was used by Milken to manipulate and trade securities on insider information. The government alleged that this arrangement began in April 1984, when Milken helped a client, Victor Posner, obtain secret control of Fischbach Corporation, a construction company, by having Boesky buy shares subject to a guarantee against loss, which was not disclosed. Posner was not indicted, though civil charges were later brought against him by the SEC. (The charge then was a classic parking allegation—having a third party buy shares of the target of a raid.)

The next transaction the government challenged involved the Golden Nugget Corporation, a major casino operation in Las Vegas and Atlantic City controlled by Stephen Wynn. The indictment charged that Golden Nugget bought 2.4 million shares of MCA in 1984 and then decided to sell rather than seek control of MCA. To sell such a large block in the market could have caused the price to collapse. The indictment charged that Milken induced Boesky to buy approximately half the shares from Golden Nugget in a block transaction and then to sell them quietly and in a way that would not drive the price down. Milken allegedly agreed to reimburse Boesky for any loss. This transaction was characterized as a manipulation, even though Golden Nugget and Wynn were never even accused of a civil violation and trying to sell shares without "dumping" them is a common Wall Street technique.

The third transaction was an abortive merger between Diamond Shamrock and Occidental Petroleum Corporation. The merger was announced on January 4, 1985, without giving any terms and omitting the ratio of Occidental to Diamond stock that would be used. On the same day, Boesky, allegedly pursuant to a share-the-profit-or-the-loss agreement with Milken, sold Diamond stock short and bought Occidental, a move that could be profitable only if the ratio had been fixed beforehand. But on January 7, when the tentative terms were first reached and announced, the Diamond Shamrock board rejected the merger, and Boesky lost his shirt. The indictment contained no specific allegation that Milken had participated in the merger negotiations or knew the exchange ratio.

The indictment was filled with unintentional ironies. Milken was the most important investment banker of his time, yet the indictment charged that, in tipping Boesky on the takeovers of Fischbach and MCA, he had bet on the wrong horse and he and Boesky lost money, which Milken had to make good through favorable bond prices. It was also alleged that Drexel had parked stock for Phillips Petroleum, and that Boesky and Milken had agreed to buy shares of Storer Communications and split the profit. The shares had allegedly been parked by

Boesky for Milken and yielded a profit of more than $1 million. Milken was accused of parking Pacific Lumber shares with Boesky when the Maxxam Group was trying to acquire Pacific, and of parking Harris Graphics stock with Boesky, as well as MGM common stock. By March 21, 1986, in the government's chronology, Milken allegedly no longer owed Boesky money for losses he had sustained. The situation was reversed, and Boesky now allegedly owed Milken $5.3 million for profits that were supposed to be split. Drexel sent Boesky a bill for $5.3 million in consulting fees to even up the account, and the payment drew Michael's brother Lowell into the case for the first time. Lowell was accused of having told Drexel accountants that the $5.3 million represented bona fide consulting fees, not a reconciliation of the profits and losses from their allegedly secret parking and trading activities.

The indictment went on to charge Milken with getting Boesky to buy Wickes common stock and Stone Container common stock to drive up their prices. It concluded with a transaction involving Princeton Newport Partners, a hedge fund run by Jay Regan; the charge was that Milken and the Drexel salesman, Bruce Newberg, had parked securities with Princeton Newport. Among the other corporations named in instances of alleged parking were COMB Corporation and U.S. Home. Also thrown in for good measure was a count that Drexel had understated its holdings of Mattel securities in its SEC filing, and another that Milken had bought Lorimar securities while in possession of insider information.

The indictment ended with a description of Milken's wealth, characterizing the various allegations of securities violations as a pattern of racketeering. It alleged that Milken made $550,054,000 in 1987, $294,799,000 in 1986, and $135,324,000 in 1985, although his profit from the transactions in the indictment and with Boesky, according to the government, amounted to $1,845,405,494. The sheer recitation of the number of securities transactions with Boesky, plus Milken's overall compensation, gave the impression of illegal activity somewhere. In other words, Ed Williams had been right: the reek of money would permeate the courtroom.

After such a long investigation—more than two years had passed since Milken first engaged us—it seemed surprising that the case turned

on the testimony of one man, Ivan Boesky. True, the government had
sprinkled allegations of insider trading through the indictment, but
what was striking to us was that, more often than not, the tips Milken
allegedly gave Boesky had proved to be wrong, and the secret joint
account that Boesky said he and Milken owned was a loser. This from
the one man on Wall Street who knew more than any other about
mergers in the works. Indeed, I later tested the charge that Milken had
given Boesky insider information on MGM, at an evidentiary hearing
prior to Milken's sentencing. On close examination, the evidence
showed that Boesky had bought MGM at all the wrong times—the very
opposite of insider trading!—and his allegation against Milken was
rejected by Judge Wood.

In a strange way, though, the handing down of the indictment, which
might have signified that a long and tumultuous courtroom struggle
was now inevitable, had the opposite effect. John Carroll, the prosecutor, once told me that he considered Milken a gamester, and that he had
enjoyed playing games with Boesky in which Boesky lost. A literature
major at Yale, Carroll said Milken was like the Icarus of Greek myth,
that he mischievously flew too close to the sun. That is how the prosecutor saw his quarry. But Carroll, I would say, had something of the
gamester in him too. He and Fardella let it be known that they were
working toward a new indictment, one that would be much broader
than the Boesky charges and based on different evidence. At the same
time, being lawyers, they expressed a willingness to talk, and so, in a
measured, almost desultory fashion at first, we reopened the dialogue.

The plea negotiations were carried out, on our side, by Flumenbaum, Litt, Sandler, Kaufman, and me, with Carroll, Fardella, and Alan
Cohen, the new head of the securities fraud unit, for the government.
Giuliani was gone by that time, which was not a good thing for us. As
tough as he was, when there was a deal to be made, Giuliani knew how
to make concessions. We knew he would have liked to leave office with
a Milken plea in his pocket. Furthermore, he wouldn't have tolerated
being overruled by bureaucrats at the Justice Department or the SEC.
Now, with only a temporary U.S. Attorney in place, the SEC and the
Attorney General's Office claimed dominion over the negotiations, and
they were both ignorant of the weaknesses in the prosecution's case and
vindictive toward Milken, whom they saw only through the lenses of
Boesky and the media.

Meeting in safe rooms in the courthouse, we kept our negotiations secret, the only time in the case when no leaks were made. While there is always a measure of posturing and bravado in the beginning of a negotiation, and ours was no exception, we ultimately hit hard ground. Milken, we said, would never, as a matter of principle, enter into a plea bargain as long as his brother Lowell remained subject to charges that he, Michael, regarded as outrageous. Second, Milken was not an insider trader, and never had been; he would not enter a plea bargain in which insider trading was part of the charges. He might as well be charged with treason. Third, the amount of the fine, while it would probably not be an obstacle to a settlement in Michael's eyes, since money meant little to him, did concern us: the amount of the fine might be equated with the gravity of the offense and so reflect on a prison sentence. Finally, the prison sentence that could be imposed on Milken was, obviously, of the utmost concern. We had to find a way, in the prevailing climate of hysteria about Milken, to reduce the risk of an exaggerated sentence.

The government didn't want to tie a dismissal of the charges against Lowell to Michael's plea. It also wanted a very significant fine. It insisted that Milken plead to more counts than Boesky had—at least five, in other words—and, more important, that the court have full discretion to impose the sentence provided by law—up to five years per count. This was something we could never accept. So while there was a will on both sides to settle, for a time the differences seemed unbridgeable.

We kept proposing new ideas and alternatives. The government kept rejecting them. But finally, we struggled forward to some compromises.

The charges against Lowell Milken would be dropped. There would be six charges in all, none involving insider trading. Milken would pay $600 million, of which $200 million would be a fine and $400 million restitution. The government would be allowed, as was standard, to point to other conduct reflecting on Milken's character that it felt should have bearing on his sentence, to which we in turn could respond. Milken would not be questioned until after his sentencing—that is, the issue of his cooperation would be postponed.

Of the charges we finally agreed upon, after hard negotiation, most concerned parking and customer-accommodation practices and violations. One charged Milken with trying *not* to spook the market by selling MCA stock, which we labeled manipulation, although it scarcely sounded felonious. Perhaps the most conventional criminal charge was that Milken had tried to accommodate a customer, David Solomon, by creating capital losses for him. None, however, accused Milken of insider trading, or of selling fraudulent junk bonds, or of RICO charges, nor, needless to say, was he accused of wrecking the savings and loan industry. These last were all inventions of the media or, in the case of the savings and loans, of politicians like William Seidman, the head of the regulatory government agency, who badly needed a scapegoat.

Finally, and essential to the plea bargain, we would agree to language that would be presented to the judge before the plea and read in open court, in which the government acknowledged that it wasn't seeking consecutive sentences on the different counts. While we knew the government couldn't bind the court to concurrent sentencing, we all believed the court would honor the government's view. In that event, Milken's exposure would be limited to five years; with parole and good behavior, he would actually serve no more than twenty months.

According to our research, the government had never before agreed to send such a message. Therefore, we set out to work on language that would be, on the one hand, subtle enough not to offend the court's sense of prerogatives, but, on the other, unmistakable enough to tell the court that the government—which, after all, knew its case best—thought a five-year sentence sufficient.

The language we finally agreed on was at first rejected—after which we broke off negotiations—and then cleared by the Justice Department. It was sent to the court the night before the plea was to be taken, along with other materials relating to the plea, and it was never disavowed or questioned by Judge Wood. It was reflected in court, the next day, in the following exchange:

Mr. LIMAN: We would like to clarify, Your Honor, one point in the plea agreement. The government has agreed that it will make no specific recommendation as to the sentence of incarceration. That means the government will not ask the court to impose consecutive sentences in this case.

THE COURT: All right. Mr. Carroll, is that correct?

Mr. CARROLL: Your Honor, that is correct. It's the general practice of our office not to recommend specific sentences, although on certain occasions we have done so. In the light of the entirety of this plea agreement, we think it's entirely appropriate to adhere to the practice in this case.

Still, we were sufficiently uneasy about the language beforehand that we tested it on a number of defense lawyers who knew the case and even some former judges. They all agreed that the signal was unmistakable: the parties to the agreement were clearly counting on concurrent sentences only, that is, a maximum of five years, and the court couldn't help but realize that the defendant had relied on the unusual language in agreeing to plead guilty. Therefore, the court would have to either reject the plea entirely, as derogatory to its authority, or honor the signal by pronouncing concurrent sentences.

Milken, meanwhile, had agonized over whether to go forward. For once, reliance on rational analysis offered no good answers. He knew that the alternative to pleading was years of further investigation and trials, that even if we won in court the first time, the government would never give up. He also understood, as we explained to him, that if he did plead, the government investigation would probably end, meaning that not just Lowell but his other colleagues would be spared indictment.

(In this we were correct. Once Michael entered his plea, no other Drexel figure was indicted. As one of the government prosecutors later acknowledged, in a speech before a bar group in Philadelphia, it had been imperative to put Milken's head on a pike in front of the Stock Exchange as a deterrent to all on Wall Street. In other words, having been a symbol of greed, he had to become a symbol of punishment.)

While it is always the client who decides whether to plea, there was one point on which Michael should have been able to rely on his lawyers, and that was when I advised him that the "no consecutive sentences" language would work.

Writing these words, seven years later, I still wince. For I couldn't have been more mistaken.

Judge Kimba Wood was new to the bench and had virtually no experience in criminal cases. Before her, she had a defendant who had been described as the greatest offender in securities history and had agreed (my old worry) to pay a record fine.

Yet the charges to which he pleaded guilty scarcely seemed monumental. On the other hand, in the poisoned atmosphere outside the courtroom, people were calling for his head.

What would be the appropriate sentence?

A more experienced judge might have worried less about that question and held the prosecutors to their plea bargain—that is, the six offenses and the exchange on nonconsecutive sentences. But Judge Wood, for whatever reasons, hesitated. Before pronouncing sentence, she decided she wanted to know more. Thereupon, she ordered an unusual presentencing hearing, a kind of second mini-trial in which the prosecution would have the opportunity to prove that Milken had in fact committed more serious crimes than those to which he had pled.

This hearing was known as a Fatico hearing, for the case *U.S. vs. Fatico*, and it had been used largely in Mafia cases. Its original purpose was to allow the government to show that a defendant had intimidated or silenced witnesses during the trial itself. The government had to prove its allegation only by a preponderance of the evidence, not beyond a reasonable doubt, and if the court so held, the defendant could then be given an enhanced sentence.

Whatever one thought of the procedure, the Supreme Court had ruled it constitutional. Now, for the first time, it was to be used in a securities case. In essence, Judge Wood was giving the government another chance to prove something that the defendant had refused to plead to and that the government itself had decided not to try in court.

Fatico hearings were almost never used in white-collar or ordinary criminal cases. They raised troubling civil liberties issues. Just before Milken entered his plea of guilty, Judge Pierre Leval, one of the country's most respected federal judges and a former federal and state prosecutor, was confronted, in a courtroom just down the hall from Judge Wood's, with the trial of Robert Freeman, the former head of risk arbitrage at Goldman Sachs. Freeman had pleaded guilty to a single count of insider trading, in exchange for which the government had dropped its other charges against him. At his sentencing, however, the government tried to introduce evidence that Freeman had in fact committed other acts of insider trading. Leval, in refusing to hear it, explained that the defendant would then be entitled to a full hearing on the new accusations. He said it would serve no useful purpose, since the court still had to sentence the defendant on the transaction to which he had pleaded guilty and could not enlarge the sentencing procedure.

Judge Leval clearly understood that to allow the government to introduce such evidence and hold a hearing on it would render the whole plea-bargaining process meaningless. Why would anyone plead guilty to charges—six in our case, the result of endless negotiations—if, at the end of the day, the court could sentence him for other offenses the government might claim he had committed?

In our case, the court explained why it felt a need to go beyond the charges to which Milken had pleaded. Fatico, it affirmed, was a way to educate the judge about the defendant's character. It noted that sentences are normally limited to a narrow range because defendants plead to a single count. That had not been the case here, and furthermore, there was a stark contrast between the defense version of the defendant's conduct and the prosecution's.

The government was as surprised as we were by the Fatico ruling. Both sides had assumed that we would file the usual sentencing briefs, the one lambasting the defendant, the other extolling him, and while the court could take our arguments into account, it would still sentence the defendant based on what he had pleaded to. That, in fact, is why we felt he faced imprisonment. But he would not be sentenced for what he refused to plead to—obstruction of justice, insider trading, or cheating clients.

This is where common sense broke down, and at the risk of repeating myself, I must state that common sense is the lifeblood of the law.

Indeed, neither side knew how to proceed in this Fatico hearing. Judge Wood initially suggested that the prosecutors choose five offenses that they thought Milken had committed and that we, the defense, pick five that he hadn't committed. I argued—perhaps it was a mistake on my part—that this made no sense. Was I to call witnesses to a lifetime of business transactions with Milken, to testify that all his dealings with them had been honest? What was the relevance if Milken had behaved impeccably with clients A through Y? If he'd given insider tips to Client Z, wouldn't he still have committed an offense for which punishment would be required?

In the end, the government was permitted to present its five alleged offenses in the hearing, and we defended against them. Judge Wood found for the government on two of these—one, an attempt at obstruction of justice, and the other, Milken's failure to disclose to Kohlberg Kravis Roberts, in its leveraged buyout of Storer Communications, that Drexel principals were receiving warrants. These alleged offenses, it should be noted, had hardly been unknown to the government during the plea bargaining. They were not charged then because they were sharply disputed. But now, through the Fatico procedure, they were transformed, as though by magic, into "findings" by the court.

The fact is that our justice system depends on certain shared assumptions and expectations among the prosecutors, the defenders, and the court. Without these guideposts—these shared assumptions and expectations—there would never have been a plea of guilty in the Milken case. For this reason alone, a just sentence, based on the plea, was as important to the U.S. Attorney's Office, and the court, as it was to us.

I return now to November 21, 1990, the Wednesday before Thanksgiving. When I picked up Michael at his hotel that morning, we were both tense—obviously—but, still and all, I felt cautiously optimistic. I thought we had every reason to hope that the sentence would be no more than two or three years. No more than five, certainly, given the "no consecutive sentences" agreement. My expectation was based in part on the fact that, in all my experience, the only client I'd had who actually served a prison sentence had received far less than he'd expected. But I also felt that we hadn't done that badly in the Fatico hearing. Of the five counts brought up by the prosecution, Judge Wood may have found against us twice, but she'd found for us three times. And then there was the probation department's report. Normally, the court relies on this for its assessment of a defendant's character, and ours couldn't have been better. The probation officer had clearly made an effort to get to know Michael and described his genuine philanthropy, his devotion to his family, his values that were based not just on money. It was the kind of report that, for any defendant other than Michael Milken, would have indicated a modest sentence consisting principally of community service.

Room 318 is the largest courtroom in the federal courthouse building in Foley Square. Defendants such as Alger Hiss have been tried there. That November day, there wasn't an empty seat. Employees of the U.S. Attorney's Office, friends and family of Milken and his defense team, and, of course, the press, crowded the courtroom.

I spoke at length about Michael's good deeds, his background, his values, and I also reminded the court, one more time, of the "no consecutive sentences" message. The prosecution made its traditional sentencing speech, stressing the importance of deterrence in white-collar crime and calling the defendant's crimes ones of greed and arrogance. Michael spoke too—briefly, for Michael—apologizing to the court and his family for his failures.

But there was only one speech that counted that day in that courtroom, and that was the court's.

Judge Wood's sentencing speech had been carefully composed, and she read it from a written text. She generalized about the obligation of the court to protect investors in the financial markets from secret manipulation, and then, zeroing in on Michael, she excoriated him. She charged him with "repeatedly conspiring to violate" the securities and tax laws so as "to achieve more power and wealth for himself and his wealthy clients." She said that only "sparse" evidence had been presented to show that the preponderance of his business was honestly conducted, and she asserted that serious crimes required serious punishment. She said to Michael, "You also committed crimes that are hard to detect, and crimes that are hard to detect warrant greater punishment in order to be effective in deterring others."

Then she asked Milken to rise.

Five *consecutive* sentences, on counts two to six of the charges, each of two years.

A total term of ten years' imprisonment.

Michael didn't seem to get it at first. He seemed dazed, as though what he'd heard hadn't registered. And then it did, suddenly. I heard him cry out involuntarily, and I think Lori Milken cried out too. Flumenbaum and I had to support him to keep him from falling.

As for me, I couldn't believe my own ears. I was stunned. After all our prolonged and arduous negotiation over that "no consecutive sentences" language, it had disappeared totally from the case, never so much as mentioned by the court!

Five two-year terms. Consecutive. Ten years.

Judge Wood indicated that, if Milken cooperated with the government, she could adjust the sentence, but that offered cold comfort. I felt that I'd let Michael down, that I'd betrayed him. And that the system had betrayed me.

Outside the courthouse building, there was total clamor, total joy. The media, now confirmed in its depiction of Milken's villainy, went wild, like spectators at some gladiatorial combat. And I retain from that moment one face, one voice. As we escaped from Foley Square, or tried to, there was one journalist—a *journalist*, mind you—who kept banging on the roof of our car and shouting, "*Ten years! Ten years!*" He haunts me still.

———

Of course, it didn't end there. A few weeks later, the court found, by a rather abstruse legal calculation, that the amount of loss involved in Milken's offenses—that is to say, the huge fines he'd paid—meant that he would be eligible for parole in about forty-four months. The prosecutors, Carroll and Fardella, whether they admitted it or not, knew the sentence was wrong. We traveled together to California to visit Michael in the federal minimum-security prison outside San Francisco, so that the government could now seek his cooperation.

Some white-collar offenders end up serving hard time in prison because they cannot adjust to the regimentation and pettiness of prison camp life. Not Milken. Probably because he was used to helping clean house in Encino and taking out the garbage, he had no objection to the most menial chores. Nor did he complain about the elbows he took playing basketball with his fellow inmates. They, it seemed, looked on him as a regular guy, if an eccentric one. I remember, in those months, receiving phone calls from him when I got to my office and hearing voices booming in the background, in unprintable language, "Hey, Michael, get off the ——— phone, it's five in the ——— morning!" He gave illiterate prisoners lessons in mathematics, teaching them his secret shortcuts, as well as other subjects, and he saw some of them through their high school equivalency exams.

To Carroll and Fardella, though, he remained elusive, sometimes maddeningly so. Milken was convinced that the Wall Street establishment did no fewer, and far more valuable, favors for its customers, including fund managers, than he had been accused of, and he repeatedly offered to review the records of other securities firms with them to make the point. The last thing Carroll and Fardella wanted was for Milken to lecture them on what else was wrong with Wall Street. He saw his discussions of the prevailing practices as valuable cooperation; they saw it as evasion. What they wanted from him were facts and names—the names of customers and fund managers who had received secret equity or favors from Drexel or parked securities for him.

To their credit, Carroll and Fardella never blamed him for the downfall of the savings and loans, nor did they ever accuse him of insider trading. They brought only one savings and loan case, charging Thomas Speigel, the head of Columbia Savings and Loan and a major client of Milken's, with receiving the opportunity to buy the equity in an LBO; Speigel was acquitted. Although they did finally use Milken as a witness in two government cases, his testimony had no discernible effect on their outcome. By that time, Milken was largely out of the news anyway, and the government prosecutors seemed to have had enough of him. In August 1992, having received a letter from the government attesting to Milken's candid cooperation, the court reduced his sentence to twenty-two months—which was within the range of sentencing he would have received if the "no consecutive sentences" plea had been observed.

Meanwhile, once Milken's guilty plea had been accepted, it was just a matter of time before the civil suits against him and Drexel's employees were settled too. The publicity surrounding the criminal proceedings had encouraged scores of buyers of securities from Drexel to bring class actions—sufficient in magnitude to drive all of the defendants into bankruptcy. Furthermore, Milken's and Drexel's guilty pleas could be used against them in the civil suits. Finally, under the random assignment system of judges in the Southern District, the class action cases landed on the docket of Judge Milton Pollack.

Whatever else one might say of him, Pollack was one of the most senior and experienced judges in the courthouse. And he was fast. "If you want justice," he told Milken, "I will give you a jury trial within the next six months. If you want compassion, I will settle the cases, leaving you with more money than the lawyers will." He didn't bother waiting for an answer.

Federal judges, by wielding the carrot and the stick, have enormous power to force a settlement. None was better at it than Pollack. He told defendants that he would try their cases within weeks—ready or not—if they weren't prepared to accept his recommendations for settlement. I saw him do exactly this to a savings and loan regulator who, until that time, had thought his regulatory agency all-powerful.

Within one year, Pollack had settled all the civil cases arising out of the Drexel-Milken matter. Everyone had to contribute to the settlement—not only Milken, who had already paid $600 million to the U.S. Attorney's Office and the SEC, but all Drexel employees who had, as part of the Drexel compensation scheme, received warrants. Ever the demagogues, the savings and loan regulators refused to take their settlement in the form of LBO equity shares, which they derided as worthless. When the markets that they, through their actions, had helped destroy returned to normalcy, the prices of LBO paper skyrocketed, and ironically, some of these same Drexel employees made new fortunes from it. Milken, however, had already given his interest to the government as part of his settlement.

In the aftermath of the case, one of the most disheartening aspects for me were the letters I got from people who said that, having admired me during Iran-Contra, they were now angry and bewildered that I would represent a Michael Milken. I replied to each and every one, saying that I would never apologize for fulfilling a fellow American's right to counsel, and that my love for the Constitution and the rule of law, which had allowed me to do my work in the Iran-Contra investigation, had also allowed me to represent Michael Milken with pride.

That is how I felt, then and now.

The attacks, of course, had started well before then, and sometimes, I admit, they hurt. Judge Rifkind himself had written a letter to the *New York Times;* the paper saw fit not to print it, but I cherished it. In an editorial dated April 26, 1990, the *Times* had complained that Milken's plea was too soft, and the editorial was followed by an essay by Benjamin J. Stein, who said that the Milken plea was a joke.

"From the beginning of the case more than three years ago," Rifkind wrote in reply,

Mr. Milken was tried and, as far as the public was concerned, was convicted in the press. A Niagara of leaks achieved that result long before he was indicted. Even the SEC staff's investigative report was leaked. Leaks reached such monstrous proportions that the District Court was obliged to order the government to investigate them.

Having been tried and convicted in the press, he is now being sentenced in and by the press. This result is aided and abetted, in part, by inappropriate statements issued by public officials, such as cries for vengeance by the Chairman of the SEC and Congressional leaders. The press reflects demands that he be sentenced not for the limited offenses which he has acknowledged but for offenses for which he has never been tried or convicted by plea or trial. This mob clamor generated through press stories has prompted a Chicago rabbi to demand that Milken be hung by his thumbs. The guilty plea, which the law has traditionally favored as acceptance of responsibility and, therefore, as a factor mitigating punishment, is being presented as a cover-up which should aggravate rather than mitigate punishment.

Ours is a society in which persons convicted of a crime are sentenced in the serene quiet of the courtroom presided over by a judge who should be insulated from public clamor and who acts in response to evidence legally established. In such a society, the shrill words of some of the press exceed the acceptable noise level.

Still and all, the outcome of the Milken case went hard with me. Even though friends and colleagues offered me solace, I found myself wondering whether I ever wanted to try a criminal case again, knowing that I might yet again face disappointments and that I would blame myself for them. On the other hand, as Oliver Wendell Holmes observed early in the century, controversial cases do not always lead to rational results.

Great cases, like hard cases, make bad law. For great cases are called great not by reason of their real importance in shaping the law of the future, but because of some accident of immediate overwhelming interest which appeals to the feelings and distorts the judgment. These immediate interests exercise a kind of hydraulic pressure which makes what previously was clear seem doubtful, and before which even well settled principles of law will bend.

That is the way I have come to see the Milken case.

This leaves Michael Milken himself.

What can I say about him without appearing the Pollyanna on the one hand, or the apologist on the other, neither of which would reflect what I feel? Our contacts have become limited with the passage of time—I no longer represent him—but whenever I think of him, I'm reminded of the first trip I made to California to meet him, when he and Lori took Ellen and me out to dinner. My exposure to restaurants in southern California had been limited to places like Spago in Beverly Hills, where you had to be a celebrity even to get a table. But the Milkens took us to a neighborhood place where we had to wait on line for more than an hour to be seated, not because the cuisine was in any way exceptional but because the prices were so moderate!

That was Michael. Throughout my career, I've known and represented some powerful figures in the financial industries, but none like him. None so modest in how they lived, or for whom money meant so little. None as committed as he was to his own visions and aspirations.

An enigmatic figure to me, even now.

But I think I can say this about him. He was the most imaginative financier of his generation. He was also the least understood—and, surely, the most demonized.

V

The Iran-Contra Investigation

20

Flouting the Constitution

I'VE OFTEN TRIED to imagine what it would have been like if the details of the Iran-Contra investigation had been leaked, Watergate-style, to a Bernstein and Woodward—day by day, item by item. The headlines might have been:

- U.S. Sold Missiles to Iran for Hostages. President Denies Authorizing Sales. Asks Attorney General to Investigate.

- White House Aides Prepared False Chronology to Cover up President's Approval.

- Aide to National Security Adviser, Lt. Col. Oliver North, Shreds Documents Before Investigation.

- National Security Adviser Fired. North Too.

- CIA Head Lied to Senate Intelligence Committee. Said President Thought Shipments to Iran Contained Oil-Drilling Equipment.

- Proceeds of Missile Sales Used Illegally to Fund Operation of Nicaraguan Contras.

- Secretaries of State and Defense Objected to Missile Sales. President Then Kept Them in Dark.

- National Security Adviser Says President Authorized Secret Assistance to Contras.

- Contra Funds Solicited from Foreign Countries by State Department Official.

- North Says He Wrote Diversion Memos to President. President Denies Knowledge.

- National Security Adviser Contradicts North, Says No Memoranda Prepared for or Sent to President.

- National Security Adviser Admits Destroying Presidential "Finding" Authorizing Arms-for-Hostage Trade.

- Witness Says North Told Him President Joked About Using Ayatollah's Money for Contras.

- North, at CIA Head's Suggestion, Created the Enterprise, a Parallel, Clandestine, Covert Action Group.

- The Enterprise a Profit-Making Organization.

- North Testifies CIA Head Told Him to Destroy All Records.

- President Tells Tower Board He Did Not Authorize Iranian Sales.

- President Retracts Testimony, Says He Authorized Iranian Missile Sales.

- CIA Head Casey Dies. Takes Secrets to Grave.

- Congressional Committees to Consider Impeachment of President.

And on and on.

Iran-Contra was a remarkable story, almost too filled with intrigue to be fully comprehensible to the public. Unlike Watergate, which was an attempt on the part of a paranoid administration to play fast and loose with our electoral politics and then to cover up what it had done, Iran-Contra actually involved our national security. The past covert actions of our intelligence agencies—some of which had had scandalous consequences—nonetheless had been carried out under the umbrella of our Constitution. But the Iran-Contra investigation unveiled a conscious attempt, on the part of a few, to set up a covert action force, a kind of parallel CIA that would, and did, function outside the restraints of our checks-and-balances democracy.

When it was all over—after forty days of public hearings—the public and the media tended to believe that the Congress had somehow "lost" and the witnesses "won." Perhaps, in some senses, this was so. But Iran-Contra wasn't about winning and losing. An attempt had been made to undermine our Constitution, to reduce the importance of the legislative process, and wittingly or not, to create an imperial presidency—ironically headed by a man who had no ambition to be an emperor.

What the investigation accomplished was to bring all of it, in all its details, to the national attention—and that took a lot of hard work.

In this sense, I believe we all won.

As Justice Brandeis said in an opinion years ago, "In a democracy, sunlight is sometimes the best disinfectant."

21

Contraband, Contra-Aid, Controversy

WHEN SENATOR George Mitchell called me, the day after New Year's in 1987, and asked whether I'd meet with him in Washington on an important matter, it couldn't have come at a worse time. I was as busy as I had ever been in my career. Just two months before, in November, Michael Milken had hired me and Edward Bennett Williams. As always, Steve Ross was considering several major transactions that would transform his company. I was on the verge of going to trial, defending the famous auction house Christie's against one Dimitry Jodido, a disgruntled Swiss art dealer whose collection of impressionist paintings had failed to sell well in a Christie's auction. A case involving works by such artists as van Gogh, Cézanne, and Renoir ought, I always thought, to be heard in a grand setting, but I ended up arguing the case in a small, dreary state courtroom in an auxiliary downtown courthouse. It was quite strange to compare the beauty of the painted canvases displayed as evidence and the dinginess of the paint flaking off the courtroom walls.

In addition, dozens of other clients had lawsuits and problems demanding my attention, and as a rainmaker at the firm, I was responsible for a meaningful part of our business. But the remarkable story unfolding in Washington made all these activities seem almost petty.

That previous November, a Lebanese magazine had reported that President Reagan had ordered the sale of missiles to Iran in order to win the release of Americans held hostage in Lebanon. At first blush, the report had seemed preposterous. Reagan had defeated Jimmy Carter six years before in part because Carter had seemed so ineffectual after radical Iranians seized the American embassy in Teheran and held its occupants hostage for more than a year. Reagan had vowed never to negotiate with terrorists. How could he now have sold missiles to the ayatollah? Denials were issued, followed, begrudgingly, by concessions that the arms sales had in fact taken place.

Then, in late November, came an even more startling disclosure. Justice Department lawyers searching the files of a National Security Council (NSC) staffer, Lieutenant Colonel Oliver North—those files, that is, that hadn't already been shredded—found evidence that proceeds from the Iranian arms sales had been diverted to support the Nicaraguan Contras, the military force opposed to that country's leftist Sandinista regime. The so-called Boland Amendment, passed by the Congress and signed into law by the president in 1984, had outlawed such direct military aid. Reagan denied any knowledge of the diversion of funds. North and his boss—the president's national security adviser, Vice Admiral John Poindexter—were fired. An independent counsel was appointed to consider criminal charges, and the Senate and House each formed a special committee to conduct investigations. The questions to be investigated were fundamental: Had the president and other high officials engaged in illegal activities? How much had they known about the NSC staff's operations? If the president had approved the diversion, or the attempted cover-up afterward, the consensus was that he could be impeached.

I had been following these events the way most Americans did, little knowing that in a few weeks I would be summoned to Washington. Mitchell was calling to ask me to become chief counsel to the Senate's select committee. I told him over the phone that I doubted whether I'd be a wise choice, but I could hardly say no to his invitation to talk about it, and I agreed to come down to Washington the following Monday.

We met in Mitchell's office in the Russell Senate Office Building that Monday afternoon. He had invited some of the select committee's other members. Usually a Senate committee is divided along party lines and has two separate staffs, but Daniel Inouye, the Democratic senator from Hawaii, who would chair the committee, wanted the ranking Republican member, New Hampshire Senator Warren Rudman, to be his vice chairman and full partner in the investigation. This meant that there would be one staff, not two, and that the chief counsel would represent the entire committee, Democrats and Republicans alike. Mitchell assured me that I could choose my own staff and that I would have an ample budget. But time was of the essence. The presidency hung in the balance, he said gravely, and the committee had to determine swiftly whether impeachment was warranted.

As attractive as the offer was, I had reasons to hesitate. For one thing, given Israel's possible involvement in the arms sales to Iran, it could be a mistake for the committee to choose a Jew as chief counsel. I mentioned this to Mitchell and the other senators. They seemed almost offended by the idea. Well, Mitchell asked me, would my religion make me pull my punches on Israel? No, I said, and I conceded that once a lawyer undertakes a matter for a client, he has no religion. Israel would certainly receive no preference from me. But what about appearance and credibility, I asked, when one of the essential goals of investigation had to be to restore faith in government?

"But I'm Jewish too," Senator Rudman said, and then Mitchell and another senator, Howell Heflin of Alabama, joined in with their support.

"If supporting Israel is a disqualification," one of them said, "then not a single solitary one of us should be serving on the committee." Indeed, simply raising the Jewish issue seemed unpatriotic to both of them.

Nevertheless, I raised another objection. Wouldn't they be better advised to choose a savvy Washington insider over a trial lawyer from New York?

Mitchell disagreed. The investigation, he told me, was going to involve complicated foreign bank accounts, transfers, and transactions.

They needed someone who'd handled complex financial cases and could track the funds in question. An outsider was precisely what they wanted, someone with no axes to grind, someone who wouldn't be political. In that sense, Mitchell said, I was the perfect candidate.

Still I hesitated. This wasn't just another case, I worried, not even another important case. I would be assisting the Senate in investigating the president of the United States. It would be a highly visible procedure. What if I failed?

Intrigued as I was, and flattered, all I could commit to on the spot was to give them a rapid response. Back in New York, two valued friends urged me not to take the assignment. One was Ed Williams, as savvy as they came with regard to how things worked in the capital. Washington, Ed said, was like Puritan Salem: they burned a new witch each month. He warned me that I'd become one. It would be impossible, he said, to convince every faction in Washington that the investigation was fair. Besides, he pointed out, the Congress was even less popular than Michael Milken. And on the other side, unless we brought down the president, the media would criticize me as blind and incompetent, and they'd do it no matter what we turned up by way of evidence.

Bill Paley was even more opposed than Williams.

"Watch out," he said. "You're talking about one of the most popular presidents in history. The better job you do, the more you'll be attacked for persecuting him."

Judge Rifkind, on the other hand, didn't hesitate for a minute. Sixteen years before, he'd advised me not to take on Attica, but he felt very differently about Iran-Contra. For one thing, he loved the Senate and vividly remembered working there as Senator Wagner's legislative assistant. This was the first time I ever heard Rifkind sound envious talking about one of my projects.

Other friends, Cyrus Vance among them, urged me to do it too, and so did my family, especially Ellen. But, to be candid, there was one compelling reason that overwhelmed all the others, both positive and negative: it was a challenge of historic proportions.

———

Later in January, I returned to Washington to meet with Senator Inouye. Inouye was, and is, a true and unabashed patriot. During World

War II, he and his family were interned in camps even though they were American citizens. His draft board classified him as "subversive," but Inouye joined the Army's Nisei battalion and fought in some of the bloodiest battles of the war in Italy and France. He lost his arm in combat and won the Distinguished Service Cross for his valor. In 1987 Inouye might have been the most beloved member of the Senate and was rumored to be a candidate for majority leader.

He told me he wanted a fair and nonpartisan investigation. Harking back to Watergate—he himself had been a member of Sam Ervin's Senate Watergate committee—he recalled that the partisanship had been so bitter that Democratic and Republican staff members had spied on each other and withheld information from the other side. This investigation, he assured me, would be different. It would have one unified staff headed by one counsel. It would be conducted privately at first. Only when we were ready—when we had looked for all the smoking guns—would the committee hold public hearings. I in turn assured him that I was not Sam Dash, that I wasn't looking for headlines, and that I would get him an authoritative account of what had happened.

At the same time, Inouye insisted we proceed with all deliberate speed. Whenever an American president has been weakened politically, he observed, the Soviet Union became more adventuresome and aggressive. We could afford to remove a president, but not to incapacitate one. If we found evidence warranting impeachment, the impeachment process would begin immediately in the House of Representatives. But just as important, if convincing evidence of impeachable conduct wasn't there, then the president had to be exonerated no matter what we ourselves believed about his conduct. Our duty to the Constitution and our country demanded no less.

I learned firsthand, that day, what Inouye meant by "deliberate speed." Although I'd brought along my partner, Mark Belnick, whom I would want to help run the investigation if I took the job, I hadn't even formally accepted. Certainly, we'd had no chance to discuss whether we could meet Inouye's timetable. But suddenly, without explanation, Inouye stood up, said we were late for a briefing, and led Belnick and me out to the Senate press gallery, where, to my astonishment, he publicly announced my appointment as chief counsel!

Whether I had been enlisted or drafted is still a good question, but there we were: no staff; no offices except a room Inouye found for us in the Hart Senate Office Building while secure offices were being built in a former gym; and no place to live for Ellen and me, though I would be spending the lion's share of my time in Washington for the foreseeable future. Mark Belnick and I didn't even have security clearances to read the documents the White House had already started producing. It would take us another month, and pressure from the committee, to obtain our clearances, but it was a sign of Inouye's clout that he got me and my top staff passes to the Senate garage, which were harder to obtain and even more envied than a top-secret classification.

For historical reasons, I decided to keep an informal diary of the beginnings of the investigation. I had to be careful what I wrote down because of the security issue, but one of my first entries followed my first visit to 1600 Pennsylvania Avenue:

> There is a smell of death around the White House. It is almost as if the professionals feel that this administration is drawing to an end, and they want to be sure that their reputations are intact for the next. The president seems to be almost a bystander in the whole investigation. Unlike Nixon, who sounded like a shyster lawyer on the tapes in attempting to direct what his staff would say and what they would produce, President Reagan says only that he is interested in finding out what happened. We thus have the absolutely amazing spectacle of the president looking forward to the reports of investigation so that he can learn whether he, in fact, authorized sales to Iran!

Our congressional investigation wasn't the only one going on. An independent counsel, Judge Lawrence E. Walsh, had been named to investigate criminal charges, and the president, meanwhile, had appointed his own panel of inquiry, headed by former Senator John Tower. The Tower Commission had no subpoena power and couldn't grant immunity. It did, however, interview the president several times—thus adding, unfortunately, to the prevailing confusion. In his first interview, the president said he had authorized the initial sale of arms to Iran, through Israel. In the second, the following day, he denied any such authorization and said he'd objected to the sale by Israel. Finally—astonishingly—the president stated that he had no actual recollection of whether he did or didn't authorize the initial sales.

As I noted, late that February:

> Washington is getting ready for a lynching, the lynching of Colonel North, Admiral Poindexter, and Bud McFarlane in the Tower Commission report. All week there have been leaks in the *Washington Post* and the *New York Times* on how critical the report is going to be. The leaks can come from one of two sources: those who will benefit by the criticism, which in this case can be the members of the Tower Commission themselves who are bathing in self-praise; or it can come from those who are going to be criticized, namely the Reagan White House, as a way of launching a preemptive strike. . . . As usual, the president will plead guilty to nonfeasance, that is, nonmanagement, since he has elevated negligence into a virtue.

When the report was released, it criticized Chief of Staff Don Regan, the secretary of state, and the secretary of defense for being deficient as a committee for someone who could not manage his own affairs. (The Tower Commission was careful not to come right out and say that the president couldn't manage his own affairs.) It was clear that the commission's conclusions were in part political.

Admiral Poindexter and Colonel North had refused to cooperate with the Tower Commission. So had Richard Secord and others involved in the arms sale and the Contra support operations. On top of that, William Casey, director of the CIA, died in December. Without these witnesses, great gaps remained in the story, and there was much the Tower Commission never found out. Still, within its limitations, the commission did a remarkable job of rescuing and putting together all the documents that had survived shredding by the NSC staff.

The Friday after the report was issued, I was at the White House with the White House counsel, reviewing the president's notes, when Regan was replaced by James Baker. It was an extraordinary moment of history. Peter Wallison, the White House counsel, received a call while we were meeting. It was Regan, who said that the president had just announced that Baker had replaced him. Nobody, it seems, had told Regan about it beforehand. Regan was furious, and Wallison was close to tears, both shocked that no one had felt it necessary to offer them the decency of advance warning or a face-to-face chat. "They play it rough in this town," read my diary entry that night.

When you lose power in Washington, it is very visible. While Regan was chief of staff, Senators Inouye and Rudman planned to attend his deposition before the committee. Once he was deposed, only Mark Belnick, my deputy Paul Barbadoro, and I went. Even the White House counsel was withdrawn from representing him. There is no transition period. After we took Regan's testimony the following Tuesday, I wrote:

> He is a broken man and was able to add little to the record except his description of the president's method of receiving briefings from the national security adviser. Traditionally, the president receives a briefing book overnight and then receives his briefing in the morning from the adviser after he's had the opportunity to read the book. This president is not a reader. As a result, the adviser gives the president a briefing and then leaves the briefing book with the president so that he can read it. Given the president's inability to concentrate for more than a few minutes, it is no wonder that he was unable to focus on the issues relating to Iran. Nor is it a surprise that he signed a finding without realizing what he was doing. Fortunately, a declaration of war was not included in his papers with the signature line.

No one spoon-fed our committee the facts. We had to dig them out, just as the Tower Commission had, and the difficulties were greater than those I'd faced in any other investigation or lawsuit. To begin with, in the other investigations I'd led, witnesses cooperated. Even if in Attica some inmates, correction officers, and state troopers refused to talk to us, there had been other witnesses to the same event. In Iran-Contra, some key facts were known only to North and Poindexter, and it was likely, if we subpoenaed them, that they and other witnesses would invoke their Fifth Amendment privilege against self-incrimination. Contemptuous of the Congress throughout the affair, they had no reason to start talking now. Congress, of course, could grant them immunity and compel them to testify, but even in 1987 that was a loaded and politically sensitive issue.

Another problem was that the Senate and House committees each wanted to control its own investigation. The two institutions are very different. The Senate tends to be more collegial and less partisan. By contrast, in the House, where congressmen must run for reelection every two years, the party in the majority usually gives the minority party little respect or power, making cooperation between Democrats and Republicans difficult. Unless the investigations were to become a circus, the two committees would have to work out consolidated public hearings—something that had never been done before. However, late in February I had lunch with the House counsel, John Nields, a skilled Washington lawyer, and wrote in my diary:

> Nields promised cooperation, offered to conduct joint dispositions, and told me that we could attend testimony that he was taking the following week of Southern Airways. Unfortunately, he neglected to tell me that he has scheduled Hasenfus's deposition later that week, with other examinations scheduled. I promised cooperation with him, but it will clearly become more difficult if he can mislead me looking me in the eyes.

Since lawyers have different questioning styles (and Nields and I were no exceptions to this rule), the question of who would question which witness was at least partially a strategic one. Near the end of March, we negotiated with Nields on the division of witnesses. We took Poindexter and gave him North. The other witnesses were divided in accordance with our interests. We focused on the decision-makers. He chose the private network.

In addition to such difficulties between the two houses, there were turf battles even within the Senate. The Intelligence Committee felt it should continue the investigation it had started in December and resented Inouye's select committee. In particular, the Intelligence Committee jealously protected its relationship with the CIA. At one point in our investigation, Senator David Boren of Oklahoma, a member of our committee but also chair of the Intelligence Committee, assailed Paul Barbadoro for being too hard in the questioning of the acting director of the CIA. Inouye and Rudman, however, told us to ignore all these complaints, and this we did.

Still another problem was that every pertinent document we needed was classified, even some that had been printed in the *Washington Post*. Every member of my staff would require a top-secret clearance, which took months to obtain, and then we had to excise from documents we used at public hearings material that was too sensitive to be made public. The Washington bureaucracy, we discovered, was obsessed about classification. To cite one Orwellian example, Mark Belnick asked the State Department to send a cable for him to the sultan of Brunei, requesting his help in tracing money he had contributed to the Contra cause. Mark drafted the cable and called it in to the State Department, but when he asked the State Department cable operator to read it back to him to make sure the wording was correct, he was told that couldn't be done.

Why not, he asked?

Because, he was told, he didn't have the proper clearance! He was "cleared" to write the cable, yes, but not to hear what he'd written!

Because the investigation was moving so fast, staffing was especially hard. We had to assemble a staff from scratch; by the end of March, there were about forty of us. Also, each committee member got to name one lawyer, and although I could have vetoed any one appointment, to have done so would obviously have offended the senator in question. Molding the resulting group into a collegial organization, one dedicated to gathering the facts whatever they might be, was one of my principal challenges. It was a little like assembling a ball team that had never played together before but was now called upon to appear in the World Series.

I was lucky to have Mark Belnick and Paul Barbadoro as my deputies. Mark knew literally everything that was going on, and in addition to his extraordinary capacity to examine witnesses, he was comfortable with computers and set up our system, which was crucial when it came to organizing our mountains of documents. Paul, who was named by Senator Rudman and is now a federal judge, took on the difficult task of investigating the CIA's role, and he accomplished it with great skill and finesse.

We were ready to start public hearings in May; by the time they ended in September, we had unraveled all the basic facts of Iran-Contra. One of the reasons we managed to move so quickly was the president's cooperation. Recognizing that it was in his interest to have the matter concluded sooner rather than later, Reagan undoubtedly believed that none of his staff would provide a case for impeachment against him and that he could survive the embarrassment of having his actions exposed to the public's gaze. We all agreed that the extraordinary act of impeaching a president of the United States would require an extraordinarily high standard of proof. Without credible, direct, and conclusive evidence of guilt, the committees would not and could not subject the country, or the Congress, to the anguish of an impeachment proceeding, nor were they going to establish a precedent that could leave the threat of impeachment hanging over the head of every future president.

Almost immediately, as I indicated, the committees faced a critical choice, one that was bound to create controversy either way. Should we, or shouldn't we, immunize the key witnesses from criminal prosecution in exchange for their testimony? The committees believed strongly that no one, particularly no one who served in government, was above the law, and therefore that the Congress could give immunity only sparingly and for exceptional cause. On the other hand, without the testimony of all the relevant witnesses—and particularly North and Poindexter—how could we possibly proceed?

Nor, when it came down to it, could we wait for Judge Walsh to finish his investigation. By the time he brought his charges, President Reagan's second term would have long since been over.

Richard Secord made the decision easy for us by agreeing to testify without immunity, but his partner, Albert Hakim, did not. The committees granted Hakim immunity because he had the records of the Enterprise; we needed those records to follow the flow of the money. As it happened, the independent counsel also struck a deal with Hakim to obtain his bank records, so that our grant of immunity did not affect any eventual prosecution of him.

But when it came to Poindexter and North, the committees agonized. The two men may have been senior government officials and high-ranking officers in the military, but neither would testify without immunity. We also knew Judge Walsh would attack us if we granted even limited immunity, and since the media and the public favored independent prosecutors over Congress, even the partial grant was bound to be unpopular.

Before he became a senator, George Mitchell had been a federal prosecutor and then a federal judge. He in particular was reluctant to grant North immunity unless the committee was sure it would get important testimony in return. As the investigation progressed and the committee wrestled its way toward a decision, Mitchell sought me out on several occasions.

What did I think? Did Oliver North have facts that could incriminate the president?

And if he did, would he actually disclose them to the committee?

These were fair questions, but the only answers I could give were intuitive.

My House counterpart, John Nields, was convinced North had such information. We had already heard from his secretary, Fawn Hall, an anorexic, somewhat faded, pale, ex–high school prom queen with unalloyed loyalty for her boss. Her concocted story, in which she blamed herself for shredding documents, altering eighteen-month-old records, and smuggling them out of the building, was thoroughly unbelievable. We knew North held a key to the puzzle, and Nields believed he would reveal it to us, but only if he was assured it wouldn't land him in jail. I relayed this to Mitchell. I also reported that North's lawyer, Brendan Sullivan, had said to me that we wouldn't regret giving North immunity.

But what did he mean by that? Mitchell asked me.

It was hard to say. Sullivan had given me no details. He was a crafty lawyer, a partner in Ed Williams's firm of Williams & Connolly, and Mitchell and I had both been around the block often enough to know that Sullivan could be trying to lure us into granting immunity with tantalizing hints—hints, needless to say, that might well turn out to be empty.

Well, Mitchell persisted, but what did I think?

What I thought was that North felt betrayed by Reagan and that he wouldn't protect him. North may well have accepted being the "fall guy" for Iran-Contra—he would testify that CIA Director Casey had told him this—but not if it meant going to jail. The bigger question for me was: could he actually incriminate the president? I myself doubted whether the two had ever had any direct conversations about North's illegal activities, and everything he'd written for the president's attention—the famous five memoranda—had gone first through Poindexter. I realized that the key to what the president knew would turn out to be not Oliver North, but Admiral John Poindexter.

Still, as I told Mitchell, the only way we and the public were ever going to hear the two men's stories was by granting them immunity. At my suggestion, Warren Rudman and several other committee members urged Judge Walsh to prosecute North immediately for obstructing justice when he shredded the documents. This more limited prosecution, they argued, could be tried immediately, and the committees would willingly defer North's testimony until after it was over.

But Walsh was adamant. He had it in mind to build a massive conspiracy case, one that would take more than a year to prepare and prosecute. This presented us finally with an unavoidable choice: either abort the investigation or grant limited-use immunity.

There was, as it turned out, a terrific irony in the Reagan administration's selection of Lawrence Walsh. A former partner of Davis Polk & Wardwell (a major New York law firm), and a former deputy attorney general, president of the American Bar Association, and federal judge, Walsh had an impeccable professional background. But clearly, as I learned the very first time I met him, from the administration's point of view, they'd found the wrong man. As I wrote at the time:

I met with the independent counsel in the company of John Nields. The independent counsel objected to our giving immunity to Poindexter. When I asked him for his grounds for the objection, he asked me whether I had considered that I might be giving immunity to Alger Hiss. I took that as a remark that wasn't serious until I met with Walsh privately. He then told me he felt he had to investigate whether Poindexter was a Soviet agent. I asked him what evidence he had that Poindexter was. Walsh's only response was that if Poindexter were a Soviet agent, he couldn't have caused more harm to the United States and that he couldn't think of any reason why Poindexter would have approved the Iran initiative unless he had improper motives. I responded by asking Walsh whether he thought Casey was a Soviet agent, or Meese a Soviet agent, or the president himself. They'd all pushed for the plan. So had Vice President Bush. It was obvious, to me, that Judge Walsh did not have the slightest feeling for the facts, and I laid them out for him. I also reminded him that the country was about to enter into serious arms negotiations with the Soviet Union and that my committee felt a responsibility to get to the bottom of this and not leave a cloud over the president.

We got off to a bad start that day, and our relations never did improve.

In the end, though, the committees had no choice. Swallowing our sense of morality, we granted immunity to both Poindexter and North. At the same time, we did all we could to minimize the damage to Judge Walsh's criminal investigation by deferring their testimony until the very end, thereby giving him as much time as possible to build his cases against them.

Just as hard for the committees was whether to accept North's demand that he give only one private deposition, which would be limited to the subject of what the president knew. I would have preferred that we reject North's terms, hold him instead in contempt of Congress, and send him to jail until he agreed to testify without conditions, but Brendan Sullivan had done his homework. The House had no civil contempt power, and although the Senate did, there was an exception in the law when it came to government employees, an exception designed to prevent the Senate from using the threat of civil contempt to exact information from an administration. North fit this exception. I even researched whether the Senate's sergeant at arms could arrest North and hold him until he agreed to testify with limited-use immunity, but no such power existed.

Judge Walsh offered to add criminal contempt to the list of charges against North, but that would have delayed North's testimony to the congressional committees for years. Once again we faced the same difficult question: how crucial was North's testimony?

This time it was Inouye and Representative Lee H. Hamilton of Indiana, chair of the House committee, who put the question to Nields and me. Could we interrogate North effectively at the public hearings if all we had ahead of time was a limited deposition?

Prosecutors, we reminded them, do this all the time when they cross-examine defendants. We both felt that we could prepare well enough with the documents at hand, which included North's diaries. North's remarkable performance-to-come at the public hearings would have nothing to do with his being deposed only once, and nothing would have changed, in my view, if he'd been deposed many times, without restrictions.

When it came to other witnesses, the committees made some important concessions to the independent counsel. For the most part, we allowed Judge Walsh to finish his interviews or depositions of witnesses before we spoke to them, so that we would not freeze their testimony. When we, in turn, discovered evidence from a nonimmunized source—for instance, that the Contras had given North traveler's checks that he'd used for personal purposes—we passed it along to Walsh's investigators.

Deferring immunity for North and Poindexter until the end of our investigation gave Judge Walsh time, as I've said, to seal independent evidence beforehand. Yet all the precautions we took on both sides failed to work. After Walsh won convictions against North and Poindexter in jury trials, both verdicts were reversed on appeal because the court found that they had been based in part on immunized testimony from our hearings. In so deciding, the federal appeals court changed and broadened the rules of immunity well beyond what we had expected, and it has since become almost impossible for the Congress to grant immunity and for the wrongdoer to whom it has been granted to be brought to justice.

Since it was our grant of immunity that allowed Poindexter and North to void their convictions, naturally the committees were blamed for having placed them above the law, but in my view, Judge Walsh must also take some of the blame. He failed to keep his cooperating witnesses from watching our televised hearings, and they were thereby tainted by North's and Poindexter's immunized testimony. Also, Judge Walsh risked calling Robert "Bud" McFarlane as a witness at North's trial. Aside from the fact that McFarlane's testimony was more favorable to North than to the prosecution, McFarlane not only had watched North's immunized testimony on television but had demanded the right to reappear before the committees as a sort of rebuttal witness.

But to argue blame and responsibility finally misses the point. Iran-Contra involved issues far more compelling and relevant to the national welfare than whether Oliver North and John Poindexter were guilty of lying or, in the case of North, of mishandling funds, or whether they should go to jail or be free—again, in the case of North—to run for the U.S. Senate. Before our investigation was very far along, I wrote my committee a private memorandum:

> This is basically a constitutional story: how the pursuit of certain policy objectives in indifference to law eventually led to the U.S. being

held hostage to a secret policy, subverting the checks and balances of representative government. First the Congress, then the departments, and eventually the electorate had to be misled by the White House; irregular channels and personnel had to be employed and the judgment of conscientious officials cut out; finally, even criminal activity had to be resorted to in a vain attempt to maintain the secrecy that had begun as an operational constraint and became a political necessity. The basic constitutional compact—that the people determine the fundamental policies of government and that their officials are faithful to the process—was broken.

Without the immunized testimony of Poindexter and North, we could never have had the real issues fully disclosed and the impeachment question could never have been resolved. In my view, the price we paid was well worth paying.

———————

Investigating a president and his aides also forced me to consider the broader effect of a host of lesser—but still significant—actions. President Reagan, for example, kept a daily diary, making entries every evening. We demanded all excerpts relating to the Contras and the Iranian arms sales. Would invading the privacy of diaries discourage future presidents from keeping them and thus deprive history of an invaluable source?

President Reagan had given his biographer, Edmund Morris, access to White House meetings so that he could write a book on the Reagan years. I thought that Iran-Contra might have been discussed at one of the meetings Morris attended and so asked to interview him. Some of the press editorialized against us, maintaining that our demand would discourage presidents from using biographers in the future. Were they right?

A further example: after suggestions in the press that North had undergone psychiatric treatment at a military facility, I subpoenaed those records. Was this, as some charged, an unfair stigmatization?

On the issue of the president's diaries, we insisted that the relevant excerpts be made available to us. Presidents, concerned about their place in history, would still keep contemporaneous records of their thoughts and actions. Morris, the president's biographer, had no objection to the interview. Indeed, he turned it into an interview of me and how we were conducting the investigation. As for North's psychiatric records, I concluded that he was entitled to the same privacy as an ordinary citizen, whose medical records are protected by privilege. The fact that, as a Marine, he had received treatment at a government hospital didn't mean he'd forfeited his rights as a citizen.

Public Hearings in the Television Age

O NE OF THE remarkable things about Iran-Contra was that it was the first time committees in the Senate and the House had agreed to hold joint investigative hearings. Their success was due to the skill and tenacity of the two committee chairs, the Senate's Inouye and Representative Lee Hamilton.

Hamilton looked Lincolnesque to me, and like Lincoln, he was forthright, honest, and fair. The last thing he wanted was for his committee's investigation to degenerate into partisan bickering. He selected Nields as majority counsel, but unlike Inouye, he had no Warren Rudman to help him with his Republican minority, which had its own counsel and its own agenda and was dedicated to protecting the president. Still, Hamilton and Inouye were quickly able to agree on combined public hearings and practicable ground rules.

While I was investigating Iran-Contra, however, some Republican members of the committees found time to conduct an investigation of their own. I learned of this when Senator Orrin Hatch of Utah, with whom I had established a cordial working relationship, asked permission during one of our sessions to read into the record some "insightful" comments about congressional investigations. He then began reading a passage of the most turgid academic writing about the dangers that congressional investigations could pose to civil liberties. A few of the words sounded familiar, but I couldn't identify the source until Hatch, in concluding, stated that the author of these wise observations had been a twenty-one-year-old Harvard senior named Arthur Liman!

To much laughter, Hatch asked whether I knew him.

I admitted ruefully that I did. I thanked the senator for publicizing a work that had sat unread for more than thirty years, and stated that I was still trying to conduct myself, and our investigation, by the principles I'd held in my youth.

One of our major goals was for the public to understand not just what had happened but why, for Iran-Contra wasn't just a series of improper actions, it was a mentality. North's secretary, Fawn Hall, captured it when, in defending what she and her boss had done, she exclaimed, "Sometimes one has to rise above the written law."

Witness after witness would express similar attitudes, exhibiting contempt for established agencies like the CIA and the Defense Department because they were subject to legal restraints, and for the Congress because it refused to go along with all aspects of the president's foreign policy. For some of the Iran-Contra participants, Vietnam had been the defining event. To them, the Vietnam War had been lost not on the battlefield but in Congress, on the evening news, and in the antiwar demonstrations. Desert One, the failed expedition to rescue the hostages in Iran, had reinforced their hostility to the traditional organs of government. Oliver North had boasted to Bud McFarlane that, while the Pentagon and the CIA couldn't transport missiles to Teheran, Secord's Enterprise could get it done in a matter of hours.

It was this so-called can-do mentality that made it patriotic to lie to Congress, to circumvent checks and balances through covert actions, and to create the Enterprise to do what the CIA was not permitted to do. To many of the Iran-Contra witnesses, it was axiomatic that, to be effective, you had to go outside the system, and this, more than anything, we wanted to bring out.

In early March, Mark Belnick, Paul Barbadoro, and I proposed in writing that the hearings proceed with a theme just like a trial. The theme would be whether constitutional processes that provided safeguards against misuse of executive power had been circumvented. We wrote:

We propose that the Committee's hearings focus on the process, not the merits, of foreign policy. They will not be pro or anti Contra, for or against the Administration, Democrat or Republican. By examining how foreign policy was made in this case, the hearings will address issues of historic dimensions—the appropriate balance between the Executive Branch and Congress in foreign policy, and the right of oversight and public debate versus secrecy in the formulation and carrying out of policy.

The evidence indicates that it would be a mistake to treat the Iran arms transactions and Contra support program as two separate operations which happened to merge at a point in time. The evidence suggests these two covert operations may have been manifestations of the same approach to foreign policy by an Administration which felt blocked from pursuing its goals by Congress and by opposition within the Executive Branch itself. The Administration, therefore, decided to use irregular channels: the NSC and an elaborate private network.

By placing the operations in the NSC, the White House was able to avoid restrictions imposed by Congress (notification requirements, arms export limitations, and prohibitions on military assistance to the Contras) and to keep even the principal organs of foreign policy within the Executive Branch largely in the dark. Laws and established procedures were regarded by NSC personnel not as guides to action, but as obstacles to be circumvented. Decisions were taken contrary to the conclusions of the intelligence and foreign policy experts.

Secrecy within the White House became more critical than ever, for not only was the policy covert—so was the policy-making.

In consequence, we ended up with two foreign policies: (1) the public policy ("We will not sell arms to Iran or bargain with terrorists or provide anything other than humanitarian aid to the Contras") and (2) the secret policy, made in an irregular manner, carried out by non-accountable private agents (some of whom were not even American citizens), and incompatible with public policy. The secret policy provided that we would sell arms to Iran, traffic with terrorists, arm the Contras and indeed run their war from the Old Executive Office Building. To achieve these secret purposes, it was necessary to bypass and mislead not just the Congress, but Cabinet members.

The purpose of the public hearings was therefore educational as well as investigative. For my part, I was determined not to allow the proceedings to be used to embarrass witnesses—as McCarthy's committee and certain other congressional committees since have done. Every witness was to be afforded the opportunity to tell his or her story. We examined or interviewed each witness fully in private before he or she was called publicly, with the sole exception of Oliver North, for the reason already described. We ourselves knew in advance what each one was going to say before the cameras.

———

Since the Senate and House committees insisted on their prerogatives as coequal institutions, Nields and I, as I have mentioned before, divided the witnesses. For the Senate, I took Poindexter, McFarlane, Fawn Hall, Secretary George Shultz, Don Regan, and Elliott Abrams, among others. Nields took North, Secord, Hakim, Edwin Meese, and Defense Secretary Caspar Weinberger. Each of us would examine all the witnesses, but one of us had the primary responsibility and the other asked follow-up questions. Equality between the two Iran-Contra committees was carried to extraordinary lengths. The hearings themselves rotated each week between the marbled caucus room of the Russell Senate Office Building and the Rayburn House Office Building, and each committee built costly two-tiered platforms for the committee members and staffs. Still, equality in responsibility does not always translate to equality in outcome, and at times during the hearings I was frustrated by the actions of the House team. In the middle of the summer, I sadly noted in my diary that I was "terribly disappointed in the House side. I thought we would have gotten more out of them. They're so yellow too."

Our first witness was Richard Secord. While his testimony illustrates how Nields and I worked together as coexaminers, it also revealed another, far more perilous aspect to the proceedings that I don't think either of us had fully anticipated.

Secord went first at his own request. A retired Air Force general and Defense Department assistant secretary, he agreed to testify without immunity so long as he was the first witness, undoubtedly believing that if he went first, he could steal the show. And he almost succeeded.

On direct examination, Nields let Secord tell his own story without interruption. Brisk and self-confident in manner, Secord quickly warmed to the task. He'd been sought out by Oliver North, he testified, in the middle of 1984 on the recommendation of CIA Director Casey. At the time, the Contra operations in Nicaragua were going poorly. The Congress, though divided and vacillating from year to year, and budget to budget, had repassed the Boland Amendment, severely restricting any aid to the Contras. The Contras themselves were disorganized and had no resupply capability. Most of them were camped across the border, outside Nicaragua, and were either unprepared or unwilling to engage the Sandinistas in combat. At the same time, Casey and the NSC staff recognized that giving money directly to the Contras would be like pouring it down a sinkhole. Instead, at Casey's recommendation, Secord was tapped to take the money the president had begun raising through foreign countries, to purchase arms with it, and to supply the Contras. Later, once the Iran initiative got into full swing, Secord's mission was broadened to include assisting in the sale of arms to Iran and funneling the profits to the Contra effort.

Casey knew the man he was recommending. Secord made it crystal clear in his testimony that he felt the U.S. capacity to engage in covert actions was diminished by congressional interference and a bureaucratic culture. He regarded the CIA as no better than a bunch of clerks in a shoe store. He was convinced that he could run covert actions as a private citizen better than the government—and, of course, without any accountability.

To accomplish his mission, Secord testified that he created "the Enterprise" (Secord's own name for it) with Albert Hakim, an Iranian expatriate who had been a commissioned agent for American companies doing business in Iran during the shah's regime. Hakim's role was to handle the finances by setting up a network of secret Swiss accounts. Secord was in charge of the field operations.

Giving Secord a platform to tell his story had a distinct downside for the committees. True, it got the hearing off to a start with something new, remarkable, and totally startling. The tale of the Enterprise was like something out of a spy novel—*Six Days of the Condor* came immediately to mind—but not only did Secord reveal its existence, he boasted of it!

Who else could have organized the resupply of the Contras? Who else could have handled the delivery of arms to the Iranians? Despite Nields's skillful examination, Secord's testimony was having the exact opposite effect of what we'd expected. Instead of frightening the public with his tale of an uncontrolled, unaccountable private CIA, he was coming across on television as patriotic, heroic, even romantic, the warrior called out of retirement to save his country from its own bureaucratic bungling.

Our "clients"—that is, the members of the Senate and House committees—were distraught. Their political antennae confirmed their fears: our very first witness was succeeding in glamorizing Iran-Contra for the "jury"—that is, the television viewers of America.

Nields and I and our staffs caucused with the committees. I told the Senators and staff that Secord was wrapping himself in the flag and that if we let him get off the stand, wrapped in the flag, we would lose the public and the truth. The unhappy members gave me the assignment, once Nields was done, of showing Secord as he really was. I wasn't to badger or denounce the witness—this too, we feared, would backfire—but I was to hammer home the unseemly side of the Enterprise.

In other words, I was to concentrate on the money.

This was something the public was sure not only to understand but, unless we were all crazy, find distasteful. Secord had denied vehemently any financial interest in the Enterprise, but I had the documents showing that he had earned "commissions" on sales, that profits from the Enterprise had been used to fund investments he and Hakim made for themselves, and that funds had been paid into an account opened for Secord at a Swiss bank.

Obviously, he wanted to be seen as a patriot, but through a series of acrimonious exchanges, I harped on the fact that he was also an entrepreneur. I had the documentation to back it up. But I was no Joseph

Welch either, that sly and endearing old lawyer who, while defending the Army, had brought Joe McCarthy down. I was a New York lawyer with, as someone said, spaghetti hair, and I was attacking a retired general of the U.S. Air Force, and almost immediately the committees began to receive bags full of hate mail directed at me. With our very first witness, we found ourselves unexpectedly on the defensive, and I became a lightning rod for right-wing attacks on the committees and on the Congress in general. One member of my committee received a threat that if I continued to challenge witnesses like Secord, a whispering campaign would be started regarding *his* personal life. While no one sought to restrain me, it was clear to the committees that we were dealing with a very different phenomenon than Watergate. Those who supported the Contras—both inside and outside the government—saw themselves as on a sacred mission, and we, the congressional committees, were anti-American for so much as questioning that mission, even if it had violated the law of the land.

I never had the slightest doubt about the fortitude of most of my senators—Inouye, Rudman, Mitchell, William Cohen, Sam Nunn, and Paul Sarbanes, among them—and none either about the Democratic majority on the House committee. But this is not to deny that political pressures exist in a congressional investigation of a kind I'd never encountered before. The simple fact that members of Congress have to run for reelection—be it every two years or every six—changes everything. Their staffs are constantly reminding them of public opinion polls and the tendencies reflected in their mail. As time went on, some of our members clearly began to worry about whether they should have accepted appointment to the committees in the first place, and for some of them, standing by me and Nields became an act of political courage.

When Robert McFarlane was called, Nields and I reversed roles. My responsibility was to let McFarlane tell his story as he saw it—in other words, to let him be McFarlane, warts and all.

Robert "Bud" McFarlane was a conflicted and tortured man who had carried out a program and engaged in activities that he knew were wrong. Just as our investigation began, he had tried to commit suicide, his suicide note an apology to several senators and representatives.

Those on our committee who knew him were sympathetic toward him, and he was, to me, that rare participant in Iran-Contra, a man with a conscience, which put him in denial over what he himself had actually done. McFarlane was central to the story of Iran-Contra. He had been President Reagan's national security adviser until December 1985. Poindexter and North had both reported to him, and it was McFarlane who had given North his assignments, both as liaison to the Contras and as the point man on the Iranian arms sales. A former Marine himself, the leader of the first full-fledged American unit to land in Vietnam, McFarlane saw in North a person who could get virtually anything done.

During the spring and summer of 1987, I interviewed McFarlane on many occasions in the presence of his lawyer, Leonard Garment. My diary entries in the early interviews were negative:

> If the committee ever needs to chew up two weeks of hearing time, we can call him as a witness. His opening statement will take at least a month. I was not able to get straight answers from him. But Leonard Garment has done a brilliant job for him.

Garment was the most psychologically oriented lawyer I'd ever met, and that, in the long run, was a great service to his client. Between McFarlane's candor and Garment's psychological insights, I came to see McFarlane, alone among the Iran-Contra figures, not as an ideologue but as a deeply troubled man, constantly caught between the demands of his conscience and his emotional need to be regarded as a tough, shrewd, political battler. Unlike Poindexter and North, he sought no immunity—to do so would have been inconsistent with his notion of public service. Nor did he share his colleagues' mistrust of the Congress. McFarlane proudly told me that his father had been a New Deal congressman from Texas who was defeated after he voted for Roosevelt's program. He had received no reward from Roosevelt for his support, McFarlane added with some bitterness, and wound up in a dead-end job in the Lands Division of the Department of Justice. (Ironically, McFarlane risked his life for his president and ended up in "ruins.")

McFarlane had worked as an aide to Henry Kissinger when Kissinger was national security adviser to President Nixon. He desperately wanted a foreign policy achievement of his own to match Kissinger's China initiative, and he'd hoped that a revived relationship with Iran might be it. But McFarlane was no Kissinger, Reagan was no Nixon, and Iran was not China. McFarlane clearly lacked Kissinger's grasp of realpolitik. He genuinely believed that he was promoting a rapprochement with Iran and dealing with a cautious group of moderate Iranian politicians. In fact, all that was involved was a sale of arms for hostages, and the so-called moderates in Iran behind the trades were part of the ayatollah's regime. McFarlane couldn't contain his revulsion when he recounted meeting the Iranian go-between, Manucher Ghorbanifar, for there was no way that even McFarlane could have confused Ghorbanifar with Zhou En-lai. Listening to the tape recordings from his secret trip to Tehran, one he'd made at Reagan's request and with Oliver North at his side, it was hard not to laugh. McFarlane had clearly wanted to be treated as the personal emissary of the president of the United States, there to discuss grand strategic matters. The Iranians, though, had wanted to talk only about arms and whether the hostages would be released in installments or at once. McFarlane, in fact, had turned against the Iranian arms sales by December 1985, but unable to stand missing the action, he'd stayed peripherally involved even after he resigned, that same month, as national security adviser.

When I pressed McFarlane as to why he'd continued to support secret military aid to the Contras even after the Boland Amendment became law, he exploded. He'd been unable to make Reagan understand the most basic strategy of our relationship with the Soviet Union, he yelled, yet there I was, criticizing him for humoring the president on something as trivial as Nicaragua!

He claimed he'd been unaware that North was directing the resupply of the Contras and insisted that he himself had never deliberately broken the law. He was in full denial about his role in the attempted cover-up when the Iran-Contra news first broke in November 1986. He had actually helped create chronologies that falsely represented that the president had known nothing in advance of the shipments of HAWK missiles by Israel to the Iranians in November 1985 when, as McFarlane knew full well, the president had authorized those shipments.

The phenomenon wasn't new to me. I'd had clients myself who rewrote history in their own minds and came to believe their versions of it simply because they couldn't face the reality of what they'd done. McFarlane, to me, was a tragic case, a victim of Iran-Contra, and while it would have been easy to discredit and humiliate him in our public hearings, I knew that in so doing we would have destroyed him as a person. History would be better served, it seemed to me, if we let him demonstrate what happens to a man with a conscience when he gets caught up in improper activities on behalf of a president of the United States. If, during his examination, Nields did confront McFarlane with his improper acts, the man came out more a flawed figure than an evil one.

I can't, though, say that we always adhered to the policy of not humiliating witnesses. One administration lawyer, who got his job through patronage, had advised the White House that the national security adviser and his staff were not bound by the Boland Amendment and were therefore free to provide military assistance to the Contras. This was dumb advice, nothing more or less, but some members of the committees insisted on calling him as a witness. During his testimony, a lawyer for the House Committee brought out that he'd flunked bar examination after bar examination. By the time we'd finished with him, he was destroyed—not just as a witness but as a person. Some partisan members of the House committee regarded this as a triumph. I saw it as a low point. But this was an exception, and when I refused to call a witness who was prepared to make sensational charges against the president but was engaging, I felt, in pure fantasy, the committees supported me.

One day a former White House staffer named Edward Radzimski came to see Mark Belnick. Radzimski claimed that he had seen—and placed in a highly confidential file—some memoranda written by North referring to the diversion and sent to the president.

If he was telling the truth—and Radzimski appeared to have no motive to lie—then he was the smoking gun.

There was no way, though, we could schedule him as a public witness before checking out his story. The FBI staff assigned to the independent counsel did the same. Virtually every lead and piece of information he gave us turned out to be wrong, and he had clearly expanded and embellished his own story with facts he'd heard only at the public hearings. He was a veritable Zelig. To test him, we made up a "fact" and, without missing a beat, Radzimski incorporated it into his story. But the crowning blow was his story about his own logs. First, he told us that his accusation could be corroborated by a handwritten log of document numbers he kept. But the log didn't support him; it contradicted him. So then he claimed that someone must have forged his log—a new and wild assertion that, according to our document examiner, could not be substantiated. Only in his final appearance before us did he acknowledge, under oath, that his recollections might have been wrong.

Nevertheless, one House committee staff member lobbied hard to have Radzimski called, convinced that his testimony would dominate the hearings and discredit the president. She even complained to Seymour Hersh, the investigative journalist, that we were covering up evidence against Reagan. But we concluded that we couldn't responsibly call such a witness, and the independent counsel reached the same conclusion. Not every congressional committee, I'm sure, declines to give a platform to witnesses who make such accusations, but Inouye, Rudman, and Hamilton had an innate sense of fairness, and in an investigation into the abuse of power by the executive branch, it would have been indefensible for the legislative branch to abuse its own investigatory power.

23

North and Poindexter:
Covert Acts and Cover-Ups

F ROM THE FIRST day I met him, I knew it was Vice Admiral John Poindexter, not Oliver North, who held Ronald Reagan's fate in his hands. North was the more colorful by far, but I wanted Poindexter as my witness.

Poindexter served as national security adviser to the president from December 1985 until his dismissal when the Iran-Contra story broke a year later. Before that, he was the assistant national security adviser under McFarlane. He had briefed the president every morning on matters affecting national security. Among the topics were the missile sales to Iran and the secret support of the Contras. More than anyone, indeed even more than the president, he knew what the president was told and what the president had authorized.

Questioning Poindexter was the decisive moment of our investigation. If he implicated President Reagan—in the diversion or in the later cover-up, or both—impeachment proceedings were a virtual certainty. Because of this, I wanted to hear his story before we began the public hearings in May. But examining Poindexter, even in private, presented a problem. The independent counsel wasn't finished with his investigation of Poindexter by early May, and he said he needed several more months. If Poindexter's private testimony were somehow leaked and became public, it could taint what the independent counsel took subsequently from other witnesses and make it impossible for him to prove that his evidence against Poindexter didn't derive, even indirectly, from the private testimony.

The Senate committee, though, came up with an ingenious solution.

In order to prevent leaks, I would take Poindexter's testimony in private before the public hearings and share the results only with John Nields. No member of the Senate or House committees would be privy to what Poindexter said, unless I concluded that his testimony gave us evidence warranting the impeachment of the president.

In this case, and this case only, I was to report to Inouye and Rudman so that the impeachment process could begin promptly. On the other hand, if I concluded, after listening to Poindexter, that there was insufficient basis for impeachment, no member of the Senate or the House would be told the contents of the deposition.

I doubt that any counsel to any congressional committee had ever been entrusted with such responsibility, and it weighed heavily on me. Not that I was unused to pressure. I'd tried cases, as I've described, in which huge amounts of money were at stake, and I'd defended clients facing the loss of liberty. But nothing prepares a lawyer for conducting an examination in which the impeachment of a president turns on the outcome.

I had no idea, either, what Poindexter would say. Would he distance himself from North? Would he claim he was out of the loop on North's activities concerning the diversion, that it was all North and Casey? And what of the president? What of the shredding of documents and the cover-up? McFarlane, for example, had maintained that he was unaware of how far North had gone. Wouldn't Poindexter try to do likewise, particularly since he could be prosecuted if he'd participated in any criminal activity?

During the week before Poindexter's deposition, I hardly slept. At the same time, I was preparing for the public hearings, including my cross-examination of Secord, and supervising twenty other lawyers plus investigators. I was also consulting regularly with the committee members, who made more demands on my time as the hearings approached and they themselves prepared to question witnesses. But most important of all, I had to pull together everything we knew about Poindexter.

We scheduled Poindexter's examination on a Saturday, May 2, to ensure secrecy. The questioning itself took place inside the "bubble," a special high-security, eavesdropping-proof metal shell the government had required us to install in our office. The bubble supposedly couldn't be penetrated even by the most sophisticated electronic listening devices.

To keep the very fact of his examination secret, we arranged for Poindexter to be spirited in and out of our offices with his attorney. I would arrive at 7:00 A.M., three hours before.

Inouye was out of Washington that weekend, so it fell to Senator Rudman, as vice chairman of the committee, to administer the oath to Poindexter and read him the immunity order. Rudman came to our office shortly before the scheduled start of the deposition, and we waited together.

Then Poindexter arrived with his lawyer. We greeted each other stiffly and without pleasantries. Poindexter was dressed in civilian clothes and held a pipe in his mouth throughout. With his rimless glasses and his pipe, he was bookish-looking—more professorial than military. He never once smiled, never exhibited the slightest warmth. He had been ordered here to give testimony against his will, he wanted to get it over with, and he wasn't going to try to charm us or persuade us. We, in short, were the enemy.

Rudman swore Poindexter in. Then I asked Poindexter his occupation, and he immediately took the Fifth—that is, he refused to answer on the ground that his answer to that question might incriminate him. A McCarthy or a Cohn, needless to say, would have harassed Poindexter with one loaded question after another, thereby forcing him repeatedly to invoke his Fifth Amendment privilege, but we didn't. Instead, Senator Rudman read Poindexter the court's immunity order and asked him whether he understood that he had to testify. Poindexter nodded, and at that point, as we'd agreed, Rudman withdrew from the bubble.

Poindexter sat across the table from me.

On one side of me was an assistant, and on the other, Nields and one of his aides.

I began with some routine questions about Poindexter's background. He answered them, but he was clearly impatient. He wanted the $64,000 question about the president without any foreplay so he could answer and leave. But I chose to get there more gradually. One reason was tactical: I was sure Poindexter had worked with his lawyer and would deliver a carefully rehearsed answer. I hoped that, if the topic came up later when perhaps he was not expecting it, he would be less able to stick to his canned answer. But I think there was another reason too. I think I was reluctant to hear his answer. Either it would destroy the president of the United States, or it would leave the rest of our investigation an anticlimax.

It seemed like a whole day, but it was only about an hour into the deposition when I turned to the diversion.

And out spilled Poindexter's story.

He alone, not Reagan, was the villain. He alone had authorized North to divert the profits from the Iranian arms sales to the Contras. He took full responsibility. The cover-up too. He'd never told the president about the diversion because he knew it would be politically explosive if it ever came out. From the beginning, he'd wanted to give the president deniability.

But didn't the doctrine of deniability, I asked, mean that a president was put in a position where he could deny what he actually knew? That was the point of deniability, wasn't it? It certainly didn't mean that aides made decisions on their own that could wreck a presidency without telling the president, did it?

But my questions didn't faze Poindexter in the slightest. None of them. He had told the president nothing.

"But do you understand," I asked him, "that by claiming to be the most senior government official who approved the diversion, you're leaving yourself without any legal defense that you were acting on presidential orders?"

This didn't faze him either.

When we stopped for a break, I asked Poindexter's lawyer the same question. Didn't he understand that his client's position was exposing him to serious criminal liability?

"He is fully aware of the consequences," Poindexter's lawyer replied. "You can believe his testimony or reject it, but as far as he's concerned, it's the truth."

At that point I was reminded of Billy Budd, Herman Melville's sailor who, upon being sentenced to death by his captain to make an example of discipline, thanks the captain for permitting him to serve.

Sometimes a witness gets flustered when confronted with an inconsistency, but not Poindexter. I couldn't shake him. He sat the whole time with his pipe between his teeth, completely at peace with himself. During one recess he told me proudly—the only emotion he ever displayed—that two of his sons were in the Navy. Probably I realized then that he wasn't going to embarrass them by becoming a snitch against the commander in chief.

Whenever necessary, he contradicted Oliver North.

North said he had written five memoranda, intended for the president, detailing the diversion?

Poindexter denied it. He also gave equivocal testimony about what the president knew about the NSC's efforts to direct the resupply and support of the Contras. According to Poindexter, yes, the president knew that North was the NSC staff officer on Central America and knew, in a general sense, that it was North's responsibility to keep the Contras alive.

But what of the Boland Amendment?

Well, in the president's view, the Boland Amendment simply didn't apply to the NSC staff.

Just as I was coming to the end of Poindexter's deposition, an urgent phone call interrupted us.

It was for me. Rudman was on pins and needles in his office.

He was about to leave for home, he said, but did I have anything to report?

I told him he could go home. That there was nothing to discuss.

I didn't have to tell him that Poindexter had just saved Reagan's presidency.

I never bought Poindexter's story.

To begin with, it would have been totally out of character for him to have authorized either the diversion or the cover-up on his own. While I was preparing for his deposition, I'd studied his background carefully, and his work habits too. First in his class at Annapolis, he'd been studious, on the dull side, dutiful with a capital "D". As he rose through the ranks of the Navy, he'd consistently received the highest ratings from his superior officers. He didn't want to be national security adviser—he'd have much preferred to command the Sixth Fleet and then become chief of naval operations, positions to which he seemed destined—but the Navy had sent him to the White House so that there would be more of a salt-water flavor to national security policy.

Throughout his career, he'd been an obedient and disciplined officer, playing everything by the book. One of his former commanders told me that Poindexter would never take an initiative without the approval of his superior, and that his obedience was almost a fault. It was inconceivable, the same man told me, that Poindexter had approved the diversion or any other illegal activities without the president's approval, and he would have insisted, furthermore, that that approval be explicit.

In this context, I would find North's testimony—that Poindexter had told him to write five memoranda for the president, describing the diversion—far more believable. Once Poindexter admitted approving the diversion, what would North possibly have to gain by implicating Reagan with some phony story about nonexistent memoranda?

Senator Sam Nunn, who was a member of the Senate committee and also the chair of the Senate Armed Services Committee, knew Poindexter well. Inouye assigned Nunn the job of questioning Poindexter at the public hearings, and so Nunn and I often speculated about him. Nunn told me that he too found it unbelievable that Poindexter would have acted without the president's knowledge.

But it was something Poindexter said about his duties as the president's national security adviser that most convinced me that he was lying. During his secret deposition, that Saturday in May, he surprised me by testifying that, once the Iran-Contra story broke in November 1986, he'd torn up an order, a presidential "finding," that was signed by the president and authorized selling weapons to Iran in exchange for the release of the hostages. This had been the only signed copy in existence. The White House now denied that the president had ever signed the finding, and the president claimed he'd gone along with selling missiles to Iran only because he thought it might encourage and promote a relationship with moderate elements inside Iran.

If Poindexter was right, the signed finding contradicted that story, and when he testified under oath, on national television, Poindexter was categorical on this point:

LIMAN: Now, Admiral, did there come a time in connection with this transaction when the CIA sent over to you a proposed finding for the president to sign?

POINDEXTER: Yes, Mr. Liman. This is the finding which I discussed with you earlier, on the second of May, which I destroyed.

LIMAN: Now, if we look at that finding, it is exhibit 18 in the book, I will put it up there. Did you receive the letter of November 26, 1985, from William Casey, addressed to you, which says, "Pursuant to our conversation, this should go to the president for his signature and should not be passed around in any hands below our level"?

POINDEXTER: I did receive that.

LIMAN: Admiral, when you saw the finding, am I correct that the finding itself was essentially a straight arms-for-hostage finding?

POINDEXTER: That is correct. . . .

LIMAN: Did the president of the United States sign that finding?

POINDEXTER: As I have testified before, he did, on or about the fifth of December.

Poindexter said further that Reagan hadn't known he was destroying the finding. He described it for the committee as follows:

POINDEXTER: Later in the afternoon or early evening [of November 21, 1986], Commander Paul B. Thompson brought into my office the envelopes that I had given him earlier containing the material we had on the Iranian project in the immediate office, which was essentially the various findings, and he pulled out this November finding—it was actually signed in December—and my recollection is that he said something to the effect that, "They'll have a field day with this."

And my recollection is that the import of his comment was that up until that time, in November 1986, the president was being beaten about the head and shoulders, that this was—the whole Iranian project was just an arms-for-hostage deal.

Well, this finding, unfortunately, gave that same impression. And I, frankly, didn't see any need for it at the time. I thought it was politically embarrassing. And so I decided to tear it up, and I tore it up, put it in the burn basket behind my desk. . . .

LIMAN: Did you regard one of the responsibilities of the national security adviser to protect the president from political embarrassment?

POINDEXTER: I think that it's always the responsibility of the staff to protect their leader, and certainly in this case, where the leader is the commander in chief, I feel very strongly that that's one of the roles. . . .

LIMAN: Now, Admiral, a finding represents a decision of the president of the United States, correct?

POINDEXTER: . . . A finding, I don't believe, is discussed in any statute. It is discussed in various presidential directives. It is an artifact of what the statute calls a presidential determination.

LIMAN: And the president, when he signed this finding, was making a determination?

POINDEXTER: That is correct. But it's important to point out that the finding, that early finding, was designed for a very specific purpose, and was not fully staffed, and did not in any way ever represent the full thinking on the subject.

LIMAN: Well, the president didn't authorize you to destroy the finding, correct?

POINDEXTER: He certainly did not.

The implications were obvious. If Poindexter saw it as his duty to destroy an official record to protect the president from political embarrassment, where did that sense of duty stop? How could we believe anything he'd told us? How, in fact, could we credit his claim that he'd destroyed the finding without the president's knowledge? Suppose that, later, the president remembered having signed the finding and asked Poindexter for it. Would Poindexter really have put himself in a position where he would have to tell the president of the United States he'd shredded a signed written order and not bothered to tell him he was doing so?

Even a far more freewheeling officer was unlikely to have done that.

Finally, there was the story of the uniform. Early in the investigation, Senator Inouye had called Poindexter and his attorney into his office to try to persuade Poindexter not to invoke the Fifth Amendment and insist on immunity. Inouye told Poindexter that he respected his constitutional rights and that he had fought a war to protect them. Then he talked about his comrades who'd lost their lives on the battlefield during World War II, and with his voice almost choking, he told Poindexter that it dishonored the uniform for a military officer to invoke the privilege against self-incrimination like an ordinary criminal defendant.

Poindexter replied that he felt the same way. But then, by way of response, he pledged to Inouye that he wouldn't wear his uniform when he testified!

He would be testifying, he said further, as the former national security adviser—a civilian aide to the president—and thus the honor of his Navy uniform wouldn't be at stake. Presumably civilian advisers, like the politicians they served, could be called upon to fudge the truth all the time. As Poindexter saw it, he'd been just a political appointee at the White House.

I was sure that if, somehow, the committees could persuade him to wear his uniform when he testified, the protective shield would drop and we would get the full facts. But it was not to be.

Many members of the committees, Republicans included, were as skeptical of Poindexter's absolution of the president as I was. At the same time, we agreed, browbeating him in front of the television cameras wouldn't have done us the slightest good. Privately, however, I was less restrained in expressing my opinions. Once, during a recess when Poindexter was testifying, Senator Nunn and I were talking when a reporter approached and asked what I thought of the testimony. Out of sheer frustration, I said bluntly, "It's bullshit." Unfortunately, we were close enough to a live network microphone, and my comment was broadcast. When the hearings resumed, the House Republicans launched such a vigorous counterattack that I leaned over to Nunn, who was sitting next to me, and commented that, while Reagan was safe, it looked like I was the one who was going to be impeached.

———

Oliver North.

I share responsibility for making him into a national hero. In retrospect, I think it was almost inevitable. North, boyishly handsome and photogenic, sat in his Marine uniform with his medals at a simple table, alone with his lawyer. Arrayed against him, on an elevated two-tier platform, sat eleven senators and fifteen members of the House committee, plus all their aides and staff. Steven Spielberg later told me that North was televised at the hero's angle, looking up as though from a pit at the committees, who resembled two rows of judges at the Spanish Inquisition. Spielberg called that the villains' angle. Unfortunately, the committees had built the platforms without any advice from a movie director.

Senator Rudman tried to persuade Inouye, when North began testifying, to wear his Distinguished Service Cross along with the Good Conduct Medal he habitually wore in his lapel. But Inouye replied that he wore the latter because he'd earned it, whereas he'd only gotten the Distinguished Service Cross by being in the wrong place at the wrong time—that is, in the line of enemy fire! For my part, if I had it to do over again, I'd hire a Vietnam War vet to examine North. As it was, the Marine lieutenant colonel could all too easily portray himself as a patriot and a war hero being bullied by politicians and their lawyers—one with long hair (John Nields) and the other crowned with "spaghetti."

Before we even knew what had hit us, the most nonpartisan hearings ever held in the U.S. Congress came across on television as unfair.

With North, as with all the other witnesses, Nields and I divided the questioning. Nields's questions, like a direct examination at a trial, were designed to bring out North's basic story, including his lying to Congress, his shredding of documents, his creating the Enterprise, the diversion, and his accepting the role of fall guy. I, in turn, would examine North about allegations that he had misappropriated money from the Enterprise for personal use.

A Washington lawyer named David Lewis, who had contacted Nields, told us that he'd had professional dealings with one Willard Zucker, an American lawyer residing in Switzerland who had handled the Enterprise's bank accounts. In the fall of 1986, Lewis claimed, Zucker had asked him to arrange a fictitious real estate commission of $200,000 to Oliver North's wife. Lewis had refused. He'd had no contact with the Norths. Zucker, in turn, had refused to cooperate with us.

Hakim, however, had testified that he asked Zucker to set up a $200,000 trust in Switzerland for North's family as an "insurance policy" for North if he was killed during his trip to Tehran. According to Hakim, however, he never told North about it.

I had also discovered, when examining Adolfo Calero, the head of the Contras, that he had given some $100,000 in traveler's checks belonging to the Contras to North. Finally, we had also established in the earlier part of the hearings that Secord used Enterprise funds to pay for a security fence around North's home and that North created false documents showing that he was the one who'd paid for the fence.

These subjects, not nearly as serious as the constitutional violations of Iran-Contra, were to be explored during my second examination.

Nields's questioning of North, over a two-day period, elicited even more damning admissions than we'd expected. North acknowledged that he'd established the Enterprise—at Casey's direction. He admitted the diversion and said that Poindexter had authorized it. (Until then, the public record had contained only the statement, from Poindexter, that he had indications of the diversion but looked the other way.) North testified that he believed the president had been aware of the diversion. At Poindexter's direction, he said, he'd written the five memoranda intended for the president that referred to the diversion. He admitted that he had shredded them when the scandal had broken, but he had missed one copy. He told of having lied to the Congress about the Contras. Assistant Secretary of State Elliott Abrams, he said, had been aware of his activities in supporting the Contras and was involved in the cover-up. (Abrams later pleaded guilty to lying to the Congress.) North admitted shredding all documents relating to his Contra and Iranian activities—at Casey's suggestion. He testified that McFarlane had asked him to alter official records to delete references to direct assistance to the Contras and that he'd helped McFarlane to prepare the false chronology in November 1986, covering up the president's role in the missile sales through Israel. He testified that Casey told him that he—North—was to be the "fall guy" for the president if the Contra and Iranian operations ever became known, and that the president, after firing him, had called him and told him there were "some things a president doesn't know."

I had rarely, if ever, seen a cooperating witness in a criminal case who admitted more than North did. But there was one salient difference. Even when making these admissions, North acted like a hostile witness. He was combative even when agreeing with Nields's questions, and he made all his illegal acts—the lying to the Congress, the diversion, the formation of the Enterprise, the cover-up—seem logical and patriotic.

Somehow, it got to John Nields, some realization perhaps that whatever crimes he'd committed, North was nevertheless emerging a national hero. Normally a mild and gentle examiner, Nields became unexpectedly and unnecessarily acrimonious. Before the eyes of the nation, an old conflict was reprised, the Vietnam veterans against the protesters—North, with his crew cut, pressed uniform, and upright military bearing, Nields with his long hair—and with it an old national perception, born out of the frustration of those years, that, even if the war had been wrong, somehow the protesters had been wrong too.

The longer the examination went on, the angrier Nields grew. And then, suddenly, he started questioning North about possible misappropriations of money—the very matters we'd agreed I would cover later.

I don't know at what moment Nields decided to do this, but the tactic backfired. North managed to deflect Nields's angry allegations. In a bravura performance, North, the can-do Marine, became the victim of Nields—an unlikely switch but one that took place right before the cameras—and the result was the overshadowing of all that Nields had accomplished in bringing out North's story by a series of essentially petty matters. In response to Nields's probing, North testified that he'd built the security fence to protect his family against a terrorist threat, and that Calero's traveler's checks had merely reimbursed him for money he'd laid out of his own pocket for the Contras.

Essentially a spectator to Nields's examination, I also got my first glimpse of how the networks were covering it. At least one of the network anchormen kept describing the hearing like a sporting event—and clearly he had North way ahead on points. It didn't seem to make a particle of difference to him—supposedly a seasoned observer of the political scene—that North was describing a deliberate and systematic operation to subvert the Constitution. The anchorman couldn't have cared less.

But not even the television coverage prepared me—or any of us—for the extraordinary public response. A veritable tidal wave of telegrams poured in to the committee members in support of North. We had no idea, at the time, that Western Union was offering a discount rate for a stock telegram supporting North, while telegrams supporting the committees were transmitted at regular rates, but at the same time, North's supporters were flooding the telephone lines of the members of the committees with calls. When I questioned North myself, I received thousands of threatening letters, including a number of ugly anti-Semitic ones, and for several days, Inouye and I had to be given special police protection.

Nields questioned North for a full two days and finished at the noon break on the third day. I had an hour to decide what to do. My choices were few.

Not that I needed further proof, but the enormity of North's popularity was also brought home to me by the Capitol police. Many had served the Congress for decades. They were proud employees, the first friendly voices you would hear in the morning, and the last in the evening. They respected and protected the senators and representatives, and they couldn't have been more cordial to me.

But they also were subject to the same emotional pulls and responses as the public. Maybe Oliver North had practically spit in the eyes of their employers, but he still came across as a patriot and celebrity. During one luncheon recess, while North was still on the stand, I'd walked back into the hearing room to retrieve some papers. An embarrassed guard tried to stop me, but too late. In the room was a line of Capitol police, maybe as many as one hundred, waiting for North to autograph some memento. I saw in that scene the transfer of loyalty from the Congress that they served to the man who, more than anyone, symbolized contempt of Congress. For the first time, I felt disillusioned. Perhaps one old guard sensed it, for he put an arm around my shoulders and escorted me out of the hearing room.

The senators, of course, were keenly aware of what was going on. All they wanted was for me to get North off the stand as quickly as possible. I myself knew I could only make matters worse by challenging him. Besides, I believed most of his story.

As with Secord, I'd prepared an examination that would focus on the attempts to launder money for North's family. Even if North were to deny knowledge of these efforts by Hakim and Zucker, I'd thought I could succeed in removing some more of the patriotic patina from the Enterprise. But after North's performance, the committees—all of us— would have been lynched if we'd made too much of the subject. So during that recess, after Nields had finished his examination, I sat with Mark Belnick, James Kaplan, a staff member, and my son Lewis, who had come down to watch. As I munched a sandwich, I cut out all my planned questions on money. I wasn't even sure I should conduct an examination at all, and several members of the committees had already suggested that I not do so. As I was working, though, Warren Rudman came in and told me that both he and Inouye wanted me to proceed, pointing up the constitutional issues, not the personal ones. I wasn't to worry about the reactions of the other members of the committees either. He and Inouye would take care of them.

Belnick and my son urged me to think of my questions not as a cross-examination in a trial but as a redirect, as though I were the lawyer who had put the witness on the stand in the first place. Redirect, needless to say, isn't a hostile examination. Its purpose is to highlight facts already brought out in direct examination, facts favorable to the questioner. I knew instinctively that they were right. Rather than attacking North, I would focus on how the Iranian arms sales, the covert Contra support, and the Enterprise had subverted our constitutional system of checks and balances. Reshuffling my papers, I went back into the caucus room to question the hero.

I chose the most dramatic and damaging parts of North's story in terms of the rule of law. I brought out again that Casey had told him to be the fall guy, to take the responsibility for any illegal or embarrassing acts. Above all else, the president had to have deniability. Once the story of Iran-Contra began leaking out, North testified, Casey had warned him that Poindexter might also have to take the fall, since North was not a senior enough official. I had him testify that he'd told the same thing to McFarlane—that he would be the scapegoat for the president and the administration.

North, however, hadn't been willing to go to jail. When, on November 25, Attorney General Meese had announced the appointment of an independent counsel, North was, as he put it, "the only person on the planet Earth" named in the independent counsel's order. That wasn't part of his deal, was it? No. And that had made him resolve to tell the whole story.

I had North repeat his testimony that the diversion was Casey's idea, that Casey had been proud to get the ayatollah's money to support American interests in Nicaragua, that North had written the five memoranda to Poindexter, and that they were intended for the president. He also repeated his testimony about lying to Congress and shredding, and he blamed Congress for creating Iran-Contra by passing laws against aid to the Contras, not the administration for evading those laws. His testimony, whatever he thought and whatever the television audience thought at the time, was a stark rejection of basic constitutional principles.

When I began, North's lawyer, Brendan Sullivan, tried to disrupt my examination with many objections. North, however, was a perceptive witness, and once he sensed I wasn't out to attack him, he started overruling his own lawyer. He was reassured further by a small incident. On that day in November 1986 when he was fired from the NSC staff, he had written a rather intimate entry in his diaries in which he'd listed his "priorities," first and foremost of which was his family. At one point, I began to question him about it, although I had some misgivings because the tone of the entry was so personal and anguished. North paused when I asked him a preliminary question, then engaged in a long discussion with Sullivan. When they'd finished, North looked back at me, and I could see he was on the verge of tears. Momentarily, I thought about going ahead anyway, but I decided instead to move on to another topic. North, I think, was the only other person who knew what had just happened, but from that point on he was noticeably less belligerent and more forthcoming, and the next day I had a handwritten note from him, thanking me for not having pressed him on the matter.

In fact, I finished my examination as quickly as I could, knowing that it stood no chance of changing the public's opinion of North. I was able to use his testimony to emphasize that Iran-Contra had never been the escapade of a single, out-of-control loose cannon of a Marine lieutenant colonel, but instead a policy, and one that, whichever side one was on, went all the way to the president. And I was able to reinforce what Nields had brought out earlier—that we were dealing with activities of a constitutional dimension, inconsistent in every way with our principles of accountability and a government under law.

24

Implausible Deniability:
Why Reagan Was Not Impeached

W E HAVE BECOME so used to accusations against presidents, particularly under the Clinton administration, that some of us may look back at Iran-Contra as just another partisan tussle between Congress and the president. But Iran-Contra was different, and in some ways it was a lot more disturbing than Watergate and the other "gates" that have happened since.

Watergate was a bungled burglary and then a cover-up. Iran-Contra, though it also involved a cover-up at the highest levels of government, was a deliberate effort—perhaps the first in our country's history—to conduct foreign policy in secret by using a private organization motivated by profit and accountable to no one.

Covert operations are inherently dangerous for our democracy. Intended, at least in theory, to further U.S. foreign policy goals, they can also undermine them. They can jeopardize relations with foreign countries, as when the downed U-2, during the Eisenhower administration, escalated tension severely with the Soviet Union, or as the Bay of Pigs did under Kennedy. Covert operations can also lead to retaliation and war. They were the prelude to our full-scale involvement in Vietnam and Cambodia.

Covert operations have also served the national interest, as when American money, funneled secretly to middle-of-the-road parties in Europe after World War II, helped prevent a Communist takeover in several different countries. But to avoid abuses and unnecessary risks, they have to be tightly controlled by the government. This is why, since the Carter administration, the law requires the president of the United States to sign off on covert operations in writing, so that he may be held personally responsible for their initiation and supervision. They must also be reported to select members of Congress—the majority and minority leaders and the heads of the intelligence committees.

Secrecy was the hallmark of Iran-Contra, secrecy above and beyond the law. President Reagan deliberately chose not to inform any members of Congress of the arms-for-hostages sale to Iran under the pretext that members of Congress could not be trusted with a secret. In his testimony, North rallied support for this position by citing two examples of alleged leaks by Congress of sensitive information with which it had been entrusted. The first was our planned air attack on Libya in April 1986. The second was our planned interception of an Egyptian airliner carrying the hijackers of the *Achille Lauro* cruise ship. In the case of the Libyan air raid, North contended that leaks by members of Congress had led to an increase in antiaircraft fire in which one American plane was downed.

North's attack on Congress for leaking was, however, too much for the media. *Newsweek*, breaking the tradition of protecting sources, said it was North himself who had leaked the *Achille Lauro* story to them. As for the Libyan air raid, Chairman Inouye cited eight news reports identifying administration officials as the source of advance information about the raid. Indeed, ABC's Sam Donaldson, referring to the administration's leaks, reported at the time: "Seldom will U.S. military action have been so widely and publicly advertised in advance."

It is common practice for the administration and Congress to trade charges of leaks. The Reagan administration, however, mounted a veritable campaign to discredit the congressional intelligence committees by accusing them of leaking. CIA Director Casey resisted all oversight by the committees and tried, in return, to undermine their credibility. His animus had an ironic edge because, as Senator Daniel Patrick Moynihan of New York, a member of the Senate Intelligence Committee, observed, the congressional committees tended to be co-opted by the CIA anyway.

Analysis of leaks during the Reagan administration showed that they almost always came from administration officials trying to advance policy goals and enlist support for the administration's foreign policy. The record of the intelligence committees for keeping secrets was, with a few exceptions, a generally good one.

In any event, "national security" was hardly a justification for keeping the Iran-Contra activities secret. The White House's support of Contra military operations was well known to the Sandinistas. Indeed, the White House *wanted* the Sandinistas to know what we were doing—as a means of intimidating them. As for the arms-for-hostages exchange, it was obviously known to the ayatollah's regime, which received the arms; in Lebanon to the Hezbollah terrorists, who held the hostages; to the shady Iranian middleman Ghorbanifar, who could never pass a CIA lie detector test; and to Albert Hakim and others. Only the leaders of Congress and the intelligence committees, it appeared, could not be trusted. The real reason, however, was perfectly clear: President Reagan wanted no debate with any member of Congress about whether he could, or should, violate American policy by selling arms to Iran or violate the Boland Amendment by supporting the Contras. Secrecy—from the Congress—was indispensable.

Looked at this way, the Enterprise was a perfectly logical creation. Indeed, it was formed because the government itself couldn't directly engage in the Contra operations. But there were no checks on what the Enterprise could do, and it was accountable to no one. Only a few government officials even knew it existed—North, Poindexter, and Casey—not the president, not the secretaries of state or defense, and certainly not the Congress.

Secord described the Enterprise as an "off-the-shelf" entity that could be used anywhere around the globe for covert operations on behalf of the United States. North testified that Casey wanted a private "stand-alone" organization that could perform the covert operations the CIA was not permitted to do and that would be free from congressional oversight and interference. Hakim drew up an elaborate organization chart, which included collecting companies to receive the money for operations, treasury companies to funnel money to operating companies, and operating companies to conduct covert operations around the world. The very complexity was supposed to ensure that if one company was exposed, the other operations would not be jeopardized. The Enterprise, meanwhile, reported to just one person in the U.S. government—Lieutenant Colonel Oliver North.

The Enterprise had its own secret Swiss bank accounts, its own aircraft used for the resupply of the Contras, even its own ship to be used in the event of operations in the Middle East. Originally, its funding came from the money the president raised from other countries for the Contras, but once the Iranian venture began, it was funded by its markup on the arms sold to Iran-Contra. It was a very profitable operation. The Enterprise's revenues from its two years of operations were almost $48 million. It spent almost $36 million on covert operations, principally the arms to be sold to the Iranians and the resupply of the Contras. The remaining $12 million was profit, some $6 million of which remained in its bank accounts after the Enterprise was shut down; Secord and Hakim, on the one hand, and the United States, on the other, have battled over that sum in Swiss courts ever since.

When I was first appointed to run the Senate investigation, I'd visited Clark Clifford, one of Washington's famous wise men whose experience went back to the Truman administration. Clifford told me the story of the Algerian colonels who, out of anger at de Gaulle for giving Algeria independence, had tried to organize a coup against the French government.

Clifford said that he suspected that frustration over the war in Vietnam had fostered similar attitudes among national security officials and that we should look for whether a secret and unaccountable government agency was being organized. In the Enterprise we found it, and I consider the exposure of the Enterprise, even though it has now been almost forgotten, as the most important accomplishment of our investigation. Privatizing the post office is something we can all argue over. But privatizing CIA operations should be left to the novelists and movie directors who entertain us.

Like Watergate, Iran-Contra also involved a cover-up, but one on a much broader scale. It began when President Reagan decided, after the Congress adopted the Boland Amendment, to seek funding for the Contras from other countries. Secretary of State Shultz objected to such solicitations; he believed that "wherever there was a quid, there was a quo." As a result, he was never told of the contribution of some $32 million that the president raised from one Middle East country with which we had an important strategic relationship and with which the State Department had constant dealings. Nor was Donald Regan, the president's own chief of staff, ever told. He wasn't trusted to keep the secret. Congress, of course, was regarded as the enemy of the Contras, and every effort was made to hide the NSC staff's role. Poindexter, North, and the assistant secretary of state for Latin American affairs, Elliott Abrams, gave deliberately misleading, and sometimes false, responses to inquiries from congressional committees. At McFarlane's request, North revised memos that Congress might see to expunge any references to the support of the Contras.

The lies had escalated in August 1986, when an Enterprise C-123K transport plane was shot down over Nicaragua. The pilot and copilot were killed, but the Sandinistas captured an American member of the crew, Eugene Hasenfus. The White House denied any involvement with the flight. The lying and secrecy had one purpose alone—to keep the Congress of the United States from learning about the Enterprise and imposing still further restrictions on the administration's foreign policy.

The same policy of concealment was followed in the sale of arms for hostages to Iran. The White House knew it couldn't defend the policy. Thus, even after his secretary of defense, Caspar "Cap" Weinberger, warned the president that the law required disclosure to the intelligence committees and the leaders of Congress, the president refused to do so. According to George Shultz, in December 1986, as the Iran-Contra story was emerging in the press, Weinberger warned Reagan that he could go to jail. Reagan replied that the American people would forgive his efforts to redeem the hostages, but if not, well . . . "visiting days were on Thursday"!

The exclamation point is mine. I'm sure the president took his insouciant line from a movie.

During the Iran initiative, the NSC staff continuously lied to the secretary of state. Secretary Shultz wasn't even told that the president had sent his former national security adviser to Tehran to negotiate with the Iranians. The lies were so pervasive within the administration that, once the stories became public, it was hard for any one person, much less the media, to keep track of them, and as I have tried to show, the concerted effort at deception didn't stop even when the investigations by the independent counsel and the special congressional committees began.

We may never know whether John Poindexter, in shielding the president in his testimony, was merely executing the role of the fall guy envisioned for North by Casey. But Secretary of Defense Weinberger did lie to us.

In an interview, Weinberger told me that he kept neither a diary nor notes of meetings. He even gave his disclaimer verisimilitude by saying he wished that he, like Henry Kissinger, had taken such notes because they would have made it easier to write a book once he left government. He told this same story to the independent counsel. But no sooner had I left the room than he made notes of our interview. Weinberger, it turned out, was a diarist too—just like Kissinger—and when the independent counsel got his hands on Weinberger's notes and diaries sometime later, they proved that he'd lied not only on the subject of note-taking but, in repeated testimony to congressional committees, on his knowledge of the missile sales to Iran, the contributions to the Contras of certain foreign countries, and other matters. The notes and diaries revealed the truth, and the independent counsel indicted him for his false statements.

President Bush later pardoned Weinberger. It was a kind gesture to an old friend but a terrible precedent, since it said that a cabinet officer could lie to a prosecutor and the Congress with impunity.

Weinberger's lies were all the more puzzling because he had been an early critic of Reagan's policy in Iran-Contra. He couldn't have been trying to protect himself when he denied that he had diaries and notes, since his objections to the arms sales made him look good. Rather, I am convinced that he regarded it as unseemly and disloyal for a cabinet officer to testify about his conversations with the president.

The Weinberger problem lurks in every investigation of a president. Appointees, be they a Poindexter or a Weinberger, regard it as their duty to protect the president from embarrassment, or worse, and are unwilling witnesses. Oliver North put it accurately when he testified that all who serve a president, be they Democrat or Republican, feel it is incumbent on them to protect the commander in chief. With that perspective, it was surprising that we found out as much as we did.

I had had some previous firsthand experience with impeachable conduct: I served as prosecutor in the proceeding that disbarred Richard Nixon from the practice of law in New York.

Prior to the presidency, Nixon had been a corporate lawyer in New York City, and even after he resigned, he still belonged to the New York bar. Cyrus Vance, then president of the Bar Association of the City of New York, believed that any lawyer who had deliberately obstructed justice, as Nixon had, should be formally punished by the bar, and he asked me and my partner, Lewis Kaplan, to take on the assignment. We agreed, though without relish.

Nixon had no intention of litigating Watergate before the disciplinary committee of the New York State bar. Instead, he defaulted in the proceedings. We still had to make our case, however, and we relied heavily on the Watergate tapes. As a result, I spent hours listening to them. They were appalling, and sad. It was disheartening to hear the president of the United States plotting false testimony just like some member of the Mob. We succeeded in our unsavory task, and in 1976 Nixon was disbarred in New York, the only state that did so.

When it came to Iran-Contra, though, we had no comparable evidence. We could never prove whether President Reagan was actually told of the diversion. Too many documents were shredded, too many witnesses gave inconsistent testimony, and too many of his aides wanted to protect him. Like me, many members of the committees believed he knew, but belief is no substitute for proof. Troubled as we were about the Enterprise, there was no proof that the president knew of that either.

The Constitution defines the grounds for impeachment as high crimes and misdemeanors, and most constitutional scholars agree that an act need not be criminal to warrant impeachment. A serious dereliction of duty could suffice. But even though Reagan had demonstrably contributed to the cover-up with his divergent stories, given his legendary lack of interest in and memory for details, the committees were not prepared to recommend impeachment on this basis alone.

Impeachment, we all believed, must be reserved for cases where the proof is virtually beyond dispute. In fact, there was never a debate on the issue among our committee members, nor did we take a vote. On May 2, as I've said, when Poindexter threw his body in front of the president, the subject was closed.

The impeachment issue aside, Reagan saved his presidency by avoiding the mistakes Nixon had made in Watergate. Reagan's innate political sense must have told him that he could cooperate fully with the investigators and survive. He waived executive privilege without qualification, waived attorney-client privilege, directed all government employees to cooperate, made available his private diaries to us, and even, as I said, arranged for his biographer to meet with us. And in the end, he came across as a bungling chief executive officer, but one whose mistakes were neither conspiratorial nor malicious.

Nevertheless, Iran-Contra will always haunt the record of his administration. The hearings showed a White House out of control—run by zealous aides who were encouraged by the president to consider him above the law and who carried out secret policies that failed. They revealed a president hiding his Iran adventures from his secretary of state. They showed a disdain for Congress and for our system of checks and balances, and a rejection of accountability, which is one cornerstone of a constitutional government.

As we noted in our final report, all of the government officials who took part in Iran-Contra believed that, since they were carrying out the president's policy, they would not be reprimanded for evading the law and lying to Congress. In fact, none received even the mildest of criticism from the president. With the majority of its Republican members assenting, my Senate committee concluded that the president, at the very least, bore the responsibility for creating a climate in the White House in which a disdain for law had flourished. Noting that, under the Constitution, the president is charged with the duty to take care that the laws are faithfully executed, we concluded that he had defaulted in that duty.

2 5

Presidential Accountability and Criminal Liability

W ASHINGTON IS A GEM of a city, and for Ellen and me, it turned
out to be a delightful place to live. But unlike New York, it is also a one-
company (that company being government) town. I found this claus-
trophobic. An instant celebrity, I was even, on occasion, asked for my
autograph, and I was glad when the time came to go back to the more
familiar anonymity of New York.

I was aware that many people considered the Iran-Contra investigation a failure, and for a while after we got home, this bothered me a
great deal. Eventually, though, I came to see my own naïveté. I had so
strongly wanted the hearings to be a lesson on the importance of adher-
ing to our Constitution and the rule of law that I'd assumed the public
and media would perceive them the same way. This was probably a
pompous expectation on my part. Certainly it was an unrealistic one.
The media and the public communicate in sound bites, and as I sug-

gested at the beginning of Chapter 20, our media cover high-profile stories, from the cold war to the O. J. Simpson trial, in terms of winners and losers. In this sense, Oliver North "won," the Congress "lost," and the constitutional threats posed by the Enterprise, which we had exposed in detail, never fit comfortably into the evening news or even the headlines of our more responsible newspapers. In this context, it is no accident that, say, the sordid sexual liaisons of a presidential media consultant are deemed more newsworthy than the tale of a secret, unaccountable organization carrying out covert operations on behalf of the government.

But the test of a congressional investigation surely involves more than who rates higher on the applause meter. Did we or didn't we bring out the facts that the public had a right to know? Did we or didn't we fill that pivotal role of the congressional committee—of providing a check and balance against a wayward administration? These tests we passed.

But there was, to me, one highly disturbing consequence of Iran-Contra. The framers of our Constitution anticipated that there would be friction between the three branches of government, and even that symbol of unity, George Washington, defied the Congress early when it asked for the negotiating history of a treaty. But the framers also provided for impeachment when the president or vice president engaged in severe misconduct, and indeed, the constitutional ink was hardly dry before an attempt was made to impeach Vice President Aaron Burr.

Watergate introduced the institution of the special prosecutor on a national level. Special prosecutors were appointed again in the Carter administration and in Reagan's first term, but they acted quickly and were willing to decline prosecution for insubstantial matters. Iran-Contra was the beginning of a new practice—turning over matters of political accountability to the criminal law enforcers.

Judge Walsh conducted his Iran-Contra investigation as if he were prosecuting a massive antitrust case, not a matter of constitutional dimensions. It mattered not a whit to him that it took six years to complete the investigation, or even that the president had long since retired. Moreover, like prosecutors who expand the reach of the criminal law, he tried to make criminal cases out of political offenses, such as the violation of the Boland Amendment. If the Congress, which had vacillated over the extent of permissible support of the Contras, felt that evasion of the Boland Amendment warranted further proceedings, it could have sought impeachment. But no member of the committees favored basing an impeachment case on what had been, after all, a rider to an appropriations bill.

Judge Walsh, moreover, saw it as his mandate to pursue criminal charges by every possible theory. He was encouraged in this by the media, which, as I have already pointed out in white-collar cases, have developed a strange and unjustified faith in the criminal process to reform society, and by the Congress itself, which is always too willing to shift responsibility for politically difficult and complex decisions to the courts. Walsh regarded the congressional investigation as interfering with his role, and his role, as he saw it, was paramount.

These were all the sorts of things that we tried so hard to avoid. We looked into an abuse of executive power without abusing congressional investigative power. No witness was ever called simply in order to have him repeatedly invoke the Fifth Amendment with all the inferences of guilt such invocation implies. We called witnesses who invoked that privilege only when we were prepared to give them immunity. We tried hard not to bully and badger witnesses. We did not call witnesses who were prepared to make accusations against others, including in one case the president, when, after investigation, we considered the accusations unfounded. We demonstrated that a committee can observe due process and still get the facts, and the facts that we brought out will long be remembered. Those facts—the sordid picture of government officials deceiving one another, breaking the law in the guise of patriotism, shredding incriminating documents, trading arms for hostages, devising a cover-up—outlast the passions of the moment. By showing what happened, I hope we make it more unlikely that such things will happen again. That alone would justify the investigation, but that can only happen when the goal of the investigators is not to serve political aims but to seek the truth.

This all seems more relevant today than it did then, given the activities of Kenneth Starr. Starr, the independent counsel investigating Whitewater, is a brilliant former judge who understands well our constitutional system. He has, however, kept alive the Walsh tradition. Unlike Iran-Contra, Whitewater involves mainly pre-presidential financial activities in Arkansas that present no constitutional issue for Congress or question of presidential accountability. Even when Whitewater has turned to such Washington matters as the handling of Vincent Foster's briefcase, the sudden appearance of Rose Law firm records, or even the accusations of Paula Jones, the issues seem to be more of character, judgment, and cooperativeness than any threat to the system. There is not the slightest evidence in any of the Whitewater investigations that the president had any interest in making money. Indeed, most evidence suggests the contrary, that the president was almost negligent in his indifference to the financial condition of his family. In a state in which three families—the Waltons, the Tysons, and the Stevens—generate many millions of dollars of legal fees, Hillary Clinton never got any referrals from them, despite her husband's political power. The few investments the Clintons appear to have made—a failed Whitewater land transaction and Mrs. Clinton's profits on cattle trades—are scarcely the stuff out of which cases are made. The president is not alone: there are independent counsels investigating cabinet officers for minor offenses of a sort any ordinary U.S. Attorney or District Attorney would have ignored.

I remember Senator Inouye's warning that the country can afford to remove a president if there is convincing proof of an impeachable offense, but it cannot afford to incapacitate a president by a drawn-out investigation questioning his legitimacy. This is not limited to the independent counsel. The Paula Jones case may be the first lawsuit against a president for alleged conduct, but if it is allowed to stand it will not be the last. In our litigious society, lawsuits can be filed at the drop of a hat. The lure of publicity and the opportunities to inflict political damage make the president a particularly inviting target. Paula Jones waited years before bringing her action, and there is no reason why she cannot now wait until the president is no longer in office. Constitutional violations are one thing, but from a policy standpoint we need to insure that our highest elected official will not be harassed and distracted in office.

This is not to say that presidents should be above the law. But there are important distinctions to be made. I do not believe that this boom of investigations and lawsuits reflects a decline in the morality of public officials. If the same standards had been applied during, say, the Roosevelt or Truman administrations, I am sure that just as many investigations could have been conducted, if not more. All it illustrates, in my view, is how quickly we now turn to criminal prosecution to solve problems that should not be treated as crimes.

We now imprison a greater percentage of our population than any democracy. This high rate is not just a result of having a permissive society still plagued by drug problems, poverty, and racism. We have always looked to criminal law to address problems that call for other solutions, and most recently to deal with flaws and failures in our political system. That is why there is an immediate call for special prosecutors today whenever a political scandal or controversy erupts. But we pay a price for our over-reliance on criminal laws: more and more, we avoid legislative and regulatory solutions to our social and political ills.

The Iran-Contra investigation was the right way to go. As I hope I've made abundantly clear in this book, I've lost my share of cases over the course of a long career. Iran-Contra, though, wasn't one of them. Whatever my own shortcomings may have been as counsel, my "clients"—those special committees of the U.S. Congress—discharged their constitutional function with flying colors.

SUMMATION

The PRACTICE OF LAW has changed enormously in forty years. When I graduated from Yale Law School in 1957, my classmates and I were imbued with idealism. A social revolution was under way. Joe McCarthy was toppled. In *Brown v. Board of Education* and other decisions, the Warren Court was remaking our fundamental law with a new sensitivity to human rights, the rights of the poor and criminal defendants. Lawyers were in the vanguard of those great social reforms. Law was a powerful engine for improving society.

John Kennedy's election in 1960 created a sense of enormous excitement for young members in the profession, and lawyers played key roles in the new administration. Robert Kennedy, as Attorney General, was a charismatic figure whose concern for the underprivileged in society infused us all with a sense of purpose and change. Kennedy's Justice Department, with Burke Marshall as head of the Civil Rights Division, stood up to state officials trying to preserve Jim Crow in their universities and began the process of desegregating the South. Arthur Goldberg, as secretary of labor, breathed life into that department, and

Sargent Shriver, another lawyer and the president's brother-in-law, formed the Peace Corps.

Many of my friends joined the Kennedy administration. Still in their twenties, they became counsels for agencies and assistant secretaries in various cabinet departments. Their zeal and public consciousness typified my generation, and the flow of lawyers to and from the public sector has continued over the years.

None of us, in my era, expected to become rich from the practice of law, nor were we materialistic by nature. I used to dream that someday I might make $75,000 a year, knowing that my family and I would be more than satisfied. We started in law firms at $5,500 a year, or $6,500 for veterans. We got raises of $1,000 a year. On the other hand, we rented apartments for less than $200 a month, and ate lunch in restaurants for $3.

The firms were much smaller too, and the bar itself far more collegial. We knew lawyers at other firms, socially as well as professionally. Litigation was a stepchild in many firms, although not at Paul, Weiss. Cases were smaller, class actions unknown. Discovery was limited. We didn't have computers, and we had no need of legions of paralegals to keep track of our documents because in a typical case the documents filled but a few file folders.

Corporate legal activity was much simpler too. Tender offers weren't in vogue, and most mergers were friendly transactions that proceeded without the threat of interference from either litigation or other potential bidders. Deadlines and time pressures, while they always existed, seemed somehow less urgent. Lawyers working on a transaction had time to consult with other lawyers in the firm, and a general excitement swept through the entire firm whenever a major transaction was completed or a new one undertaken.

Above all, there were enduring relationships between lawyers and their clients. Lawyers came to know their clients, and clients their lawyers, and they became friends. In the prevailing intimacy of such relationships, lawyers could give advice tailor-made to the client's needs. We were truly a personal-service profession.

All this changed, as I have tried to describe, and the profession has also been affected—or infected—by many of the ills that have afflicted the society at large in the 1980s and 1990s: the rampant materialism, the sense that somehow we have sacrificed our souls and hearts for a cold-blooded, bigger-is-better efficiency, the more clamorous, in-your-face style that has replaced our older cultural humanism, as well as a growing and generalized mistrust of government. Why, after all, should a lawyer want to take a government position when the agency in question may be a candidate for extinction? Who wants to be an assistant secretary when the principal job duty may be to fire other people and cut back on programs? Even the Democratic Party is now running against government and voting to scale down or eliminate the great social programs of the New Deal and the Great Society, and a pervasive political cynicism has supplanted the idealism of my generation.

Still, the qualities bred in lawyers that have enabled us to play our manifold roles have not disappeared. Law schools still train students to challenge every premise, to take nothing for granted. The precedents we read as students still remind us of the darker days of racism, prejudice, religious conflict, denial of civil rights, and inhuman working conditions. Trained to work with precedents, lawyers have a stronger sense of history than many people. We still recoil from injustice, and we have all studied how, in the evolution of the law, our legal institutions and our profession have, overall, worked to improve society.

I decided to write this book after almost forty years of practicing law, because I am convinced that the greatest threat to our justice system is not the occasional miscarriage of justice, but cynicism about the rule of lawyers and doubt that the process serves justice. Law can and should be an honorable profession, but not if we discourage decent young women and men from choosing it as their career.

The heroes of the legal profession are not the lawyers who achieve celebrity status by self-promotion or mugging for the cameras but the often unsung and young lawyers (some just out of law school) who brought about the social revolution in this country that led to the repeal of the Jim Crow laws; the lawyers in Connecticut who won the case establishing a right of privacy to keep government out of personal decisions relating to reproductive freedom; and the lawyers who, for little or no fee, take on the defense or appeals in cases for indigent defendants who have no means of obtaining effective representation and whose trials are often over almost before they begin. These are the lawyers against whom we should measure ourselves.

The winds of change are nonetheless stirring, it seems to me, and not only in my field of litigation, where virtually every bar group is proposing reform. Just as the economic and social upheavals of the 1960s and 1970s, and the new laws that accompanied them, made it possible for smaller independent firms like Paul, Weiss to grow and flourish, so the great changes of the 1990s—the downsizing of the old, the emergence of the new and the entrepreneurial in so many different fields of activity—will make it possible, indeed inevitable, for small new firms, built on collegiality, high morale, and the free exchange of ideas among their members, to provide excellent service to the new clients of the twenty-first century. Creativity is scarcely the monopoly of the large law firms. In my view, the day is already at hand when the larger firms themselves will have to become more collegial, more caring, and more fun to work at if they are to attract their share of the best young lawyers and survive.

It is a myth that lawyers of my generation had opportunities handed to them on a silver platter, just as it is a myth that such opportunities no longer exist. They are there, in fact, in every era. It is a question of identifying them, of seizing them, and of running the risks that they inevitably entail.

In this context, I wonder about that anonymous Paul, Weiss lawyer—the one I mentioned before who told *American Lawyer* he'd rather be a shoe salesman.

What disillusioned him so? And what's become of him?

Perhaps he really wanted to be a shoe salesman? If so, then I hope that's what he's doing. But if not, and if he was only speaking out of frustration or boredom or weariness or any of those afflictions that, from time to time, affect us all, then I hope like anything he's stuck it out, if not at Paul, Weiss, then on any of a number of career paths many of his predecessors have followed—in the public sector, in another law firm, in the companies and corporations and the nonprofits of our society. And I say this simply because the law is a great apprenticeship, and its practice a great profession, with room in it for all manner of temperaments, all kinds of intelligence and talent and ambition, and because it offers so many opportunities not only to contribute to the welfare of the society at large but to achieve a most rewarding, and deeply satisfying, life.

If I've made that clear, then I've accomplished something.

The Legacy of Arthur Liman

SITTING AT LINCOLN CENTER at the memorial service for Arthur Liman in the fall of 1997, I listened as twelve speakers talked about what Arthur had meant to their lives and to the world. One example captured many. Senator Warren Rudman, who chaired the investigation of what is popularly known as "Iran-Contra," described Arthur as an unusual chief counsel, "not the Democrats' or the Republicans' chief counsel but the committee's chief counsel." Senator Rudman paid tribute not only to Arthur's capacity to bring together a disparate group of people, but also to Arthur's moral authority. At one point, Arthur was faced with what to do about a witness who had played a peripheral role. Arthur advised the committee not to call the witness; he said that the contribution to the investigation from testimony was minor at best while the harm to the individual from being the focus of national media attention would be enormous. Arthur, as lawyer for the senators, advised them to "do the right thing," to respect individuals as well as to work for the public good. And, they listened.

The theme of wise counsel, mixed with what Senator Rudman described as "special humanity and compassion," was repeated by an array of clients, colleagues, family, and friends in their memorial tributes. Arthur had the distinctive capacity to care passionately about the particulars (as illustrated by the rich details of these memoirs), yet also to care about the implications and consequences of decisions made. That Arthur Liman was both wise and unusually smart marked him as one of a few outstanding attorneys. That he also cared passionately about social justice and devoted himself to its pursuit marked him as one of even fewer great lawyer-citizens. Arthur's contribution to the legal profession consists of his insistence on the two interwoven purposes of his career: that lawyering required giving clients honest advice attuned to the consequences to clients as well as to third parties, and that lawyering required devotion to the pursuit of fairness for everyone, not only one's own clients. In the last meeting I had with Arthur, he bemoaned the turn of lawyers away from these lawyerly attributes and into what he termed "accountants," by which he meant individuals concerned more with profit margins than with wisdom, fairness, and the public good.

Arthur's significance was sufficiently plain to those around him that they wanted to express their respect for him in a way that had special meaning to him. They translated their admiration for Arthur Liman into gifts to the Yale Law School, establishing a chaired professorship in his honor; a fellowship program for Yale Law School graduates to work for one year in public interest law; and the Liman Public Interest Fund, which provides grants to individuals or organizations that work in the public interest.

The Liman Public Interest Fellowship and Fund at Yale Law School has sponsored fellows to work on an array of projects, ranging from criminal justice reform to advocacy for the institutionalized elderly to protection of employment rights of "workfare" workers and efforts to ensure that migrant and seasonal farm workers are not denied Social Security and unemployment benefits. Funds have been provided to institutions involved with legal issues relating to substance abuse and AIDS, as well as to a pilot project for college students to have summer public interest fellowships before returning to school to serve as advisers to other students. Yale Law School has hosted a colloquium of legal professionals from around the United States to address legal services for the poor. The Law School will also publish essays written by judges, lawyers, law students, and law professors about legal services in a symposium entitled "The Future of Legal Services."

In short, work and thought about public service and unmet legal needs goes forth in the name of Arthur Liman. His own career decisions provide the model that informs our choices and presses us to find the energy and resources to work toward a justice that remains elusive. A wonderful tribute to Arthur's legacy is in the daily work of the current and former law students, who make the Liman Program—and Arthur's legacy—live through their personal commitment to social welfare.

—JUDITH RESNIK,
Arthur Liman Professor of Law,
Yale Law School

INDEX

A&P, 98–99
ABC, 165
Abdullah, crown prince of Saudi
	Arabia, 111
Abercrombie & Fitch, 38
A block (Attica Correctional
	Facility), 179, 182–183, 187
Aboodi, Oded, 127, 147, 150,
	153–155
Abram, Morris, 59–60
Abrams, Elliott, 320, 338, 347
Abrams, Floyd, 65
Acheson, Dean, 4, 22, 172
Achille Lauro, 344
Adams, Sherman, 238
Adelson, Merv, 150
Advicorp Advisory and Financial
	Corporation, 113, 117,
	119–120

Affirmative action, 172, 234
Affirmed (horse), 86
Agger, Carolyn, 59, 92
Agnew, Spiro, 58
AIDS discrimination, 212
Alcohol abuse, 211
Alcohol tax laws, federal, 41–42
Allied Crude Vegetable Oil Refining
	Corporation, 68
American Bar Association, 188, 312
American Express, 67–84, 146
American Lawyer, 236
American Leduc Petroleum Ltd., 51
American Stock Exchange, 51
Americans with Disabilities Act, 212
Anderson, Robert, 204–205
Andrews, Julie, 101
Anti-Semitism, 9, 10–11, 20–21, 194,
	202

Antitrust law, 27–30, 98–99
Arbitrageurs, 269
Arizona, 19
Armstrong, Michael, 141–143, 272
Army, U.S., 13–14
Arthur Young, 147
Asbestos cases, 58
Ashley, Ted, 127, 128, 135
Ashley Famous, 127
AT&T, 262–262
Atari, 136–139
Attica Uprising (1971), 172,
    175–194. *See also* McKay
    Commission
  criminal charges against inmates,
    188–190
  filmed by state trooper, 186
  hostage taking and, 175, 176, 179,
    187–188
  negotiations during, 176, 185–186
  Quinn's death, 185–186
  racism and, 188, 194
  Rockefeller and, 175–176,
    187–189
Attorney's Office, U.S., Southern
    District of New York, 33,
    34–35, 37–53, 172
  appointment of Liman to, 33,
    34–35, 37
  insider trading and, 269–270

Bache & Company, 114–115
Baer, Harold, 39
Baird, Bruce, 273
Baker, James, 306–307
Baltimore Colts, 130
Banque de l'Indochine, 109–110
Barbadoro, Paul, 307–309, 319
Bartholet, Elizabeth, 211
Batavia Club (Attica), 181
Bausch & Lomb, 230–231

Bay of Pigs invasion, 344
Bell, Griffin, 171–172
Bellacosa, Joseph, 191
Bell & Howell, 203–204
Belnick, Mark, 304, 305, 307, 309,
    319, 326, 340
Bergerac, Michel, 165, 237
Bergman, Ingrid, 127
Berkeley, California, 265
Beverly Hills, California, 267, 274
Beverly Hills Hotel, 125
Bhopal, India, 250
Birrell, Lowell McAfee, 49–53
Black Law Students Association (Yale
    Law School), 180
Black Muslims, 173
Black Power, 180
Black Rock (New York City), 163,
    165, 167
Bluhdorn, Charles G., 95, 96–106,
    153
  background of, 96
  Dolkart case, 100–105
  OPEC cartel and, 98–100
  patriotism of, 97, 106
Boesky, Ivan, 252, 269
  Milken and, 269–270, 272,
    278–281
Boies, David, 247–248
Boiler rooms, 43, 44
Boland Amendment, 301, 321, 325,
    326, 332, 345, 347,
    352–353
Bonds, 265–268
Boren, David, 308
Boston Herald, 4
Boy Leading a Horse (Picasso), 160
Brandeis, Louis, 299
Brandeis University, 59
Brandel Trust, 44–48
Brazil, 49, 50, 52

Breach of contract, 198, 199–200
Breach of warranty, 198, 199–200
Brennan, William, 64
Brenner (Haupt partner), 83
Broderick, Vincent, 39
Brooklyn Law School, 39
Brown, Harold, 165
Brownell, Herbert, 64
Brown Paper, 98
Brown v. Board of Education, 13, 357
Bruggen, Richard, 201–202
Brunei, sultan of, 309
Bucks County, Pennsylvania, 50
Bunge Corporation, 68, 75, 76–77
Burger, Warren, 235
Burr, Aaron, 352
Bush, George, 172, 218, 241, 348
Butler, Sam, 148, 165

Cable television, 146–147, 155
Cadwalader, Wickersham & Taft, 50
Cahill Gordon and Reindel, 272
Calabresi, Guido, 28
Calero, Adolfo, 337, 339
California, 19, 234
Calley, John, 131
Capital Cities, 165
Capital Defender Office (New York
  City), 172, 218–219
Capital gains, 160
Capital punishment, 216–219
Capital Transit, 86
Carberry, Charles, 269, 273
Carey, Hugh, 19, 146, 191, 210, 217
Car rentals, 126–127
Carroll, John, 273, 275, 281,
  283–284, 289–290
Carter, Jimmy, 171–172, 240, 301,
  344, 352
Casa de Campo (Dominican
  Republic), 105–106

Casey, William, 95
  Iran-Contra and, 306, 321, 338,
    341, 344–346, 348
Cash funds, secret, 144
Castro, Fidel, 96
CBS, 159–167
  diversification of, 161
  headquarters, in New York, 163
  leveraged buyout of, 161–162
  stock buyback plan, 160–162
  Tisch and, 162–166
  Turner bid for, 159–160
CBS Records, 166
Central Intelligence Agency (CIA),
  308, 309, 318, 321
Chambers, Whittaker, 46
Chantilly, France, 116–118
Chiang Kai-shek, Mme., 18
Chicago Board of Trade, 114
Chicago Sun, 18
Chicago Tribune, 18
China, 108
Chris-Craft Industries, 94–95,
  145–146
Christie's, 300–301
Churchill, Winston, 34
Chutzpah, 73–74
CIA (Central Intelligence Agency),
  308, 309, 318, 321
Cities Service, 27–29
City College of New York (CCNY),
  12, 16
Civil law, 270–271
Civil rights, 211, 357
Civil Rights Division, Justice
  Department, 176, 218, 357
Clark, Ramsey, 60
Clark, Richard X, 182–183
Class actions, 210–212, 234
Clifford, Clark, 346
Clinton, Bill, 17, 64, 343, 354

Clinton, Hillary, 354
Closing arguments (summations), 48,
    83, 91, 206
CNA (insurance company), 162
Coca-Cola, 165–166
Cohen, Alan, 127, 130, 281
Cohen, William, 323
Cohn, Roy M., 13–14
    Army-McCarthy hearings (1954),
        13
    bribery and, 14
    Subcommittee on
        Investigations hearings
        (1954), 3–9, 13
    temperament of, 4, 9, 14
Cole Porter Musical and Literary
    Property Trusts, 18
Collective bargaining, 17
Colorado River, 19
Colt Industries, 196
Columbia Law School, 16, 17
Columbia Pictures, 132
Columbia Spectator, 26
COMB Corporation, 280
Commission on Mayoral
    Appointments (New York
    City), 172
Committees, congressional. *See*
    House of Representatives,
    U.S.; Senate, U.S.
Commodities industry, 111–113
Commodities Exchange, 113,
    114
Commonwealth United, 101–102,
    128–131
Communist Party, 4–8, 344
Compliance lawyers, 271
Congress, U.S., 211, 218, 307. *See
    also* House of Representatives,
    U.S.; Senate, U.S.
    leaks and, 344–345

Congressional investigations,
    351–352. *See also* Iran-Contra
    investigation
    political pressures in, 323
Connecticut, University of, 200
Connery, Sean, 127
Consolidated Cigar, 97
Consolidated Electronics
    Corporation, 203
Constitution, U.S., 299, 304, 338,
    349, 352. *See also specific
    amendments*
ContiCommodity Services, Inc.,
    110–124
Continental Grain Company,
    107–124
    Banque de l'Indochine and,
        109–110
    De Angelis (salad oil) case and,
        67, 68–83
    formation of ContiCommodity
        Services, 111–112
    as privately held company, 107,
        108
Contract, breach of, 198, 199–200
Contras, Nicaraguan, 301, 314, 315,
    319–326, 328, 331, 332,
    337–339, 341, 345, 347, 348,
    352. *See also* Iran-Contra
    investigation
Coppola, Francis Ford, 97
Cornell University, 34
Cornfeld, Bernard, 130
Costikyan, Ed, 26, 27, 36
Cottonseed oil, 68, 72–73
Coughlin, Father Charles E., 10
Court of Appeals, New York, 23–24,
    237–238
Covert operations, 343–344. *See also*
    Iran-Contra investigation;
    Watergate

Cravath, Swaine and Moore, 148,
  158, 248
Crime, 209–210
Crime in America (Clark), 60
Criminal justice programs, 210
Criminal justice system, 172,
  209–210
  in New York, 214
Criminal law, 209–210, 270–271
Cronkite, Walter, 165
Cross-examinations, 40, 48, 201–204
Cuban cigars, 38
Cuomo, Mario, 191, 217

Dahl, James, 276
Daily Worker, 5
Dallas (TV show), 161
Dalton, Harlon, 180
Darling Lili (film), 101
Darrow, Clarence, 22
Dash, Sam, 304
Davis, Martin, 106, 153
Davis Polk & Wardwell, 312
DC Comics, 127
De Angelis, Anthony "Tino," 67–84
  American Express and, 68, 69–72
  background of, 67–68
  bankruptcy of, 68, 70, 71
  cross-examination of, 76–81
  monopoly goals of, 68
  vegetable oil futures and, 72–74
  warehouse receipts issued by,
    68–71
Death of a President, The
  (Manchester), 19
Death penalty, 216–219
Dechert, Price & Rhoads, 240
DeDavega (inventor), 203–204
"Deep freeze," 129–131
Defense Department, U.S., 318
Defense lawyers, 88–89

De Kooning, Willem, 134, 156
De la Renta, Oscar, 105
De Laurentis, Dino, 105
Democratic Party, 22–23, 27, 33–34,
  171–172, 359
Deniability, doctrine of, 331
DeSapio, Carmine, 27
Desegregation, 13, 185, 357
Desert One, 318
Desilu Productions, 97
Devoe & Raynolds, 86
Diamond Shamrock, 279
Diary of Anne Frank (play), 26
Diller, Barry, 98, 162
Di Maio, Dominick, 223
Dinkins, David, 172
Disabled persons, 215
Discovery, misuse and abuse of,
  234–235
Discrimination, 181, 212, 233–234
Distinguished Service Cross, 337
Dolkart, Joel, 100–105
Dominican Republic, 105–106
Donaldson, Sam, 344
Donovan, Ray, 148
Douglas, William O., 16, 18
Doyle, Kevin, 219
Dressen, Chuck, 51
Dressmaking business, 12
Drexel Burnham and Lambert,
  266–277, 289–292. See also
  U.S. v. Milken
  campaign of intimidation against,
    275–276
  civil suits against, 290–292
  compensation scheme, 276–277,
    291
  compliance lawyers at, 271
  plea agreement, 277
Drug abuse, 211
Drug cases, 40–41

Drug laws, 40–41, 193, 210
Dunaway, Faye, 154
Dunne, John, 218, 219
D yard (Attica Correctional Facility),
    175, 176, 179, 183, 186–187

East Hampton, New York, 156–157
Ecker, Allan, 127, 129, 130
Edwards, Blake, 101
Eisenhower, Dwight D., 17, 22, 64,
    171, 238, 344
Electronic eye equipment, 203
Emmett, Jay, 127, 139–144
Empire State Building (New York
    City), 23–25
"Enterprise, the," Iran-Contra and,
    310, 318, 321–322, 337,
    338, 340, 341, 345–347, 349,
    352
Entertainment industry, 125–158. *See
    also specific individuals and
    companies*
    legal restrictions in, 132–133
Environmental cases, 58
Episcopalians, 11
Ervin, Sam, 304
ET (video game), 137
Evans, Robert, 97, 98
Exorcist, The (film), 131
Expert witnesses, 202–204

Fagen, Leslie, 139, 197, 206
Fardella, Jess, 273, 275, 281,
    289–290
Far Rockaway, Queens, 9
Fatico hearings, 285–287
FBI (Federal Bureau of
    Investigation), 46, 140–141
Federal Building (Boston), 4
Federal Bureau of Investigation
    (FBI), 46, 140–141

Federal Farm Board, 34
Federal government, 229–232
Field, Marshall, 18
Fifth Amendment, 5, 6, 140, 307,
    330, 335
"Fifth Amendment Communist," 5,
    8
Figel, Reid, 273
First Amendment, 58, 65
First Boston, 244
Fischbach Corporation, 279
Fischer, Richard, 189
Fleming, Peter, 118–124, 143,
    272
Flom, Joseph, 63
Flood, Curt, 60
Florida, 191
Flumenbaum, Martin, 269, 272, 273,
    281, 288
Forbes magazine, 133–134
Ford, Gerald, 18
Ford Foundation, 188
Fordham Law School, 39
Fortas, Abe, 59, 92–93
Foster, Vincent, 354
Frank, Anne, 26
Frank, Otto, 26
Frankel, Marvin, 191
Frankfurter, Felix, 10, 217, 234
Freeman, Robert, 285
Fribourg, Jules, 108
Fribourg, Michel, 108–110, 115, 118,
    122–123
Fribourg family, 108, 124
Fribourg Gestion, 109–110
Friendly, Fred, 188
Fuller, Vincent, 272
Furry, Wendell, 5–8
Fustok, Mahmoud, 110–111, 113,
    115–124
Futures, 72–73, 111–115

GAF Corporation, 249–264. See also
  U.S. v. GAF
Garcia-Rivera, Oscar, 180
Garment, Leonard, 324
Garrison, Lloyd K., 18, 69, 70
Garrison, William Lloyd, 18
General Electric, 8, 165
General Motors, 85–86
Gerard, Emanuel, 129, 136–139
German Jews, 17
Getty, Gordon, 240–243
Getty, J. Paul, 240, 241
Getty Museum, 240–242, 244–246
Getty Oil, 20, 239–248
  Pennzoil Company and, 241–244
  standstill agreement, 240
  Texaco and, 244–245
Gevertz, John, 263
Ghorbanifar, Manucher, 325, 345
Gilpatric, Roswell, 165
Gitter, Max, 101, 103, 104, 106, 140,
  221
  GAF case, 253, 262–264
  Gulf & Western case, 101, 103,
  104, 106
Giuliani, Rudolph, 281
  Milken case, 269, 273, 278, 281
  Westchester Premier Theatre
  affair, 142–145, 148
Glanville, James, 241
Godfather, The (film), 97–100
Goldberg, Arthur, 60, 61, 357
Golden Nugget Corporation, 279
Goldfine, Bernard, 238
Goldschmidt, Walter, 114, 115–124
Goldstein, Eric, 272
Goodale, James, 65
Goodrich, Frances, 26
Gorham, Moulton, 241
Gould, Robert, 183
Grain futures, 111–112

Grande, Charles A., 51
Gray, Robert, 79–81
Green Giant, 161
Greenhill, Robert, 153
Griffinger, Miss, 36
Gross, Elliott M., 220–225. *See also*
  Medical examiner's office, New
  York City, investigation of
  classification of deaths by,
  221–223
  lack of leadership by, 223, 224
  staff allegations against, 223–224
Gulf & Western, 96–106, 153
Gulf Coast Leaseholds, 43–49

Hackett, Albert, 26
Hagen, Cecil, 43–48
Hagenbach, Paul, 44–48
Hakim, Albert, 310, 320, 321–322,
  337, 340, 345–346
Hall, Fawn, 311, 318, 320
Hamilton, Lee H., 313, 317, 327
Hammerman, Steven, 52
Hand, Learned, 11
Harris Graphics, 280
Hart Senate Office Building
  (Washington, D.C.), 305
Harvard College, 4–7, 12
Harvard Law School, 211
Hasenfus, Eugene, 347
Hatch, Orrin, 318
Hawaii, 128–129
Hebrew language, 15
Heflin, Howell, 302
Henix, Amos, 177
Herlands, William B., 52, 53
Hersh, Seymour, 327
Hertz, Seymour, 241
Heyman, Samuel, 249–251, 263
High-yield bonds, 265–268
Hiss, Alger, 46, 287, 312

Hitler, Adolf, 216
HIV discrimination, 212
Hoffa, Jimmy, 148
Hoffman, Dustin, 154
Holmes, Oliver Wendell, 292
Holocaust, 10
Homelessness, 215
Homicide, 222–224
Hoover, J. Edgar, 46
Horse racing, 86, 111
Horwitz, Leonard, 139–144
House of Representatives, U.S.
    House Oversight and
    Investigations subcommittee,
    277
    Iran-Contra and, 307–308, 320
Hunt, Lamar, 111, 113, 114–115
Hunt, Nelson Bunker, 111, 113,
    114–115
Hunt, William Herbert, 111, 113,
    114–115
Hunter College (New York City), 12
Huntington, Sam, 4, 5, 7
Hyde Park, New York, 34

Icahn, Carl, 248
Impeachable conduct, 304, 310, 329,
    349–350
Imprisonment, 210, 355
Incentive compensation, 135
Independent counsel, Iran-Contra,
    305, 310, 312–314, 341, 348.
    See also Walsh, Lawrence E.
    immunity pleas and, 314
    North and, 253, 312, 313–314
    Poindexter and, 329
    Radzimski and, 326, 327
    Weinberger and, 348–349
Independent counsels, 352–354
Independent News Corporation, 145
Industrial code, 17

Inouye, Daniel, 302, 307, 308, 313,
    344, 354
    Liman's first meeting with,
    303–305
    North and, 337, 339, 340
    Poindexter and, 329, 330, 333,
    335–336
    at public hearings, 317–318,
    323
Insider trading, 230–231, 269–270,
    278–279, 282
Internal Revenue Service (IRS), 21
International Rescue Committee,
    251
Investment-grade bonds, 266
Investors Overseas Services, 130
Ira Haupt & Company, 68, 69–83
Iran, 99, 100. *See also* Iran-Contra
    investigation
    arms-for-hostages sale to, 301,
    305–306, 344, 347
Iran-Contra investigation, 3, 147,
    173, 297–355. *See also*
    Independent counsel, Iran-
    Contra
    classification of documents,
    308–310
    consequences of, 352
    difficulty of, 307
    equality between committees, 320
    final report, 350
    Hakim and, 310
    hearings, 309–310, 313, 317–327,
    329–330
    imaginary headlines about,
    297–298
    immunity and, 310–315, 353
    Liman appointment as chief
    counsel, 304–305
    Liman invitation to join, 301–303
    McFarlane and, 323–327

North and, 307, 310–311, 313, 336–342
perception of failure of, 351–352
Poindexter and, 307, 328–336
Reagan and, 309–310, 315–316
Radzimski and, 326–327
Regan and, 307
Secord and, 321–323, 330, 337, 345
secrecy and, 344
staff assembly, 309
television coverage of, 339, 351–352
Tower Commission, 305–307
Watergate compared with, 299, 343, 347
Whitewater compared with, 353–354
witnesses, 307, 308, 310–315, 318–321, 353
IRS (Internal Revenue Service), 21
Israel, 302, 305–306, 325

Jamail, Joseph, 243, 246–248
J. A. Winston & Company, 51, 52
Jefferies, Boyd, 251–264, 270. See also *U.S. v. GAF*
Jefferies & Company, 251–252, 254–258, 260, 264
Jodido, Dimitry, 300
Johnson, Lyndon, 60, 92–93
Johnson, Philip, 167
Jones, Paula, 354
Jones, Quincy, 157
Joseph, Fred, 268–270, 277
Junk bonds (high-yield bonds), 265–268
Jury consultants, 252, 260
Jury deliberations, 48, 83–84

Jury selection, 252–253, 260–261
race and, 252–253
in white-collar criminal case, 253
Justice Department, U.S., 171–172, 281, 301, 357
Antitrust Division, 98–99
Civil Rights Division, 176, 218, 357
GAF and, 251

Kamerman (head of Haupt), 83
Kamin, Leon, 5, 8
Kaminer, Peter, 70
Kaplan, James, 340
Kaplan, Lewis, 231, 349
Kaufman, Steve, 39
GAF case, 253–254, 259, 261, 264, 281
Kaye, Judith, 75–79, 82, 84, 218
Kaye Scholer Fierman Hays & Handler, 231–232
Keating, Charles, 231–232
Kelly, Roy B., 43–48
Kennedy, John F., 33, 35, 59, 60, 95, 344, 357–358
Kennedy, Robert, 216, 357
Keyser Ullman, 69, 71
Kidder Peabody, 240
Kimmel, Caesar, 133
King, Rodney, 252
Kinney National Service, 126–127
Forbes magazine article (1970), 133–134
name change to Warner Communications, 131–132
offices of, 128
Warner-Seven Arts acquisition, 128–131
Kissinger, Henry, 324–325, 348
Kleinbard, Martin, 26
Klementine, 154

Kleven, Mr., 87–88
Kline, Franz, 163
Kluge, John, 237–238
Knapp Commission, 142
Koch, Ed, 172, 213
   medical examiner cover-up case, 220, 225
   R–46 subway car case, 196–197, 207
Kohlberg Kravis Roberts, 286
Kollek, Teddy, 163
Kosow, Joseph, 85–93. See also *U.S. v. Wolfson*
Kroll International, 262
Kuntsler, William, 60

Labor practices, 17
Laissez-faire theories, 173
Lancaster, Burt, 127
Lang, Eugene, 275
Larré's (New York City), 59
La Société Continental de Gestion Finantiçère, S.A. (Fribgest), 109–110
Law, practice of, 357–360
   changes in 1980s, 232–237
   costs and, 215, 234–236
   materialism and, 236, 358–359
   minorities at, 233–234
   use of teams of lawyers, 235–237
   women in, 233
Law firms, 232–237, 358
   anti-Semitism at, 20–21
   partners at, 233
Lawrence, New York, 10
Law schools, 359
Lawyer-client relationship, 63–64, 358
Lazard Frères, 110, 127, 148, 239
Leaking, 344–345
Lebanon, 301, 345

Legal Action Center (New York City), 172, 193, 210–212
Legal Aid Society of New York, 53, 172, 212–216
   Civil Division, 214–215
   Criminal Division, 213, 214
   financial problems at, 214
   funding of, 212
   labor relations at, 213–214
   lawyers at, 213, 215–216
   Liman as president of, 213, 215
   management at, 215–216
   origins of, 212
   Volunteer Division, 215
Legal realism, 13, 30
Legal theory, 13
Leval, Pierre, 39, 285–286
Levi, Edward, 99
Levin, Gerald, 147, 150–158
Levin, Meyer, 26
Levine, Dennis, 269–270, 278
Lewis, David, 337
Lewis, Sandy, 270
Libel, 18, 133–134
Libya, 344
Liedtke, Hugh, 239–245
Life magazine, 93
Liman, Arthur
   background of, 9–10
   birth of, 9
   courtroom style, 32, 36, 40, 49, 199
   cross-examination style, 254–255
   education of, 12, 13
   first interest in legal profession, 12–13
   first interest in tax law, 21–22
   growing up a Jew, 10–11
   "Liman letter," 151–152

switch to trial law, 22
U.S. Attorney's Office
appointment, 33, 34–35, 37
Liman, Chaim (great-grandfather), 9
Liman, Ellen Fogelson (wife), 35, 37,
57, 63, 136, 156, 293, 303, 305
Liman, Gladys (sister), 10–11
Liman, Harry (father), 9, 11–12
Liman, Lewis (son), 35, 35n,
340–341
Liman, Louis (grandfather), 9–10, 12
Liman, Mrs. (mother), 11–12
Lin Broadcasting Corporation,
237–238
Lincoln Savings Bank, 231–232
Lipton, Martin, 63, 240, 242–246
Litt, Robert, 272, 276, 281
L. Liman & Son, 12
Loews Corporation, 162
Lord, Day & Lord, 64
Lorillard Corporation, 162
Lorimar Telepictures Corporation,
149–150
Luce, Henry, 150–151
Lynch, Gary, 273

McCarthy, Joseph, 274, 323, 357
Army-McCarthy hearings (1954),
13–14
Subcommittee on Investigations
hearings (1954), 3–9, 13
McCormick, Robert, 18
McFarlane, Robert "Bud," 118, 314,
318, 320, 324–325, 328
North and, 329, 338, 341, 347
public hearing, 323–327
McKay, Robert P., 176–177, 184,
188, 190
McKay Commission, 176–194
black and Hispanic lawyers on
staff, 180

Clark interview, 182–183
first visit, 175, 179
formation of, 176–177
guards and inmates relationship,
182, 183, 185
guards' reluctance to speak,
178–179, 181–182
hearings, 184, 186–188, 190
impact of, 190–194
inmates' reluctance to speak, 177,
178–179, 181–183
interviews, 178, 180–183, 189
investigation, 178–186
Mancusi interview, 179
political sophistication of inmates
and, 180
prison conditions, 183, 184–185,
193–194
prison gates and, 179
Quinn's death and, 185–186
report, 184, 188, 190–191
Rockefeller and, 187–188
sentencing reforms after, 190–193
special prosecutor efforts to
subpoena files, 188–190
staff recruitment, 179–180
television report, 184, 188
women lawyers on staff, 181
Madison Square Garden (New York
City), 96
Mahoney, Andrew, 39
Manchester, William, 19
Mancusi, Vincent, 179, 184
Margolis, David, 196
Marshall, Burke, 176, 180, 190, 357
Martin, John, 39
Maultasch, Cary, 276
Maximum-security prisons, 178–179,
184–185. *See also* Attica
Uprising
rehabilitation and, 190–191

Maxxam Group, 280
Mayoral Appointments, Commission on (New York City), 172
MCA, 279, 282
Medical examiner's office, New York City, investigation of, 220–225
Attica experience similar to, 221
classification of deaths and, 221–223
findings, 223–224
institution of office, 222
interviews, 223
policy of office, 222–223
recommendations, 224
staff allegations about Gross, 223–224
staff assembly, 221, 223
Stewart case, 222, 224
Times reporting and, 220, 222, 223–224
Meese, Edwin, 312, 320, 341
Melton, James, 251, 253, 258–264
Melville, Herman, 332
Meretz, Lithuania, 15
Mergers and acquisitions, 63
Merritt-Chapman & Scott, 86, 87, 91
Methadone treatments, 211, 212
Metromedia, 237–238
Metropolitan Transit Authority (MTA; New York City), 31, 195–208, 211
Mexico Fund, 274
Meyer, André, 110, 127
MGM, 162, 280, 281
Michigan Bumper, 96
Michigan Law School, 50
Milken, Lori, 276, 288, 293
Milken, Lowell, 272, 277, 278, 280, 282, 284

Milken, Michael, 229, 231, 249, 265–293, 300. See also *U.S. v Milken*
Boesky charges against, 270, 273
civil suits against, 290–292
education of, 265–266
high-yield bonds, 265–268
letter to *New York Times*, 266
temperament of, 267, 277
vilification of, 274, 275, 288–289
Wall Street and, 267–268
Minnesota, 191
Minow, Newton, 59, 165
Mistrials, 257
Mitchell, George, 311–312, 323
Liman invitation to join Iran-Contra investigation, 300, 301–303
North immunity and, 311–312
Mitchell, John, 93
Mollo, Silvio, 38–39
Montgomery Ward & Company, 86
Moody's, 266
Morgado, Robert, 146
Morgan, J. P., 112
Morgan Stanley, 153
Morgenthau, Henry, 10, 33–34
Morgenthau, Henry, Jr., 34
Morgenthau, Robert M., 33–53, 118–119, 191, 214
background of, 33–34
love of cigars, 38
Rifkind compared with, 37
temperament of, 38
Morris, Edmund, 315–316
Motion picture rights, 18
Moynihan, Daniel Patrick, 345
MTA (Metropolitan Transit Authority; New York City), 31, 195–208, 211
MTV, 146–147

Munro, Richard, 148–151, 153
Murdoch, Rupert, 145
Museum of Television and Radio
    (New York City), 167

Nader, Ralph, 64
Nahas, Naji Robert, 111, 112–113,
    115–124
Narcotics cases, 40–41
Nathan's, 134
National Book Award, 190
National Cleaning Contractors, 127
National Industrial Recovery Act
    (1933), 16–17
National Labor Relations Board, 17,
    18
National Recovery Administration
    (NRA), 16–17
National Security Council (NSC),
    301, 321, 332, 347–348
Nation of Islam, 183
Navy, U.S., 332–333, 336
Nazism, 10, 21
NBC, 165
Netherlands, the, 21
Newberg, Bruce, 278, 280
New Deal, 16
New Jersey Zinc Company, 97
Newsweek, 344
New York (city)
    arraignment process in, 214
    financial crisis, 19–20, 198, 208
    police brutality cover-up. *See*
        Medical examiner's office, New
        York City, investigation of
    subway system, 195, 198–199. *See*
        also R–46 subway car case
New York (state), 191
    death penalty in, 217, 218–219
New York Court of Appeals, 23–24,
    237–238

New York Hospital, 167
New York Knicks, 96
New York Post, 18
New York Produce Exchange, 72–77,
    83
New York Rangers, 96
New York Shipbuilding Corporation,
    86
New York State Legislature, 174
New York State Special Commission
    on Attica. *See* McKay
    Commission
New York Stock Exchange, 127
New York Times, 64–65, 176, 266, 291
    medical examiner cover-up and,
        220, 222, 223–224
New York Transit Authority, 31,
    195–208, 211
New York University Law School,
    176
Nicaraguan Contras, 301, 314, 315,
    319–326, 328, 331, 332,
    337–339, 341, 345, 347, 348,
    352. *See also* Iran-Contra
    investigation
Nicholas, Nicholas, 148–156
Nickelodeon, 146–147
Nields, John, 308, 311–313, 317
    division of witnesses, 308,
        320–321
    McFarlane and, 326
    North and, 337, 338–339
    Poindexter and, 329, 330–331
    Secord and, 321, 322
Nixon, Richard, 93, 171, 305, 324,
    349–350
North, Oliver, 253, 301, 320,
    336–342, 347, 352
    Casey and, 345–346
    contempt for Congress, 318, 344,
        347

North, Oliver *(cont.)*
  duty to protect the president and,
    348–349
  firing of, 301
  hearings, 336–342
  immunity and, 307, 310–313
  independent counsel and, 312,
    313–314
  McFarlane and, 324, 325
  Poindexter and, 332, 333, 338,
    341
  psychiatric treatments of, 315,
    316
  public support for, 336–340
  Secord and, 321
  Tower Commission and, 306
NSC (National Security Council),
    301, 321, 332, 347–348
Nunn, Sam, 323, 333, 336
Nussbaum, Bernard, 100

Occidental Petroleum Corporation,
    279
O'Donnell, Jack, 75, 82
O'Herron, Jon, 148
Oil companies, 27–30
Oil prices, 98–100
Onassis, Jacqueline Kennedy, 18–19
One-person-one-vote principle, 59, 61
OPEC cartel, 98–100
Opening statements, 49, 73, 75, 91,
    199–200
Orange juice futures, 112–113
Oresman, Don, 101, 104, 106
Orla, 9, 10
OTS (Office of Thrift Supervision),
    231–232

Pacific Lumber, 280
Paley, William S., 65, 159–168, 303
  apartment of, 160, 163, 168
  management style of, 161, 163

Tisch and, 163–164, 166–167
  Wyman and, 159, 160–161
Paley Park (New York City), 161
Palmieri, Edmund, 89–92, 270
Paramount
  name change from Gulf &
    Western, 153
  Time Warner and, 153–154
Paramount Pictures, 96–101, 132,
    145
Paris, 115–116
Pataki, George, 217
Patterson, Belknap & Webb, 33, 34
Paul, Randolph, 18, 96
Paul, Weiss, Rifkind, Wharton &
    Garrison, 17, 18–19, 21–22,
    35–36, 50, 57–66
  changes in 1980s, 232–234
  collegial atmosphere at, 59, 236
  Committee on Committees,
    61–62
  compensation at, 62
  conflict-of-interest dilemmas,
    236–237
  Deciding Group, 62
  democratic principles of, 19,
    61–62, 236
  diversity of practice, 58–59
  formation of, 17–19
  Liman joins, 19, 21–22
  Liman leaves, 35–37
  litigation department, 22, 25–27
  minorities at, 233–234
  open-door policy, 61
  public service and pro bono cases,
    173–174
  recruitment at, 59–61
  Rifkind joins, 17, 18–19
  Stevenson and, 22–25
  tax department, 21–22
  women at, 233

Payola, 133
Payson, Martin, 127, 139
Peace Corps, 358
Pearson, Drew, 18
Pennsylvania, University of, 266
Pennzoil Company, 239–248. See
    also *Pennzoil v. Texaco*
    Getty Oil and, 241–244
Pennzoil v. Texaco, 237, 245–248
    appeal, 20, 248
    Jamail summation, 246–247
    Liman handshake and, 243–244
    Liman testimony, 245–246
    verdict, 247–248
Pentagon, 318
Pentagon Papers, 64–65
Perella, Joseph, 244
Perelman, Ronald, 237
Perjury, 88
Peterson, Sidney, 240, 243
Phi Beta Kappa, 11–12
Phillip Morris, 17
Phillips NKV, 21
Phillips Petroleum, 279
Picasso, Pablo, 160, 161, 163
Pillsbury, 161
Piper Aircraft, 94, 145
Plea negotiations, 278
Pogroms, 9
Poindexter, John, 310–312, 320,
    328–336, 347, 348, 350
    firing of, 301
    hearing, 333–335
    immunity and, 310–313
    implausibility of story,
        332–336
    independent counsel and, 314
    McFarlane and, 324, 328
    North and, 332, 333, 338, 341
    secret deposition, 329–331, 333
    Tower Commission and, 306

Poison pill, 240
Police brutality, medical examiner's
    cover-up of. *See* Medical
    examiner's office, New York
    City, investigation of
Pollack, Milton, 290–291
Pollak, Irving, 95
Pollak, Walter, 18
Poor, the, 172, 212, 214–216
Porter, Cole, 18
Posner, Victor, 279
Postal Service, 211–212
"Predators' Ball," 274
President, U.S., 354
    duty to protect, 348–349
Princeton-Newport Partners, 270,
    280
Princeton University, 200
Prisoners' rights, 190
Prisons. *See also* Maximum-security
    prisons
    sentencing reforms and, 190–193
Pro bono cases, 173
Process control equipment,
    203–204
Procter & Gamble, 72
Property tax, 23–25
Prosecutors, federal, 37–53, 89. *See
    also* Independent counsel, Iran-
    Contra; Independent counsels
    special, 352–354
Proust, Marcel, 25
Proxy fights, 86
Public bonds, 266
Public schools, 275
Public service, 171–174, 209
Pulitzer Prize, 26
Pullman, Inc., 195, 196, 200, 202

Puzo, Mario, 97, 99

Quinn, William, 179, 185–186

Racism, 180, 182, 188, 194, 220
    death penalty and, 216–217
Radzimski, Edward, 326–327
Ramadan, 183
Rangel, Charles, 39, 184
Rayburn House Office Building
    (Washington, D.C.), 320
Re (father-son team), 51
Reader's Digest, 96
Reagan, Ronald, 215, 230, 301,
    305–306, 309–311, 325, 344,
    347–350. *See also* Iran-Contra
    investigation
    leaking and, 344–345
    North and, 333, 338
    Poindexter and, 328–329, 331,
        333–336
    private diary of, 315–316
Reality House (New York City), 177
Record industry, 133
Redstone, Sumner, 106
Regan, Donald, 306–307, 320, 324,
    347
Regan, Jay, 280
Registration statement, 129–131
Reprise, 131
Republicans, 171, 172
Repurchase agreements, 87–90
Revlon, 236–237
Revson, Charles, 236–237
R–46 subway car case (1980; New
    York City), 195–208
    closing argument, 205–207
    cross-examinations, 201–202,
        204–205
    opening statement, 199–200
    retrofit solution by Rockwell, 196,
        204, 205
    technical material and, 196, 198,
        199
    trial theme, 197–199

verdict, 207
witnesses, 200–201
Richards, Charles, 154
Richards, Layton and Finger, 154
RICO (Racketeer-Influenced and
    Corrupt Organizations) Act,
    229, 275–277, 280
Rifkind, Simon H., 15–32
    appointment as U.S. District
        Judge, 17
    Attica assignment and, 177
    background of, 15
    Cities Service case (1956), 27–30
    on class action lawsuits, 211
    Continental Grain and, 110
    courtroom style of, 31–32, 36, 49
    death of, 20
    democratic principles of, 19
    education of, 16
    Empire State Building appeal
        (1958), 23–25
    Iran-Contra and, 303
    joins Weiss firm, 17, 18–19
    Kosow case (1968), 85–86, 92
    legal legislation of, 16–17
    Liman and, 27–28, 31–32, 35,
        36–37, 49, 65–66, 89
    as mentor to Liman, 27–28,
        31–32, 35, 36–37, 49
    Milken and, 291–292
    Morgenthau compared with, 37
    office of, at 575 Madison, 36
    Pennzoil case, 20, 248
    public assignments of, 19–20
    recruitment of, 59–61
    Revlon and, 236–237
    S. J. Klein case, 31
    temperament of, 16
    on trial lawyers, 30–32
    work principles of, 19, 61–62
Rittmaster, Alexander, 90–92

Ritz-Carlton (New York City), 165
Robinson, Linda, 248
Rockaway Hunt Club (New York), 10
Rockefeller, Nelson, 37, 142
    Attica uprising (1971) and, 175–177, 187–189, 193
Rockefeller Plaza, 128
Rockwell International, 195–208. *See also* R–46 subway car case
Rohatyn, Felix, 239
    Ross and, 127, 130, 135, 137, 148, 150
Roman Catholic Diocese, 176
Roosevelt, Franklin Delano, 10, 12, 16–18, 34, 171, 324
Rosenbloom, Carroll, 130, 131
Ross, Courtney, 132, 155
Ross, Nicole, 132
Ross, Steve, 95, 98, 125–158, 300
    Atari crisis, 136–139
    background of, 126
    CEO bylaw provision, 149, 150–152
    collecting of, 134
    compensation negotiations, 135
    counselors to, 127–128
    deal-making strategy of, 129
    death of, 156–157
    Emmett and, 139–141
    enters entertainment industry, 132–133
    Forbes magazine article (1970), 133–134
    Kinney National and, 126–127
    lifestyle of, 134
    Liman and, 125–127, 132, 135–136
    "Liman letter" and, 151–152
    Lorimar acquisition, 149–150

    management style of, 129, 131–132, 135, 149
    media relations, 133–134
    Nicholas rupture with, 155–156
    resignation offer, 156
    Sardinia vacation, 154–155
    Siegel and, 145–147
    temperament of, 126
    Time Warner merger, 147–156
    Warner-Seven Arts acquisition, 128–131
    Westchester Premier Theatre affair, 139–144
Rubenstein, Ernie, 21, 22
    Empire State Building appeal (1958), 23–25
Rudin, Milton "Mickey," 131, 133
Rudman, Warren, 302, 307–309, 312, 317, 323, 327, 329, 330, 332
    North and, 337, 340
    Poindexter and, 329, 330, 332
    public hearings, 317, 323, 327
Russell Senate Office Building (Washington, D.C.), 302, 320
Russian Jews, 9

Saarinen, Eero, 163
Sabrett, 161
Sackett, Robert, 180
Salad oil scam, 67–84
Salomon Brothers, 253
Samuels, Leroy, 40–41
Sandinistas, 301, 321, 345, 347
Sandler, Richard, 272, 281
Sarbanes, Paul, 323
Sardinia, 154–155
Saudi Arabia, 111
Savage, Royce, 28–30
Savings and loans, 290
Scanlan, Robert, 201

Schiavone Construction Company, 148
Schuman, Daniel, 230–231
Schwartz, Alan, 196–197
Schwebel, Mac, 130, 131
"Scottsboro Boys," 18
Sebastiano, Joe, 200
SEC. *See* Securities and Exchange Commission
Second World War, 10, 21, 65, 108, 109, 231, 303–304, 335
Secord, Richard, 310, 320, 345–346
  public hearing, 321–323, 330, 337, 345
  Tower Commission, 306
Secretary of the Treasury, 34
Secret cash funds, 144
Section 7(a) of the National Industrial Recovery Act (1933), 17
Securities and Exchange Commission (SEC), 42, 43, 53, 63, 89–91, 95–96, 270–271, 281
  Atari and, 138–139
  Bausch & Lomb, 230–231
  Birrell case (1967), 49–51
  budget cuts at, 43
  Commonwealth United and, 129–131
  compliance departments and, 271
  Drexel Burnham and, 271–272
  GAF and, 251, 255–256
  Gulf Coast Leaseholds case (1962), 43, 46
  Gulf & Western and, 100–105
  Liman's relationship with, 95–96
  Merritt-Chapman case (1963), 87–88

Milken and, 273–274, 277
Warner Communications and, 141–143
Securities cases, 39–40, 42–53
Securities industry, 270–271. *See also* Wall Street
Securities laws, 35, 42–43, 51, 62, 89
Segregation, 13, 185, 357
Seidman, William, 283
Select Committee, U.S. Senate, 3, 301–303, 308. *See also* Iran-Contra investigation
  House committee and, 307–308, 320
  lack of party line division, 302
Selznick, David, 18
Senate, U.S.
  Armed Services Committee, 333
  Government Operations Committee, 4
  Intelligence Committee, 308, 345
  Permanent Subcommittee on Investigations, 3–9
  Select Committee. *See* Select Committee, U.S. Senate; Iran-Contra investigation
Sentencing guidelines, 40–41
Sentencing reforms, 190–193
Seymour, Whitney North, 99
Share parking, 89, 270, 278–280
Sherwin, James, 251–264. See also *U.S. v. GAF*
Shor, Toots, 51
Shriver, Sargent, 358
Shultz, George, 320, 347–348
Siegel, Herb, 94–95, 145–148, 156
Siegel, Martin, 240, 270
Sills, Beverly, 157
Silver bullion, 111–124
Silver futures, 111–124

Silverman, Samuel J., 25–27, 35
  courtroom style of, 25
  Diary of Anne Frank case, 26
Silver sheiks case, 107, 110–124
Silver Thursday (March 27, 1980),
  114–115
Simon, Paul, 157
Simon & Schuster, 96, 98
Simpson, O. J., 252
Simpson, Thacher & Bartlett,
  99–101
Sinatra, Frank, 130–131
Sistrom, Peter, 219, 272–273
S. J. Klein (New York City), 31
Skadden Arps, 63
Slobotnik, Mr., 238
Smith College, 10–11
Snyder, Richard, 98
Social Security, 215
Solomon, David, 283
Sorensen, Ted, 58, 60
South Puerto Rican Sugar, 97
Soviet Union, 108, 124, 304, 325,
  344
Special prosecutors, 352–354
Speigel, Thomas, 290
Spielberg, Steven, 137, 157, 336
Sporkin, Stanley, 95, 100–105
Sprizzo, John, 39
Stalin, Josef, 8
Standard and Poor's, 266
Starr, Kenneth, 353–354
State Department, U.S., 309
Stein, Benjamin J., 291
Stein, Gertrude, 161
Stevenson, Adlai, 8, 22–25, 59
  courtroom style of, 24–25
  Empire State Building appeal
  (1958), 23–25
  joins Weiss firm, 22
Stewart, Michael, 222, 224

Stock fraud, 34–35, 42–53
Stockholder suits, 27
Stock manipulators, 110–111
Stock parking, 89, 270, 278–280
Stone, Chris, 218, 219
Stone Container, 280
Storer Communications, 279, 286
Streisand, Barbra, 154, 157
Subway car case, New York City. *See*
  R–46 subway car case
Subway Sam (New York City), 31
Suez Canal, 27–28
Sullivan, Brendan, 311, 313, 341–342
Summations (closing arguments), 48,
  83, 91, 206
Supreme Court, U.S., 13, 60, 145,
  211
  briefs, 27
  Colorado River water rights, 19
  habeas corpus, 218
  sentencing guidelines and,
  192–193
Swan-Finch Oil Corporation,
  50–52
Syracuse University, 50

Tammany Hall (New York City), 27
Tarrytown, New, 139–144
Taubman, Al, 241
Tax law, 21–22
Television, 133, 145, 149–150
Texaco, 20, 237, 241–248. *See also*
  Pennzoil v. Texaco
  bankruptcy filing, 248
  Getty Oil and, 244–245
Texas, 234
Theatrical law, 18
Thomas, Franklin, 39, 165
Thrift Supervision, Office of (OTS),
  231–232
Time Inc.

CEO bylaw provision with Ross and, 149, 150–152
"Liman letter" and, 151–152
management style at, 149
Warner merger with, 147–156
Time magazine, 148
"Times Square" (Attica Correctional Facility), 179
Time Warner, Inc., 125, 153–156
Levin named sole CEO, 156, 158
Tisch, Billie, 162, 163
Tisch, Laurence A., 162–166, 241, 266
management style of, 163
Paley and, 163–164, 166
Wyman and, 164–165
Tisch, Robert, 162
Topkis, Jay, 26–27, 36
Cities Service case (1956), 27–30
Toshiba, 155, 156
Tower, John, 305
Tower Commission, 305–307
Tramiel, Jack, 139
Transit Authority, New York (MTA), 31, 195–208, 211
Tree, Marietta, 165
Trial lawyers, 22, 30–32, 58, 237
courtroom style, 31–32
settlements and, 122–123
Trial themes, 197–198
Triangle Shirtwaist Factory fire (1911), 177–178
Triboro Bridge (New York City), 174
Troy, New York, 205
Truman, Harry S., 22, 346, 354
Tulsa, Oklahoma, 28
Turner, Ted, 159–160
Turner Broadcasting, 159–160
20th Century-Fox, 145

Uniform partnership agreement, 18
Union Carbide, 250–259, 264. See also *U.S. v. GAF*
Universal Finance Company, 44–48
Universities, Jewish quotas at, 10
U.S. Attorney's Office for Southern District of New York, 37–53, 172
appointment of Liman to, 33, 34–35, 37
insider trading and, 269–270
U.S. Home, 280
U.S. v. GAF, 229, 231, 249–264
appeal, 264
conviction, 263
first trial, 252–257
first witnesses, 253
invoice, 258
Jefferies and, 253–257, 261
jury deliberations, 260
jury selection, 252–253, 260–261
Melton and, 258–259
Milken case similarities with, 249
mistrials, 257, 260
second trial, 257–260
summation, 259
third trial, 260–263
typewriter experts, 258
WATS telephone service, 258–263
U.S. v. Leroy Samuels, 40–41
U.S. v. Milken, 231, 271–292
Boesky charges, 270, 273
defense team, 235, 272–273
Fatico hearing, 285–287
GAF case similarities with, 249
indictment, 278–280
plea negotiations, 278, 281–284
prosecution, 273
sentencing, 287–289

sentencing negotiations, 282,
284–285, 287, 288
subpoenas issued, 271
U.S. v. Wolfson, 85–93
appeal, 92
background of, 86–87
cross-examinations, 90–91
government witnesses, 89–90
judge for, 89, 91
Rittmaster and, 90–91
summation, 91
U.S. vs. Fatico, 285

Van Allen, John, 43–48
Vance, Cyrus, 303, 349
Vanity Fair, 94
Variation margin, 72
Vegetable oil market, 67–84
Vera Institute of Justice (New York
City), 210
Veterans Administration, 211
Viacom, 106
Video games, 136–139
Vietnam War, 59, 173, 180, 318, 324,
337, 344, 346
Vogel, Harold, 73–75

Wachtell, Herbert, 154
Wachtell Lipton, 63, 154, 240
Wagner, Robert F., 16–17
Wagner, Robert J., 178
Wagner Act, 17
Walla Walla, Washington, 16
Wallison, Peter, 306–307
Wall Street (New York City)
anti-Semitism on, 20–21
dislike of Milken on,
267–268
stock fraud and, 34–35,
42–53
Wall Street Journal, 248

Walsh, Lawrence E., 305, 310,
312–314, 352–353. *See also*
Independent counsel, Iran-
Contra
Waltuch, Norton, 113
Ward, Robert, 231
Warner Brothers Records, 131
Warner Brothers Studio, 128,
131–132
Warner Communications, 125–158
Atari crisis, 136–139
Lorimar acquisition, 149–150
as Murdoch takeover target,
144–145
name change from Warner-Seven
Arts, 131–132
Ross compensation negotiations,
135
Time merger with, 147–156
Westchester Premier Theatre
affair, 139–144
Warner Pictures, 145
Warner Records, 133
Warner Reprise, 131
Warner-Seven Arts, 128–131
name change to Warner
Communications, 131–132
Warranty, breach of, 198, 199–200
Warren, Earl, 60, 64, 357
Washington, George, 352
Washington Post, 308–309
Wasserstein, Bruce, 244
Watergate scandal, 304, 343, 347,
349, 350, 352
Iran-Contra compared with, 299,
343, 347
Water rights, 19
Weinberger, Caspar, 320, 347–348
Weinfeld, Edward, 197
Weiss, Louis, 17–18
Weiss, Solomon, 140–144

Weiss & Wharton, 17–18
Welch, Joseph L., 14, 322–323
Westchester Premier Theatre
 (Tarrytown, New York),
 139–144
Westinghouse, 167
Wharton, John F., 17–18
Wharton School of Business, 266
White-collar crime, 34, 38, 50,
 85–93, 210
White Plains, New York, 212
Whitewater, 353–354
Wicker, Tom, 176
Wickes, 280
William Paley Foundation, 167
Williams, Edward Bennett, 92, 221,
 238, 259, 273, 274, 300, 303
 Dolkart case, 102–105
 Milken and, 272, 280
Williams, Harold, 240, 241
Williams, Milton, 179
Williams & Connolly, 102, 272, 311
Willis, Charles, 179
Wilson, Woodrow, 33–34

Winchell, Walter, 18
Winokur, Barton, 240–241
Winthrop Simpson & Ross, 70
Wirtz, Willard, 59
Wisconsin Law School, 18
Witnesses
 attacking, 201–204
 expert, 202–204
Wolfson, Louis E., 85–93, 270. See
 also *U.S. v. Wolfson*
Wood, Kimba, 265, 283–288
Woodstock (film), 131
World War II, 10, 21, 65, 108, 109,
 231, 303–304, 335
Wyman, Thomas H., 105, 159–166
Wynn, Stephen, 279

"Yacht Club," 112
Yale Law Journal, 21
Yale Law School, 13, 20–21, 28, 57,
 99, 176, 180
Yiddish, 15

Zucker, Willard, 337, 340

PUBLICAFFAIRS is a new nonfiction publishing house and a tribute to the standards, values, and flair of three persons who have served as mentors to countless reporters, writers, editors, and book people of all kinds, including me.

I. F. STONE, proprietor of *I. F. Stone's Weekly*, combined a commitment to the First Amendment with entrepreneurial zeal and reporting skill and became one of the great independent journalists in American history. At the age of eighty, Izzy published *The Trial of Socrates*, which was a national bestseller. He wrote the book after he taught himself ancient Greek.

BENJAMIN C. BRADLEE was for nearly thirty years the charismatic editorial leader of *The Washington Post*. It was Ben who gave the *Post* the range and courage to pursue such historic issues as Watergate. He supported his reporters with a tenacity that made them fearless, and it is no accident that so many became authors of influential, best-selling books.

ROBERT L. BERNSTEIN, the chief executive of Random House for more than a quarter century, guided one of the nation's premier publishing houses. Bob was personally responsible for many books of political dissent and argument that challenged tyranny around the globe. He is also the founder and was the longtime chair of Human Rights Watch, one of the most respected human rights organizations in the world.

·　　·　　·

For fifty years, the banner of Public Affairs Press was carried by its owner, Morris B. Schnapper, who published Gandhi, Nasser, Toynbee, Truman, and about 1,500 other authors. In 1983 Schnapper was described by *The Washington Post* as "a redoubtable gadfly." His legacy will endure in the books to come.

Peter Osnos, *Publisher*

CPSIA information can be obtained at www.ICGtesting.com
Printed in the USA
BVOW08s2355110716

455220BV00002B/5/P